What were the boundaries between "official" and "subversive," "orthodox" and "dissenting" practices in medieval literary theory and allied fields of knowledge? Placing medieval critical and intellectual discourses within their cultural and ideological frameworks, *Criticism and dissent in the Middle Ages* examines conflicts of gender, violence, academic freedom, hermeneutical authority, sacramentalism, and heresy among so-called official as well as dissenting critical orders. Pedagogies, theories of grammar and rhetoric, poetics and hermeneutics, academic "sciences," clerical professionalism, literacy, visual images, theology, and textual cultures of heresy are all considered. This collection of new essays by major scholars examines medieval critical discourses – theories of textuality and interpretation, and representations of learning and knowledge – as contesting and contested institutional practices within and between Latin and vernacular cultures.

CRITICISM AND DISSENT IN THE MIDDLE AGES

CRITICISM AND DISSENT IN THE MIDDLE AGES

EDITED BY

RITA COPELAND

CAMBRIDGE
UNIVERSITY PRESS

CAMBRIDGE UNIVERSITY PRESS
Cambridge, New York, Melbourne, Madrid, Cape Town, Singapore, São Paulo

Cambridge University Press
The Edinburgh Building, Cambridge CB2 2RU, UK

Published in the United States of America by Cambridge University Press, New York

www.cambridge.org
Information on this title: www.cambridge.org/9780521453158

First published 1996
This digitally printed first paperback version 2006

A catalogue record for this publication is available from the British Library

ISBN-13 978-0-521-45315-8 hardback
ISBN-10 0-521-45315-1 hardback

ISBN-13 978-0-521-02443-3 paperback
ISBN-10 0-521-02443-9 paperback

Contents

Contents

Illustrations

ix

Contributors

Sarah Beckwith, Department of English, University of Pittsburgh, is the author of *Christ's Body: Identity, Culture, and Society in Late Medieval Writings* (1993)

Michael Camille, Department of Art History, University of Chicago, is the author of *The Gothic Idol: Ideology and Image-Making in Medieval Art* (1989) and *Image on the Edge: The Margins of Medieval Art* (1992)

Janet Coleman, Government Department, London School of Economics, has most recently published *Ancient and Medieval Memories: Studies in the Reconstruction of the Past* (1992). Among her other publications are *Against the State: Studies in Sedition and Rebellion* (1990), *English Literature in History, 1350–1400: Medieval Readers and Writers* (1981), and *Piers Plowman and the Moderni* (1981).

Rita Copeland, Department of English, University of Minnesota, Minneapolis, is the author of *Rhetoric, Hermeneutics, and Translation in the Middle Ages: Vernacular Traditions and Academic Texts* (1991).

Jody Enders, Department of French, University of California, Santa Barbara, is the author of *Rhetoric and the Origins of Medieval Drama* (1992).

Ralph Hanna III, Department of English, University of California, Riverside, has most recently published *Pursuing History: Middle English Manuscripts and Their Texts* (1996). His other publications include *A Handlist of Manuscripts Containing Middle English Prose in the Henry E. Huntingdon Library* (1984), and (with David Lawton) an edition of *The Siege of Jerusalem* (1996).

Martin Irvine, Department of English, Georgetown University, is the author of *The Making of Textual Culture: Grammatica and Literary Theory, 350–1100* (1994).

Steven Justice, Department of English, University of California, Berkeley, is the author of *Writing and Rebellion: England in 1381* (1994).

James Simpson, Faculty of English, University of Cambridge, has most recently published *Sciences and the Self in Medieval Poetry: Alan of Lille's Anticlaudianus and John Gower's* Confessio Amantis (1995). He is also the author of Piers Plowman: *An Introduction to the B-Text* (1990), and *A Handlist of Manuscripts Containing Middle English Prose in Parisian Libraries* (1989).

Marjorie Curry Woods, Department of English, University of Texas at Austin, edited and translated *An Early Commentary on the* Poetria nova *of Geoffrey of Vinsauf* (1985), and coedited the volume *The Uses of Manuscripts in Literary Studies: Essays in Memory of Judson Boyce Allen* (1992).

Nicolette Zeeman, King's College, University of Cambridge, is the coeditor of *English and International: Studies in the Literature, Art, and Patronage of Medieval England* by Elizabeth Salter (1988), and *Fourteenth-Century English Poetry* by Elizabeth Salter (1983). More recently she coedited *Displacement and Recognition: A Special Issue on Medieval Literature*, a volume of the journal *Paragraph* (1990).

Acknowledgments

Grateful acknowledgment is made to the following libraries for permission to reproduce illustrations: Bamberg, Staatsbibliothek; Berne, Burgerbibliothek; Besançon, Bibliothèque municipale; Cambridge, Corpus Christi College Library (by permission of the Master and Fellows of Corpus Christi College); Cambridge, St. Johns College Library; Chicago, Newberry Library (for the reproduction from Murner's *Logica memorativa*); Darmstadt Bibliothek; Dublin, Trinity College Library; Heiligenkreuz Abbey Library; Oxford, Bodleian Library; and Paris, Bibliothèque nationale.

The editor and contributors would also like to thank Kevin Taylor and Josie Dixon of Cambridge University Press for their expert and patient supervision of this project at its earlier and later stages, respectively.

Introduction
Dissenting critical practices

RITA COPELAND

The history of medieval critical discourse as ideological form and cultural practice has yet to be written. Recent turns in literary studies toward a socially reflexive analysis of critical theory as an institution have, with unreflecting consensus, established the modern period (sometimes incorporating early modern precedent) as the *terminus a quo* for any historical inquiry about how criticism has been and continues to be practiced as intellectual and cultural work.[1] Where medievalists have contributed to debates about the politics of theory, it has been mainly in connection with the politics of post-structuralist theory as it has redefined the work and concerns of medieval studies: where does the study of medieval texts fit into ongoing debates about theories of representation and the writing of history? How do changing practices of theory and historiography – theorizing gender and sexuality, social formations, race, and empire – shift the categories for historicizing medieval cultures? What stake does medieval studies have in present reconfigurations of academic critical discourse?[2]

But these debates about contemporary institutions of theory and the place of medieval studies within current practices also invite a return to medieval traditions of theory and criticism, that is, discourses of textuality and interpretation, and representations of learning and knowledge. To historicize medieval critical practices within their own ideological contexts opens these institutions of learning to visibility on their own grounds, as systems that are themselves politically multivocal. Perhaps because of the religious freighting of the study of medieval critical systems – so much of medieval interpretive practice and textual theory is built around the universalizing claims of Scripture, and its modern study was developed largely out of the resources made available by clerical scholarship – it has seemed something of an irrelevant impiety to address such questions.[3]

Conversely, challenging older reigning orthodoxies about the ideological unity of medieval culture (here resisting those orthodoxies of cultural representation handed down by the Middle Ages itself) has been the *métier* of progressive literary scholars, for whom, of course, literary history dominates the scene: literary historians have looked to medieval literary milieux, not to academic and other critical discourses, as the objects of revisionist cultural inquiry. The demand for a multivocal account, a nuanced ideological reading of medieval culture, has not fully extended to critical or "clerical" discourses of the Middle Ages. Indeed, the supposedly monolithic character of such critical discourses has been deployed as a foil to purely *literary* practices that are seen to assert their multivocal dynamism through opposing a static universalism of clerical discourse.[4] Historicism has left hermeneutics and its allied discourses in a political vacuum.

The essays in this volume examine medieval critical discourses as contesting and contested institutional practices within, as well as between, Latin and vernacular cultures. The term "criticism" in the volume's title represents the nexus of intellectual and disciplinary interests that constituted interpretive practices in the Middle Ages, as opposed to the narrower definition of "critical theory" in modern literary usage. Thus the essays here move among considerations of pedagogy, rhetoric and grammar, poetics and hermeneutics, academic classifications of the sciences, clerical professionalism, literacy, visual images, theological discourses, and the social--textual intersections of heresy.

As practices, medieval critical discourses are heterogeneous, contingent, and conflictually invested, even within their own established orders. Through the narrative conventions of intellectual and literary history, the critical practices of the Middle Ages have been represented as having a consistency of motive and a logic of relation and historical progression that fix them as secure frames of reference for more problematized work on other aspects of medieval culture. Medieval pedagogies, the textual theories embodied in the systems of grammar and rhetoric, the grand classificatory schemes of the sciences, the apparatuses of poetics and hermeneutics, and even traditional demarcations of language use (for example, the domains of Latinity), have thus figured as stable ideological articulations, as a unitary backdrop, *against which* can be judged the force of dissenting practices in social history and in the cultural history of literature. On the terms of such historiographical conventions, historians have recognized critique and dissent as responses to established critical orders, but not as inevitably constitutive of those orders themselves. Scholarly projects of "mapping" medieval critical systems have tended to emphasize discursive unity. Michel de Certeau has observed (in the context of broader considerations about the writing of history) how the labor of forming continuous historical narratives:

promotes a selection between what can be *understood* and what must be *forgotten* in order to obtain the representation of a present intelligibility. But whatever this new understanding of the past holds to be irrelevant – shards created by the selection of materials, remainders left aside by an explication – comes back, despite everything, on the edges of discourse as in its rifts and crannies: "resistances," "survivals," or delays discreetly perturb the pretty order of a line of "progress" or a system of interpretation.[5]

As de Certeau goes on to suggest, the writing of intellectual history especially prizes unities and organizing principles as a reaction against disciplinary specialization.[6] Within and around the discourses of medieval criticism, the "remainders" and "resistances" that are never really forgotten, even while often consigned to the margins of intellectual historiography, are the very possibilities of ideological difference and dissent within the "official" domains of academic or clerical discourses as well as the more commonly recognized conflicts between the "official" and the "heterodox." Reading practices that refuse assimilation to dominant epistemologies; the originary violence (both real and narrativized) of pedagogies and intellectual disciplines; subversive ambiguities within the pedagogical performance of gender: these are the estranged and repressed political motives and dissenting voices that return to "perturb" but also to animate historical representations of medieval critical culture.

On these terms, the project of this volume is also to restore to the notion of dissent its dynamism and elasticity as a gesture of difference, and thus to exemplify and historicize the various manifestations of dissent among medieval critical practices. Official systems of interpretive discourse in the Middle Ages encountered sharp challenges from outside the clerical establishment, such that we can surely speak of certain critical postures in the stark terms of orthodoxy and dissent. But the polarization between authoritarian orthodoxy and equally resolute resistance may best be seen as a radical rhetorical effect, an outward projection of the internal pressures, discontinuities, and differences that drive any critical practice, orthodox or not. Of course, such radical polarization was no less real for being rhetorical: medieval history gives us too many examples of the political consequences of retreating into hardline critical positions. Under such conditions we can say that dissent is "summoned" or "hailed" through what is necessarily an oppositional recognition, the juridical reprimand that compels dissent into its subjected and thus knowable status, naming it as heterodoxy, heresy, or sedition.[7] But the juridical denunciation of dissent as illicit resistance, as in the prosecution of heresy, is only one possible manifestation of "disobedience" and estrangement.[8] Dissent is a range of practices: as R. I. Moore's important work on social relations in the central Middle Ages suggests, the "habit" of dissent found expression through the vehicle of popular heresies, but as "habit" dissent also exceeds and precedes the formal boundaries of what is pronounced heretical or illicit.[9]

But restoring an elasticity to our understanding of dissent in history, and in the history of critical practices, is not to dissipate the force of our analysis. Dissent as attitude, habit, or action, from unvoiced deviation to open disobedience, speaks to the complex distributions and appropriations of power among critical and social orders. In what ways does such a reading of dissenting critical practice make visible the political constitution of medieval theoretical discourses? The open challenges of critical dissenters, interrogating the universalist claims of official intellectual paradigms, from Christian de Pizan refusing to "read like a man" to Lollard polemic contesting the adequacy of clerical exegetical methods, may have served to expose to the participants of such polemics the institutional and social contingencies of accepted practices. They certainly have served in this way for modern historians of medieval criticism. But curiously, the conspicuousness of the dissenting stance as overt resistance to official systems also works to mask, from modern readers, the very social "situatedness" and the self-dislocation of those official systems. Quite simply, modern readers do not feel called to read medieval criticism as ideological when there is no outward sign of rupture or difference. We read gender in medieval critical discourses when the conflicts of gender announce themselves through expressions of resistance to established interpretive practices; we read contestations over exegetical authority where lay, vernacular readers voice urgent claims to hermeneutical agency, claims that manifest themselves through overt political critique. Conversely, but by a similar logic, such overt critiques of official critical convention invite us to read them as somehow self-consistent, without

4

their own disguised dissonances, because as particularized critiques they can make their ideological investments so explicit. But to read politically is also to read the counterpractices of dissenting discourses against their own teleological claims.[10] As this volume will suggest, dissent itself is not homogeneous or univocal.

Such readings of critical dissent also encourage us to reimagine the historiographical landscape on which we map medieval criticism. Modern scholarship has tended to visualize medieval critical discourses on the terms of grand scientific *récits* inherited from the nineteenth century: the macro-structures of theology, learned systems of exegesis, philology, and the subdisciplines – but still macro-structures – of poetics, stylistics, and literary history. These scientific narratives, proceeding through chronological trajectories, providing *termini a quo* and *ad quem*, mark out large political and institutional territories of inquiry for the historian. While work in other areas of medieval studies – notably literary studies – has turned to various historicist methodologies to reimagine textual and historical relations in smaller, more local, and yet synchronically more complex terms, medieval critical "theory" continues to be read and represented, by literary scholars as well as intellectual historians, as a complete and unitary language with a beginning and an end that can absorb all of its minor aberrations in between. That the "univocality" of clerical purpose persists until contested or exploded from without by the claims of emergent political subjectivities is one of the mythic structures of modern narratives about medieval intellectual culture. But to reconceive this landscape is also to resist the temptation to replace one sort of continuist narrative of history with another, to resist substituting a history of dissenting discourses for a history of orthodox discourses. Dismantling the binarism of orthodoxy/dissent calls for a practice of "dissenting reading" in which the writing of history can take on a certain force of political intervention: to read dissent, both where it advertizes itself as dissent and where it does not, as that which also in some measure escapes representation, as the excess of meaning that we must nevertheless situate among determinate political, social, and textual relations.

To place these observations in a concrete micro-history of a medieval critical practice, I want to turn here to an example of an institutional context for the generation and application of critical theory: classrooms and their effects on the human beings who actualize theoretical discourse.

5

The medieval classroom is the historical site where the *ars grammatica* is produced and reproduced as the fundamental program of textuality. Grammar shapes students and their environment, and it is continually shaped in and by student culture. Grammar as discipline comes into being as it is materially enacted in the classroom. As the most physically embodied of the *trivium* arts (with its emphasis on tongue and mouth for pronouncing words, and the formation of letters inscribed on parchment or wax by fingers correctly holding pens), it is also enacted on and through the bodies of the students learning its rules. Thus grammar is an embodied relationship between students and teachers in the physical locus of the classroom, a place consigned to the authority of the teacher, who dispenses knowledge of scientific "disciplines" and – as part of that pedagogical regimen – enforces order through coercive "discipline." As we know from countless images of the medieval schoolroom and from iconography of Lady Grammar herself, often depicted with flagellum in hand, the teaching of grammar is inextricably linked in ancient and medieval imaginations with violence to the body.[11]

The fundamentals of grammatical knowledge are thus transmitted to young students through the quotidian environments of classrooms, institutional structures that, for all their mythical authority, are hardly univocal. One narrative about the classroom, a motif that is reprised in several forms and with varying interpretations of motive from ancient historical writing to late antique martyrology and medieval chronicle, tells a story of violent rebellion by students against pedagogical authority. The earliest full version of the story occurs in Livy's *Ab urbe condita* 5.27, but the versions that I will consider here, representing either end of the martyrological development of the legend, are Prudentius' account (fourth century) of the martyrdom of St. Cassian of Imola in *Peristephanon* 9 and William of Malmesbury's chronicle accounts (twelfth century), derived from Prudentius, of the death of John Scotus Eriugena.[12]

Prudentius' poem tells of a vision of the martyr Cassian:

> plagas mille gerens, totos lacerata per artus,
> ruptam minutis praeferens punctis cutem.
> innumeri circum pueri, miserabile visu,
> confossa parvis membra figebant stilis,
> unde pugillares soliti percurrere ceras
> scholare murmur adnotantes scripserant.   (lines 11–16)

6

[bearing a thousand wounds, lacerated through all his joints, and showing his skin broken with tiny pricks. Countless boys around him – pitiful sight – pierced his limbs full of holes with little styluses with which they used to traverse their wax writing tablets, writing down the droning lesson in school.][13]

The explanation of this strange martyrdom in which the styluses, the material instruments of grammatical instruction, become the instruments of death, is actually more a story of the teaching of grammar and the culture of the classroom than a martyrology. Cassian had been a schoolmaster, a "magister litterarum" who sat surrounded by a great swarm of students:

> verba notis brevibus conprendere cuncta peritus,
> raptimque punctis dicta praepetibus sequi.   (lines 23–24)

[he was skilled in putting every word in *notis brevibus* {shorthand marks, or small characters},[14] and in following spoken words quickly with nimble pricks {on the wax writing tablets}.]

But the crucial correlative is that his lessons were also severe and his attitude harsh, and he was much resented by the "childish mob": "nec dulcis ulli disciplina infantiae est" (line 28) [no discipline is ever sweet to childhood], where the term *disciplina* carries not only the meaning of intellectual training but also that of punishment, a second valence the term had acquired by late antiquity.[15] Singled out for persecution by the local governor for his Christian beliefs, Cassian was dragged from his classroom and delivered to the punishing hands of his students, the "flogger" (*verberator*) given as a captive gift to the children to suffer the torture of their choice. Prudentius' text deserves to be quoted here at length:

> vincitur post terga manus spoliatus amictu,
> adest acutis agmen armatum stilis.
> quantum quisque odii tacita conceperat ira,
> effundit ardens felle tandem libero.
> coniciunt alii fragiles inque ora tabellas
> frangunt, relisa fronte lignum dissilit. . .
> inde alii stimulos et acumina ferrea vibrant,
> qua parte aratis cera sulcis scribitur,
> et qua secti apices abolentur et aequoris hirti
> rursus nitescens innovatur area.
> hinc foditur Christi confessor et inde secatur;
> pars viscus intrat molle, pars scindit cutem. . .

7

"quid gemis?" exclamat quidam; "tute ipse magister
istud dedisti ferrum et armasti manus.
reddimus ecce tibi tam milia multa notarum,
quam stando, flendo te docente excepimus.
non potes irasci quod scribimus; ipse iubebas
numquam quietum dextera ut ferret stilum.
non petimus totiens te praeceptore negatas,
avare doctor, iam scholarum ferias.
pangere puncta libet sulcisque intexere sulcos,
flexas catenis inpedire virgulas.
emendes licet inspectos longo ordine versus,
mendosa forte si quid erravit manus.
exerce imperium: ius est tibi plectere culpam,
si quis tuorum te notavit segnius."
talia ludebant pueri per membra magistri. . .
(lines 43–48, 51–56, 69–83)

[So he is stripped of his garments and his hands are tied behind his back, and all the band are there, armed with their sharp styles. All the hatred long conceived in silent resentment they each vent now, burning with gall that has at last found freedom. Some throw their brittle tablets and break them against his face, the wood flying in fragments when it strikes his brow. . .Others again launch at him the sharp iron pricks, the end with which by scratching strokes the wax is written upon, and the end with which the letters that have been cut are rubbed out and the roughened surface once more made into a smooth, glossy space. With the one the confessor of Christ is stabbed, with the other he is cut; the one end enters the soft flesh, the other splits the skin. . ."Why do you complain?" calls one; "you yourself as our teacher gave us this iron and put the weapon in our hands. You see we are giving you back all the thousands of characters which as we stood in tears we took down from your teaching. You cannot be angry with us for writing; it was you who bade us never let our hand carry an idle style. We are no longer asking for what was so often refused when we were under your instruction, you stingy teacher, – a holiday from school. We like making pricks, twining scratch with scratch and linking curved strokes together. You may examine and correct our lines in long array, in case an erring hand has made any mistake. Use your authority; you have power to punish a fault, if any of your pupils has written carelessly on you." Such sport the boys had on their master's body. . .]

There is nothing very mysterious about the affective import of this story in which the instruments of writing write death on the body, in which the

8

grammatical discipline of writing itself (the manual skills of "twining scratch with scratch and linking curved strokes together") is given its most powerful embodiment as excavation in the flesh (literally instantiating what Elaine Scarry has called the "language-destroying capacity" of torture), and in which the students are licensed to fulfil a fantasy of vengeance.[16] And yet, within the sanctioned structure of a martyrology it tells a story, or stories, that cannot otherwise be told. As a horror-fantasy of student rebellion, it imagines the counter-institutional possibility that children really might have power in the classroom (it is, of course, the very imagining of this possibility that is enlisted to legitimize the repressive severity of classroom law). But this is also a story of dissent circumscribed by the structures of civic law: the children are given *license* by the pagan governor to take vengeance on the "confessor of Christ" so that they are no more than deputies of a civic mechanism of persecution. Moreover, the narrative as rhetorical product is circumscribed and defined by the explanatory structures of Christian martyrology: the narrative action in which the boys reverse the violence of the schoolroom to torture their Christian teacher is assimilable to the generic conventions, the didactic framework, of martyrology. So the pupils' dissent against pedagogical law is tidily reabsorbed first into the authority of civic law and ultimately of Christian law.[17]

But the story of dissent that cannot be reabsorbed is the story of grammar's own institutional dislocation. Grammar is embodied in the living presence and authority of teachers, and the authority of grammar is contingent on the power of teachers to exercise physical and, even more, academic and public authority at any given historical moment. This is, then, also a story of the limits of grammar's authority and institutional power as the *origo et fundamentum liberalium litterarum*.[18] In the mockery of the boys, the grammar teacher's power to punish a fault, to correct an erring stroke or chastise an idle hand, leads not to entry into the formal hierarchies of the liberal arts, but to death itself. The story does not ask us to distinguish between the grammar teacher and the office of grammarian: the pupils appropriate the teaching of grammar and its making of language, and convert them into the destruction of language itself. That the grammar teacher can be killed off by his own pupils, by the recipients of his scientific knowledge who turn the very tools of his office into instruments of bodily torture, suggests that the disciplinary practice of grammar itself, as symbolic entity, is under siege.

9

Probably no grammarian ever died in this way, but in late antiquity the grammarian's authority and the disciplinary claims of grammar were subject to contestation and restriction within academic and social orders, even while the conservational role of *grammatica* placed it at the very center of imperial interests.[19] In the fourth century in the Latin West, teachers of reading and writing (among whom we could place the martyr Cassian) whose duties covered the rudiments of grammatical instruction, occupied the very bottom of pay scales for teachers. Even the grammarians proper, who taught the more advanced parts of the grammatical curriculum (as well as, at times, the basic subjects of reading and writing), took second place in pay and prestige to the rhetoricians, who had asserted institutional and disciplinary dominance since the days of the Roman Republic. In many cities of the late Empire where both grammarians and rhetoricians could use their positions for climbing the social and professional ladder, rhetoricians seem to have far outstripped grammarians in opportunities for professional advancement and economic success, even as grammarians clearly outnumbered rhetoricians. Accorded some measure of social esteem, the grammarian was still economically and institutionally vulnerable.[20] And despite its foundational value within the curriculum, grammar's disciplinary competence was still constrained by the powerful territorial claims of rhetoric, which relegated grammar to the intellectual status of a propaedeutic. Most typically, then, it is in the person of a poorly remunerated and professionally subordinate schoolmaster that the authority of grammar is invested and embodied at the specific historical moments when that knowledge is imparted in a classroom.

When the "death by stylus" story reappears in William of Malmesbury's account of the death of John Scotus Eriugena, it seems to be no longer a story about grammar. The plot has been almost entirely extracted from its explanatory circumstances and projected on to the figure of Eriugena seemingly as pure martyrology. William of Malmesbury gives two accounts of Eriugena's death, one in the *Gesta regum Anglorum* (first composed *c.* 1125), and another amplified version in the *Gestum pontificum Anglorum* (begun *c.* 1125) (this second version is reprised in a letter that William composed [possibly *c.* 1140] on the history of Eriugena):

Succedentibus annis munificentia Elfredi allectus venit Angliam, et apud monasterium nostrum a pueris quos docebat grafiis, ut fertur, perforatus, etiam martyr aestimatus est.   [*Gesta regum Anglorum*][21]

[In the following years, drawn by the munificence of Alfred, he came to England, and at our monastery, as the story goes, the boys whom he taught pierced him with their pens; and so he was deemed a martyr.]

Propter hanc ergo infamiam, credo, teduit eum Frantiae, venitque ad regem Elfredum. Cujus munificentia illectus, et magisterio ejus, ut ex scriptis regis intellexi, sullimis, Melduni resedit. Ubi post aliquot annos, a pueris quos docebat grafiis foratus, animam exuit. Tormento gravi et acerbo, ut, dum iniquitas valida et manus infirma sepe frustraretur et sepe impeteret, amaram mortem obiret.   [*Gesta pontificum Anglorum*][22]

[On account of this notoriety {suspicions of heresy surrounding his writings}, I believe, he grew weary of France and came to King Alfred. Drawn by the king's munificence and, as I have read in the king's own writings, honored as the king's teacher, he went to live at Malmesbury. There, some years later, he died, pierced with styluses by the boys whom he taught. With terrible and painful torment he suffered a bitter death, as vigorous crime and weak hand many times fell short and many times renewed the attack.]

Both versions go on to quote a verse epitaph commemorating his martyrdom. The story of a schoolroom rebellion is so powerful that it seems to be able to translate itself into a new setting without accompanying motivation. Except for the actual instrument of death, the students' styluses, the ulterior story of grammar's dislocation from its own practice has disappeared. But while it is no longer a story explicitly *about* grammar, it is a story *of* grammar, that is, a story materially generated by the grammatical curriculum of the monastery of Malmesbury itself.

William's account of the death of Eriugena is a composite of sources. Notable among these are Asser's account, in the *De gestis Alfredi*, of a monk of Old Saxon origin named John, who at Alfred's invitation came from France to become abbot at Athelney, and who was attacked in the church by two young pupils of the monastery; and a local Malmesbury legend of John the Sophist who was celebrated for his intellect.[23] William of Malmesbury's account of Eriugena's death was produced, no doubt, by a certain confusion of "Johns." Perhaps it is this confusion that allows William to place the death of Eriugena in his own monastery of Malmesbury, a rather self-reflexive irony for the monastic chronicler. But overlaying this confusion of identities there is also the traceable influence of Prudentius' story of Cassian of Imola. This is obvious in the detail of the styluses as the instruments of death (a detail that is not present in Asser's account of the Abbot John). Moreover, William's second version of the story contains distinct verbal and thematic echoes of Prudentius' poem. Prudentius offers details about the particular pain and suffering inflicted by the weaker boys who could not deliver death blows but could only prick the flesh, thereby prolonging the martyrdom:[24]

> maior tortor erat qui summa pupugerat infans,
> quam qui profunda perforarat viscera;
> ille, levis quoniam percussor morte negata
> saevire solis scit dolorum spiculis. . .
> sed male conatus tener infirmusque laborat;
> tormenta crescunt dum fatiscit carnifex. . .
> nec longa fessum poena solvebat virum.   (lines 59–62, 67–68, 84)

[A greater torturer was the child who only pricked the surface than he who bored deep into the flesh; for the light hitter who will not wound to the death has the skill to be cruel with only the piercing pains. . .But the young boys from lack of vigour fail in their efforts and begin to be fatigued; the torments worsen while the tormentors grow faint. . .yet the long-drawn suffering was not releasing him from his weariness.]

It is readily apparent that William of Malmesbury's amplified version of the story is actually an abbreviation of details in Prudentius. How may we understand the value of this late antique story of schoolroom insurrection in a twelfth-century English chronicle?

As I have suggested above, while this no longer seems to be a story about grammatical instruction, it is a story *of* the grammatical curriculum, a text that inscribes in itself the institutional history of grammar, that embodies that tradition in its very making. By the Carolingian period, the works of Prudentius had become literary staples of grammatical teaching of the *auctores*, and were widely copied in single-author codices as well as compilations. The *Peristephanon* (known in the Latin Middle Ages as the *Liber ymnorum*) had somewhat less currency than the better known *Psychomachia*, but still appears regularly in booklists of monastic libraries.[25] The small library of Malmesbury Abbey, of which William himself was librarian by the 1120s, had a codex of the works of Prudentius from the tenth or eleventh century (now Corpus Christi College, Cambridge MS 23) with many illustrations and extensive glossing.[26] In that manuscript William would have had at hand the story of Cassian of Imola. Thus the very handing down of an *auctor* of the grammatical curriculum, and the survival of the art through the teaching of such an *auctor*, ensures the survival of a story about the death of a grammarian.[27]

Here in the environment of medieval monastic learning, in which grammar has achieved uncontested disciplinary primacy as the art of reading and the vehicle of cultural conservation, the story of a revolt against grammatical instruction is reconfigured through the quintessential grammatical exercise of amplification and abbreviation, William's abridging of Prudentius' story to embellish his own narrative of Eriugena.[28] William of Malmesbury's account of Eriugena's "death by stylus" is a story that harbors the cultural memory of grammar's imagined death. It is of course the very survival and curricular ascendancy of grammatical study that enables this suppressed rehearsal of its loss in the person of a martyred grammarian; and it is grafted here on to the life-story of a controversial philosopher–theologian of the ninth century, who began his intellectual career as a grammarian at the court of Charles the Bald, whose own thought was contested, and whose own writings (and sometimes even name) were suppressed by his contemporaries and later generations.[29] The oblique presence of grammar's imagined loss here, in the context of the undisputed institutional dominance of the *ars grammatica*, is all the more powerful because it is the most repressed matter of the monastic chronicler's borrowing from the resources of his own library. It expresses itself only in the instruments of death.

In Prudentius and even more in William of Malmesbury, this is a story that contains both an overt gesture of dissent, the classroom rebellion against pedagogical discipline, and a repressed gesture of difference, grammar's dislocation from its institutional power. Thus the "habit" of dissent is to be found even in the material story of grammar's ascendancy: the institutional conditions of grammar's conservational and self-preserving power – the monastic library, the librarian–chronicler's own compositional strategies – preserve the textual acknowledgment of grammar's institutional contingency. The story in which the scene of writing and of the transmission of knowledge is a scene of violent death is codified in subsequent textual traditions of learning: William of Malmesbury's account of Eriugena's death is reproduced by various chroniclers, scholars and even antiquarians through the late Middle Ages and beyond.[30] This story of the violence of intellectual transmission also has remarkable resonances with later humanist textual practices in which representations of political violence are assimilated into the morally prescriptive topical registers of the literary canon, where encoded or sublimated forms of cultural violence come to dominate the "scene of writing."[31]

Whether we speak of critical discourses or of political experience itself, dissent is that dissonant modality that resists explanation in the normalizing terms of narrative representation. As the transformations of the "death by stylus" legend might suggest, it is not enough to read the "politics" of a critical practice (in this case the science of grammar and its attendant pedagogies) without also considering the technologies of suppression whereby critical systems convert political contradictions into naturalized patterns of dominance and even violence. But this reading may also suggest how the explorations of dissenting practices in this volume do not take for granted the polarity of victim and oppressor, or resistance and authority. For this binarism too is the product of normalizing historical narratives that want to assimilate the habit of dissent into knowable and interpretively actionable forms of representation. Such a "normalizing" history might, for example, render Prudentius' legend as no more than a cautionary tale of student rebellion against pedagogical severity. Indeed, such normalizing historical narratives would reproduce the mechanisms of law itself (pedagogical law, the "law" of the Christian *imperium*) which summons dissent into legally or symbolically actionable forms of representation. But the modulations of resistance in this story, from the violent rebellion in the grammar classroom to the institutional dislocation of *grammatica* itself, are precisely what resist linear representation through the binarism of "orthodoxy" and "dissent."

In the largest terms, then, dissent may be cast as the hermeneutical moment that finds no adequate articulation or representation, that key moment in ideological formation that Althusser (drawing on Lacan) describes in terms of the "structure of misrecognition" between the law and the subject that it commands, where the meanings produced by either side confound and exceed all signifying intentions.[32] In the records of political experience, dissent itself resists containment by the mechanisms of legal and narrative representation. The records of heresy inquisitions may show the accused affirming formal lists of orthodox beliefs that they never claimed to disavow, or making abjurations from formulaic lists of heretical articles that do not fully correspond with, or at times even fathom, the beliefs the suspects were likely to have held.[33] Sometimes the nature of a dissident's intention is precisely what the official record chooses to ignore. The Lollard priest Richard Wyche, imprisoned in 1403 by Walter Skirlawe, Bishop of Durham, was offered the opportunity to take an ambiguous oath: as "custodian" of his own conscience, to swear obedience to the law of the church "insofar as it pertained to him," to make his oath "with mental reservations" ("iuramentum limitatum in corde meo").[34] Here (at least in the initial formulation of the bargain) the law allows a gap in its power of representation over the dissenter, exercising its power to compel the dissenting subject by acknowledging that it cannot fully narrate the subject. The heretic, in turn, is willing to consent to partial representation under the law, at least initially allowing the law to contain him, but only subversively, through the "structure of misrecognition," here the unmapped, unregulated area of "mental reservations."

The structure of misrecognition is writ large in intellectual traditions, even where the political content is not overtly visible. Their political dissonances are registered, as the essays in this volume suggest, in various ways: in the disciplinary memory of imperial violence (Enders); the pedagogical spectacle of sexual violence (Woods); or in the less spectacular but no less forceful resistance to clerical proprieties of gender (Irvine), poetic encoding (Zeeman), and iconic representation (Camille). Enders and Woods each read the pedagogical tradition from inside out, to force it most where it resists political explanation. For Enders, the rhetorical canon of *memoria* is the contested site for rhetoric's own disciplinary memory, where its narratives of its own mythic origin link it with a history of political subjugation recast as voluntary submission to the rule of "democratic" civilization. This memory – and forgetting – of violence resurfaces in every institutional manifestation of rhetoric, from courtroom to classroom. Woods' essay returns us to this latter forum, the classroom and its textual canonization of violence. Where traditional histories of medieval education accept pedagogical and curricular practices on their own terms, content to note the transmission of classical texts through the medieval classroom, Woods asks us to consider how the sexual roles in the classical rape narratives used as primers for reading and composition played out in the same-sex, adolescent environment of medieval schools, where they offered subversive possibilities in the formation of masculine identities. Irvine also considers the displacement of gendered identity, here in relation to the disciplinary formation of *grammatica*, where Heloise's letters imagine the grammatically impossible "feminine *litteratus*." Like Woods,

15

Irvine moves beyond questions of gender and literary form to historicize the gendered construction of intellectual disciplines. Camille's essay revisits the scene of writing, here the historical moment at which older monastic traditions of "living speech" were being eroded by new, hierarchical disembodied modalities of reading and writing, and in which the iconic text (Matthew Paris' image of Socrates as "writer") is a regressively defiant presence that embodies (in a way almost prescient of the post-modern) a sense of its own radical historical alterity. And Zeeman takes us to the "scene of reading" in clerical commentary on poetics, where the governing epistemology of ethical mimesis in poetic discourse cannot suppress or contain a competing view of tropology as irresolvable, evasive, oblique. Ethical evaluations of poetry in clerical commentary are much less homogeneous than modern scholarship has recognized. It is such heterogeneity in the clerical tradition of teaching on language that vernacular poetics can render as radical when it opens ambiguous questions of class and sexuality.

Hanna and Justice situate their readings, more specifically than the other authors, at the historical juncture of a radical dissenting movement. Both examine critical discourses associated with the Lollard heresy of England in the late fourteenth and the fifteenth centuries. But even though engaged with the records of political history, neither of these essays takes dissent as something that it is possible to represent conclusively as a critical and political gesture. Dissent becomes visible only on the terms of hermeneutical desire, whether the appropriative desire of the English Lollard writer for a vernacular that can achieve a canonical parity with the Latinity of Wyclif's own academic exegesis (Hanna), or the intentionalist desire of modern scholarship to fortify its own investments in the knowability of the past through the explanatory powers of historicist practice (Justice). But the Lollard dissent also figures as a reference point of institutional and hermeneutical disruption in Simpson's analysis of Langland's desiring reader, in Beckwith's revaluation of sacramentalism and symbolic formation in the Corpus Christi drama, and in Coleman's synthetic account of the disciplinary formation of politics itself *as* an object of study in the arts faculty of fourteenth-century Oxford. As Beckwith observes, "dissent as critical consciousness is intrinsic to symbolic formation as such. . .[it] does not need to be understood as a purely doctrinally-driven set of precepts which exist as a set of merely propositional terms to counter orthodox dogma, but might rather be understood as a component part of a vigorous lay and vernacular religiosity" (pp. 265 and 278). Dissent as critical consciousness serves to articulate the complex relations between intellectual discourses (hermeneutics, politics as academic science, theology and its symbolic regimes) and the social and political systems which they inhabit: Simpson's study of Langland's "voluntarist" hermeneutics that conforms to neither orthodox nor heterodox institutions of reading, Coleman's account of the retreat of Oxford's arts faculty from "politicized" engagement with the practical science of politics, and Beckwith's reassessment of Corpus Christi as both mystery and resistance in the civic theater of York.

The dialogues that emerge among these diverse critical perspectives serve to reframe categories of historical inquiry about dissent and orthodoxy. Hanna and Simpson read Lollard exegetical discourses both within and against their own revisionist claims, underscoring the commonality of their most radical positions with orthodox models of intention and reception; similarly Camille positions the "dissenting image" within conservative resistance to changes in technologies of writing. Conversely, the encoding of hermeneutical orthodoxies, whether poetic or sacramental, generates its own necessary mechanics of doubt and difference, as the essays by Zeeman and Beckwith suggest; along related lines, Coleman's account of academic conceptions of the "science" of politics shows how the most conservative intellectual methodologies could foster the most liberal forms of intellectual inquiry. In their explorations of the enfolding of the intellectual with the political, these essays also work toward reimagining that historiographical landscape in which the boundaries between the spheres of intellectual and political have been rigidly maintained. In this sense the manifold discourses of criticism are actively constitutive of the "social field," a continuous incorporation and reincorporation of the social and political into the textual community.[35] What Gramsci called the "intrinsic nature of intellectual activity" is itself organized and inflected as political discourse, as Enders shows in her reading of the history of memorial theory as a narrative "commemoration" of pedagogical and juridical coercion; and as we see in the essays by Woods and Irvine, which trace how the very inscription of gender constitutes a radicalizing alterity – the difference that matters – in the curricular and textual institution of grammar. And Justice redefines the very criterion of intellectual activity – where we find it, how we distinguish it – by calling our attention to the "intentionalities" of both entitled speakers (medieval clerks, modern critics) and those whose speech defies professional categories of intellectual representation, the individual Lollards at Norwich who perform the function of intellectuals within their own social nexus, elaborating the beliefs that bring together their particular heretical communities.[36]

The heterogeneity of this volume is deliberate. Neither singly nor collectively do these essays seek to replace one continuist history with another or to produce a "unified picture" of dissenting critical practice. The authors here demonstrate their indebtedness to modern and older work in intellectual and literary history, those scholarly precedents out of which their own investigations grow and to which they are also responses. Nor is this a handbook on dissent in the Middle Ages, or a macro-survey of critical practice as social history. It is not possible – and probably not desirable – for one volume to synthesize the multiple histories and critical productions of monastic, cathedral, and university schools with grammar schools and colleges, noble courts, and judiciaries, and write their economic and social relations across Europe and the Mediterranean, and across a millennium. Some individual studies, notably those by Alexander Murray and Brian Stock, have performed massive archeologies of intellectual and cultural histories to illuminate somewhat more specified historical periods.[37] By contrast this volume presents a range of historical and generic interests out of which two foci emerge most prominently (here with some valuable overlapping): the Latin academic cultures of late antiquity and the high Middle Ages (Enders, Woods, Irvine, Camille, Zeeman, Coleman) and English social and critical practices in the fourteenth and fifteenth centuries (Coleman, Simpson, Hanna, Beckwith, Justice). But the topical relations among these essays, their dealings with certain "genres" of critical discourse, traverse the more obvious pattern of a progressive historicality: the critical "genres" of pedagogies (Enders, Woods, Coleman); hermeneutics (Irvine, Camille, Zeeman, Simpson, Hanna); institutional sciences (Coleman, Irvine); and theology and heresy (Simpson, Beckwith, Hanna, Justice).

In his essay Steven Justice poses the problem of what "side" we are to take when we study distant political histories, where our own interpretive agencies create the spaces that we occupy as *interested* readers in making meaning out of the utterances of the past. This can remind us of the limits of our own ambitions to intervene in the past, and of our own hermeneutical intentionality in representing dissent. But despite its diverse manifestations and even its resistance to systematic representation, dissent

Introduction: dissenting critical practices

is always a point of reference, even at a historical remove, and to write of it does ask us in some ways to take sides. It is to be hoped that the work of this volume can demonstrate some possibilities for rethinking our own connections to the historically distant manifestations of dissent that we study and teach, and more importantly, for re-evaluating the adequacy of our own critical models of representation in those arenas where how we choose to represent can still matter.

Notes

1 See especially Terry Eagleton's now classic Marxist study, *The Function of Criticism: From the Spectator to Post-Structuralism* (London: Verso, 1984). Among more recent examples see: Bruce Robbins, ed., *Intellectuals: Aesthetics, Politics, Academics* (Minneapolis: University of Minnesota Press, 1990); *PMLA*, "The Politics of Critical Language" special issue of *PMLA* (Fall, 1990); Robert Young, *White Mythologies: Writing History and the West* (London: Routledge, 1990; rpt., 1992).

2 On this last question see, notably: Marina S. Brownlee, Kevin Brownlee, and Stephen G. Nichols, eds., *The New Medievalism* (Baltimore: Johns Hopkins University Press, 1991); Allen J. Frantzen, *Desire for Origins: New Language, Old English, and Teaching the Tradition* (New Brunswick: Rutgers University Press, 1990); and Louise Fradenburg, with Carla Freccero, "The Pleasures of History," *GLQ: A Journal of Gay and Lesbian Studies* 1 (1995): 371–84, the introductory essay to a special issue on "Premodern Sexualities," eds. Fradenburg and Freccero. Fradenburg's essay in particular elaborates this question to envision how medieval studies can intervene in contemporary debates about gender and history, considering how refigurations of the pre-modern challenge theoretical assumptions about modernity.

3 And here medieval studies has often internalized and replicated humanist constructions of the Middle Ages as a monolithic other. As Alastair Minnis has recently noted, the very project of writing a nuanced history of medieval literary theory represents a challenge to still-prevailing humanist orthodoxies about the homogeneously theocratic constitution of medieval society; see A. J. Minnis and A. B. Scott, with David Wallace, eds., *Medieval Literary Theory and Criticism c. 1100–c. 1375: The Commentary-Tradition* (Oxford: Clarendon, 1988), p. 5 (citing W. K. Wimsatt and Cleanth Brooks).

4 See for example Lee Patterson's rejection of the universalist picture of medieval ideology promoted by Robertsonian readings of clerical exegesis

Rita Copeland

(*Negotiating the Past: The Historical Understanding of Medieval Literature* [Madison: University of Wisconsin Press, 1987], pp. 32–34). For Patterson the counter-instantiation is to be found in medieval *literary* texts – primarily late medieval, primarily vernacular – which provide multivocal, localized narratives of medieval ideologies. Under this recuperative move, medieval academic discourses, clerical practices of exegesis, still remain invisible to, or untouched by, historicist inquiry. Compare the analysis of this issue in Nicolette Zeeman, "Alterations of Language," *Paragraph* 13 (1990): 219.

5 Michel de Certeau, *The Writing of History*, trans. Tom Conley (New York: Columbia University Press, 1988), p. 4.

6 *Ibid.*, p. 27.

7 See Louis Althusser, "Ideology and Ideological State Apparatuses (Notes Towards an Investigation)," in *Lenin and Philosophy and Other Essays*, trans. Ben Brewster (New York: Monthly Review Press, 1971), pp. 170–77. On dissent as "heresy" on the one hand and as "sedition" on the other see David Aers, "Reading *Piers Plowman*: Literature, History and Criticism," *Literature and History* new series 1 (1990): 4–23.

8 On heretical manifestations of dissent, see most recently Peter Biller and Anne Hudson, eds., *Heresy and Literacy 1000–1530* (Cambridge: Cambridge University Press, 1994). On disobedience as a range of practices, see Judith Butler, "Gender is Burning: Questions of Appropriation and Subversion," in Butler, *Bodies that Matter: On the Discursive Limits of "Sex"* (London: Routledge, 1993), pp. 121–40.

9 R. I. Moore, *The Origins of European Dissent* (Oxford: Blackwell, 1977; 2nd edn., 1985), p. ix.

10 On this see the essays in this volume by Ralph Hanna (on Lollard polemic) and James Simpson (on Langland's "voluntarist hermeneutics"). Steven Justice broadly explores the fissures within formal heterodoxy and the disjunctions between dissenting critical practice and political action in *Writing and Rebellion: England in 1381* (Berkeley and Los Angeles: University of California Press, 1994); see especially ch. 2, "Wyclif in the Rising."

11 This is only one among many features of Grammar's iconic repertoire (which can also include, for example, mother, physician, and gardener); see Ayers Bagley, "Grammar as Teacher: A Study in the Iconics of Education," *Studies in Medieval and Renaissance Teaching* new series 1 (1990): 17–48. Compare Martianus Capella's representation of Grammar with a paring knife (*scalprum*) for scraping pupils' tongues and mouths and thus clearing the way for proper pronunciation. See *De nuptiis Philologiae et Mercurii*, book 3, in *Martianus Capella*, ed. James Willis (Leipzig: Teubner, 1983), p. 60, line 224.

20

12 A general survey of the hagiographical versions of this story is by F. Lanzoni, "Le leggende di San Cassiano d'Imola," *Didaskaleion* new series 3.2 (1925): 1–44. Other martyrological versions of the story include one by Gregory of Tours, *Gloria martyrum* 42, in Gregory of Tours, *Opera*, part 2, eds. W. Arndt and B. Krusch (Hanover, 1885), published in *Monumenta Germaniae historica, Scriptores rerum Merovingicarum* 1: 516–17; by Flodoard of Rheims, *De Christi triumphis apud Italiam* 14.8, in J.-P. Migne, ed., *Patrologia latina* (Paris, 1844–55), 135: 857–58; and a long prose version, based directly on Prudentius, by the monk Hucbald of Saint-Amand, (*c.* 840–930), ed. François Dolbeau, "Passion de S. Cassien d'Imola composée d'après Prudence par Hucbald de Saint-Amand," *Revue Bénédictine* 87 (1977): 238–56. See also Julia M. H. Smith, "The Hagiography of Hucbald of Saint-Amand," *Studi Medievali*, 3rd series 35 (1994): 517–42.

13 Text and translation in *Prudentius*, trans. H. J. Thomson, vol. II, Loeb Classical Library (Cambridge, Mass.: Harvard University Press, 1953). The translations here and in the next quotation have been slightly altered.

14 On "characters" see Martin Irvine, *The Making of Textual Culture: "Grammatica" and Literary Theory, 350–1100* (Cambridge: Cambridge University Press, 1994), pp. 97–101.

15 H.-I. Marrou, " 'Doctrina' et 'disciplina' dans la langue des Pères de l'Eglise," *Bulletin du Cange* 9 (1934): 5–25; Jean Leclercq, "Disciplina," in Charles Boumgartner et al., eds., *Dictionnaire de spiritualité*, III (Paris: Beauchesne, 1957): 1291–302.

16 Elaine Scarry, *The Body in Pain: the Making and Unmaking of the World* (New York and Oxford: Oxford University Press, 1985), p. 20.

17 It is worth noting that the postscript to Hucbald's prose redaction of Prudentius' version reinforces the motif's absorption into the explanatory structures of martyrology, and within this didactic emphasis also turns the narrative to an explicit pedagogical lesson, exhorting his own monastic pupils to love and revere their teachers; see Dolbeau, "Passion de S. Cassien," 255–56.

18 This is the well-known formulation by Isidore of Seville, *Etymologiae*, ed. W. M. Lindsay (Oxford: Clarendon, 1911), 1.5.1. But this notion is familiar from classical and late classical contexts as well: for sources see Irvine, *The Making of Textual Culture*, pp. 12–13.

19 On the political value of grammar and grammarians for generating and cultivating an imperial mythology in late antiquity, see Irvine, *The Making of Textual Culture*, pp. 78–87.

20 Robert A. Kaster, *Guardians of Language: The Grammarian and Society in Late Antiquity* (Berkeley and Los Angeles: University of California Press, 1988), pp. 100–34; and R. R. Bolgar, *The Classical Heritage and its Beneficiaries*

(Cambridge: Cambridge University Press, 1954; rpt. 1973), p. 33, both drawing on the information about Bordeaux in Ausonius' *Commemoratio Professorum*. Grammarians certainly did use their positions to move up professional and social ladders. On bleaker conditions in Republican Rome, see Henri-Irénée Marrou, *Histoire de l'éducation dans l'antiquité* (Paris: Editions du Seuil, 1950), p. 370.

21 William of Malmesbury, *De gestis regum Anglorum*, ed. William Stubbs, I (London: Rolls Series, 1887): 131.

22 *De gestis pontificum Anglorum*, ed. N. E. S. A. Hamilton (London: Rolls Series, 1870), p. 394. See the text of William's letter, printed by Stubbs in *De gestis regum Anglorum*, I: cxliii–cxlvi.

23 Maïeul Cappuyns, *Jean Scot Érigène: sa vie, son œuvre, sa pensée* (Louvain and Paris, 1933; rpt. Brussels: Culture et Civilisation, 1964), pp. 256–60.

24 The crucial parallel between Prudentius and the expanded version of William's account was first noted by Ludwig Bieler, "Vindicta scholarium: Beiträge zur Geschichte eines Motivs," in Robert Muth et al., eds., *Serta Philologica Aenipontana*, Innsbrucker Beiträge zur Kulturwissenschaft 7–8 (Innsbruck: Felizian Rauch, 1962), pp. 383–85.

25 For accounts and contents of library books, see Irvine, *The Making of Textual Culture*, pp. 315–16, 340–44, 356–57, 364. The *Liber ymnorum* appears in Conrad of Hirsau's *Dialogus super auctores*, ed. R. B. C. Huygens (Leiden: Brill, 1970), pp. 97–98.

26 Pointed out by Bieler, "Vindicta Scholarium," p. 385, establishing a material connection between Prudentius' text and William of Malmesbury's account of Eriugena. On the manuscript see M. R. James, *Descriptive Catalogue of the Manuscripts of Corpus Christi College, Cambridge*, I (Cambridge: Cambridge University Press, 1912): 44–46. On Malmesbury's ownership of the manuscript see also Rodney M. Thomson, *William of Malmesbury* (Woodbridge, Suffolk: The Boydell Press, 1987), pp. 78, 113–14. On William as librarian of Malmesbury Abbey, see Stubbs, introduction to *Gesta regum Anglorum*, pp. xvi, xxvi, and *Gesta Pontificum*, ed. Hamilton, p. 431; and see Thomson, *William of Malmesbury*, ch. 3.

27 On William's own classical reading, in the conservatory tradition of grammatical learning, see the articles by Neil Wright, "William of Malmesbury and Latin Poetry: Further Evidence for a Benedictine's Reading," *Revue Bénédictine* 101 (1991): 122–53, and "'Industriae Testimonium': William of Malmesbury and Latin Poetry Revisited," *Revue Bénédictine* 103 (1993): 482–531.

28 While the exercises of amplification and abbreviation are conventionally associated with the prescriptive (rhetorical) *artes poetriae* of the twelfth and thirteenth centuries, they are in fact holdovers from ancient grammatical

practice in composition, as for example in Quintilian, *Institutio oratoria* 1.9.2.

29 On Eriugena's career as a grammarian, see Hans Liebeschütz, "The Place of the Martianus *Glossae* in the Development of Eriugena's Thought," in John J. O'Meara and Ludwig Bieler, eds., *The Mind of Eriugena* (Dublin: Irish University Press, 1973), pp. 49–58.

30 Cappuyns, *Jean Scot Erigène*, pp. 253–54.

31 See Stephanie Jed, "The Scene of Tyranny: Violence and the Humanistic Tradition," in Nancy Armstrong and Leonard Tennenhouse, eds., *The Violence of Representation: Literature and the History of Violence* (London and New York: Routledge, 1989), pp. 29–44.

32 Althusser, "Freud and Lacan," in *Lenin and Philosophy*, p. 219; see the excellent discussion of this in Butler, "Gender is Burning," in *Bodies That Matter*, p. 122.

33 On the first, see, for example, Moore, *Origins of European Dissent*, pp. 10–16, on the heresy investigation at Arras in 1024, where Bishop Gerard of Cambrai interrogated a group of suspected heretics whose own professed beliefs did not conflict or even overlap with the list of orthodox beliefs to which the Bishop had them swear. On the second, formulaic lists of heterodox beliefs to be abjured, see Anne Hudson, "The Examination of Lollards," originally published in *Bulletin of the Institute of Historical Research* 46 (1973); rpt. in Hudson, *Lollards and Their Books* (London: Hambledon Press, 1985), pp. 125–39, especially p. 131 on the East Anglian Lollards, and pp. 135–39.

34 Wyche's letter, written (according to its own account) while he was still imprisoned, is edited by F. D. Matthew, "The Trial of Richard Wyche," *English Historical Review*, 5 (1980): 530–45; see especially p. 534.

35 See Gilles Deleuze, "On the Line," in Constantin V. Boundas, ed., *The Deleuze Reader* (New York: Columbia University Press, 1993), pp. 232–34.

36 Antonio Gramsci, "The Formation of the Intellectuals," in *Selections from the Prison Notebooks*, eds and trans. Quintin Hoare and Geoffrey Nowell Smith (New York: International Publishers, 1971; rpt. 1989), p. 8.

37 Alexander Murray, *Reason and Society in the Middle Ages* (Oxford: Clarendon, 1978; rpt. 1985), and Brian Stock, *The Implications of Literacy: Written Language and Models of Interpretation in the Eleventh and Twelfth Centuries* (Princeton: Princeton University Press, 1983), both of which bring their remarkable syntheses of earlier materials to bear on the period after the millennium.

I

Rhetoric, coercion, and the memory of violence

JODY ENDERS

> There is perhaps nothing more terrible in man's earliest history
> than his mnemotechnics.
>
> Friedrich Nietzsche, *Genealogy of Morals*

"And don't you forget it!"

The phrase resonates for almost anyone, conjuring images of the imposition of a moral lesson – pedagogical, parental, societal. The imperative not to forget is a threat; and it is a threat that implicates the memory. In this essay, I propose to explore the ways in which medieval rhetorical theory and pedagogical practice enact and dramatize, perpetuate and subvert, a mnemonic system that was often born of violence.

For the modern critic, the famous description from the *Rhetorica ad Herennium* of purple-cloaked *imagines agentes* moving about a kind of psychodramatic (and also protodramatic) stage within the mnemonic imagination has largely conjured visions of a stately allegorical dance – a delicate iconography of personified figures enclosed like a tableau within a painter's frame or a dramatist's theatrical space: "we ought, then, to set up images of a kind that can adhere longest in the memory. And we shall do so if we establish likenesses as striking as possible; if we set up images that are not many or vague, but *doing something* [*agentes*]; if we assign to them exceptional beauty or singular ugliness; if we dress [*exornabimus*] some of them with crowns or purple cloaks, for example, so that the likeness may be more distinct to us. . ."[1] Yet even as the Pseudo-Cicero continues to muse about the engenderment of those images, he oscillates between beauty and ugliness, between forming and deforming, betraying a preoccupation with disfigurement which is as intense as that with figures: "if we somehow disfigure them [*deformabimus*], as by introducing one

24

stained with blood or soiled with mud or smeared with red paint, so that its form is more striking, or by assigning certain comic effects to our images, for that, too, will ensure our remembering them more readily" (*Ad Herennium* book 3.37). While I am by no means implying that memory *phantasmatae* could *not* be lovely or stately, I wish nonetheless to stress the importance of the violent context in which many narratives of the origins of mnemotechnics occur. There may no longer be any doubt about the paramountcy of memory theory in learned medieval literary representation: but the twentieth-century critical imagination has tended to preserve rhetorical *imagines agentes* as if on our own memory stage – and with all the appropriate aesthetic distance a classical theatrical metaphor would imply: a safe barrier between the dramatic illusions of a mnemonic *théâtre vitrine* and our own position as thinking spectators.[2] Notwithstanding such notable exceptions as Mary Carruthers and Eugene Vance,[3] virtually nowhere within the space of that critical stage have scholars made room for the memory image that is violent and frightening.

Memoria was the rhetorical canon that offered orators a pictorial script whence to deliver their performances: "the arrangement and disposition of the images [is] like the script" (*Ad Herennium* book 3.30). It conjoined epistemology, invention, mental picture, and delivery (*actio, pronuntiatio*, or *hypokrisis*), reuniting the visual psychodrama with a dramatic rhetorical performance.[4] Furthermore, rhetorical theorists had long explored the political and pedagogical power of those performances. For his part, Plato identified memory as a mighty force by which lawmakers might impose the proper visions of civilization upon society. Like poets, those lawmakers were the masters of illusion – societal or dramatic: "distance has the effect of befogging the visions of nearly everybody, and of children especially; but our lawgiver will reverse the appearance by removing the fog, and by one means or another – habituation, commendation, or argument – will persuade people that their notions of justice and injustice are illusory pictures. . ."[5] So it was that judicial and poetic communities alike targeted the memory vision in order to regulate desired social performances on the stage of the world – and to do so by replacing one public picture with another. The nature of that ideological substitution is profoundly coercive; and its ramifications for medieval forms of indoctrination must be explored.

If, as Aristotle observes in *De anima*, the soul "never thinks about a mental picture," then what happens when the picture is violent?[6] If memory was the "guardian of all the parts of rhetoric" (*Ad Herennium* book 3.28), then what are the ramifications of its custodianship of violence? If, as Longinus reminds us, the key function of any memory image was to "engender speech,"[7] then just what kind of speech would a violent image engender? And finally, if a quintessentially violent mnemonic scene could literally "set the stage" for dramatic delivery (as it did for Lucian of Samosata, who cited Mnemosyne as the premier quality of pantomime),[8] is it not possible that, in some cases, the memory image would generate not only violent speech but violent action? And that such violence would then inform the spectacularity of the "rule of the rod" in the medieval classroom?

Focusing here on the insights of such theorists as Cicero, the Pseudo-Cicero, Quintilian, Augustine, John of Garland, and Thomas Murner, I respond to those questions with the suggestion that the violent origins of memory theory laid the foundations for a pedagogy that was violent, coercive, spectacular, and rife with self-contradictions. While Quintilian proclaimed with the utmost confidence that "rhetoric is not self-contradictory (nam rhetorice non est contraria sibi). The conflict is between case and case, not between rhetoric and itself;"[9] rhetoric was indeed self-contradictory – a status that is best revealed by the inability of theorists to address their own need to create a rhetorical counter-discourse *against* violence within the very discipline that depended on violence for its own genesis. I argue below that theorists endeavored to conceal the violence of mnemotechnical systems by fabricating an illusion of creativity, beauty, and mediation in the name of civilization, a fiction that destruction could be reconfigured as generation.[10] As we shall see, that process has particularly harrowing ramifications for the interplay (both medieval and modern) among coercion, educational institutions, the invention of literature, the performance of pedagogy, the cultural construction of gender, and the very nature of transgression. And nowhere is that more clear than in the well-known narrative of the apocryphal origins of memory itself.

It is a legend of the origins of mnemotechnics, a legend of how Simonides is called away from a lovely evening of banquet revelry. No sooner does he cross the threshold on his way out when the entire building collapses on top of the guests, crushing and mutilating them to such an extent that the relatives who come to identify their loved ones are unable to do so from the isolated body parts protruding here and there from the rubble. Simonides purportedly saves the day through his astonishing ability to remember exactly where each guest had been seated at table and thus allows the victims of an isolated violent incident to be identified, buried, and commemorated.[11] Notwithstanding the apparently happy ending implied by that onomastic return to order, this is a narrative that stages the genesis of mnemotechnics as a response to a need that arose from sudden and violent death. The apocryphal origins of memory are played out in a tale of dismemberment, corporeal order, reconstruction, and reconstitution: mnemonics is the science born of accidental violence to the body.

"Let art, then, imitate nature," writes the Pseudo-Cicero of the artificial memory: "find what she desires, and follow as she directs. For in invention, nature is never last, education never first; rather, the beginnings of things arise from natural talent, and the ends are reached by discipline [*disciplina*]" (*Ad Herennium* book 3.36). But how and why a rhetorician would imitate nature in a bloody scene of dismemberment in order to invent, to engender, and to preserve the various discourses of the state is indeed a dilemma. In their various ways of addressing it in their conceptualizations of the *ars memorandi*, classical and medieval theorists do far more than express contentment with the birth of their *techne*: they actually refocus the Simonides story on the didactic ramifications of mnemonic systems that respond to acts of violence that are not accidental but intentional, not "natural" but unnatural, not dead but reborn. By thus substituting beauty for violence and intention for accident, they problematize one of the great debates within the history of rhetoric itself: whether that discipline in general (and memory in particular) is natural or artificial. Indeed, a closer reading of early memory theory shows that, despite the best rhetorical efforts to "naturalize" violence in the polis or in the classroom, there was, in fact, no more "artificial" construction than that very "naturalness."

After all, Simonides' building was constructed by men and destroyed by nature: so what rhetoricians discovered in the rubble was an artificial science that could concern itself with violent acts which were natural to nature but "unnatural" to humankind. In other words, while the *techne* which imitates natural violence is artificial, the initial crypt of Simonides' building – its object of imitation – is not. The *ars memorandi* artificially or "unnaturally" imitates the natural violence of nature in order to reconstruct, to re-create from death.[12] In what follows, I suggest that it is because mnemotechnics *imitates* nature that memory is artificial; but it is also because it imitates nature successfully that it is able to "engender speech" in violence: in the courtroom, in the classroom, and on the stage.[13] And if the consequences of such an analysis are troubling in that they point to the possibility that rhetorical narratives of the beauty of rhetorico-literary creation have always been violent and disfigured, that is a conclusion that is reinforced by another apocryphal tale of origins: that of rhetoric itself.

As the legend goes, the art of rhetoric was born at the same moment as the political hegemony, its advent explained in terms of the need for a peace-keeping, mediatory discourse that simultaneously facilitated empowerment, domination, and discipline. For Cicero, eloquence arose from the impossibility that a "mute and voiceless wisdom could have turned men suddenly from their habits and introduced them to different patterns of life. . .How could it have been brought to pass that men should. . . become accustomed to obey others voluntarily. . .? Certainly only a speech at the same time powerful and entrancing could have induced one who had great physical strength to submit to justice without violence. . ."[14] And in the eighth century, Alcuin argued in his *Dialogue with Charlemagne* that civilization was founded when the first eloquent man discovered in rhetoric a linguistic means of subjugating the inhabitants of the earth who were "made gentle and mild from being savage and brutal." It was rhetoric which turned them "against their previous habits, and [brought] them to the diverse pursuits of civilized life" (47–51).[15] But here, rhetoric is necessarily identified with the imperialistic imposition of social constructs of civilized law.[16] No matter how "voluntary" the participation of a given community, the coercive status of a civilizing rhetoric defies the concomitant theoretical articulation of that discipline as non-violent and mediatory. Emerging from the apparent need to replace militaristic rule-by-force with democratic rule by participation, rhetoric remains dependent nonetheless on the violence it claims to replace. It needs not only souls and minds but bodies.

In medieval England, for example, the need for actual bodies as the recipients of rhetorical lessons was enacted spatially during the Rogation or Gangdays, one of the Maytime festivities which was typically held on Monday, Tuesday, and Wednesday before Ascension. During the ritual and commemorative delineation of a civic space, the boundaries of a medieval town were literally marked upon the bodies of its young male citizens:

Led by the priests and carrying the Cross, banners, bells, and lights, the men of a village went in perambulation about the boundaries of the village. They *beat its bounds*. The small boys who went with the procession were thrown in to the brooks and ponds or had their buttocks bumped against the trees and rocks which marked the bounds, so that they should *remember* them better. And at certain customary points in the ganging, at every "Holy Oak of Gospel Tree" the procession stopped, and the priest offered up prayers and blessed the growing crops.[17]

Given this explicit bodily equation of remembrance with the spatial circumspection of the polis, it is difficult to accept Jacques Derrida's belief that discourse, "if it is originally violent, can *only do itself violence*, can only negate itself in order to affirm itself, make war upon the war which institutes it without ever *being able* to reappropriate this negativity, to the extent that it is discourse."[18] Derrida understands very well the ideological contortions of a mnemotechnical system that denies the very violence it engenders: but the flogged young men of Mayday would scarcely have agreed that an originary violent discourse "can only do itself violence."

It thus becomes especially urgent that we resituate the memory image within the performative and disciplinary rhetorical context for which it was intended, all the while recalling how its virtual violence would be translated into speech. Given the imperialistic "intent" of rhetoric as betrayed by the tale of its own origins, and given the status of memory as the epistemological site for the translation of intention into the delivered performances of civilized law, there arose a need to rationalize those paradoxes within the collective memory of rhetoric and its audiences. It is in their theorizations of mnemotechnics that rhetoricians grapple uneasily with an ideological discrepancy of their own creation: the discrepancy between an ennobled theory of civilization as indoctrination and the violent performance practices necessary for that indoctrination.[19] Classical and medieval rhetoricians consistently praise the "good" or necessary violence of rhetoric as well as its literal status as "discipline": but at the same time, they conceptualize their discipline as non-violent and mediatory because the rhetorics of law and civilization cannot create a *mise-en-abîme* of themselves and continue to generate, enact, and preserve the social "truths" they claim to transmit.[20] Therefore, when rhetoricians wish to justify, enforce, and perpetuate the "voluntary submission" to the common good which heralds the birth of civilization, they create a history of camouflage and subterfuge. In the rhetorical interplay among violence, memory, discipline, and performance, the hegemony attacks the very weapons it requires for its continued imposition of itself: rhetoric must construct itself as a non-violent way to mediate the violence which it both condemns and requires – a phenomenon that extends far beyond antiquity and the Middle Ages into the present day.

In his recent re-evaluation of historian Marc Bloch's statement that violence was "deep-rooted in the social structure and in the mentality " of the Middle Ages, Peter Haidu asserts that "we will not begin to make headway with our own versions of the issue [of violent transgression] until we grasp the continuity between those contemporary versions and the bases laid down in the Middle Ages upon which our struggles with violence are founded."[21] The history of mnemotechnics provides a particularly effective way to prove that claim historically.

Despite the critical currency of the Pseudo-Ciceronian *imagines agentes* in modern scholarly literature, those are not the first images of mnemotechnics to be invoked in the *Rhetorica ad Herennium*. Rather, the author begins his analysis of memory with a vision of murder for money, highlighting both the motive and the means of death. The art that had originated with Simonides' response to the destructive forces of nature (the collapse of a building) is no longer "natural": instead an apparently "unnatural" violence is the result of human – and in this case – criminal agency:

[H]oc modo, ut si accusator dixerit ab reo hominem veneno necatum et hereditatis causa factum arguerit et eius rei multos dixerit testes at conscios esse. Si hoc primum, ut ad defendendum nobis expeditum sit, meminisse volemus, in primo loco rei totius imaginem conformabimus; aegrotum in lecto cubantem faciemus ipsum illum de quo agetur, si formam eius detinebimus. . .Et reum ad lectum eius adstituemus, dextera poculum, sinistra tabulas, medico testiculos arietinos tenentem. Hoc modo et testium et hereditatis et veneno necati memoriam habere poterimus. (*Ad Herennium* book 3.33)

For example, the prosecutor has said that the defendant killed a man by poison, has charged that the motive for the crime was an inheritance, and declared that there are many witnesses and accessories to this act. If in order to facilitate our defence we wish to remember this first point, we shall in our first background form an image of the whole matter. We shall picture the man in question as lying ill in bed, if we know his person. . .And we shall place the defendant at the bedside, holding in his right hand a cup and in his left tablets, and on the fourth finger a ram's testicles. In this way we can record the man who was poisoned, the inheritance, and the witnesses.

30

To introduce the topic of *memoria* in this way is to stage a scene of impending disfigurement – the ultimate and intentional disfigurement of murder as a prelude to the theorization of mnemotechnics and its translation into a dramatically delivered rhetorical performance in the courtroom. But paradoxically, one of the ways in which theorists subvert that violence even as they articulate it is by emphasizing the artifice of the performances to which memory gives rise.

For example, Quintilian praises Cicero for capitalizing on the spirit of the memory image during courtroom performances by exhibiting the physical evidence that would commemorate and vivify violent acts metonymically: "blood-stained swords, fragments of bone taken from the wound, and garments spotted with blood" (*Institutio oratoria* book 6.1.30).[22] Thus, when Cicero displayed the blood-stained, purple-bordered toga of the murdered Caesar, he did considerably more than demonstrate how images are remembered more readily "if we somehow disfigure them [*deformabimus*], as by introducing one stained with blood or soiled with mud or smeared with red paint, so that its form is more striking" (*Ad Herennium* book 3.37): he also brought "such a vivid image of the crime before their minds [*repraesentavit imaginem sceleris*], that Caesar seemed not to have been murdered, but *to be being murdered* before their very eyes" (*Institutio oratoria* book 6.1.31; emphasis mine). Quintilian's emphasis on the outcome of memory in violently dramatic delivery facilitates a kind of ideological cleavage between the epistemology and the performance of violence – even as he stresses the status of memory as the birthplace of performance. Indeed, in a triumph of counter-intuition, Quintilian even goes so far as to acknowledge the power of theatrical violence, only to claim that delivery is actually that which precipitates the *forfeit* of rhetorical power – a power that must be controlled or "moderated" by the juridical powers of the State: "to-day a rather more violent [*agitatior*] form of delivery has come into fashion and is demanded of our orators: it is well adapted to certain portions of a speech, but requires to be kept under control. Otherwise, in our attempt to ape the elegances of the stage [*actoris captamus elegantiam*], we shall lose the authority which should characterise the man of dignity and virtue" (*Institutio oratoria* book 11.3.184). After all, forensic rhetors had generated their mnemonic images in order to ensure justice, to punish criminals, and to protect society from the very acts of violence now represented iconically and discursively before judge, jury, or audiences.

Continuing to emphasize the "artificial" mnemonic spectacle of intentional violence, Quintilian rehearses the violent memory scene as a dramatic and participatory spectacle designed to make audiences "feel as if they were actual eyewitnesses of the scene [of the crime]" (*Institutio oratoria* book 4.2.123). His orator is to re-create a drama of criminal activity on his own memory stage in order to place the audience of delivery at the re-enacted scene of that violence:

I am complaining that a man has been murdered. Shall I not bring before my eyes [*in oculis habebo*] all the circumstances which it is reasonable to imagine must have occurred in such a connexion? Shall I not see the assassin burst suddenly from his hiding-place, the victim tremble, cry for help, beg for mercy, or turn to run? Shall I not see the fatal blow delivered and the stricken body fall? Will not the blood, the deathly pallor, the groan of agony, the death-rattle, be indelibly impressed upon my mind?   (*Institutio oratoria* book 6.2.31–32)

When Quintilian stages delivery as the place where real violence is re-enacted dramatically, when he applauds Cicero's exploitation of actual commemorative objects rather than of images (or in addition to images), the result is that the violence of the mnemonic image appears almost non-violent by comparison, appears somehow cleansed by the purity of its intentions to do "good violence." Since violence is conceived epistemologically as the virtuality of memory, and since rhetorical delivery constitutes the locus for enacting and re-enacting that violence, the originary mnemonic images of disfigurement and deformation seem neutralized even as their violence reaches fruition. The artifice of the "artificial memory" is consigned to delivery in an ideological feat which naturalizes that which is violently artificial.

In the thirteenth century, it seems that the death-rattle emanating from Quintilian's man abed was heard by John of Garland, whose *Parisiana poetria* bespeaks an equally subtle conception of the violent genesis of mnemotechnics. Although John portrays the traditional columnar locus in his treatment of "The Art of Remembering," it is in the section that immediately precedes it that he lays the literal foundation for the intentional violence to which arts of memory must respond.[23] To illustrate the style of "Complex Embellishment," John chooses an image of violation "in which a master complains to his bishop of a violent assault [*de violenta manuum iniectione*]." Yet when the victim describes the Everyman knight who attacked him, the exposition is rife with mnemonic imprints that seem to anticipate eerily the Derridean *trace*: a sword metonymically cast as the "wound-making steel" as well as the familiar description of memory as a stomach-like receptacle for the food and drink of the mind – transposed here as a criminal mind feeding on blood.[24] Moreover, that this section precedes John's discussion of memory suggests a veritable restaging of the Simonides legend: the prelude to the codification of the art of memory is no longer an accident, but an intentional act of violence committed by a criminal and conveyed through re-enactment:

> I flee to your Holiness's footsteps, most pious Father, to complain that R., knight of such-and-such a place, brandishing the *wound-making steel*, and his satellites. . .assaulted me with a good deal of sweat. . .In the end the aforesaid knight, with all his house, *fed his crime-infected mind to satiety on my blood*, and leaving the *marks* of his livid hatred on me, dismissed me for dead. . . Wherefore, in accordance with your clemency, I beg you to offer 'the chalice of salvation' (Ps. 115: 13) to me as I keep my couch by listening to the *gasping groans* of my voice. And I beg you so to purge the bilge water of crime in that knight that through the punishment of the presumptuous insolence of one many may cringe in *terror*.   (*Parisiana poetria*, 51–68; emphasis mine)

John's victim pleads that his Bishop elevate to the status of coercive exemplarity a scene of intentional violence which will strike terror in the hearts of future criminals and regulate their conduct. Like Plato's law-maker, John thus utilizes visions in order to deter criminal behavior; like Cicero and Quintilian, he exploits the metonymic power of the mnemonic object (in this case, the weapon) in order to generate *visiones*; and like the Pseudo-Cicero, he brings *imagines agentes* to life as disfigured images of the body. Ultimately, however, when the Pseudo-Cicero, Quintilian, and John of Garland oppose the virtuality of violent memory epistemology to the performed violence of crime and of delivered speeches about crime, they obscure the insight that it is largely *because* of memory that the violence is inevitable.[25]

Given that inevitability, the question arises as to how theorists manage to attribute a positive valence to the very violence that they seek (however subtly) to conceal. Early rhetorical narratives reveal that they do so by figuring destruction (or destructive intention) as beautiful generation or birth. Indeed, according to Elaine Scarry, the Bible itself provides the quintessential demonstration of a larger socio-cultural intuition to conflate violence with creation: "this intuition is obscured and deconstructed, as the activity of creation becomes conflated with the activity of wounding; in turn. . .the deconstruction is itself re-constructed, the original intuition is itself rescued, and creating and wounding are once more held securely in place as separable categories of action" (*Body in Pain*, pp. 184). Yet the rhetorical tradition betrays a similar oscillation between wounding and birth which is further reinforced by the oscillation between virtual and actual violence. In the *Poetria nova*, for example, Geoffrey of Vinsauf conflates wounding and creation only to separate them. In a violent *ludus* of wrestling, his psyche literally tortures itself in a struggle to invent beautiful poetry:

> Non venit ex facili res ista nec absque labore;
> Sed mens quando studet, tanquam pugil, anxia pugnat.
> Pugnat enim secum. Petit ut sibi consulat, et non
> Consulit ipsa sibi. Repetit patiturque repulsam
> Ipsa secunda sibi: ferventius instat et ipsa
> Perstat adhuc contra se, curis anxia torquet
> Se, tandem quod vult extorquet vi violenta
> A se. Sicque simul victrix et victa triumphat
> De se. (1754–62)[26]

The matter does not come easily or effortlessly; but when the mind is eager, like a champion, it struggles over-anxiously. For it fights with itself. It desires to take counsel of itself, and it does not. It tries again, and suffers repulse, being its own worst enemy. More determinedly it presses on, and yet it still stands firm against itself: *it torments itself*, afflicted by cares; *with violent force it finally wrests what it seeks from itself*. Thus at once conqueror and conquered, it triumphs over itself. (Gallo, p. 109)

Geoffrey figures poetic production as the positive creation of the violence which engenders it. But here, the very concept of generation demands much closer scrutiny, especially with regard to its harrowing ramifications in two crucial cultural arenas: the construction of gender and the performance of pedagogy.[27]

The refiguration of violence as creation is unmistakable in Thomas Bradwardine's *De memoria artificiali*, which features bloody images connected by acts of beating and of childbirth. In the same way that during the Rogation days, a mnemonic beating of the male body was accompanied by prayers for germinating crops, this is a mnemonic beating which takes place at the epistemological level. In order to teach techniques for memorizing the signs of the zodiac, Bradwardine stages a bloody Taurus who is being kicked in his engorged testicles on one side by Aries the Ram while, on the other side, the bull's blood spills over a woman in

34

painful labor with Gemini's Twins. Violence is a *figure* of birth which simultaneously dis*figures*. And, in a vision of "economy" that would leave the heads of most post-modern critics spinning, Bradwardine even finds in memory a means by which to assimilate from women the entire birthing process:

Constituat ergo sibi iuxta principium primi loci arietem candidissimum stantem et erectum super posteriores eius pedes cum cornibus si voluerit deauratis. Taurum quoque rubissimum ponat ad dextram arietis cum pedibus posterioribus percutientem arietem; aries vero stans erectus dextro pede percutiat taurum super *testiculos eius magnos* et ultra modum *inflatos ad effusionem sanguinis copiosam.* Et per *testiculos* memorabitur quod sit taurus, non bos *castratus* nec vacca. Similiter taurum anteponatur mulier quasi *laborans* in partu, et in *utero* eius quasi *rupto* a pectore fingantur duo gemelli *pulcherimi* exuentes, et cum cancro horribili et intense rubro *ludentes,* qui unius parvulorum captam manum detineat, et sic ipsum ad fletum et ad signa talia compellat, reliquo parvulo admirante et nihilominus cancrum pueriliter contrectante. Vel ponantur ibi duo gemelli *non de muliere* sed de tauro *mirabili modo nasci,* ut rerum paucitas observetur.[28]

One places a very red bull to the right of the ram, *kicking* the ram with his rear feet; standing erect, the ram then with his right foot kicks the bull above his *large and superswollen testicles,* causing a *copious infusion of blood.* And by means of the *testicles* one will recall that it is a bull, not a *castrated* ox or a cow. In a similar manner, a woman is placed before the bull as though *laboring in birth,* and from her *uterus* as though *ripped open* from the breast are figured coming forth two most beautiful twins, playing with a horrible intensely red crab which holds captive the hand of one of the little ones and thus compels him to weeping and to such signs, the remaining child wondering nonetheless caressing the crab in a childish way. Or the two twins are placed there *born not of a woman* but from the bull in a marvellous manner, so that *the principle of economy of material* may be observed.

While Carruthers observes of this passage that "what is most surprising, to a puritan-formed sensibility, is the emphasis on violence and sexuality which runs through all the interaction of the figures in each scene" (*Book of Memory,* p. 134), the violent conjunction of bloodshed and birth is not so surprising when we recall the violent genesis of mnemotechnics itself. Bradwardine stages that violent genesis literally by attaching its pedagogical efficacy to the infliction of blows upon male and female reproductive organs. For example, his depiction of the womb is consistent with that of Honorius Augustodunensis, who deemed it a mere receptacle for male impressions: "the womb, indeed, is certainly the receptacle of the semen; it is lined within with villi so as to retain it better, and is composed of seven cells with the shape of a man *stamped* on them as if on a coin."[29] And more interesting still is his representation of the testicles, which harks back to the Pseudo-Cicero's long perplexing image of the ram's testicles (*testiculos arietinos tenentem*) which signify the presence of witnesses (*testes*) (*Ad Herennium* book 3.33; cited above, p. 30). Combining connotations of testimony, sexuality, and spectatorship, the term *testis* spotlights the status of men as *witnesses*; whereas the uterus is only a space (however generative) upon which violent imprints are inflicted.

If ever there were a narrative that anticipates Antonin Artaud's dark metaphysics of theatre, it is Bradwardine's birth of memory. "All the great Myths are dark," writes Artaud, "so that one cannot imagine, save in an atmosphere of carnage, torture, and bloodshed, all the magnificent Fables which recount to the multitudes the first sexual division and the first carnage of essences that appeared in creation."[30] If ever there were a demonstration of the deliberate staging of brutalized bodies as a necessary topos of culture, it is the cruelty of this astrological vision: cruelty, insist Gilles Deleuze and Félix Guattari, "has nothing to do with some ill-defined or natural violence that might be commissioned to explain the history of mankind; cruelty is the movement of culture that is realized in bodies and inscribed on them, belaboring them. That is what cruelty means."[31] And all these blows, all the stamping, all the cruelty participate in a disfiguring mnemotechnics which founds trenchant distinctions between men and women as the recipients of pedagogical violence.

Medieval and early Renaissance pedagogues had their own violent ways of ensuring that students would not forget as the classroom became a kind of stage on which the "rule of the rod" was enacted as a mode of desirable violence. Contributing to that larger spectacle of violence was first, the space of the classroom itself. In the same way that Cicero had pronounced that all memory imagery required "an abode, inasmuch as a material object without a locality is inconceivable" (*De oratore*, book 2.358), so too did the actual physical space of the classroom constitute a kind of Burkean "predisposing structure" for violence.[32] In fact, one of the premier functions of that space was to set the scene for the potentially violent inculcation of intellectual and social norms. So it was that in the Renaissance, Erasmus believed that "even the schoolroom walls and the fixtures all around the pupils offered lessons about how one should think and behave."[33] Yet, to borrow Scarry's terms from her analysis of torture, even a room could become a weapon: space is "converted into a weapon, deconverted, undone. Made to participate in the annihilation of the prisoners, made to demonstrate that everything is a weapon, the objects themselves, and with them the fact of civilization, are annihilated: there is no wall, no window, no door. . .only weapons" (*Body in Pain*, p. 41). Second, because of its own designs on remembrance, pedagogy frequently reproduces violence as the space of the classroom becomes a locus of spectacular torment, display, and discipline. The translation of memory visions of intellectual discipline into actual pedagogical discipline was not only impressed on young minds: it was inflicted by means of blows upon young bodies. And once again, the pain and suffering of the pedagogical process is figured as positive, salubrious, or, as many medieval dramatists apparently saw it, entertaining.[34]

My intention here is neither to suggest that all pedagogical spaces were violent, nor to perpetuate the recent theories of pedagogy as victimization which have been so aptly refined by Marjorie Curry Woods. In questioning what she calls the debilitating "fear of teaching topos" in which "having taught" becomes synonymous with "having oppressed," Woods emphasized the "ageism and academic self-hatred that we support when we accept the suppression of the pedagogical aspects of the history of our profession."[35] However, I do wish to emphasize that many of the mnemonic techniques of early pedagogy were indeed violent and oppressive. Nor had there been much change over the years in Plato's initial conception of the lawmaker as one who corrects the "foggy vision" of his charges by replacing one image of society. As late as 1858, Henry Adams complained of his training in the German *gymnasium* that "the arbitrary training given to the memory was stupefying; the strain that the memory endured was a form of torture."[36] Indeed, as we shall see, even modern theorists of pedagogy rehearse anew all the anomalies of the history of rhetoric, denying or rationalizing the violence on which teaching has historically depended.

In his fourth-century *Confessions*, no less an authority than St. Augustine agreed that pedagogy was torture. Comparing the relationship of master to disciple with that of torturer to victim, Augustine invokes the actual *tormenta* "which we school-boys suffered from our masters." "Is there any man," he asks, qui tibi pie cohaerendo ita sit affectus granditer, ut *eculeos et ungulas atque huiscemodi varia tormenta*, pro quibus effugiendis tibi per universas terras *cum timore magno* supplicatur, ita parvi aestimet, diligens eos, qui haec acerbissime formidant, quemadmodum parentes nostri *ridebant tormenta*, quibus pueri a magistris affligebamur?[37]

who by devoutly applying himself unto thee, is so resolutely affected that he can think so lightly of those racks and strappadoes, and such varieties of torments, (for the avoiding whereof men pray unto thee with so much fear all the world over), that he can make sport at those who most bitterly fear them; as our parents laughed at these torments, which we school-boys suffered from our masters? For we were no less afraid of the rod, nor did we less earnestly pray to thee for the scaping of it, than others did of their tortures.

When Augustine casts pedagogues as punishers, he also emphasizes the symbolic power of the figure of the master himself, especially the Master of Grammar so frequently depicted in the iconography of the Middle Ages and Renaissance with whips in hand.[38] Medieval *magistri* wielding the weapons of their trade were expert in glossing the signs of fear, as when Geoffrey of Vinsauf offers the following illustration of the plain style: " 'When he looked at the rods, the color left the boy's cheeks and his face was pale.' Such a figure of rhetoric indicates that he was afraid" (*Poetria nova*, p. 97). But even more important, they were expert in *creating* fear, creating the very signs they wished to gloss, in reading its traces and creating future traces upon the bodies of their students. Geoffrey of Vinsauf's teacher might well have seen the signs of fear *before* the beating; but others would interpret afterward the physical traces inscribed upon the beaten student body. Guibert of Nogent portrays in his *Memoirs* the experience of being "pelted almost every day with a hail of blows and harsh words" by his schoolmaster, the traces of which caused his mother to grieve at "the very savage punishment inflicted on my tender body":

I went to my mother's knee after a more severe beating than I had deserved. And when, as often happened, she began to ask me repeatedly whether I had been whipped that day, I, not to appear a telltale, entirely denied it. Then against my will she threw off my inner garment (which is called a shirt or *chemise*) and saw my little arms blackened and the skin of my back everywhere puffed up with the cuts from the twigs.[39]

Mnemonic preservation of the pedagogical experience of violence is thus figured in the traces left by switches upon the body of the student/victim. Indeed, according to Avicenna, memory was the faculty by means of which pain could be accessed, as when he chose to illustrate his own theory of mnemotechnics with a beating whose pain could only be apprehended by the mnemonic imagination: "one feels pain from a beating [*verbera*] and the accident of pain is in the body, while the pain is had in the [internal] senses according to what it means [intention] to sense something whilst the cause of the pain is in the body. . .Imagination comes from what is apprehended rather than from what is experienced by the body."[40]

In what may well be the most sinister representation of all of the virtuality of memory, Thomas Murner (1475–1537) offers a visual mnemonic which actually anticipates such traces. Murner was the author of the *Logica memorativa* or *Chartiludium logice* (*Mnemonic Logic* or *Logical Card Game*) first published in 1509. A Franciscan religious satirist and anti-Lutheran writer, Murner reworked Peter of Spain's thirteenth-century *Summulae logicales* in his own emblematized game, approximately one third of which comprises woodcut illustrations.[41] The work begins with a glossary of signs designed to assist the reader in glossing text and pictures: a sleigh bell signifying an enunciation, a lobster a predicable, a fish a predicament, a syllogism an acorn, a coronet a fallacy, and so on. But, as Walter Ong emphasizes in his own assessment of Murner, when that key is used to interpret the violent memory image of a schoolmaster holding three bundles of switches (fig. 1.1), the pedagogical repercussions are "terrifying" (*Rhetoric, Romance, and Technology*, p. 125).

For Murner's destined reader – the "soft youth" of his generation – the image of the schoolmaster is to be glossed as follows: the weight in his hand is an affirmative proposition, the cord a negative proposition, the birds of different species propositions with no common term, and most relevant here, the three switches signify three questions to be imprinted on and rehearsed within the memory: "what? what kind? and how many?" In terms strikingly reminiscent of the definition of torture from the Justinian *Digest* as "torment and corporeal suffering and pain employed to extract the truth" from the body of the victim, Murner writes that "it is with the aid of the switches that the answers to these questions are extracted from the pupils" (triplici virga: triplex esse quesitium nam virgis iuvenes inquirimus).[42] So, while Ong concludes that this image is "calculated to *beat* the terms and rules into little boy's heads if not really to teach any genuinely formal logic" (*Ramus*, p. 85), the question is: what, then, does it teach? In Murner's pedagogical invocation of memory, interrogation,

Primus

Applicatio tertia

1.1 Master of grammar with switches, from Thomas Murner, *Logica memorativa*. Strasbourg, 1509

beating, and extraction, his woodcut becomes more than a memory image, more than an iconographic representation of mnemotechnics as menacing, disciplinary, literally dependent on the whip or *disciplina*: it is a memory image of torture or, rather, an image of torture as the ultimate mnemonic. Like some kind of coercive human metronome, Murner's schoolmaster wields his switches as one who is empowered to beat the "truth" not only *out of* but *in to* the bodies of his students – his intended audience, his intended victims.

Centuries before Friedrich Nietzsche enumerated his own list of tortures in the service of memory, medieval and early Renaissance pedagogues had already recognized the function he described: "by such methods the individual was finally taught to remember five or six 'I won'ts' which entitled him to participate in the benefits of society; and indeed, with the aid of this sort of memory, people eventually 'came to their senses.' "[43] The beatings threatened by Murner's *magister* are not internalized as they were in Geoffrey of Vinsauf's description of the self-inflicted tortures of poetic invention: they are directed at others. Indeed, his pedagogy is a discipline which demands an Other to serve as victim of the violent mnemonic imprints of others – a violence which is cast not only as birth but as love. Similarly, like Virgil and Ovid before him, Guibert de Nogent invokes *saevus amor*, loyalty, and gratitude for his tormentors. While he finds his teacher's punishments cruel and unjust, they engender enough feelings of love – even of sublimated sexual love – that the very violence of the mnemonic indoctrination can reach its desired counter-intuitive conclusion: to be forgotten:

Now my teacher had a *harsh love* for me, for he showed excessive severity in his unjust floggings, and yet the *great care* with which he guarded me was evident in his acts. Clearly I did not deserve to be beaten, for if he had had the skill in teaching which he professed, it is certain that I, though a boy, would have been well able to grasp anything that he taught. . . .I conceived much love for him in response, in spite of the many weals with which he furrowed my tender skin, so that not through fear, as is common in those of my age, but through a sort of love deeply implanted in my heart, I obeyed him *in utter forgetfulness* of his severity. (Guibert, pp. 48–49; emphasis mine)

In that sense, the accounts of Guibert and of Thomas Murner do far more than presage René Girard's theorization of a "good violence" which depends on surrogate victims who enable societies to conceive of violence as ritualized, "creative and protective in nature" (*Violence and the Sacred*,

p. 144). They view the rule of the rod as a crucial cultural tool by which society may purge itself of an undesirably "soft male youth" by reforming their bodies, by beating the effeminacy out of them. This is a complex epistemological move according to which softness is cast as feminine – and then beaten out of men at the same time that masculinity is beaten in.

Although there is no doubt about the highly coercive register of the mnemonic techniques employed against men, early theorists make some crucial distinctions between men and women as possessors of mem-ory and as recipients/victims of the mnemonic indoctrination of others. Male students upon whom the lessons of the hegemony are violently inscribed may well be victims: but they are also the future victimizers, the future inflicters of violence. Their bodies and memories were marked and tormented so that boys might participate as teachers in the violent pedagogical ethos described in the twelfth century by John of Salisbury. His medieval master was both architect and brutalizer, a militaristic commander who was to build character as follows:

In military matters, a commanding officer must first see that his army is properly supplied with arms and other military equipment. The architect-builder with his tools first determines and obtains materials he will use in his construction. . .In like manner, the contriver of the science of reasoning, the drill-master [*campidoctor*] of those who profess to be logicians, has. . .provided the means of disputation, and stacked in the arena arms for the use of his students. . .His next step is to show his disciples how they may use these instruments, and somehow to teach them the art of engaging in [argumentative] combat.[44]

Moreover, while mnemonic thrashings ultimately enable men to speak and to teach, they tend not only to silence women but also to prefigure future violence against them. Unlike men, women cannot be teachers, as Juan-Luis Vives reminds us: she must be denied the right to teach young boys "lest when she hath taken a false opinion. . .she spread it into the hearers, by the authority of mastership."[45] The male student is both target and targeter; and the female student is target alone. If male students were brutalized, they were also comforted, as when Guibert's mother discovers the traces of her son's classroom beating. Virtually suckling him on her knee, she reads the signs of his body:

Grieved to the heart by the very savage punishment inflicted on my tender body, troubled, agitated, and weeping with sorrow, she said: "You shall never become a clerk, nor any more suffer so much to get an education." At that, looking at her with what reproach I could, I replied, "If I had to die on the spot, I would not give up studying my lessons and becoming a clerk."

(Guibert, p. 50)

Yet Guibert criticizes his mother for her pity and concern. Her capacities as a reader of signs are limited insofar as she does not understand the salubrious violence of her son's training. And her limited role of comforter is a potential impediment to his education and part of the effeminate traits Guibert and Murner wished to expunge. But, however defective the source of comfort may be, Guibert is comforted nonetheless. And no such comfort was available to women: rather such a student as Abelard's Heloise actually served to provide sexual comfort to her abuser as he translates the violence inflicted upon her memory and body into a comforting male vision of erotic love.

When Abelard identifies Heloise in the *Historia calamitatum* as someone "fortunate" enough to be considered for instruction, the objectified girl is passed from her uncle to her teacher (and later, her husband). The beatings she endures at his hands are represented not only as violent pedagogical imprints, but as signs of love:

For when he handed her over to me not only to teach but to discipline, what else was he doing but giving free rein to my designs, and opportunity, even if I were not seeking it, easily to subdue her by threats and stripes if blandishments did not work. . .? And the better to prevent suspicion, I sometimes struck her not through anger or vexations but from love and affection which were beyond the sweetness of every ointment. No sign of love was omitted by us.[46]

In that sense, although Carruthers concludes from her own reading of Heloise that all subjectivity is located in the memory (*Book of Memory*, pp. 180–82), the female memory remains elusive insofar as female subjectivity has itself been objectified. For example, Andreas Capellanus writes that woman "is like melting wax, always ready to assume fresh shape and to be moulded to the imprint of anybody's seal" (est enim mulier tanquam *cera* liquescens, quae semper est sigilli cuiuslibet impositionem mutari).[47] But that troubling invocation of the traditional mnemonic wax tablet denies to woman even the possession of a memory upon which to inscribe the lessons of the hegemony. Unlike Heloise, she is not even an intellect who endures a mnemonic thrashing. Rather, woman is the receptacle upon which men inscribe and enact their own lessons – violently, and often sexually as her own memory is itself neutralized.

That sinister process is particularly clear in the prosecution and

43

persecution of witches as elaborated in the notorious *Malleus maleficarum* by Heinrich Krämer and Jacob Sprenger. There the two authors literally demonize the female memory by implying that, even if woman does possess a memory, it is a faculty governed by the Devil. There are more female than male witches, they explain, because women "have weak memories; and it is a natural vice in them not to be disciplined, but to follow their own impulses without any sense of what is due; this is her whole study, and that she keeps in her memory."[48] The perfidious female memory is then further anathematized both by the denial of any real "intellectual understanding" to women and the attribution to women of a power to create diabolical illusions which confuse men:

For by the power of devils, with God's permission, mental images long retained in the treasury of such images, which is the memory, are drawn out, not from the intellectual understanding in which such images are stored, but from the memory, which is the repository of mental images, and is situated at the back of the head, and are presented to the imaginative faculty. And so strongly are they impressed on that faculty that man has an inevitable impulse to imagine a horse or a beast, when the devil draws from the memory an image of a horse or a beast; and so he is compelled to think that he sees with his external eyes such a beast when there is actually no such beast to see; but it seems to be so by reason of the impulsive force of the devil working by means of those images.

(*Witchcraft*, pp. 146–47)

In the deft ideological sleight of hand, Krämer and Sprenger manage to transmute the theoretically *active* faculty of memory into one that is necessarily *passive* if possessed by women. They problematize the very nature of female subjectivity by creating the ultimate oxymoronic construct: objectified subjectivity.

In the last analysis, however disturbing the distinctions made between men and women, one common denominator of violent memory imagery is its performative potential in pedagogy. Early theories of mnemotechnics demonstrate a penetrating awareness of the "psychological axiom" that would be articulated by Friedrich Nietzsche in his own discussion of the creation of remembrance for a human species that incarnated forgetfulness: " 'A thing is *branded* on the memory to make it stay there; only what goes on hurting will stick.'. . .Whenever man has thought it necessary to create a memory for himself, his effort has been attended with torture, blood, sacrifice" (*Genealogy*, pp. 192–93). Similarly, when Deleuze and Guattari extrapolate from Nietzsche that societies record their essence in such

44

violent operations as "tattooing, excising, incising, carving, scarifying, mutilating, encircling, and initiating" with the design of "creating a memory for man" (*Anti-Oedipus*, pp. 144–45), they too stress the importance of a primordial cultural drive to invent a collective memory from violence. But long before modern critics posed their own questions about the memory of violence, ancient and medieval authors had already rehearsed the answers in a violent rhetorical scene that was didactic, disciplinary, corrective, and coercive. If Nietzsche, Deleuze, and Guattari invoke the pain of branding, if they confirm the artifice of invention, they also reaffirm the principle that memory is a learned rather than an inborn ability.

The notion that mnemonic violence is both necessary and artificial prompts certain final questions about its historical presence in the classroom: namely, if mnemotechnics has always been concerned with the infliction of intentional violence, then why has that violence come to be seen as so "unnatural?" If violence is indeed a norm in education, then why does the modern audience remain shocked by it? How is it that, even today, academics find themselves surprised, ruffled, or angry when academic debate becomes contestatory? Given the salubrious violence of early educational theory, how does the illusion of a naturally peaceable dialogue come to overshadow the reality of corporal punishment and violent indoctrination?

While many medievalists may well be grateful that our current debates have not yet led to the situation of *c.* 1450, where, as Durkheim reminds us, "people even reached the point where they kicked, punched and bit one another. Wounded and dead were lying on the floor"; still, the agonistic tenor of early education tends to be categorized under the convenient rubric of "alterity."[49] In a practice of ideological subterfuge, not unlike that in which early theorists of mnemotechnics indulged, contemporary societies deem pedagogical violence transgressive and deny its prevalence, even though that finding is regularly contradicted by each daily disclosure in the evening news of beatings, rapes, and abuses in American elementary, secondary, and post-secondary schools. Peter Haidu, for example, eloquently exposes the "hypocrisy" of the contemporary cultural assumption that peace is the "desired and desirable norm" and violence its negativized opposite: "in respect to the practices of violence, modernity is medieval: it continues the practices of the Middle Ages, differentiating itself primarily in the amount of violence produced, and in its hypocritical disguisement" (*The Subject of Violence*, pp. 3 and 193–94).

And earlier, René Girard agreed, commenting that "we believe the normal form of desire is nonviolent and that this nonviolent form is characteristic of the generality of mankind. . .[but] this hopeful belief is clearly without foundation" (*Violence and the Sacred*, p. 144).

Yet civilized societies depend on such hopeful beliefs. If the explicitly coercive register of pedagogy were to be acknowledged, those hopes would vanish and Derrida's worst fear would be realized: "the horizon of peace would disappear into the night" (*Writing and Difference*, p. 130). Teresa de Lauretis' contention would become all too clear: "once a connection is assumed between violence and rhetoric, the two terms begin to slide, and, soon enough, the connection will appear to be reversible."[50] And outrage against school violence would itself become an illusion, its primary function being to secure the myth of a non-violent pedagogy.

In his re-evaluation of the modern tendency to celebrate dialogue over brainwashing, James Berlin identifies a contemporary revisionist fable according to which dialogue has always been the best and only way to learn: "disruptions in this trajectory [of dialectic]. . .are to be explained away as the products of failed cultures – the most frequently named being that of the Middle Ages and the nineteenth century."[51] And yet, there was nothing dialogic about John of Salisbury's footsoldiers or Murner's schoolmaster with his bundle of switches. In essence, these fictions are entrenched in the same myths of creation and civilization rehearsed by the origins of an imperialistic rhetoric. Inasmuch as the ostensibly mediatory powers of a rhetoric grounded in the memory must originate in violence, rhetoric itself must remain at odds with itself and civilization must be paired with cruelty.

"Life," writes Derrida, "is already threatened by the origin of the memory which constitutes it" (*Writing and Difference*, p. 202). And, historically speaking, one important moment at which that threat was addressed was the eighteenth century, when such moral philosophers as Adam Smith offered to substitute empathy for cruelty: indeed, Smith reconfigures violence as the very origin of empathy. In his *Theory of Moral Sentiments* (1759), he turns to torture in order to argue that empathetic identification on the part of an observer/witness can only be achieved through the memory. Evoking the incapacity of the senses to convey the suffering of "our brother upon the rack," Smith employs such profoundly mnemonic terms as imagination, representation, copies, and impressions:

It is *by the imagination only* that we can form any conception of what are his

46

sensations. Neither can that faculty help us to this in any other way, than by *representing* to us what would be our own, if we were in this case. It is the *impressions* of our own senses only, not those of his, which our imaginations copy. By the imagination we place ourselves in his situation, we conceive ourselves enduring all the same torments, *we enter as it were into his body*, and become in some measure the same person with him, and thence form some idea of his sensations. . .[52]

But again, centuries earlier, Cicero and Quintilian had already linked mnemonic *visiones* and *phantasiai* with role-playing, empathy, and theatricality. The former cited mnemonic branding as a prerequisite for the theatrical enactment of memory during delivery: "it is impossible for the listener to feel indignation, hatred or ill-will, to be terrified of anything, or reduced to tears of compassion, unless all those emotions, which the advocate would inspire in the arbitrator, are visibly *stamped or rather branded* on the advocate himself (impressi esse atque inusti videbuntur)" (*De oratore* book 2.189; emphasis mine). And the latter directed that "the prime essential for stirring the emotions of others is. . .first to feel those emotions oneself" (*Institutio oratoria* book 6. 2.26). Quintilian then likened that situation to actors who are still drowned in the tears of their role after the play is over, concluding that "we must identify ourselves so strongly with the persons of whom we complain. . .and must plead their case and for a brief space feel their suffering as though it were our own" (*Institutio oratoria* book 6.2.34–35). This entire phenomenon is less a history of the engenderment of empathy and more a camouflage of the fact that a violent memory epistemology appears necessary for its theatrical construction.

Finally, to come full circle to the image with which I began – the theatrical space of the violent memory scene and the questionable safety of its boundaries – Constantin Stanislavski's theory of the emotion memory serves as a fitting conclusion. In *An Actor Prepares*, actor Kostya learns from his mentor that emotion memory is important because "just as your visual memory can reconstruct an inner image of some forgotten thing, place or person, your emotion memory can bring back feelings you have already experienced."[53] It cannot be coincidental, however, that when Kostya learns how to access the "memory of life" rather than the "theatrical archives of your mind," his epiphany occurs when he recalls and relives the violence of an isolated vehicular accident which had dismembered its victim – an incident which constitutes a compelling rearticulation of the Simonides legend:

47

On a boulevard we ran into a large crowd. I like street scenes, so I pushed into the centre of it, and there my eyes fell on a horrible picture. At my feet lay an old man, poorly dressed, his jaw crushed, both arms cut off. His face was ghastly; his old yellow teeth stuck out through his bloody moustache. A street car towered over its victim. . .This picture made a deep impression on me. . .In the night I awoke, and the visual memory was even more terrifying than the sight of the accident itself had been. Probably because at night everything seems more fearful. But I ascribed it to my emotion memory and its power to deepen impressions. (*An Actor Prepares*, pp. 170–71)

For Kostya, it is the relived and remembered terror prompted by this violent accident which engenders good acting and even "acting good." Moreover, in the same way that the Simonides legend sparked the genesis of *technē*, Stanislavski's equally arbitrary scene of violence also has a happy ending. It is a self-affirming, life-affirming, naturalizing dismemberment which gives birth to empathy:

I passed by the scene of the accident and involuntarily stopped to recall what had happened so recently. All traces were obliterated. . .As I thought, my memory of the catastrophe seemed to become transformed. At first it had been raw and naturalistic, with all the ghastly physical details, the crushed jaw, the severed arms, the children playing with the stream of blood. Now I was shaken as much by my memory of it all, but in a different way. I was suddenly filled with indignation against human cruelty, injustice, and indifference.

(*An Actor Prepares*, p. 171)

In a sense, it is not surprising that an intellectual subculture would prefer pathos to brutality. After all, moral philosophers have traditionally exalted the virtues of compassion and community – however violent their origins. For reasons that remain embedded in the very language of rhetoric, violence, and aesthetics, societies prefer to tell themselves stories of empathy and civilization rather than to unmask the ways in which those very stories promote the violence necessary to their own construction.

Notes

1 [Cicero], *Rhetorica ad C. Herennium*, ed. and trans. Harry Caplan, Loeb Classical Library (1954; rpt. Cambridge, Mass.: Harvard University Press, 1977), 3.37. I analyze mnemonics as protodrama in *Rhetoric and the Origins of Medieval Drama* (Ithaca: Cornell University Press, 1992), pp. 44–54. For premier critical discussions of memory, see especially: Frances Yates, *The Art of Memory* (Chicago: University of Chicago Press, 1966); Mary

Carruthers, *The Book of Memory* (Cambridge: Cambridge University Press, 1990); Janet Coleman, *Ancient and Medieval Memories* (Cambridge: Cambridge University Press, 1992); M. T. Clanchy, *From Memory to Written Record: England, 1066–1307* (Cambridge, Mass.: Harvard University Press: 1979); Walter J. Ong, *Rhetoric, Romance, and Technology: Studies in the Interaction of Expression and Culture* (Ithaca: Cornell University Press, 1971), ch. 4; and Paul Zumthor and Bruno Roy, eds., *Jeux de mémoire: Aspects de la mnémotechnie médiévale* (Paris: Vrin, 1985). I wish to take this opportunity to thank several colleagues for invaluable intellectual feedback on this study: Rita Copeland, Eugene Vance, Sharon Farmer, Louise Fradenburg, Elizabeth MacArthur, and an anonymous reader for Cambridge University Press.

2   Recently, modern theorists of performance have called into question the safety of this barrier: see, for example, Geoff Pywell, *Staging Real Things: The Performance of Ordinary Events* (Lewisburg, Pa.: Bucknell University Press, 1994); and David Graver, "Violent Performances: Aggression, Pain, and the Protocols of Theater," paper presented at "Unnatural Acts," Riverside, California, February 13, 1993.

3   See Carruthers, *Book of Memory*, pp. 130–38; Eugene Vance, *Merelous Signals: Poetics and Sign Theory in the Middle Ages* (1986; rpt. Lincoln: University of Nebraska Press, 1989), pp. 24–26, 53–55; and Michael Roberts, *Poetry and the Cult of the Martyrs: The* Liber Peristephanon *of Prudentius*, Recentiores: Later Latin Texts and Contexts (Ann Arbor: University of Michigan Press, 1993), pp. 55–77.

4   For example, in the *Poetria nova* (*c.* 1210), Geoffrey of Vinsauf finds that memory is the conduit between the imaginative visualization of "wandering images" and languages that should be heard *in recitante, The* Poetria Nova *and its Sources in Early Rhetorical Doctrine*, ed. and trans. Ernesto Gallo, (The Hague: Mouton, 1971), lines 2022, 2036.

5   Plato, *Laws*, 2 vols., Loeb Classical Library (1926; rpt. Cambridge, Mass.: Harvard University Press, 1942), 663b–c. Elsewhere, Plato identifies lawyers as the rivals of poets (817b); see also Kathy Eden's compelling analysis of this material in *Poetic and Legal Fiction in the Aristotelian Tradition* (Princeton: Princeton University Press, 1986), pp. 29–30.

6   Aristotle, *De anima*, ed. and trans. W. S. Hett, Loeb Classical Library (Cambridge, Mass.: Harvard University Press, 1935), 432a; see also see Eden, *Poetic and Legal Fiction*, p. 80; and Yates, *Art of Memory*, pp. 32–33.

7   Longinus, "On the Sublime," ed. and trans. W. Hamilton Fyfe, in *Aristotle, Longinus, Demetrius*, Loeb Classical Library (Cambridge, Mass.: Harvard University Press, 1927), 15, 1–2. See also Vance, *Merelous Signals*, p. 70; and Charles Segal, *Euripedes and the Poetics of Sorrow: Art, Gender, and*

Commemoration in Alcestis, Hippolytus, *and* Hecuba (Durham: Duke University Press, 1993), ch. 7.

8   Lucian of Samosata (*c.* 125–180), "Saltatio," ed. and trans. A. M. Harmon, *Works,* vol. V, Loeb Classical Library (1936; rpt. Cambridge, Mass.: Harvard University Press, 1972), 36.

9   Quintilian, *Institutio oratoria,* ed. and trans. H. E. Butler, 4 vols., Loeb Classical Library (1920; rpt. Cambridge, Mass.: Harvard University Press, 1980), 2.17.33. Even though the *Institutio oratoria* was only partially accessible to the early Middle Ages in the mutilist tradition, Quintilian's influence at that time was greater than once thought, as James J. Murphy shows in "The Influence of Quintilian the Middle Ages and Renaissance," paper presented at Seventh Conference of the International Society for the History of Rhetoric, Göttingen, Germany, July 28, 1989; see also his *Rhetoric in the Middle Ages* (Berkeley and Los Angeles: University of California Press, 1974), pp. 123–26.

10 For an important discussion of that phenomenon, see Elaine Scarry, *The Body in Pain: The Making and Unmaking of the World* (1985; rpt. New York: Oxford University Press, 1987), p. 184, which I discuss at greater length later.

11 The story of Simonides appears in numerous rhetorical treatises, including Cicero's *De oratore,* eds. and trans. E. W. Sutton and H. Rackham, 2 vols., Loeb Classical Library (1942; rpt. Cambridge, Mass.: Harvard University Press, 1976), 2.351.55; and Martianus Capella, *De nuptiis Philologiae et Mercurii,* ed. Adolfus Dick (1925; rpt. Stuttgart: Teubner, 1969), 177g.

12 See Peggy Kamuf's analysis of the Derridean crypt as both disguise and commemoration of death in *Fictions of Feminine Desire: Disclosures of Heloise* (Lincoln: University of Nebraska Press, 1982), p. xi; and Patrick Geary, *Phantoms of Remembrance: Memory and Oblivion at the End of the First Millennium* (Princeton: Princeton University Press, 1994).

13 The scope of this essay is limited to courtroom and classroom: I explore the ramifications of violence for theatrical practice in a forthcoming book on "The Medieval Theatre of Cruelty."

14 Cicero, *De inventione,* in *De inventione* and *Topica,* ed. and trans. H. M. Hubbell, Loeb Classical Library (1949; rpt. Cambridge, Mass.: Harvard University Press, 1968), 1.3; see also his *De oratore* 1.30–35.

15 Alcuin, *The Rhetoric of Alcuin and Charlemagne,* ed. and trans. Wilbur Samuel Howell (Princeton: Princeton University Press, 1941), pp. 43–51.

16 In this sense, rhetoric may inform contemporary discussions of imperialism and political colonialization, see, for example: Carol Dougherty, *The Poetics of Colonization: From City to Text in Archaic Greece* (Oxford: Oxford University Press, 1993), p. 41; Louise Fradenburg, "Troubled Times:

Margaret Tudor and the Historians," in Sally Mapstone and Juliet Wood, eds., *The Thistle and the Rose: Late Medieval and Renaissance Scottish Culture* (Canongate Academic Press, forthcoming); and Jonathan Dollimore, *Radical Tragedy: Religion, Ideology, and Power in the Drama of Shakespeare and his Contemporaries* (1984; rpt. Durham: Duke University Press, 1989), p. 14.

17 George Caspar Homans, *English Villagers of the Thirteenth Century* (1941; rpt. New York: Norton, 1975), p. 368; emphasis mine.

18 Jacques Derrida, *Writing and Difference*, trans. Alan Bass (Chicago: University of Chicago Press, 1978), p. 130.

19 In theatre studies, compelling critical analyses of imperialism include: Anthony Kubiak's brilliant *Stages of Terror: Terrorism, Ideology, and Coercion as Theatre History* (Bloomington: Indiana University Press, 1991); Michael Lieb, *Milton and the Culture of Violence* (Ithaca: Cornell University Press, 1994); and two essays in Thomas Postelwait and Bruce A. McConachie, eds., *Interpreting the Theatrical Past: Essays in the Historiography of Performance* (Iowa City: University of Iowa Press, 1989): Erika Fischer-Lichte's "Theatre and the Civilizing Process: An Approach to the History of Acting," pp. 19–36, and Bruce A. McConachie's "Using the Concept of Cultural Hegemony to Write Theatre History," pp. 37–58.

20 In our own era, that paradox has been analyzed insightfully by René Girard, who notes that "evil and the violent measures taken to combat evil are essentially the same. . .Ritual is nothing more than the regular exercise of 'good' violence," *Violence and the Sacred*, trans. Patrick Gregory (Baltimore: Johns Hopkins University Press, 1977), p. 37. See in this connection Rita Copeland's theory that theorists assign rhetoric itself a body in order to subject it to discipline, "The Pardoner's Body and the Disciplining of Rhetoric," in Miri Rubin and Sarah Kay, eds., *Framing the Medieval Body* (Manchester: Manchester University Press, 1994), pp. 138–59.

21 Peter Haidu, *The Subject of Violence: The Song of Roland and the Birth of the State* (Bloomington, Indiana University Press, 1993), p. 195. The citation from Marc Bloch appears in *Feudal Society*, 2 vols., trans. L. A. Manyon (1961; rpt. Chicago: University of Chicago Press, 1974), I: 411.

22 See also Vance on memory, commemorative objects, and re-enactment in *Mervelous Signals*, pp. 53–54.

23 John of Garland, "The Art of Remembering," *The Parisiana Poetria of John of Garland* [c. 1220], ed. and trans. Traugott Lawler, Yale Studies in English, 182 (New Haven: Yale University Press, 1974), 2.92–110. Other discussions of the pillared memory stage include the *Ad Herennium* 3.31–34; and Cicero, *De oratore* 2.351–60.

24 For the *trace*, I refer to Jacques Derrida's *Memoirs for Paul de Man*, trans.

Cecile Lindsay, Jonathan Culler, and Eduardo Cadava (New York: Columbia University Press, 1986); and for the alimentary register of memory, see, for example, Geoffrey of Vinsauf and Quintilian on memory as a *cellula* or *vasculum* to be filled in moderation with food and drink in *Poetria nova*, 1972–82; and *Institutio oratoria* 1.2.28; 11.2.40–42.

25 In "The Feminist Mnemonics of Christine de Pizan," I argue that the only possible way to avoid this theoretical cleavage is to insist that performance never occur, by assigning violence to eternal virtuality (*Modern Language Quarterly*, 55 [1994]: 231–49).

26 What compels our attention is that Geoffrey speaks of violent extraction (*extorquere vi violenta*) in terms that recall the juridical vocabulary for torture from the Justinian Digest: "by 'torture' we should understand, torment and corporeal suffering and pain employed to extract the truth" ('Quaestionem' intelligere debemus tormenta et corporis dolorem ad eruendam veritatem), *Digesta*, ed. T. Mommsen, in *Corpus iuris civilis* (Berlin, 1877): 47.10.15.41. This text is discussed by Edward Peters, *Torture* (New York: Blackwell, 1986), p. 28; and Peter Garnsey, *Social Status and Legal Privilege in the Roman Empire* (Oxford: Clarendon Press, 1970), p. 141. In "The Medieval Theatre of Cruelty," I argue that the rhetorical truth of torture is undermined by the tendency to figure it in terms of dramatic verisimilitude, theatricality, illusion, subjectivity, and aesthetics.

27 Here I extend Vance's argument that violence may stem "from the very necessities of the mnemonic process itself" and that it "may be seen not only as the 'subject' of oral epic narrative, but also as an *aide-mémoire* or as a generative force in the production of such narrative" (*Mervelous Signals*, pp. 53–54).

28 Thomas Bradwardine, *De memoria artificiali*, Fitzwilliam Museum, Cambridge, MS. McClean 169, quoted in translation by Carruthers in appendix C of her *Book of Memory*, pp. 283–84; for the Latin, see Carruthers, "Thomas Bradwardine, 'De memoria artificiale adquirenda,'" *Journal of Medieval Latin* 2 (1992): 37; all emphases mine. For more on the particular significance of Gemini, see Jerome Mazzaro, "*Mnema* and Forgetting in Euripides' *The Bacchae*," *Comparative Drama* 27 (1993): 286–305. I explore the rhetorical ramifications of assimilated birth at greater length in the "The Medieval Theatre of Cruelty," including the even more explicit formulation of Juan-Luis Vives: "Does he indeed who gives birth to the body do more for the child than he who stirs the mind to action? In truth, insofar as the mind is more truly the essential part of the man than the body, the teacher may be said to be more truly the parent," *Vives on Education (De tradendis disciplinis)*, trans. Foster Watson (1913; rpt. Totowa, N.J.: Rowman and Littlefield, 1971), p. 86.

29 Honorius cited by Marie-Christine Pouchelle in *The Body and Surgery in the Middle Ages*, trans. Rosemary Morris (New Brunswick: Rutgers University Press, 1990), p. 137. For the bodily architecture of feminine memory spaces, see her complex discussion of the surgeon Henri de Mondeville, Brunetto Latini, Jean de Meun, and the Song of Songs (pp. 130–49); see also Page duBois's ch. 14 on "Women, the Body, and Torture," in *Torture and Truth* (New York: Routledge, 1991).

30 Antonin Artaud, *The Theater and its Double*, trans. Mary Caroline Richards (New York: Grove Weidenfeld, 1958), p. 31.

31 Gilles Deleuze and Félix Guattari, *Anti-Oedipus: Capitalism and Schizophrenia* (Minneapolis: University of Minnesota Press, 1983), p. 145. Even their statement that social organization "which traces its signs directly on the body, constitutes a system of cruelty, a terrible alphabet" (pp. 144–45) is a veritable paraphrase of the definition of *memoria*, which functioned as just such an alphabet.

32 Kenneth Burke, *The Philosophy of Literary Form: Studies in Symbolic Action*, 3rd edn. (1941; rpt. Berkeley: University of California Press, 1973), p. 106.

33 Erasmus, *Education of A Christian Prince*, pp. 144–45; cited by Edward Erdman, "Imitation Pedagogy and Ethical Indoctrination," *Rhetoric Society Quarterly* 23 (1993): 2.

34 In "The Medieval Theatre of Cruelty," I analyze numerous medieval and early Renaissance plays – comic and serious – which stage violent pedagogical indoctrination as ludic.

35 Woods, "Among Men – Not Boys: Histories of Rhetoric and the Exclusion of Pedagogy," *Rhetoric Society Quarterly* 22 (1989): 18. For other revisionist pedagogies, see Jane Gallop, ed., *Pedagogy: The Question of Impersonation* (Bloomington: Indiana University Press, 1995).

36 Henry Adams, quoted by Harry Caplan, "Memoria: Treasure-House of Eloquence," ch. 9 of Anne King and Helen North, eds., *Of Eloquence: Studies in Ancient and Medieval Rhetoric* (Ithaca: Cornell University Press, 1970), pp. 244–45.

37 Augustine, *Confessions*, trans. William Watts, 2 vols., Loeb Classical Library (Cambridge, Mass.: Harvard University Press, 1950): 1. ch. 9; emphasis mine.

38 See, for example, Emile Durkheim, *L'évolution pédagogique en France: des origines à la Renaissance* (Paris: Félix Alcan, 1938), pp. 198–99.

39 Guibert of Nogent, *Self and Society in Medieval France*, ed. John F. Benton, Medieval Academy Reprints for Teaching, 15 (Toronto: University of Toronto Press, 1989), pp. 47, 49–50.

40 Sed dolorem habet propter verbera et propter permutationem complexionis, et hoc accidens habet esse in corpore: solutio enim

continuitatis et complexio sunt dispositiones corporis ex hoc quod est
corpus, et etiam hic dolor habet esse in sensu sentientis secundum quod
est sentiens, sed causa corporis.

> (*Avicenna Latinus, Liber de anima seu sextus de naturalium*, ed. Simone
> van Riet [Louvain, 1972], IV: 60–61, quoted and translated by
> Janet Coleman, *Ancient and Medieval Memories*, p. 357)

41 Rarely treated by historians of rhetoric, Murner's text is discussed briefly by
    Walter J. Ong in *Rhetoric, Romance, and Technology*, p. 125; and at greater
    length in his *Ramus, Method, and the Decay of Dialogue* (1958; rpt.
    Cambridge, Mass.: Harvard University Press, 1983), pp. 83–91. For his
    part, Peter of Spain was a contemporary of Aquinas who had also studied
    with Albert the Great at Paris.

42 Thomas Murner, *Logica memorativa, Chartiludium logice, sive totius dialectice
    memoria; et Nonus* [i.e. *novus*] *Petri Hispani textus emendatus, cum
    iucundopictasmatis exercitio. . .*, (Strasbourg, 1509), fols. Bv^{vo}–Bvi^{ro}, quoted in
    translation by Ong, *Rhetoric, Romance, and Technology*, p. 125. The *Logica
    memorativa* is also available in a facsimile edition (Nieuwkoop: Miland
    Publishers, 1967). For the Justinian Code, see above n. 26.

43 Friedrich Nietzsche, *The Birth of Tragedy and the Genealogy of Morals*, trans.
    Francis Golffing (Garden City, N.Y.: Doubleday, 1956), p. 194.

44 John of Salisbury, *The* Metalogicon *of John of Salisbury: A Twelfth-Century
    Defense of the Verbal and Logical Arts of the Trivium*, ed. and trans. Daniel D.
    McGarry (Berkeley: University of California Press, 1955), p. 189.

45 See Joan Gibson's discussion of this passage in "Educating for Silence:
    Renaissance Women and the Language Arts," *Hypatia* 4 (1989): 18–19.
    She notes that humanistic educational treatises advocating curricular
    reform, "show a strongly gender-related understanding of all education and
    attempt to reconcile women's education with conventional norms of sex-
    stereotyped behavior, emphasizing chastity, silence, and obedience for
    women, courageous and active virtue for men" (p. 10). See also the larger
    historical treatment of this topic recently elaborated by Helen Solterer in
    The Master and Minerva: Disputing Women in Old French Literature (Berkeley
    and Los Angeles: University of California Press, 1995).

46 Abelard, *The Story of Abelard's Adversities: A Translation with Notes of the
    Historia Calamitatum*, trans. J. T. Muckle (Toronto: Pontifical Institute,
    1964), p. 28.

47 Andreas Capellanus, *On Love*, ed. and trans. P. G. Walsh (London:
    Duckworth, 1982), 3.83. pp. 312–13; emphasis mine. For memory as a
    wax tablet, see Plato, *Theaetetus*, trans. Francis MacDonald Cornford (1957;
    rpt. Indianapolis: Bobbs-Merrill, 1977), 190e–195b.

48 Cited in translation by Alan C. Kors and Edward Peters, *Witchcraft in*

Europe 1100–1700: A Documentary History (1972; rpt. Philadelphia: University of Pennsylvania Press, 1986), p. 24.

49 I cite from the English translation of Durkheim by Peter Collins, published as *The Evolution of Educational Thought* (London: Routledge, 1977), p. 142. For the concept of medieval alterity, see especially: Rainer Warning, "On the Alterity of Medieval Religious Drama," *New Literary History* 10 (1979): 265–92; and Hans-Robert Jauss, "The Alterity and Modernity of Medieval Literature," *New Literary History* 10 (1979): 181–227.

50 Teresa de Lauretis, *Technologies of Gender: Essays on Theory, Film, and Fiction* (Bloomington: Indiana University Press, 1987), p. 34.

51 James Berlin, "Revisionary Histories of Rhetoric: Politics, Power, and Plurality," in Victor Vitanza, ed., *Writing Histories of Rhetoric* (Carbondale: Southern Illinois University Press, 1994), p. 234.

52 Adam Smith, *The Theory of Moral Sentiments*, 11th edn. (London, 1812), p. 2; emphasis mine. For an important discussion of this text, see David Marshall, *The Surprising Effects of Sympathy: Marivaux, Diderot, Rousseau, and Mary Shelley* (Chicago: University of Chicago Press, 1988), pp. 4–5; see also Ronald J. Pelias, "Empathy and the Ethics of Entitlement," *Theatre Research International* 16 (1991): 142–52. In this connection, see also Eugene Vance's contention that "in a commemorative culture, events of violence (sacrifices, circumcisions, tortures, crucifixions, burnings, etc.) are given great prominence so that the collective memory will be duly impressed with the *pathos* of 'history' as it is deployed: violence as semiosis" (*Mervelous Signals*, p. 54).

53 Constantin Stanislavski, *An Actor Prepares*, trans. E. R. Hapgood (New York: Theatre Arts, 1936), p. 168.

2

Rape and the pedagogical rhetoric of sexual violence¹

MARJORIE CURRY WOODS

From Statius' *Achilleid* (*c.* 95–96 CE):

> et densa noctis gavisus in umbra
> tempestiva suis torpore silentia furtis
> vi potitur votis et toto pectore veros
> admovet amplexus; vidit chorus omnis ab alto
> astrororum et tenerae rubuerunt cornua Lunae.
> illa quidem clamore nemus montemque replevit. . .   (I. 640–45)

[. . .and in the thick darkness of the night, rejoicing that the unstirring silence gives timely aid to his secret deeds, he gains by force his desire, and with all his vigour strains her in a real embrace; the whole choir of stars beheld from on high, and the horns of the young moon blushed red. She indeed filled grove and mountains with her cries. . .]²

From the *Ars amatoria* of Ovid (43 BCE–17 CE):

> uim licet appelles: grata est uis ista puellis;
>   quod iuuat, inuitae saepe dedisse uolunt.
> quaecumque est Veneris subita uiolata rapina,
>   gaudet, et inprobitas muneris instar habet.
> at quae, cum posset cogi, non tacta recessit,
>   ut simulet uultu gaudia, tristis erit.   (I. 673–78)

[It's all right to use force – force of *that* sort goes down well with
    The girls: what in fact they love to yield
They'd often rather have stolen. Rough seduction
    Delights them, the audacity of near-rape
Is a compliment – so the girl who *could* have been forced, yet somehow
    Got away unscathed, may feign delight, but in fact
Feels sadly let down.]³

Rape and the pedagogical rhetoric of sexual violence

From the anonymous *Pamphilus* (twelfth century):

> Pamphile, tolle manus! Te frustra nempe fatigas,
>   Nil ualet iste labor, quod petis, esse nequit.
> Pamphile, tolle manus! Male nunc offendis amicam
>   Iamque redibit anus: Pamphile, tolle manus!
> Heu michi, quam paruas habet omnis femina uires,
>   Quam leuiter nostras uincis utrasque manus!
> Pamphile, nostra tuo cur pectore pectora ledis?
>   Quod sic me tractas, est scelus atque nephas.
> Desine! Clamabo! Quid agis? Male detegor a te.
>   Perfida, me miseram, quando redibit anus?
> Surge, precor: nostras audit uicinia lites.
>   Que tibi me credit, non bene fecit anus.
> Vlterius tecum me non locus iste tenebit
>   Nec me decipiet, ut modo fecit, anus.
> Huius uictor eris facti, licet ipsa relucter,
>   Sed tamen inter nos rumpitur omnis amor.   (681–96)

[Pamphilus, take your hands off me!
You are wearing yourself out in vain!
This labor won't get you anywhere!
What you want cannot be!
Pamphilus, take both your hands off!
Now you badly offend your sweet friend,
And soon the old woman will return: take your hands off![4]
Alas, how little strength we women have;
how easily you hold fast each of my hands!
Pamphilus, you're hurting my breasts with your breast.
Why are you treating me like this?
It is a crime and a sin!
Stop it! I'll scream.
What are you doing?
It is wrong to take my clothes off!
Oh poor me, when will that treacherous woman return?
Get off, I beg you. The neighbors will hear!
She did wrong, that old woman, entrusting me to you.
I'll never come here again;
she will not deceive me a second time.
    You've conquered me, however strongly I resisted,
but all hope of love is shattered between us – forever.][5]

These three quotations describing rape, from works written more than a thousand years apart, were widely used as school texts during the second half of the Middle Ages. As I have argued elsewhere, sexual imagery is omnipresent in the texts used to teach Latin to medieval boys, and rape is a common narrative vehicle in these texts.[6] Although in recent years there has been much important and provocative work on images of rape in medieval literature,[7] almost no studies have been done on the most widely read texts using this theme: those that were read in the classroom for centuries. By "widely used" I mean over time and space: the medieval audience in which I am interested is limited in age and gender.

These three exemplary texts quoted above appear in the order in which a classroom might have read them, rather than in order of composition. The two classical texts were among the most widely used works in the medieval classroom. The *Achilleid* (along with, among other texts, Claudian's *De raptu Proserpine*), was one of the works collected into the famous *Liber Catonianis* or *Cato Book*, a basic reader for medieval boys.[8] It was, therefore, a text through which basic literacy was acquired. Ovid's *Ars amatoria* was never part of the *Liber Catonianus* (although its sequel, the *Remedia amoris*, was sometimes substituted in this collection for the fifth-century *Elegiae Maximianae*);[9] but the significant numbers of manuscripts of it that have survived, often collected with other school texts, guarantee its widespread influence and use in schools. As Ralph Hexter points out in his important study of *Ovid and Medieval Schooling*, the *Ars amatoria* was "the earliest significantly glossed Ovidian text."[10] The medieval *Pamphilus* may have been even better known than the *Achilleid* and the *Ars amatoria*. It was ubiquitous, "die wohl bekannteste Komödie des Mittelalters,"[11] "recognized and quoted by almost every man of learning from the Middle Ages to the Renaissance."[12] In his *Registrum multorum auctorum* of 1280, Hugh of Trimberg lists *Pamphilus* as a basic school text to be read after Maximianus.[13] The other contents of the manuscripts in which it is copied emphasize its presence in the classroom.[14]

These texts present an increasingly complex, some would say increasingly "realistic," depiction of rape, from Statius' somewhat distant summary to Ovid's arch advice about female psychology to the orchestrated rape scene in *Pamphilus* complete with the victim's explicit vocal objections quoted above. Recently, the *Pamphilus* has been praised by women scholars for the realism of Galathea's objections to Pamphilus' actions. Elliott argues, for example, that "*Pamphilus* is an attempt to apply Ovid's precepts, the 'comandemanz d'Ovide,' to real people and to see what happens."[15] Ann Schotter argues that the play "explore[s] a real world social problem."[16] I have benefited greatly from Elliott's and Schotter's work on *Pamphilus* and disagree with them here not in disparagement but in sympathy. Women readers do react strongly to this text; my women students often want to know if it could have been written by a woman, and it is significant that the most recent revival of attention to this text is the work of women.

But Schotter accurately acknowledges that her argument for the realism of the text is limited by whether women are included in its audience. As she points out, "The later audience, extending through the fifteenth century and mixed in gender (because it read the poem in vernacular versions as well as in Latin), would have responded to. . .Galathea's strong voice."[17] Schotter contrasts this "later audience" with the "original twelfth-century audience – young, clerical, and male – for whom the poem was a school exercise, [who] would most likely have been amused by the rape. . .[and for whom] the poem may have truly been a comedy."[18] Schotter's distinction between the audience of the Latin and vernacular versions of the work is important, but I want to reverse her rhetorical emphasis and concentrate on those "young, clerical, and male" students. They are the most important and consistent audience of texts about rape read during the Middle Ages and one that the vernacular tradition supplants but does not displace.[19]

It is true that Galathea would not have spoken, in fact probably would not have appeared at all, in one of the Roman comedies of Terence from which come Pamphilus' name and his position as hero of the drama:[20] "unmarried citizen girls are generally not allowed to speak in New Comedy. . .With youthful sons (*adulescentes*) as stock characters, Roman comedies present far more dialogue about the conflicts and negotiations over their sexual relations and marriage [than about those of youthful daughters]."[21] While rape is a staple element in Terentian drama, it takes place offstage and often before the action of the play occurs. Even when it is the initiating element of the action, as in the *Andria*, the "Girl from Andros" who is "seduced" and made pregnant by Pamphilus (she is married to him by her father at the end of a series of misunderstandings) does not even appear on stage at all; and in the *Hecyra*, as the second-century summary by Gaius Sulpicius Apollinarus tells us, the plot is initiated when

Vxorem ducit Pamphilus Philumenam,
cui quondam ignorans uirgini uitium obtulit,
cuiusque per uim quem detraxit anulum
dederat amicae Bacchidi meretriculae.   (1–4)

Pamphilus marries Philumena, the girl he once assaulted, without knowing
who she is and that it is her ring he took by force and gave to his mistress, the
courtesan Bacchis.[22]

What I want to explore here, however, is not the relationship of
Pamphilus to Terentian or other sources, but rather the long-standing
schoolroom tradition of teaching texts describing rape of which *Pamphilus*
is a significant part. The apparent "realness" of *Pamphilus* as a text and the
seeming "strength" of its heroine are, I argue, the effects of rhetorical
techniques taught in the classroom; these techniques are of classical origin
and documented medieval usage. They do challenge traditional power
structures and provide evidence of psychological acumen of a specific kind,
but one as I acknowledge in my conclusion that is likely to make us
uneasy. I want to argue that the young male student audience for the
poem was looking for and found something in the story of Pamphilus and
in texts like the *Achilleid* more serious and more important to them than
amusement.

It is useful to examine first some of the conventions of rape as it appears
in classroom narratives. The most significant of these is that, when the
protagonist is young, the rape signifies the onset of his manhood. That
this development is presented in an approving way does not mean that
there was no artistic condemnation of violent rape in the Middle Ages. For
example, Diane Wolfthal has demonstrated a tradition of unambiguously
negative depictions of rape in twelfth- to fourteenth-century manuscripts
with extensive Old Testament picture cycles.[23] But along with the biblical
tradition that condemns forced sex with an unwilling victim, the Middle
Ages also inherited two intertwined traditions from the classical world
that cast a different light on such an action.

The first is that of "'heroic rape,' myths or legends in which the
assailant is a Greek or Roman god or hero."[24] The victim is usually a naive
virgin, and the act confers on the victim enhanced status and, when the
victim is a woman,[25] semi-divine offspring. Mary F. Lefkowitz calls these
rapes "beneficial and honorific seductions" and argues that "the consequences of these unions are usually glorious for the families of the mortals
involved, despite and even because of the suffering that individual

members of the family may undergo."[26] The rape in the *Achilleid* is of this type, as we see when immediately after the rape Achilles solaces Deidamia in part as follows: "quid defles magno nurus addita ponto? / quid gemis intentes caelo paritura nepotes?" ["Why dost thou weep who art made the daughter-in-law of mighty ocean? Why dost thou moan who shalt bear valiant grandsons to Olympus?" (I. 655–56)].[27]

When the perpetrator is a young hero, the experience constitutes his own sexual initiation.[28] In the central book of the *Achilleid* according to the medieval division of the text (1.397–674),[29] the young Achilles, at his worried mother's insistence, is hiding out in drag in order to escape fighting in the Trojan War. Given the emphasis on gender ambiguity in the text – Achilles is described as beautiful in either gender ("et sexus pariter decet et mendacia matris" [605]) – the rape is a kind of reassurance to the readers as well as to Achilles himself. As a prelude to the rape, Achilles whips himself into a frenzy of self-excoriation, ending with "quonam usque premes urentia pectus / vulnera, teque marem – pudet heu! – nec amore probaris" ["How long wilt thou conceal the wound that galls thy heart, nor even in love – for shame! – prove thy own manhood!" (638–39)]. The *accessus* or introduction to a thirteenth-century commentary on the *Achilleid* edited by Paul Clogan states that the "materia huius actoris est Achilles et eius forcia facta. intencio actoris est non tantum de illis agere que Achilles egit circa Troiam, sed quomodo eum Chiron nutrivit et mater sua Thetis in aula Licomedis eum abscondidit." ["The author's subject is Achilles and his brave (or 'manly') deeds. The author's intention is to treat not only those deeds that Achilles accomplished around Troy, but also how Chiro raised him and his mother Thetis took him in the Licomedian court"].[30] It is Achilles' transformation from a boy under both the tutelage of a centaur and the control of his mother into the hero of the male world of the Trojan War which the author intends to describe. The rape is one of the signs of that transformation.

The second classical tradition is that of rape as a seduction gambit in which both participants are willing; here the woman – this tradition, unlike the first, is almost exclusively heterosexual – says "No" when she really means "Yes." Much has been made of the fact that the advice of Ovid quoted at the beginning of this essay describes sexual foreplay between adults, in which resistance is a kind of coy come-on. According to this argument, Ovid does not mean to urge rape, and when Venus quotes Ovidian advice concerning rape to Pamphilus who then acts on it, Ovid is being misused. But one widespread medieval tradition definitely defines the sexual object as girls, as we see in this "canonical"[31] *accessus* to the text: "Intentio sua est in hoc opere iuvenes ad amorem instruere, quo modo debeant se in amore habere circa ipsas puellas. . .Modus istius operis talis est, ostendere quo modo puella possit inveniri, inventa exorari, exorata retineri." ["Ovid's purpose in this work is to teach young men about love – how they ought to conduct themselves in their love affairs with girls. . .The method of the work is as follows: to show how a girl can be found; once found, how wooed; once wooed, how won."][32] And in the text itself Ovid links the two traditions of rape as both an act of manhood and an act desired by the young and virginal victim: in the section of the *Ars amatoria* immediately following the quotation given at the beginning of this essay, Ovid offers several examples of women, including Achilles' Deidamia, who really "wanted it." The anecdote is introduced by describing the absurdity of Achilles in women's clothes and how he should be wielding his "hasta" ("spear" [I. 696]) instead.[33] According to Ovid the rape that follows fixes the problem: "haec illum stupro comperit esse uirum. / uiribus illa quidem uicta est (ita credere oportet), / sed uoluit uinci uiribus illa tamen" ["The king's daughter, Deidamia / Who shared his room soon proved / That manhood through rape. Her seduction must have been forceful, / But to *be* forced was what she desired" (698–701)].[34]

Although Pamphilus himself is definitely not of heroic stock or stature (more about this below), we find evidence of both the heroic and the seductive classical traditions of rape in *Pamphilus*. The anxiety about manhood comes in the Old Woman's advice to Pamphilus, should her machinations to get him alone with Galathea be successful, that he "esse uirum" ["be a man" (546)]. The question of whether the girl wants it is expressed in Galathea's internal debate about whether to accept him as a lover. Although some of her indecision seems to be about whether to talk to him alone, it has been prefaced by the play's opening scene in which Ovidian advice from the *Ars amatoria* (1.665–66) has been paraphrased for Pamphilus by Venus, to whom he has appealed for help:

> Si locus est, illi iocundis uiribus insta!
> Quod uix sperasti, mox dabit ipsa tibi.
> Non sinit interdum pudor illis promere uotum,
> Sed quod habere cupit, hoc magis ipsa negat.
> Pulcrius esse putat ui perdere uirginitatem,
> Quam dicat: "De me fac modo uelle tuum!" (109–14)

[If you get the chance, woo her with gentle violence.
What you scarcely hoped for soon she will offer herself.
Modesty now and then may keep her from admitting desire;
what she most desires to have she denies most strongly,
thinking it better to lose her virginity by force
than to say, "Do with me what you will."]

Later, when Galathea is addressed by her neighbor, the Old Woman, who has been hired by Pamphilus at Venus' direction to further his case, Galathea is definitely intrigued and titillated by what the woman tells her about Pamphilus' feelings for her (which is the truth) and about Pamphilus' noble and wealthy background (which is not). Galathea admits to feeling physical desire that she fears to act upon:

> Me premit igniferis Venus improba sepius armis,
>   Nunc michi uim faciens semper amare iubet.
> Me iubet econtra pudor et metus esse pudicam
>   Hijsque coacta meum nescio consilium.   (573–76)

[Venus the cruel oppresses me with burning thoughts;
doing me violence, she continually orders me to love.
Yet modesty and fear bid me to be chaste.
With such compelling arguments on both sides
I don't know what to do.]

Later, she continues:

> O Deus, in quantis animus uersatur amantis,
>   Quem timor hac illac pellit amorque grauis!
> Hij duo discordes hunc nocte dieque fatigant,
>   Esse quod optat amor, hoc uetat esse timor.   (619–22)

[O God! with what indecision is a lover's heart torn;
fear pulls it one way, great love the other.
These two enemies assail me day and night.
Love says "Yes," and fear says "No."]

She expresses none of her indecision to Pamphilus, however – only to the Old Woman, who counsels her to give in to her desires (and who is the one who urges Pamphilus to prove his manhood). But, as Schotter points out, Galathea is not given the chance to be seduced.[35] Pamphilus' only words after the exit of the Old Woman and before the rape are the following:

> En modo dulcis amor uiridisque iuuenta locusque
>   Nos, Galathea, mouent pascere corda iocis.

63

En lasciua Venus nos ad sua gaudia cogit
  Inque suos usus nos iubet ire modo.
Quid moror? Huius ope supplex mea uota requiram?
  Tu paciens facti te precor esto mei.   (675–80)

[Look how sweet love, blooming youth, and opportunity
all urge us, Galathea, to feed our hearts with sport.
Lascivious Venus compels us to taste her joys,
orders us now to go on. Why do I delay?
Shall I, a suppliant, seek her aid for my desires?
I beg you now, be obedient to my will.]

This short passage is in stark contrast to Pamphilus' confused and
extended speech of exculpation after the deed, which may be paraphrased
as follows: first he feels guilt but no regret; next it is not his fault because
her flirtations drove him to it; then she is the one who is really guilty; and
finally they are both guilty (701–23). This exculpatory exercise is as
psychologically coercive (and to modern readers appallingly insensitive) as
his physical actions have been earlier. Yet an important *accessus* to the work
implies no criticism of Pamphilus' words or actions:

Materia huius libri sunt istae tres personae Pamphilus, Galathea et anus,
intentio auctoris est tractare de amore Pamphili et Galatheae, utilitas est ut hoc
libro perlecto unusquisque sciat sibi pulcras invenire puellas, vel utilitas est
cognitio eorum quae continentur in hoc libro.

[The subjects of this book are the three persons Pamphilus, Galathea, and the
Old Woman; the intention of the author is to treat of the love of Pamphilus and
Galathea; the usefulness is that, after this book has been read thoroughly,
anyone should know how to get beautiful girls for himself; or, the usefulness is
the knowledge of those things which are contained in this book.][36]

The students who read this text are to identify with Pamphilus and to
learn his technique in order to gain the same results.

How, then, did the medieval teachers who taught the *Achilleid*, the *Ars
amatoria*, and *Pamphilus* discuss the material related to rape? The commentators writing for the schools, particularly for the younger students, do not
allegorize or moralize these texts. Rather, they clarify them by explaining
in the interlinear and marginal glosses the meanings of individual words
and phrases or grammatical relationships among them.

The rape in the *Achilleid*, as we saw above, is treated in an almost
offhand manner, a minor but symbolic part of what the Vatican Commentator calls Achilles' "facta virtuosa."[37] This commentator does not

criticize the rape but makes clear the nature of the act: the interlinear gloss over "vi" ["by force" (642)] is "violencia." The marginal gloss on this word adds, "VI quia manifestavit se, primitus enim erant ficti" ["BY FORCE since he shows himself, for to begin with things were deceitful"], again interpreting the rape as an act of male self-definition on the part of Achilles. Just before the rape, when Achilles urges himself to prove himself in love, "amore" is glossed in the commentary as "effectu amoris scilicet coitu" ["by the effect of love, namely coitus"]. The commentator does say that the reason that the moon is blushing is "quia virgo erat" ["because Deidamia was a virgin"], and he makes sure that his students know that it is Deidamia whose "clamor" fills the landscape: "*illa* scilicet Deidamia." A little later, when Deidamia is described by Statius as "dubiam" ["uncertain" or "anxious" (649)] after the rape, the commentator explains that she is "DUBIAM utrum deberet Achilles eam violasse. . ." ["UNCERTAIN whether Achilles ought to have violated her."][38] The point is not judgment but clarification, although modern readers would disagree about what needs to be clarified.[39]

Ralph Hexter notes a similar approach in school commentaries on the *Ars amatoria*. For the youngest students, as in the ninth-century "Classbook of Saint Dunstan," the focus is on explaining the grammar and vocabulary, on making the text comprehensible. As Hexter notes, "the primary function of the *Ars amatoria* glosses is to ease the reading and increase comprehension of Ovid's text. It is also clear that this is in the service of improving the students' grasp of Latin by special attention to grammar."[40] Such attention to grammar is indicated by the high percentage of glosses that supply the antecedents of relative and demonstrative pronouns.[41] For more advanced students, as in a twelfth-century manuscript in Copenhagen, the rhetorical and structural organization of the work is emphasized; the focus is still on making the text comprehensible, but in a more sophisticated way.[42] For these older students the sexual material is simply grist for the pedagogical mill: "Near the end of both books 2 and 3 Ovid discusses sexual intercourse very openly. The commentator makes no protests or condemnations. That the comments continue through these passages shows that he did not expurgate them: he expected his students to study them, and with the same aid he gave them throughout the poem. When he feels Ovid is speaking obscurely, he clarifies things."[43]

Unfortunately, the manuscripts of *Pamphilus* that I have examined so far have not been accompanied by marginal or interlinear commentaries. But

Becker's manuscript descriptions indicate that for the *Pamphilus*, too, the emphasis of the glosses is on clarification, rather than interpretation or moralization.[44] Grammatical relationships are clarified, the action is summarized, and the speakers are identified, as in a note on Pamphilus' first speech to Galathea at line 163: "In hoc loco loquitur panphilus ad amicam suam de amore suo acquirendo" ["Here Pamphilus speaks to his friend about acquiring her love."][45] In other manuscripts, synonyms of certain words are supplied, either in lists or individually.[46] The only notes on Galathea's objection to the rape that Becker cites are "uerba gala ad panphilum" ["the words of Galathea to Pamphilus"] at the first line of Galathea's objection to the rape (681)[47] and the singular "utraque" over the plural "utrasque" ("each" [684]) with regard to Galathea's hands being held.[48]

This straightforward treatment in the medieval schoolroom of what we consider to be particularly sensitive (or insensitive) subjects is less surprising when we remember that there was an established medieval tradition of letting boys read texts that were considered problematic for adults. Peter Allen notes that St. Jerome "deemed love poetry acceptable reading matter for schoolchildren but declared it sinful for their elders,"[49] and Ralph Hexter cautions us that "in the monasteries and in the schools within their walls there was not the antipathy to eros with which contemporary imagination credits them, nor even the squeamishness many nineteenth- and twentieth-century scholars have shown or have felt compelled to show when dealing with certain aspects of the classics. . ."[50]

In fact, scenes of erotic violence were an established pedagogical tool for teaching verbal skills long before the Middle Ages. Relevant to my argument here is the ancient (both Greek and Latin) exercise known as the declamation, in which students practiced extemporaneous oral arguments based on lurid legal cases, many of which were apocryphal. A substantial number of the most popular subjects for declamation – some of which are extant in several versions – involved circumstances of transvestism, prostitution (including male prostitution), rape (including gang-rape), and adultery. The point of the exercise was to develop verbal skills in arguing both sides of a case using arresting if implausible examples to generate interest and memorability.[51] D. A. Russell describes exercises in which aspects of a rape case are argued, such as that in which a man rapes a blind man's daughter, and the blind man, hearing her scream, walks over a cliff; "the rapist offers a recognized fine, but the girl charges him with causing

66

her father's death." In another example, "A rich man goes to dinner in a poor man's house. His host's pretty daughter waits at table. The rich man asks if she is a slave or a free woman. The father is ashamed [that his daughter is serving?], and says she is a slave. The guest rapes her. The law is that the penalty for the rape of a free woman is death, for that of a slave a fine of 100 talents. The rich man offers the money; the poor man demands his death."[52] Note the overlap of parent/child relationships with rape scenes in these Greek examples, a phenomenon that also occurs with some regularity in Roman declamation.

The best-known collection of Roman declamations is the *Controversiae* of Seneca the Elder. These are display pieces, and they overlap but are not identical with extant legal circumstances. Among the laws that generate the greatest number of cases in Seneca's collection is the following: "Rapta raptoris aut mortem aut indotatas nuptias optet" ["A girl who has been raped may chose either marriage to her rapist without a dowry or his death"]. The cases organized around this law include the "Raptor Duorum: Una nocte quidam duas rapuit; altera mortem optat, altera nuptias" ["The Man Who Raped Two Girls: On a single night a man raped two girls. One demands his death, the other marriage." (1.5)].[53] A second example is "Mutanda optio raptore convicto: Rapta producta nuptias optavit. Qui dicebatur raptor negavit se rapuisse. Iudicio victus vult ducere; illa optionem repetit." ["The Change of Choice to be Made after the Conviction of a Rapist: A girl who had been raped was brought to court and asked for marriage. The alleged rapist said he was not responsible. The judgement has gone against him; he is ready to marry her – but she wants to have her choice all over again" (7.8)] We also find "Pater Raptam Continens: Raptor postulat ut rapta educatur. Pater non vult" ["The Father Who Detained His Daughter: A rapist demands that the girl he raped be brought before the magistrate [in order to make her choose]. The father refuses" (3.5)]. A fourth case involves this law and a second one;[54] the summary is as follows:

Exul Raptae Pater: Quidam, cum haberet filiam et filium, inprudentis caedis damnatus in exilium abiit. Filia eius rapta est; raptor ad patrem puellae se contulit, impetravit ab illo ut iuberet filiam nuptias optare et epistulam daret ad filium. Fratre auctore mortem optavit puella. Pater rediit; abdicat filium.   (4.3)

[The Exile Whose Daughter Was Raped: A man who had a son and a daughter was convicted of unintentional homicide and went off to exile. His daughter got raped; the rapist sought out the girl's father, and got him to order the girl to choose marriage and give him a letter to his son. On her brother's advice the girl chose death. The father returned, and disinherits the son.]

I have quoted so many examples here (the debates about the cases go on for pages and pages) because they indicate two aspects of the way that rape functions as a subject in these works: (1) the reaction of the rape victim to the rape is the focus of the *law*; and (2) the reaction of the father is often the focus of the *case*. Another law focuses explicitly on parental reaction in terms of the rapist as well as the victim: "Raptor Patrem Non Exorans: Raptor, nisi et suum et raptae patrem intra dies triginta exoraverit, pereat. Raptor raptae patrem exoravit, suum non exorat. Accusat dementiae." ["The Rapist who Failed to Win Over his Father: A rapist shall die unless he wins over his own father and the girl's within thirty days. A rapist won over the father of the girl he had raped; he is unable to win over his own, and accuses him of insanity." (2.3)]

In fact, the great majority of the cases that Seneca quotes involve parent/child relationships.[55] Most of these revolve around the father/son relationship, using bizarre circumstances in which traditional patterns of control and decision-making are disrupted. Other cases involve such issues in terms of father/daughter, husband/wife, or master/slave relationships, and these serve to reinforce the father/son paradigm as the basic one in that the girls, women, and slaves seem to serve as even more extreme cases of young men. In the first two of the ten books of *Controversiae* alone, in a total of fifteen cases (one of which has already been quoted), we find the following filial issues noted in the titles of the cases: "Archipiratae Filia" ["The Pirate Chief's Daughter, " (1.6)]; "Adoptandus Post Tres Abdicatos" ["The Man Faced with Adoption after the Disinheritance of Three Sons," (2.1)]; "Nepos Ex Meretrice Susceptus" ["The Taking In of the Grandchild Born of a Prostitute" (2.4)]; and "Pater et Filius Luxuriosi" ["The Father and Son Who Became Debauchees," (2.6)].[56] The *Controversiae* stand as the Roman declamation text *par excellence* and the one most often cited by modern scholars as indicative of Roman educational techniques,[57] sometimes much to the scholars' consternation, as when Bonner, author of the classic study of Roman declamation, is forced to concede that "No doubt the adventurous escapades of youths and maidens among pirates, and mysterious murders and poisonings made a great appeal to the young imagination, but the recurrent treatment of adultery and divorce, rape and incest, strikes a modern student as an incredible foundation for education. . ."[58] The first two books of the *Controversiae* alone include all of the topics that Bonner mentions.

As I have hinted earlier, however, it is not just their luridness that made such cases appealing for schoolroom use; it is also their unreality, their elements of projection and wish-fulfilment. In the declamation the power structure of the real world could be reversed. Here the weak – children, the poor, even rape victims – can win (albeit often winning approval from a father). As Michael Winterbottom points out in a recent edition of extracts from Roman declamations, "[The] inhabitants [of the world of declamation] are stock characters, sympathetic (raped girls, disowned sons, tyrant killers) or unsympathetic (pirates, strict fathers, tyrants). . ."[59] The very power of the reversal is directly proportional to the victimized status of the weaker half of the polarity. Russell points out that "In the Greek declaimers. . .the conflict between rich and poor is very much a political one" and one in which "the rich are always unjust and cruel and the poor are innocent victims"; in the same way, "Sympathy is usually with the children," and "the schoolmaster's concern with parent–children conflicts had some sort of cathartic effect."[60] George Kennedy notes that "Most of the subjects of declamation were, of course, designed to be exciting and to interest the young. Many of them are built around problems of adolescence and young manhood."[61] It is possible, then, to see the school tradition as a place where adolescence is a site of anxiety about control in two directions: those who control the boy and those whom he might be able to control.[62]

While it is impossible to argue for a direct link between ancient declamation and later medieval school exercises, we know that training in declamation directly influenced authors such as Ovid, who was a staple of the medieval schoolroom. Seneca even records Ovid's own arguments for one case that he records (*Contr.* 2.2.8–12), and the *Heroides*, Ovid's evocation of victimized women's epistolary outpourings to the men who wronged them, "reveal the influence of his declamatory exercises."[63] Bonner notes that a number of the declamations have a "romantic" plot, and "[t]here is also evidence that the erotic themes of the rhetorical schools had their influence upon contemporary Roman elegy, as well as the later amatory epistle, and that they form one of the sources of the collections of monks' tales, known as *Gesta Romanorum*."[64] Further, Bonner notes that the stock characters that recur in the declamations (mentioned above by Winterbottom) come from Greek and Roman comedy, and that this fact was commented on by Quintilian, who advises his own rhetoric students to study Menander.[65] The comedies of Terence, which I mentioned earlier as texts where rape occurs offstage, focus on the nexus of father–son power struggles and courtship and marriage as the site of those struggles. In Roman drama, as Richard Saller points out, the basic conflict involves a boy's power struggle with his father in determining his wife or a continuing sexual relationship with a courtesan: "The plots of many of the plays revolve around a conflict between a son wishing to pursue his youthful passion for a woman not of his status and his father who presses his son to enter a respectable and prosperous marriage."[66] In these plays the offstage rape helps the comedy to its "happy" conclusion.

With these issues in mind, let us return to *Pamphilus*. The *accessus* to the play quoted earlier also provides a summary of the plot: "Pamphilus fuit quidam qui quandam puellam, scilicet Galatheam, valde diligebat et eam nullo modo habere poterat. Tandem ivit ad Venerem, cuius consilio acquisivit sibi interpretem eiusque auxilio habuit eam. Unde compositus est liber iste." ["Pamphilus was someone who loved a certain girl and was not able to have her in any way. Then he went to Venus, by means of whose advice he acquired a go-between for himself, and by means of her help he was able to have her (Galathea). From this the book is composed."][67] Thus, for medieval students *Pamphilus* is a play about a boy who in the beginning could not get a girl but was able at the end to get her. Pamphilus says at the start of the play that he cannot aspire to marry Galathea because she is "me nobilioribus orta" ["more nobly born than I," (47)] and because "Nec michi sunt dotes, decus ingens, copia grandis / Sed quod habere queo, quero labore meo" ["I have neither gifts to give / nor shining honor nor great wealth. / All that I have, I get by my hard work." (51–52)]. Galathea is a girl ("puella," [35]) of rank and wealth; Pamphilus has neither and, consequently, cannot have her. But, as the *accessus* tells the students, by following the advice of Venus and acquiring a go-between, the boy gets the girl – and gets to marry her. And, as the *accessus* had just stated, by learning this text the student learns how to go about getting beautiful girls for himself in the same way. Pamphilus transcends the limitations of his background (his parents, unlike hers, are not mentioned in the story).

If what we have in the *Pamphilus* is new, it is new in its combination of stock elements, not in the elements itself. What feels most real to us as modern readers (particularly to those of us who are women readers) is, I would argue, highly conventional. And what may be most new in the setting of classically shaped rape *materia* in this text may be Pamphilus himself, acting and achieving on his own, without parental conflicts, ties, or responsibilities, getting a girl who has all of these. Unlike, say, Achilles or any of Terence's young protagonists, Pamphilus gets to decide his own marital fate. He gets his advice and help from females, it is true, but there is nary another male in sight.[68] Pamphilus does, as he says, have to work for everything he gets (much attention has been paid to the emphasis on *labor*, especially its sexual connotations, in the play), but he is able to make the decisions about what and who that is.[69]

Galathea, on the other hand, is appropriately obsessed with what others, especially her parents, might think of her actions. Most of her hesitations about becoming Pamphilus' lover and her greatest fear after the rape comes from well-founded anxiety about her social standing and the reaction of her parents. The end of her lament after the rape has been justly praised by modern scholars (although the old woman says that such intensity is unwise: "Ut graviter dolet, non pertinet ad sapientem" [769]):

> Et modo quid faciam, fugiam captiua per orbem?
> Ostia iure michi claudet uterque parens.
> Meciar hac illac oculis uigilantibus orbem,
> Leta tamen misere spes michi nulla uenit.   (765–68)

> [But now, what am I to do?
> Am I to flee through the world, already caught?
> {By law, both parents may close their doors to me.}
> I shall wander the earth, searching,
> but nowhere shall I find happiness,
> poor betrayed wretch that I am.]

While it is true, as was mentioned earlier in this essay, that in Terence's comedies such female distress about rape is not usually depicted during or immediately after the act, unhappy and sympathetic female victims do occur with some regularity in the declamations, and in other narratives like the *Achilleid* and *Metamorphoses*, where Galathea's last lines would fit comfortably.[70] My point here is that the exploration of what passes in medieval literature for feminine psychology (women *in extremis*, lamenting) was a standard part of the medieval as well as the classical boy's schoolroom repertoire, a creative exercise bounded by extremely long-lasting conventions and topoi.

From a medieval perspective, Galathea's reaction to the rape is less important than some of her other emotional expressions. The *florilegia* containing excerpts from the text indicate that the parts of *Pamphilus* that were most valued for their reusability are the *sententiae* or general statements that could be applied by students and others to the widest variety of kinds of writing and various contextual circumstances.[71] Hugh of Trimberg describes *Pamphilus* as a work "lascivius / Comptis et proverbiis ad mala non proclivus" ("exuberant [and surely other connotations of *lascivius* reverberate here] in quips and proverbs not directed toward evil things," [730–31]]). I had once thought, indeed hoped, that the other "usefulness" of *Pamphilus* according to the *accessus* quoted above (p. 64), the "cognitio earum quae continentur in hoc libro" ["knowledge of those things which are contained in this book"], might refer to Galathea's resistance to the rape. But the *florilegia* make it clear that the most "useful" words in the text are such set pieces as selections from the advice of Venus (71–143),[72] Pamphilus' seduction lines (for example, 207–8[73]), and cynical or manipulative statements about human nature by the Old Woman (for example, 525–26,[74] 645–46,[75] and 769–71[76]). Galathea's objection to the rape is not excerpted, but lines of hers that are popular include her dismissal of Pamphilus' first approach to her as a joke (173–74),[77] her fear of what can happen to a young girl who gives in to love (413–20),[78] and her condemnation of the Old Woman's part in the affair (730–31).[79]

Pamphilus and Galathea participate along with the characters in almost all of Ovid's works in the translation of texts from the schoolboy world to the adult and mixed gender world of the vernacular in the latter centuries of the Middle Ages. Like Ovid's *Ars amatoria*, *Pamphilus* was itself widely translated and served as the inspiration for a number of late medieval texts.[80] As I mentioned above, it is these translated texts that have recently been receiving the most attention among scholars and particularly feminist scholars. But it is in the world where women do not belong – except as sex objects – that the rape tradition has its longest and most continuous presence.[81] The absence of women in the school context in which Latin literacy was taught to boys and male adolescents seems to me to be particularly important and worthy of attention. The invoking of heterosexual desire (and often consequent misogyny) in this homosocial environment needs further study and analysis.[82] The continuity of this tradition of using rape for pedagogical purposes is disturbingly powerful – and disturbingly overlooked. Much more attention has been paid to Ovid as the author behind the scenes of the vernacular courtly love tradition, a tradition centuries shorter than the schoolboy one, but a tradition with an audience of adults, and adults of mixed gender. We know that Ovid's works were translated by other authors who, partially via his influence, were known for their insight into women.[83] And the issue of whether women are in the audience has been a recent criterion for taking works seriously. But Ovid's works were edited differently for vernacular audiences. As Peter Allen points out, the *Remedia amoris* replaces book 3 of the *Ars amatoria* in thirteenth-century translations of the text so that the advice to women is removed.[84] These changes make the text read much more like Andreas Capellanus' *De arte honeste amandi*: advice to men on how to seduce women, followed by a retraction. And this is a sign that sexual texts may have been censored more for adults of both genders than for (only male?) children in the Middle Ages.

Thus, women learned about how to get sexual partners or objected more freely to unwanted sex in texts read only by boys and young men, and young boys learned about sexual violence as a method of defining their manhood and controlling their own lives. That all of this takes place in the context of acquiring language gives new meaning to the association of the body with the text that has been the focus of much modern criticism. But while we may object to medieval schoolboys working out their anxieties about adulthood on the bodies of literary ladies (or rather girls), we should be careful not to dismiss that arena of learning as irrelevant or simply amusing. If, as I suggested above, the schoolboy's anxiety about power went in two directions, then exploring the role of powerless victim was as important to the male adolescent as the role of powerful perpetrator of violence.[85] From this perspective the victim is real insofar as s/he expresses what the schoolboy thinks that he might express in similar circumstances, rather than what a "real" girl would.[86] The gender split encourages individual readers to bifurcate themselves – boys can try out the roles of both genders. This aspect of projection is the basis, I would argue, for Galathea's spirited but unsuccessful appropriation of male, i.e. schoolboy, rhetoric in her ruminations and objections. In these texts rape is clearly an issue of power and violence rather than sex, which is why Galathea is not given a chance to be seduced; her potential pleasure is not an issue here. Rape scenes function in this tradition as the paradigmatic site for working out issues of power and powerlessness.[87]

We should not be surprised, therefore, to realize that Pamphilus the lovesick fool, pining away at the beginning of the text for a woman whom he thinks that he cannot have, rather than Pamphilus the successful rapist, was the most distinctive creation of the author, becoming a byword for absolute amatory fixation.[88] In the same way, Achilles the gender bender is, literally, the central focus of the medieval *Achilleid*; in book 3 according to the medieval division of the text, he must learn to be a woman before he can become a man.[89] This education in female qualities is combined in a single book of the *Achilleid* with the journey thither of those who in the subsequent book reveal the new manhood of Achilles. But this manhood has been earned by the experience in the women's world that culminates in the rape and subsequent fatherhood at the end of book 3.[90]

This emphasis on exploring both sides of the struggle for power, on being both victim and perpetrator of violence in the passage to adulthood, is predicated upon both the youth and the maleness of the audience of the work.[91] Or rather, it is dependent upon the single sex of the students and their shared anxiety about the transition from child to adult, which bifurcates in the pedagogical experience.[92] Material about women victims was expressed and explored when boys read about rape but not when adult men (who are also the beneficiaries of vernacular translations) or adult men and women read it. What we would call sexual orientation is irrelevant here; it is the lack of female presence in the canonical classroom as much as the female's status in the "real" world that make her the perfect projected victim in the schoolroom.[93] Premodern teachers drew on knowledge of the fears of youth and adolescence in using such texts not just for generations but for centuries. This absolutely patriarchal tradition was neither simplistic nor psychologically crude, and while we may be repelled by its very success, it behooves us to understand what we can of its processes.

Notes

1 I would like to thank Rebecca Baltzer, Mary Blockley, Rita Copeland, Karen Gould, Geraldine Heng, Joan Holladay, Jacqueline Long, Martha Newman, and Richard Tarrant for valuable references and comments.

2 Text and translation in *Statius*, trans. J. H. Mozley, vol. II, Loeb Classical Library (Cambridge, Mass.: Harvard University Press, 1969). The medieval manuscripts of the *Achilleid* divide the unfinished work into five books and complete it with a couplet. See Paul M. Clogan, *The Medieval Achilleid of Statius* (Leiden: E. J. Brill, 1968), pp. 3–4. I have retained the classical book and line numbers in my citations for ease of reference.

3 Text in P. Ovidi Nasonis, *Amores; Medicamina faciei femineae; Ars amatoria; Remedia amoris*, ed. E. J. Kenney (Oxford: Clarendon, 1961). Translation in Ovid, *The Erotic Poems: The Amores, The Art of Love, Cures for Love, On Facial Treatment for Ladies*, trans. Peter Green (London: Penguin Books, 1982).

4 Elliott's translation (see note following), which I use here for its vitality, is rather free and omits part of line 683 and all of line 684. I have supplied the translations of these lines and altered the translation of one phrase in line 686.

5 Text in Franz G. Becker, *Pamphilus; Prolegomena zum Pamphilus (de amore) und kritische Textausgabe*, Beihefte zum "Mittellateinischen Jahrbuch" 9 (Ratingen: A. Henn Verlag, 1972). Translation in Alison Goddard Elliott, *Seven Medieval Latin Comedies*, Garland Library of Medieval Literature, Series B, 20 (New York: Garland Publishing, 1984), p. 21.

6 "The Teaching of Writing in Medieval Europe," in James J. Murphy, ed., *A Short History of Writing Instruction From Ancient Greece to Twentieth-Century America* (Davis, Calif.: Hermagoras Press, 1990), pp. 77–94.

7 Besides those cited in the notes to this article, see also: Leslie Cahoon, "Raping the Rose: Jean de Meun's Reading of Ovid's *Amores*," *Classical and Modern Literature* 6 (1986): 261–85; Dietmar Rieger, "Le Motif du viol dans la littérature de la France médiévale: entre norme courtoise et realité courtoise," *Cahiers du Civilization Médiévale X–XIIIᵉ Siècles* 31 (1988): 241–67; John M. Clifton-Everest, "Knights-Servitor and Rapist Knights: A Contribution to the Parzival/Gawain Question," *Zeitschrift für deutsches Altertum und deutsche Literatur* 119 (1990): 290–317; Peter Meister, "A Little Acknowledged Theme in the Courtly Romance: Rape," and Mary Lynn Dittman, "Reply," *Quondam et Futurus* 1 (1991): 23–38.

8 The classic and still most useful study of the *Liber Catonianis* is M. Boas, "De Librorum Catonianorum historia atque compositione," *Mnemosyne* new series 42 (1914): 17–46. During the later Middle Ages, this group of texts was altered in order to give it a more moral emphasis. See also Elisabeth Pellegrin, "Les 'Remedia amoris' d'Ovide, texte scolaire médiévale," *Bibliothèque de l'Ecole des Chartres* 115 (1957): 172–79; and Y.-F. Riou, "Quelques aspects de la tradition manuscrite des Carmina d'Eugène de Tolède du 'Liber Catonianus' aux 'Auctores octo morales'," *Revue d'histoire des textes* 2 (1972): 11–44. *De raptu Proserpine* is not a focus in this essay because the *raptus* in the title refers literally to abduction, and the physical rupturing and violation is metonymically expressed in Pluto's piercing the earth's covering; see Woods, "Teaching of Writing," p. 88.

9 In the medieval schoolroom Ovid's explicit descriptions of how to discourage passion were judged "moins nocif pour les enfants" (Pellegrin, "Les 'Remedia amoris,'" 173, paraphrasing Boas, "De Librorum," 39) than

Maximianus' recollections of moments of impotence and intense sexual embarrassment.

10 Ralph J. Hexter, *Ovid and Medieval Schooling. Studies in Medieval School Commentaries on Ovid's* Ars Amatoria, Epistulae ex Ponto, *and* Epistulae Heroidum, Münchener Beiträge zur Mediävistik und Renaissance-Forschung 38 (Munich: Bei der Arbeo-Gesellschaft, 1986), p. 32.

11 Becker, *Pamphilus*, p. 10.

12 Thomas J. Garbáty, "The *Pamphilus* Tradition in Ruiz and Chaucer," *Philological Quarterly* 46 (1967): 457; quoted in Elliott, *Seven Medieval Latin Comedies*, p. xxxiii.

13 *Das Registrum multorum auctorum des Hugo von Trimberg*, ed. Johannes Huemer (Vienna: F. Tempsky, 1888), lines 730–33. *Pamphilus* should be followed, according to Hugh, by "Ovidius dictus puellarum / Quem in scolis omnibus non credo fore rarum" (734–35). This is a reference to the *Liber trium puellarum*, a work attributed to Ovid during the Middle Ages (as was *Pamphilus* in some manuscripts); see Karl Bartsch, *Albrecht von Halberstadt und Ovid im Mittelalter* (Quedlinburg, 1861; reprinted Amsterdam: Editions Rodopi, 1965), pp. ix–x. But, as the author of the most exhaustive study of *Pamphilus* has noted, "der Stil ist einfach, die Sprache die des Alltags" (Wilfred Blumenthal, "Untersuchungen zur pseudo-ovidianischen Komödie 'Pamphilus,'" *Mittellateinisches Jahrbuch* 11 [1976]: 280). It could easily have been read earlier than "real" Ovidian texts in the curriculum.

14 For example, Becker, *Pamphilus*, pp. 15, 17, 19, 37–38, and 39. A number of the manuscripts that Becker uses are from the fifteenth century, especially those containing "medieval" schoolbooks, which emphasizes the continuity of the school text tradition in the face of changes argued for or assumed by pedagogues.

15 Elliott, *Seven Medieval Latin Comedies*, p. xxix.

16 Anne Schotter, "Rhetoric versus Rape in the Medieval Latin *Pamphilus*," *Philological Quarterly* 71 (1972): 243–60. Schotter makes this statement at the very end of her paper, in reference to how it would have been read later, but her emphasis throughout the article is the importance of Galathea's objection.

17 *Ibid.*, 257.

18 *Ibid.*

19 See above, n. 14.

20 I do not enter into the debate about whether *Pamphilus* was staged; the terms "comedy" and "drama" are used for convenience here.

21 Richard P. Saller, "The Social Dynamics of Consent to Marriage and Sexual Relations: The Evidence of Roman Comedy," in Angeliki E. Laiou, ed., *Consent and Coercion to Sex and Marriage in Ancient and Medieval Societies*

(Washington, D.C.: Dumbarton Oaks Research Library and Collection, 1993), pp. 87, 89.

22 Text in *P. Terenti Afri Comoediae*, eds. R. Kauer and W. M. Lindsay, trans. W. M. Lindsay (Oxford: Clarendon, 1959); translation in Terence, *The Comedies*, trans. Betty Radice (London: Penguin Books, 1976), p. 289.

23 " 'A Hue and a Cry': Medieval Rape Imagery and Its Transformation," *Art Bulletin* 75 (1993): 39–64. Wolfthal's article, which is part of a forthcoming full-length study of the visual depiction of rape in the western tradition, is an excellent bibliographical source.

24 *Ibid.*, 39.

25 The Ganymede legend is, of course, a staple of the mythological tradition, and it has received much attention of late; see, for example, James M. Saslow, *Ganymede in the Renaissance: Homosexuality in Art and Society* (New Haven: Yale University Press, 1986); and Leonard Barkan, *Transuming Passion: Ganymede and the Erotics of Humanism* (Stanford: Stanford University Press, 1991). For the medieval period, see the numerous references in John Boswell, *Christianity, Social Tolerance, and Homosexuality: Gay People in Western Europe from the Beginning of the Christian Era to the Fourteenth Century* (Chicago: University of Chicago Press, 1980) and Thomas Stehling, *Medieval Latin Poems of Male Love and Friendship*, Garland Library of Medieval Literature 7 (New York: Garland Publishing, Inc., 1984). But the homoerotic tradition, with a few noteworthy exceptions such as the Vézelay Capital (see Wolfthal, " 'A Hue and a Cry,' " 40, n. 8, with whom I disagree here), is in general presented in a less violent light. See Froma Zeitlin, "Configurations of Rape in Greek Myth," in Sylvana Tomaselli and Roy Porter, eds., *Rape: An Historical and Cultural Enquiry* (Oxford: Blackwell, 1986), p. 144: "The iconography. . . distinguishes for the most part between the [heterosexual and homosexual rape] by depicting the male gods as more menacing towards the maidens they pursue. . ." And although Ganymede does occur in texts used in the schools, he is more likely to generate associations of sensuality rather than assertiveness.

26 Mary R. Lefkowitz, "Seduction and Rape in Greek Myth," in Laiou, ed., *Consent and Coercion*, pp. 35 and 17. In this essay Lefkowitz argues that "in the case of myths involving the unions of gods and goddesses with mortal men and women, we should talk about abduction or seduction rather than rape, because the gods see to it that the experience, however transient, is pleasant for mortals" (p. 17). The Latin, as opposed to the Greek, tradition, at least as it was inherited in the medieval schools via Ovid, includes reactions that are less than pleasant; see Leo C. Curran, "Rape and Rape Victims in the *Metamorphoses*," *Arethusa* 11 (1978): 213–41.

27 See Lefkowitz, "Seduction and Rape in Greek Myth," "Even though the

77

encounters between gods and mortal women are almost always of short duration, they have lasting consequences not only for the females involved but for civilization generally, since the children born from such unions are invariably remarkable, famous for their strength or intelligence, or both," (p. 21).

28 See Zeitlin, "Configurations of Rape in Greek Myth," p. 124: "[M]yths often focus on that critical period of passage to adulthood which for Greek society, as for many others, is a moment of acute crisis that crystallizes the continuing social concern with defining (and maintaining) the boundaries between those all-inclusive categories of 'nature' and 'culture.'"

29 See Clogan's synopsis of the *Achilleid* in its medieval format of five books, *The Medieval Achilleid*, pp. 3–7.

30 *Ibid.*, p. 21, with the glosses of MS Vat. lat. 1663, thirteenth century. Translations of these glosses are my own.

31 The term is Hexter's, *Ovid and Medieval Schooling*, p. 46.

32 Text and translation (slightly altered from that) in Alison G. Elliott, "*Accessus ad auctores:* Twelfth-Century Introductions to Ovid," *Allegorica* 5 (1980): 29. Elliott uses the edition of the *Accessus ad auctores* by R. B. C. Huygens (Leiden: Brill, 1970) for her text. But see the *accessus* by Arnulf of Orleans for a different interpretation (*ibid.*, pp. 12–13). Ralph Hexter makes a strong case for the overwhelming importance of the discussion of *intentio* in medieval *accessus* (pp. 212–13), and I have greatly benefited from his argument in my work on this essay.

33 Ostensibly this reference is to a "real" weapon, but the context and Ovid's penchant for innuendo make the phallic association unavoidable.

34 Statius is greatly indebted to Ovid, although the schoolboy chronology presented here obscures this fact; see Daniel Mendelsohn, "Empty Nest, Abandoned Cave: Maternal Anxiety in *Achilleid* 1," *Classical Antiquity* 9 (1990): 296.

35 Schotter, "Rhetoric versus Rape," 243.

36 This *accessus* is printed in Huygens, *Accessus ad auctores*, p. 53. The translation is my own, although other examples from this collection are translated in Elliott, "*Accessus ad auctores*," and in A. J. Minnis and A. B. Scott, with David Wallace, eds., *Medieval Literary Theory and Criticism c. 1100–c. 1375: The Commentary-Tradition*, (Oxford: Clarendon, 1988), pp. 12–36.

37 One reason for this offhandedness may be that the act has been foreshadowed by Achilles' first view of Deidamia, a sight that convinces him to go along with his mother's scheme. His reaction is belligerently male:

ut pater armenti quondam ductorque futurus,
cui nondum toto peraguntur cornua gyro,
cum sociam pastus niveo candore iuvencam
aspicit, ardescunt animi primusque per ora
spumat amor, spectant hilares obstantque magistri.   (313–17)

[As when a bullock, soon to be the sire and leader of a herd, though his horns have not yet come full circle, perceives a heifer of snowy whiteness, the comrade of his pasture, his spirit takes fire, and he foams at the mouth with his first passion; glad at heart the herdsmen watch him and check his fury.]

38 More glosses are found in Clogan, *The Medieval Achilleid*, pp. 88–89. Another commentary on the *Achilleid*, in the famous Petrarch manuscript of Virgil, glosses *dubiam* "vtrum diceret achillem eam uiolasse an taceret" ["whether she should say that Achilles has violated her or be silent about it" (fol. 242v)]. This manuscript, Milan, Ambros. S. P. Arm. 10 scaf. 27, is available in a facsimile: G. Galbiati, ed., *Francisci Petrarchae Vergilianus codex*. . .(Milan: in aedibus Hoepliani, 1930).

39 This approach is common to all school commentaries, even in the fifteenth century. For example, in Prague University Library MS VIII.H.22, the commentator with regard to the bull simile (see above, n. 37) notes in the margin simply, "hic ponit quamdam comparationem" ["here he puts a comparison," (fol. 130v)]; the interlinear glosses identify terms and grammatical relationships. Unfortunately the marginal glosses in this manuscript cease before the rape scene.

40 Hexter, *Ovid and Medieval Schooling*, p. 32.

41 *Ibid.*, p. 39.

42 *Ibid.*, pp. 42, 51–54, in Copenhagen, Kongelige Bibliothek Gl. Kgl. S. 2015. Hexter emphasizes the differences between these commentaries; I emphasize their similarities for my own rhetorical purposes.

43 *Ibid.*, p. 72; Hexter adds in a footnote to this passage, "This is more than can be said for numerous commentators of the eighteenth, nineteenth, or even twentieth century, who, in contrast, are positively 'medieval.'" None of the examples that Hexter cites are from the passage under consideration here.

44 See Becker, *Pamphilus*, pp. 14, 23, 27, 38 (n. 5), 41 (n. 2), 42, 47 (n. 4), 51 (n. 4), 64 (n. 2), 86 (n. 4), and 87 (n. 6).

45 *Ibid.*, p. 14 (n. 6), citing Berlin, Deutsche Staatsbibliothek cod. Diez. B. Sant. 4, fourteenth century.

46 *Ibid.*, pp. 28 (n. 6), 33 (n. 3).

47 *Ibid.*, p. 25 (n. 3), from Breslau, Biblioteka Uniwersytecka, cod. IV 2° 42,

from the end of the fourteenth century. A second scribe added this and other identifications (for example, "panphilus loquitur ad galatheam" ["Pamphilus speaks to Galathea"] at l. 245, "verba panphili ad anum" ["the words of Pamphilus to the Old Woman"] at l. 495.

48 *Ibid.*, p. 41 (n. 2), citing Karlsruhe, Badische Landesbibliothek cod. Ettenheimmünster 35, d. 1474.

49 Peter L. Allen, *The Art of Love: Amatory Fiction from Ovid to the Romance of the Rose* (Philadelphia: University of Pennsylvania Press, 1992), p. 40. Actually, according to Hagendahl, Allen's source, the classics could be taught to boys but not girls (Harlad Hagendahl, *Latin Fathers and the Classics: A Study on the Apologists, Jerome and Other Christian Writers*, Studia Graeca et Latina Gothoburgensia 6 (Göteborg: Elanders Boktryckeri Aktiebolag, 1958), pp. 196, 325–26).

50 Hexter, *Ovid and Medieval Schooling*, p. 25. The periodic condemnations of using texts like this for schoolroom use is a sign that this practice continued unabated; thus I am in disagreement with arguments such as that given by John Dagenais in " 'Se usa e se faz': Naturalist Truth in a *Pamphilus* explicit and the *Libro de buen amor*," *Hispanic Review* 54 (1989): 423 (n. 6):

> My general impression is that the Middle Ages came closest to our own concerns about the moral content of literature when children were involved. See, for example, the *De eruditione filiorum nobiliorum* of Vincent of Beauvais: "At quid enim usque hodie paruulorum sensus et lingue poeticis fabulis ad luxuriosis figmentis imbuuntur? Nam et si doctrina poetica sit utilis quantum ad regulas metricas inutilis tamen est, immo perniciosa quantum ad fabulas predictas" (23) ["For to what purpose are the senses and tongues of children today imbued with poetic fables and lustful fictions? For even if this poetic learning is useful for the rules of metrics, it is nevertheless useless and even pernicious in so far as the aforesaid stories are concerned."] Note here, however, that the text's usefulness as a guide to metric composition is weighed carefully in the balance before Vincent rejects the works of the poets.

But Dagenais' final note is useful for my own argument in its association of these texts with the study of literary language.

51 See Mary Carruthers, *The Book of Memory: A Study of Memory in Medieval Culture* (Cambridge: Cambridge University Press, 1990), pp. 130–37, on the usefulness of lurid images in committing texts and concepts to memory, so basic a part of the pre-modern educational process. In discussing Thomas Bradwardine's method of memorizing the signs of the zodiac, Carruthers notes that "what is most surprising, to a puritan-formed

sensibility, is the emphasis on violence and sexuality which runs through all the interaction of the figures in each scene" (p. 134).

52 D. A. Russell, *Greek Declamation* (Cambridge: Cambridge University Press, 1983), pp. 35, 29.

53 Text and translation in *The Elder Seneca Controversiae*, trans. M. Winterbottom, 2 vols., Loeb Classical Library (Cambridge, Mass.: Harvard University Press, 1974). Winterbottom sometimes changes "for the sake of variety" the translation to "seduction" or "ravisher" although "[i]t is rape that is in question" (1.5, pp. 120–21 [n. 3]). I have silently emended the translation to the more direct term each time. I have also silently omitted the restatement of the law "Raptor Duorum," which occurs in each case between the title and the summary.

54 "Imprudentis cadis damnatus quinquennio exulet" ["One convicted of unintentional homicide shall go into exile for five years" (4.3)].

55 The same is true with the Greek declamations that Russell examines.

56 See also Seneca, *Con.* 3.2, 3.3, 3.4, 4.5, 4.6, 5.2, 5.4, 6.1, 6.2, 6.7, 7.1, 7.3, 7.4, 7.6, 8.5, 8.6, 9.3, 9.4, 9.5, 9.6, 10.1, 10.2, 10.3.

57 In other rhetorical collections with pedagogical associations rape is also a paradigmatic subject:

> It is true that to supplement Seneca on the *educational* use of declamation we need to look at another source, the collection attributed to the great teacher Quintilian and known as the Minor Declamations. From this we learn that in a *controversia* the schoolteacher would propose a theme (e.g., "A rapist hung himself. The girl he had raped chooses his property"), often related to a stated law (in this case "a Girl who has been raped may choose her seducer's death or his property"). He would then give advice on the treatment (the sections entitled *sermo*), and a model speech (*declamatio*), put in the mouth either of one of the parties in the case or of an advocate. The schoolboys (of what we should call secondary age), would give speeches of their own, on one side or the other.
>
> (Winterbottom, ed., Seneca *Con.*, I: x–xi.)

58 S. F. Bonner, *Roman Declamation in the Late Republic and Early Empire* (Liverpool: University Press of Liverpool, 1949), p. 41; see Bonner's n. 2 for reactions of other scholars to the subject matter of the declamations.

59 Michael Winterbottom, ed., *Roman Declamation* (Bristol: Bristol Classical Press, 1980), p. 10.

60 Russell, *Greek Declamation*, pp. 27, 31.

61 George Kennedy, *The Art of Rhetoric in the Roman World, 300 B.C.–A.D. 300* (Princeton: Princeton University Press, 1972), p. 334. For Kennedy, the "best example is the recurring question of the relationship of children

to parents"; Kennedy perceives the psychological advantages of such an approach and argues for its universality: "This is the great problem which every adolescent is facing or avoiding; today we favor school texts which relate to the problem in some way: versions of the Orestes or Electra or Oedipus story, *Hamlet, David Copperfield, Tom Sawyer, Sons and Lovers, Portrait of the Artist, Catcher in the Rye*" (*ibid.*). Note the prevalence of incidents of incest, rape, and sexual initiation in these texts and the way in which they are interwoven with issues of parent–child relationships in the coming-to-manhood adventure that most of them depict.

62 With regard to this sense of self as controlling and controlled on the part of the adolescent, see Zeitlin, "Configurations of Rape":

> The Greek notion of eros as a wilful and overpowering divinity, granted immortal status by reason of its superior strength and eternal durability, also sees masculine sexuality as motivated by an external force too strong to resist. It is paradoxical that whereas phallic desire represents the aggressive impulse of eros, the individual male is himself overcome by a power difficult or impossible to control. Hence, his submission to eros is simultaneously a sign of both strength and weakness. (p. 145)

63 Bonner, *Roman Declamation*, p. 151.
64 *Ibid.*, pp. 37–38; see also Winterbottom, *Roman Declamation*, p. 70.
65 Bonner, *ibid.*, p. 37.
66 Saller, "The Social Dynamics of Consent to Marriage and Sexual Relations," p. 85.
67 Huygens, *Accessus ad auctores*, p. 53.
68 See Schotter, "Rhetoric and Rape," 245–50, for a discussion of male vs. female rhetoric in this text.
69 What Evesque argues is true for both Pamphilus and Galathea seems to me applicable only to him, although her strong presence in the text generates a sense of greater equality: "Les jeunes gens, libres de disposer d'euxmêmes par le seul fait qu'ils ont la liberté d'aller et de venir, le font suivant les penchants de leur cœur"; Eugène Evesque, ed. and trans., *Pamphilus*, in Gustave Cohen, *La "Comédie" latine en France au xiie siècle*, II (Paris: Les Belles-Lettres, 1931): 172.
70 As Leo Curran has pointed out in his important study of rape victims in the *Metamorphoses*, "Ovid does not simply take the role of woman as victim for granted and get on with the story at hand; rather he draws out its implications. He shows that there are few from whom the victim can expect sympathy or comfort. She and not the rapist is the one who must bear the injury, the guilt, society's blame, and the punishment" ("Rape and Rape Victims in the *Metamorphoses*," 223).

71 Becker, *Pamphilus*, pp. 90–117; see also Blumenthal, "Untersuchungen zur. . .'Pamphilus,'" 288. This sense of the text as a collection of information to be applied elsewhere may also be what is referred to in the explicit discussed by Dagenais: "Explicit *pamphilus* valde notabilis et sententia mente tenenda quia in eo totum verum continetur et hodie utitur" ["Here ends *Pamphilus*, extremely noteworthy and with a *sententia* to be kept in mind since in it all truth is contained and is used today"; my translation] (418, quoting Paris, Bibliothèque nationale MS lat. 8513, fol. 110r). See also Becker, *Pamphilus*, pp. 53–54. Bonner, *Roman Declamation*, p. 151, argues Ovid's importance as the source of *sententiae*, particularly "amatory maxims," of the kind for which *Pamphilus*, too, was mined in the *florilegia*. In "The Amatory Excerpts of Ovid in the *Florilegium Gallicum*: Evidence of the Knowledge of this Poet in the Twelfth Century," *Florilegium* 8 (1986), Sally A. Rackley argues that the purpose of the *Florilegium Gallicum* "was the transmission of moral *sententiae*, with a secondary purpose of instructing in Latin composition" (74). Ovid's advice about rape in 1.673–78 is not excerpted in this collection.

72 Bits and pieces of this speech are quoted in almost every collection cited by Becker, *Pamphilus*, pp. 90–117; see also Blumenthal, "Untersuchungen zur. . .'Pamphilus,'" 288.

73 Becker, *Pamphilus*, pp. 90–117 *passim*.

74 *Ibid.*, pp. 93, 94 (twice), 95, 96, 97, 100, 101, 104, 106, 108, 112, 114, 115 (twice).

75 *Ibid.*, pp. 93, 94, 95, 96, 100, 101, 107, 108, 112, 115 (twice).

76 *Ibid.*, pp. 93, 96, 97, 104, 106, 109, 115.

77 *Ibid.*, pp. 91, 92, 106, 107, 112.

78 *Ibid.*, pp. 91, 93, 94, 96, 112.

79 The first line is an aphorism, "Fructibus ipsa suis, que sit, cognoscitur" ["A tree is known by its fruit"], which is sometimes but not always excerpted with the condemnation in the following line: "Tuque michi factis nosceris ipsa tuis" ["and you will be known by your deeds"]; see Becker, *ibid.*, pp. 91, 100, 107, 113.

80 See, for example, Allen, *The Art of Love*, pp. 38–78; Garbáty, "The *Pamphilus* Tradition"; and Blumenthal, "Untersuchungen zur. . . 'Pamphilus,'" 283–97.

81 It would be almost impossible to overemphasize the continuity of specific themes and characters in the schoolboy tradition of the pre-modern West. For example, one exercise that was a "regular feature of the Greek *progymnasmata* or preliminary rhetorical exercises" was the theme of "what might Niobe say over the bodies of her dead children" (Winterbottom, *Roman Declamation*, p. 52), while two of the very few medieval school

exercises that have come down to us have Niobe as their subject (Woods, "Teaching of Writing," pp. 84–86).

82　It is significant that, while we have homoerotic material produced by and perhaps even read in the medieval schools (for example, Boswell, *Christianity, Social Tolerance, and Homosexuality*, pp. 83, 239, 248–49, 255–56 [n. 49], perhaps also 218–19 and 261–62; Stehling, *Medieval Latin Poems*, pp. 22–23, 147), we do not have manuals that tell one how to go about seducing young boys. In fact, almost the only such text that I know about is in a letter-writing manual in which the seduction ploy is the first of a pair of letters; in the second the boy successfully counters his teacher's attempt ("Two Letters from a French Treatise on Composition," in Stehling, *ibid.*, pp. 90–93, 156–157). See also above, n. 25. There are cases of homosexual rape that occur in the declamation exercises (for example, Russell, *Greek Declamation*, p. 9, and Seneca, *Contr.* 5.6, although the latter is a case involving a man who was raped while wearing women's clothes).

83　Cf. Kathryn Gravdal, who asks, "why [Chrétien de Troyes] has long been viewed as a beloved master of medieval literature and an expert in the representation of feminine psychology," *Ravishing Maidens: Writing Rape in Medieval French Literature and Law* (Philadelphia: University of Pennsylvania Press, 1991), p. 15. The same question could, of course, be asked of Chaucer.

84　Allen, *The Art of Love*, pp. 55–56:

> Fragments of one thirteenth-century Latin "pseudo-*Ars*" and "pseudo-*Remedia*" remain, and five French versions of the works are extant, produced by Maistre Elie, Jakes d'Amiens, Guiart, and two anonymous authors.
>
> 　Each of these versions attempted to accommodate the *Ars* to the literary conventions of the day. One of the most striking changes they made was to eliminate *Ars amatoria* 3 – a symptom of the period's growing uneasiness toward women. . . .And every medieval version of the *Ars* is accompanied in its manuscript by a version of the *Remedia*, even in cases in which the two texts were composed by different authors.

The "canonical" *accessus* to the *Ars amatoria* described by Hexter in *Ovid and Medieval Schooling* creates much the same effect with its emphases: "[The commentator] expresses Ovid's aim for the first two books only, as if the entire *Ars amatoria* were solely addressed to men. . . .He analyzes the final cause (in other words, the utility), only in terms of Ovid's male addressees" (pp. 46–47). But the alterations in the vernacular translations preclude the possibility of any other interpretation.

85　The medievalist Carol J. Clover's recent book, *Men, Women, and Chain Saws:*

Gender in the Modern Horror Film, makes a similar argument for the identification of the audience of these films, composed primarily of adolescent boys (pp. 3, 4, 6, 23) with the female victim as well as the male killer: "by any measure, horror is far more victim-identified than the standard view would have it. . .And just as attacker and attacked are expressions of the same self in nightmares, so they are expressions of the same viewer in horror film. . .[T]he force of the experience, in horror, comes from 'knowing both sides of the story' " (pp. 8, 12). Clover draws on "a premodern sense of sexual difference" (p. 15) for her arguments, which she also explores in her recent article in *Speculum*: "Regardless of Sex: Men, Women, and Power in Early Northern Europe," 68 (1993): 363–88. See especially 380: "What I am suggesting is that this is *the* binary, the one that cuts most deeply and the one that matters: between strong and weak, powerful and powerless or disempowered,. . .winners and losers." For my focus on medieval adolescent males, however, her study of modern films is, paradoxically, more relevant; see especially the introduction of *Men, Women, and Chain Saws*, "Carrie and the Boys," pp. 3–20, and from my perspective very felicitously titled chapter 1, "Her Body, Himself," pp. 21–64.

86 Cf. Thomas Lacquer: "The body with its one elastic sex was far freer to express theatrical gender and the anxieties thereby produced than it would be when it came to be regarded as the foundation of gender," *Making Sex: Body and Gender from the Greeks to Freud* (Cambridge, Mass.: Harvard University Press, 1990), p. 125; cited in Clover, *Men, Women, and Chain Saws*, p. 16.

87 The same issues of power may be deployed around a different site of violence in other cultural contexts; for example, rape is the least relevant issue for my studies in Clover's analysis of victim status in horror films (see Clover, *ibid.*, p. 46 (n. 2), and her discussion of rape-revenge films on pp. 114–65).

88 Blumenthal, "Untersuchungen zur. . .'Pamphilus,' " 283–97.

89 The medieval abridgements of the text emphasized the importance of his mother's coaching in the ways of women, which follows that of Chiron in matters military and moral; see C. Jeudy and Y. F. Riou, "L'*Achilléide* de Stace au moyen âge: abrégés et arguments," *Revue d'histoire des textes* 4 (1974): 143–80.

90 Statius' own division of the incomplete text, in which the end of the first book comes more than two hundred lines after the rape scene, frames the rape scene within Thetis' dominance at the beginning of the work; see Mendelsohn, "Empty Nest, Abandoned Cave," especially 302–07.

91 When there is a mixed audience, women identify with females, men with males. Clover in *Men, Women, and Chain Saws* points out that, when the

themes of horror movies move into upscale and adult films, the identification with the female victim – and her function in these films as eventual hero(ine) – is watered down and taken over by males or male-identified institutions (see, for example, pp. 60–61, 145–51, 232–35). Clover locates her arguments within specific temporal frameworks and anxieties about feminism and changing roles of women, but I wish to emphasize in my use of her work the timeless aspects of the associations of gender formation with both victim and perpetrator experience.

92 In the case of the reading of such texts in women's communities or schools, which were rarer and tended to concentrate more but not exclusively on religious texts, the bifurcation could function in a complementary way.

93 Projection and identification on the part of readers and writers are often particularly powerful when they transcend gender; see Constance Penley, "Brownian Motion: Women, Tactics, and Technology," in Constance Penley and Andrew Ross, eds., *Technoculture* (for the Social Text collective), Cultural Politics, III (Minneapolis: University of Minnesota Press, 1991): 135–61.

3

Heloise and the gendering of the literate subject

MARTIN IRVINE

In the twelfth century, a literate woman found herself circumscribed in a textual culture in which literacy was obtained through a male rite of passage in the grammatical schools. Participation in textual culture and the performance of literate practices – interpreting canonical texts and writing conventional genres – were encoded as masculine. The literate person, whose distinctive subjectivity was constituted by participating in this culture, was known only by a masculine name in Latin, the *litteratus*.[1] Much has been recovered recently about women writers in the Middle Ages,[2] but we still know little about the large social effects of the highly masculinist culture of the *litteratus* and how both women and men appropriated, negotiated, or resisted the gendered subject positions that were securely in place before anyone read or wrote a text. The collected letters of Abelard and Heloise, written *c.* 1132–*c.* 1136, open up the question of gendered subjectivity in an unusually explicit way, and disclose the possibilities for a woman to appropriate the power of Latin culture but resist its totalizing or essentializing force.

Heloise's letters reveal a highly skilled writer who negotiated a new space within literate culture – that of the woman as *litteratus* and friend (*amicus*). Abelard, after his physical and political emasculations, worked out a strategy to maintain his masculine authority while frequently writing from a feminized position, excluded from the circles of authority and power that once included him. Heloise in her letters negotiated and redefined her identity and subjectivity to write like a *litteratus* and as a woman. This essay is an attempt to describe the nature of this newly negotiated position in her correspondence with Abelard and within twelfth-century culture.[3]

Current scholarship has, thankfully, dismantled most of the earlier arguments against the authenticity of the letters of Heloise and Abelard.[4]

After studying in detail the five main manuscripts of the collected correspondence of Abelard and Heloise and comparing these manuscripts to other letter collections from the twelfth century,[5] I can find no reason to question the unanimous manuscript attributions to their authors. If there had been any doubts about authorship, they certainly would have been raised by the thirteenth century, when Jean de Meun translated letters 1–7 and the abbey of the Paraclete had grown into a large and flourishing institution. It seems highly unlikely that an institution as well-known and as close to Paris as the Paraclete could have successfully promoted a forgery: there were certainly enough people in Paris in Jean de Meun's day who would have been in a position to know about Paraclete traditions. The Abelard and Heloise correspondence bears all the marks of a canonical letter collection, and was almost certainly compiled and edited at Heloise's convent of the Paraclete.[6]

The letters in the canonical collection, conventionally numbered 1–8, were written at least sixteen years after Abelard and Heloise had been lovers in Paris. After the catastrophic outcome of their relationship and marriage, Abelard first placed Heloise in the convent of Argenteuil and then entered the abbey of St. Denis (1117–1119). Abelard founded the convent of the Paraclete near Troyes as a community for women in 1123. Heloise shortly afterwards become Abbess of the Paraclete, and in 1125 Abelard became Abbot of St. Gildas de Rhuys in Brittany. He probably wrote his first letter to an unnamed friend, known now as the *Historia calamitatum*, in around 1132, and the collected letters were probably exchanged sometime between 1132 and 1136, when Abelard had returned to Paris to teach again.[7] When the letter exchange began, Abelard was in his early fifties, Heloise in her early thirties. Abelard seems to have been adrift, without a secure place to showcase his talents; Heloise was a successful abbess with a growing community. Although separated, he and Heloise continued their collaboration in building up the Paraclete community, arguably their spiritual child and life's work.[8]

The collected correspondence, however, is not a complete collection of the letters of Abelard and Heloise. They wrote letters to each other both before and after the time represented by the canonical collection, and therefore Heloise's letters to Abelard need to be placed in the larger context of letters written from their early years in Paris (now lost) to letters that record their collaboration on monastic education and liturgy at the Paraclete.

THE KNOWN CORRESPONDENCE BETWEEN ABELARD AND HELOISE

Letters exchanged during their time together in Paris[9]

The collected correspondence:[10]

1 Abelard, *Epistola ad amicum pro consolatione* (*Historia calamitatum*)
2 Heloise, first letter to Abelard
3 Abelard, first reply to Heloise
4 Heloise, second letter to Abelard
5 Abelard, second reply to Heloise
6 Heloise, third letter to Abelard
7 Abelard, third reply to Heloise (*De origine sanctimonialium*)
8 Abelard, *Regula sanctimonialium*

Abelard, letter 9, To Heloise and the nuns of the Paraclete, *De studio litterarum*[11]
Heloise, prefatory letter to Abelard at beginning of her *Problemata*[12]
Abelard, prefatory letter to Heloise at beginning of his *Expositio in Hexameron*[13]
Abelard, prefatory letter to Heloise at beginning of his *Sermones*[14]
Abelard, prefatory letter to Heloise at beginning of his *Hymni*[15]

It seems there was seldom a time in Abelard's life – from his meeting Heloise in 1116 till the time of his trial at the Council of Sens in 1140 – when he was not writing letters to Heloise.

Because they are parts of an ongoing exchange, each of Heloise's letters needs to be read dialogically: the letters represent stages in a sequence of responses, not isolated statements. The correspondence developed both intertextually, presupposing the genre of the Latin literary epistle, specific letter collections, and other classical and Christian literature, and intratextually, constructed with self-reflexive gestures and references to earlier statements in their own exchange. While they are writing new letters, the authors are aware of the design of the whole; the collection itself becomes a text, a record of their lives archived by and for the Paraclete community. Each of Heloise's letters has its own rhetorical shape, strategies for argument, and ways of positioning the writer in relation to her correspondent and to the genre in which she is participating.

FRIENDSHIP, GENDER, AND GENRE

Rather than cobbling all of Heloise's letters together in the search for some unifying gendered quality or in the hope of establishing unifying themes external to a rhetorical and historical context, I would like to follow her first two letters in their dialogic context and disclose how Heloise carefully constructs her own position and invents a space for feminine literate subjectivity and for a feminine, eroticized friendship (*amicitia*). The developing rhetorical and dialogic context alone discloses Heloise's participation in mainstream literate discourse and genres, her resistance to taking on the identity and subject positions constructed for her in Abelard's letters, and her striking move to invent a feminine position within the traditional discourse on friendship.[16]

A key to understanding Heloise's letters and the identity that she negotiates in them is understanding the genre that she is using – the Latin, literary *epistola*, particularly the Senecan letter to a friend, a genre that took on new life in the twelfth century. During the 1130s, when Abelard and Heloise were exchanging letters, monastic culture was being redirected by a new emphasis on the affective dimensions of spirituality, largely from the Cistercian movement.[17] The twelfth century was an era of heightened interest in spiritual friendship:[18] there was a renewed interest in the classical values of friendship expressed in Cicero's *De amicitia* and in Seneca's letters to Lucilius, and the literary *epistola ad amicum* expanded in all directions.[19] Some of the monastic literature on friendship, like Baudri of Bourgueil's poems and Aelred of Rievaulx's *De spirituali amicitia (On Spiritual Friendship)*, is openly erotic and homoerotic,[20] combining *amor* and *amicitia* in ways parallel to Heloise's affirmations of sexual love and friendship with Abelard.

The Latin literary letter, however, should not be confused with the modern personal letter. The *epistola* was a formal, literary, and public genre, considered to be an occasion for a rhetorical performance on whatever themes the correspondents chose.[21] Abelard and Heloise also knew some of the techniques of the *ars dictaminis*, which provided formal generic rules for salutations and structure.[22] An *epistola* could often be a simple pretext for an essay, argument, or, like Abelard's first letter, a personal *apologia* or *consolatio*. Many letters were designed to be compiled into a formal letter collection, like those of Peter of Blois, Bernard of Clairvaux, and Peter the Venerable, and the letters of Abelard and Heloise closely follow established conventions.

By the middle of the twelfth century, writers could look to model letter collections by Seneca, Jerome, and Augustine, as well as by eleventh- and twelfth-century writers. But the genre was not unitary: there were actually many subgenres and traditions for letters, including letters of direction and monastic vocational letters.[23] One of the major conflicts in the identity negotiations between Abelard and Heloise is registered in the way they use the discourse and form of various subgenres and traditions in medieval letter-writing. Heloise follows Abelard's example in his first letter to an unnamed friend – which Heloise refers to as *ad amicum pro consolatione epistola* – by sending a Senecan *epistola ad amicum* to Abelard. Abelard, on the other hand, does not play the same literary game. His letters to Heloise are not Senecan but Jeromian: he understands clearly the genre-encoding that Heloise has initiated, but he responds by writing in the tradition of the Jeromian letter of direction to nuns and others under his authority. In other words, if we miss the presuppositions of genre and form when reading the letters of Abelard and Heloise, we risk gross errors of misreading, chief of which can be misinterpreting personal agency or intention in the expectations and conventions of genre.

While encoding the subtle distinctions and variations of genre, the letters of Abelard and Heloise also participate in the multiple discourses of love, friendship, and sexuality at work in the twelfth century. On the topic of *amor* and *amicitia*, the monastic tradition, typified by William of St. Thierry and Aelred of Rivaulx, deployed discourse from Ovidian, Ciceronian, and Augustinian traditions, often with an ambiguous interpenetration of rhetoric.[24] By the end of the twelfth century, there were at least five heterogeneous, though often combined, discourses of love and sexuality in Northern France – Augustinian patristic, Galenic/medical, Ovidian/literary, vernacular–romance, and vernacular–fabliau.[25] Although Abelard and Heloise clearly signal the discursive traditions within which their arguments are generated, a reader must attend carefully to the multiplicity of discourses and the heterogeneous domains and ideologies represented in their writings. Heloise was especially adept at combining the seemingly conflicting discourses of Ovidian *amor* and Christian *amicitia* for both rhetorical effect and new self-definition.

Let us consider first Heloise's use of the Senecan form of the *epistola ad amicum* and her appropriation and modification of the classical idea of friendship or *amicitia*.[26] This genre provided the form for her new negotiations of identity and participation in the twelfth-century ideal of friendship, which was still considered a male social value: the subject position of the *amicus* within the discourses on friendship was understood to be filled by men. Senecan assumptions about *amicitia*, however, permeate Heloise's first two letters – which she clearly marks as Senecan before modifying her form in her third letter to match Abelard's – and many of her arguments presuppose the formal requirements of the *epistola ad amicum*. But what is more significant is that Heloise's negotiates a new kind of *amicitia*: she motivates Abelard to write to her by requesting a letter of consolation like the one he wrote to a male friend, and then she appeals to the debts of both their *amor* and *amicitia*, attempting to create a new space where she can be both *amicus* and *amica* for Abelard, thus defining a dual-gendered *amicitia*. Writing from the position of the literate subject, she both appropriates the authority of the masculine *litteratus* and resists the totalizing force of this gendered position: she writes like an *amicus* but as a woman.

To mark the subgenre she is using, Heloise writes as Abelard's friend in the opening to her first letter, taking the position of a receiver of Abelard's first letter and of the conventionally male *amicus*. By writing to Abelard in this genre, Heloise positions herself as the writer of a letter to an *amicus*, assuming the kind of literate subjectivity taken by the writer of this form of letter. Heloise thus aligns herself with two conventional masculine subject positions, the writer who speaks in the first person to a (male) equal and the addressee who shares a like subjectivity with the writer of a letter.

Heloise's opening sentence refers to Abelard's letter to a friend and reveals that her letter is a response to it: "Missam ad amicum pro consolatione epistolam, dilectissime, vestram ad me forte quidam nuper attulit" ("Recently, my beloved, someone brought to me by chance your letter sent to a friend for consolation.")[27] The phrase *ad amicum pro consolatione epistola*, which Heloise uses twice in this letter, constitutes a witness to an earlier name for what we now call Abelard's *Historia calamitatum*.[28] Abelard's letter, of course, has exactly the rhetorical form designated by Heloise. Heloise's opening posture is that of another friend to whom someone brought the letter by chance (*forte*). She states that she read the letter ardently after seeing that it was from Abelard, thus placing herself in the position of the male *amicus*-addressee. She briefly summarizes his letter and then requests that he write to her and his other handmaids (*ancillulas*) directly. This is the first of her several requests for letters: Heloise repeatedly requests to be the addressee and recipient of a letter of consolation like the one Abelard sent to his male friend, and she frames the main body of her letter with references to "frequent letters" (*crebris litteris, crebris epistolis*)[29] which could form a statement of the bonds of their *amicitia* and their need for mutual *consolatio*.

It should thus be recognized that the entire collected correspondence of Abelard and Heloise – letters 1 through 7 and the *Regula sanctimonialium* – is a result of Heloise's prompting and initiation. Although Abelard's *epistola ad amicum* was the occasion for Heloise's first letter to Abelard, the subsequent exchange was initiated by Heloise.

Much of Heloise's first letter can be read as a personal commentary on the main terms of her opening sentence – *amicus* (and, by extension, *amicitia*), *consolatio*, and *epistola*. Heloise proceeds to explain her desire for a letter in which she and her community are addressees by an appeal to classical *amicitia*: by writing to her, Abelard can have partners or sharers (*participes*) of grief or joy.

We beg you, through Christ, who even now protects you in some way, that you consider it worthwhile to write frequent letters to his handmaids and yours about those things which even now you are tossed about in shipwreck, so that we at least – who remain for you alone – can have a share in your pain or joy. Those who grieve together [*qui condolent*] usually give some consolation to the one in pain, and whatever burden is placed on several is carried more lightly or removed.[30]

Heloise is gesturing toward the Senecan ideal of friendship, like that expressed in Seneca's *Epistle* 6:

tunc amicitiae nostrae certiorem fiduciam habere coepissem, illius verae, quam non spes, non timor, non utilitatis suae cura divellit, illius, cum qua homines moriuntur, pro qua moriuntur. Multos tibi dabo, qui non amico, sed amicitia caruerunt. Hoc non potest accidere, cum animos in societatem honesta cupiendi par voluntas trahit. Quidni non possit? Sciunt enim ipsos omnia habere communia, et quidem magis adversa. (*Ad Lucilium epistulae morales*, 6.2–3)[31]

[I should begin then to have a surer trust in our friendship, the true friendship, which hope and fear and concern for self-interest cannot tear apart, the friendship with which and for the sake of which people die. I can show you many who have lacked, not a friend, but friendship. This cannot happen when an equal purpose draws souls together in a companionship of honorable desire. And why can't it happen? Because they know that they have all things in common, especially their troubles.]

Seneca's ideal for friendship is *par voluntas* (like or equal will and purpose) and the commonality of things, including *adversa*, troubles or misfortunes.

Heloise not only echoes Senecan language, she quotes Seneca directly as part of her own argument. A passage from Seneca's *Epistle* 40 allows her to identify with the male writer who is writing as the receiver of a letter from an absent friend:

Quam jocunde vero sint absentium littere amicorum, ipse nos exemplo proprio Seneca docet, ad amicum Lucilium quodam loco sic scribens: "Quod frequenter mihi scribis, gratias ago: nam quo uno modo potes, te mihi ostendis. Numquam epistolam tuam accipio, quin protinus una simus. Si imagines nobis amicorum absentium jocunde sunt, que memoriam renovant et desiderium absentie falso atque inani solatio levant, quanto jocundiores sunt littere, que amici absentis veras notas afferunt [Seneca, *Epist.* 40.1]"? Deo autem gratias, quod hoc saltem modo presentium tuam nobis reddere nulla invidia prohiberis, nulla difficultate prepediris, nulla, obsecro, negligentia retarderis.[32]

[But how pleasant are the letters of absent friends, as Seneca himself shows us with his own example when he wrote this passage to his friend Lucilius: "I thank you for writing to me often; for you are revealing yourself to me in the one way that you can. I never receive a letter from you without the sense that we are together. If the pictures of absent friends are pleasing to us, renewing our memory and lightening our desire of the one absent with false and empty comfort, how much more pleasant is a letter which brings us real signs of an absent friend" [Seneca, *Epist.* 40.1]. God be thanked that at least in this way no malice can prevent you, no trouble hinder you, nor, I beg you, any negligence delay you in restoring your presence to us/me.]

Heloise has been anticipating this quotation from the beginning of her letter. In her second sentence, the phrase *ut. . .verbis. . .ejus quadam imagine recreer* ("that I would be renewed by its [the letter's] words with a kind of picture") anticipates Seneca's *imagines. . .amicorum absentium. . .quae memoriam renovant* ("pictures of absent friends which renew our memory.") Abelard's letter – addressed not to her but to a friend – bears the marks, signs, or traces (*veras notas*) of Abelard's presence (*presentia*), which Heloise says she desires like Seneca for his friend Lucilius. Heloise thus readily adopts the position of the masculine *amicus*-addressee and writes to Abelard like Seneca to Lucilius.

But Heloise omits a telling sentence from the *locus* she has cited, the place in Seneca's letters that she invokes. Seneca concludes the above thought with an even stronger statement of the link between writing and the physical traces of the absent writer: "Nam quod in conspectu dulcissimum est, id amici manus epistulae inpressa praestat, agnoscere"[33] ("for that which is sweetest when face to face, the same stands out in the impress of a friend's hand on his letter – recognizing)." Heloise suppresses at this point the more direct link between the two forms of physical recognition between friends, the recognition that happens face to face and the recognition in the traces that the hand leaves on the writing material and in the shape of the letters. Heloise does not follow Seneca in arguing for the physical connection between Abelard's letter and his own body. Most likely she had a copy of the letter, the original itself copied out by a secretary, as was the common practice; perhaps she suppresses a too vivid reminder of what she desires. Heloise, however, uses the terms "presence" and "absence" in rhetorical contrast many times in this letter, desiring letters from Abelard that can substitute for his physical presence.[34] This language is clearly Ovidian, recalling the desire of separated lovers (*absentes*) and the loss of the tragic survivors of *amor* in the *Heroides*.

It should be noted at this point that some thirteenth-century readers also placed the correspondence of Abelard and Heloise in a Senecan context. The compiler of Reims, Bibliothèque municipale MS 872 (s.xiii/ xiv),[35] a compilation of the works of Seneca and the letters of Heloise and Abelard, placed the collected letters of Abelard and Heloise after Seneca's letters to Lucilius. It would have made perfect sense to a thirteenth-century compiler to include the collected correspondence of Abelard and Heloise after the canonical letter collection of Seneca.

Pivoting on the central, and as yet not explicitly acknowledged, issue of the gendering of friendship, Heloise then expands her argument about *amicitia* by invoking the debts and obligations shared by friends. Heloise says that Abelard, in writing a letter of consolation to his friend (*amicus*), honored a debt of friendship while exposing his neglect of an even greater obligation to her and her community, his female friends (*amicae*):

Morem quidem amico et socio gessisti et tam amicitie quam societatis debitum persolvisti, sed majore te debito nobis astrinxisti, quas non tam amicas quam amicissimas, non tam socias quam filias convenit nominari, vel si quod dulcius et sanctius vocabulem potest excogitari.[36]

[You have done the will of your friend and ally, and have honored your debt to friendship as well as loyalty. But you have bound yourself to us by a greater debt, us who properly can be called not so much female-friends as closest-female-friends, not so much female-partners as daughters, or rather, if it can be devised, a name more dear and sacred.]

Here grammatical gender is used for rhetorical effect: Abelard may have fulfilled a debt to an *amicus*, but he has forgotten his *amica* and *amicae*, indeed, even his *amicissimae*, his closest-female-friends. The term "debt" in this context, furthermore, cannot but invoke St. Paul's admonition about the marriage debt in 1 Corinthians 7.3 (*uxori vir debitum reddat*). The ambiguity in *amica*, the feminine form of *amicus*, is striking: it ordinarily means girlfriend, lover, or mistress – an identity Heloise, of course, enthusiastically accepts in the context of this letter – or, more rarely, a female friend (ally, supporter).[37] Heloise leaves the erotic associations of *amica* and *amicissima* suspended in the rhetoric of her argument. She also clearly uses *amica* to mean the feminine equivalent of the masculine *amicus*, that is, a female participant in *amicitia* between equals. The term *socia*, female partner or associate, which she also uses here, reinforces the idea of a bond between the partners. Because the bonds of support and obligation can extend in either direction, she is also gesturing toward her ongoing support of Abelard in the political context of their monastic life. She and her community are truly his closest friends in that they rely on his authority and direction and are his faithful supporters in a world of misfortunes.

We should not miss the radically new statement about friendship that Heloise is making in this letter. She calls for a new kind of *amicitia*, for which the term *amica* becomes a rhetorically forceful emblem. Heloise positions herself as the equal of a male *amicus*, desiring the intimacy and loyalty of classical *amicitia*, which was ordinarily reserved for same-sex friendships or alliances between men.[38] But she also defines herself as Abelard's *amica* – his *unica*, one and only true lover. She is attempting to unite or merge what had been distinct forms of emotional, sexual, and intellectual intimacy – *amicitia* (between men) and *amor* (between men and women). Here *amica* has a double valence – female friend and lover – and by writing this kind of letter she defines herself as a feminine *amicus* while still being Abelard's very female *amica*.

Heloise continues the theme of indebtedness, but shifts the metaphor to disclose another aspect of their gendered identities: Abelard is the author and builder of the Paraclete and the father of a community of daughters. Indeed, Heloise represents Abelard as the father of a feminine child – the Paraclete community. As father and creator, Heloise argues, he owes a special debt to his creation and daughters:

For you alone after God are the sole founder [*fundator*] of this place, the sole builder [*aedificator*] of this community. You have built nothing here upon another foundation. Everything here is your own creation [*tua creatio*].[39]

Heloise further implies that Abelard's "creation" results from his fertility and potency, since it sprang up in an empty and waste land. The community is gendered as a feminine dependency (*tua creatio*), a fragile, new plantation requiring Abelard's paternal care:

Tua itaque, vere tua hec est proprie in sancto proposito novella plantatio, cujus adhuc teneris maxime plantis frequens ut profitiant necessaria est irrigatio. Satis ex ipsa feminei sexus natura debilis est hec plantatio et infirma, etiamsi non esset nova. Unde diligentiorem culturam exigit et frequentiorem, iuxta illud apostoli: "ego plantavi, Apollo rigavit, Deus autem incrementum dedit" [1 Cor. 3.6].[40]

[And so, this is yours, truly your own, this new plantation for a sacred purpose, stocked with still very delicate shoots. Watering is needed for them to survive. From the nature of its feminine sex, this plantation is weak and frail even if it were not new. It follows that it needs a more careful and frequent cultivation, according to what the Apostle said: "I planted, Apollos watered, but God granted the growth."]

The figural gendering of the Paraclete community could hardly be clearer. Heloise begins the emphatic statement of Abelard's paternity with the feminine adjective *tua* with rhetorical repetition. Abelard is represented as the progenitor, father, and caretaker of female offspring. As a feminine child, the *novella plantatio* of the Paraclete is in the traditional position of dependency on Abelard. In rhetorical terms, Heloise plays the gender card to appeal to Abelard's need for masculine authority, to motivate his direct, paternal care at least through letters.

Heloise then returns to the topic of consolation, which she introduced in her opening comments on Abelard's letter of consolation to a friend. Her grief is so great, she states, because of the way in which she lost Abelard, and his debt to her is therefore all the greater because of her great love. Heloise now shifts her language to the discourse of *amor* and the nature of her love for Abelard, the other side of the *amica* coin. Heloise's love language is based on classical or pre-romance models: her discourse is like that of Ovid's *Heroides* and the declamatory exercises in which the writer speaks as Dido would have spoken upon learning of the loss of Aeneas.[41] She even refers to her love as *insania*,[42] madness, in that it caused her to change her outward clothing and her mind so that she could show Abelard that he was the owner of her body and mind alike.

Heloise repeats and then goes beyond the language Abelard uses to describe her and their marriage. In his letter he refers to her as his *amica* and *uxor*, mistress/lover and wife, and he summarizes her objections to their marriage. Note the key terms used by Abelard:[43]

Ilico ego ad patriam meam reversus *amicam* reduxi ut *uxorem* facerem. . .[44]

[Instantly I returned to my native land and brought back my mistress to make her my wife. . .]

Addebat. . .quam sibi carius existeret mihique honestius *amicam* dici quam *uxorem* ut me ei sola gratia conservaret, non vis aliqua *vinculi* nuptialis constringeret.[45]

[She went on to argue that it was dearer to her and more honorable to me to be called "mistress" rather than "wife," so that love alone would keep me for her; some force of the marriage bond would not constrain her.]

In what is probably the most famous passage of her first letter, Heloise extends the *amicus/amica* theme, affirming that she prefers the name "lover/mistress" (*amica*) over "wife" (*uxor*), and goes beyond Abelard's narrative of her position to one much more rhetorically charged:

Et si uxoris nomen sanctius ac validius videretur, dulcius mihi semper extitit amice vocabulum aut, si non indigneris, concubine vel scorti; ut, quo me videlicet pro te amplius humiliarem, ampliorem apud te consequerer gratiam, et sic etiam excellentie tue gloriam minus lederem. Quod et tu ipse tui gratia oblitus penitus non fuisti in ea quam supra memini ad amicum epistola pro consolatione directa, ubi et rationes nonnullas quibus te a coniugio nostro et infaustis thalamis revocare conabar exponere non es dedignatus, sed plerisque tacitis quibus amorem coniugio, libertatem vinculo preferebam. Deum testem invoco, si me Augustus universo presidens mundo matrimonii honore dignaretur, totumque mihi orbem confirmaret in perpetuo possidendum, karius mihi et dignius videretur tua dici meretrix quam illius imperatrix.[46]

[If the name "wife" seems more sacred and more sound, sweeter to me always is the word "mistress" [*amica*] or, if it does not offend you, concubine or whore, so that the more I humbled myself for your sake, the more I would win your gratitude, and thus likewise hurt your distinguished reputation less. You yourself for your own sake did not completely forget this in your letter of consolation sent to a friend that I mentioned above. There you did not distain to set out some of the reasons I tried to call you off of our marriage and unfortunate marriage-bed, but you left the arguments silent in which I preferred love to marriage and freedom to chains. I call God as my witness, if Augustus, ruler of the whole world, thought me worthy of the honor of marriage and conferred the whole world on me for eternal possession, it would seem dearer and worthier to me to be called your whore than his empress.]

There are some striking rhetorical structures in this passage which state to Abelard, in effect, "here is the language in your account of my arguments and here is where I stand now. You still don't understand what it means for me to be your *amica*." Heloise repeats Abelard's terms (*amica, uxor, vinculum*), but in a new rhetorical context. Two phrases of rhetorically contrasting terms stand out:

amorem conjugio, libertatem vinculo

. . .

tua dici meretrix quam illius imperatrix

In the first phrase, *amorem* (love) and *libertatem* (freedom), in the accusative case as objects of "prefer," contrast with *conjugio* (marriage) and *vinculo* (chain/bond) in the dative; the grammatically agreeing terms rhyme, heightening the contrast between the terms that do not. In the second phrase, *meretrix* (whore) and *imperatrix* (empress) are also syntactically balanced with a rhyme that highlights the contrast.

But there is far more in this passage than a striking rhetorical performance. First, here, and through the remainder of this letter, Heloise merges the traditional discourse of monastic humility and submission to authority with the language of erotic submission by a willing lover. This is not the voice of a submissive woman attempting to placate male authority, but a voice of resistance to and even defiance of the obvious structures of authority in which twelfth-century people lived and moved and had their being. Heloise states here, and again in her second letter, that she accepted marriage and even religious vows to please Abelard, to demonstrate that she was totally his.[47] She did not submit to his authority in traditional social terms – as a woman under male authority – but as his lover (*amica*). She was his to command. In what is surely one of the most extraordinary passages of medieval Latin prose, Heloise deftly weaves the language of erotic submission into the fabric of religious humility and constructs a position of defiant submission, explicable only in terms of *amor*, not religious devotion or deference to male authority.

Second, Heloise here begins a strategy that she continues throughout her first two letters: she will not simply occupy the position constructed for her by Abelard, either in his narrative of their lives or as the kind of subject constructed as Abelard's addressee in his subsequent letters. She rewrites his narrative of her position – both her philosophical and emotional stand on marriage and her subject position as agent and actor in the drama of their lives — and represents herself as exceeding all of Abelard's attempts to contain her in the kind of narrative that he deployed for his own self-representation. In other words, she is marking off a space for her own self-representation, one that is not defined or contained by Abelard's writing about her or to her.

After asserting that she loved Abelard only for himself and praising his many attractive virtues, a bold *captatio benevolentiae* before her final critique, Heloise returns to the theme of their *amicitia* and *amor*.

Dic unum, si vales, cur post conversionem nostram, quam tu solus facere decrevisti, in tantam tibi negligentiam atque oblivionem venerim ut nec colloquio presentis recreer nec absentis epistola consoler; dic, inquam, si vales, aut ego quod sentio immo quod omnes suspicantur dicam. Concupiscentia te mihi potius quam amicitia sociavit, libidinis ardor potius quam amor. Ubi igitur quod desiderabas cessavit, quicquid propter hoc exibebas pariter evanuit.[48]

[Tell me one thing, if you can: why, after we took up the life of religion, which you alone decided to do, I have fallen into such neglect and disregard by you so that I am neither restored by your conversation in person nor consoled by a letter in absence? Tell me, I say, if you can, or I will tell you what I think, or rather what everyone suspects. Desire rather than friendship joined you to me, the flame of lust rather than love. When what you desired came to an end, then whatever you used to show for it likewise vanished.]

The first part of this passage is Senecan, echoing the opening of Heloise's letter. The second part states her view of the kind of *amor* and *amicitia* that she desires. In the calculus of her carefully chosen terms, *concupiscentia* (desire) parallels *libidinis ardor* (the flame of lust) and contrasts with the other parallel terms, *amicitia* and *amor*. In the context of her argument, their *amor* becomes a foundation for a special kind of *amicitia*. Heloise concludes her first letter by justifying her request for letters from Abelard:

Memento, obsecro, que fecerim et quanta debeas attende. Dum tecum carnali fruerer voluptate, utrum id amore vel libidine agerem incertum pluribus habebatur; nunc autem finis indicat quo id inchoaverim principio. . .Per ipsum itaque cui te obtulisti Deum te obsecro ut quo modo potes tuam mihi presentiam reddas, consolationem videlicet mihi aliquam rescribendo, hoc saltem pacto ut sic recreata divino alacrior vacem obsequio. Cum me ad turpes olim voluptates expeteres, crebris me epistolis visitabas, frequenti carmine tuam in ore omnium Heloysam ponebas; me platee omnes, me domus singule resonabant. Quanto autem rectius me nunc in Deum, quam tunc in libidinem excitares? Perpende, obsecro, que debes, attende que postulo; et longam epistolam brevi fine concludo vale, unice.[49]

[Remember, I beg you, what I have done and consider how much you owe me. When I enjoyed with you the pleasure of the flesh, many were uncertain whether I did this through love or lust; but now the end proclaims what I started at the beginning. . .And so, through God, to whom you have dedicated yourself, I beg you to restore your presence to me in the way that you can, namely by writing a reply to me in the form of a consolation, so that, in this way at least, renewed, I may be free to devote myself to divine obedience more eagerly. When you once longed for base pleasures, you used to send me frequent letters. You used to put your Heloise on everyone's lips in frequent songs; every street and every house echoed with my name. How much better for you to arouse me for God now than for lust then? Consider, I beg you, what you owe me, attend to what I demand, and I will conclude a long letter with a brief ending: farewell, my one and only.]

This passage is an extraordinary interweaving of the discourses of *amicitia* ("consider how much you owe me," "a reply to me in the form of a consolation"), *amor* ("when I enjoyed with you the pleasure of the flesh," "'farewell, my one and only'"), and religious devotion ("through God, to whom you have dedicated yourself," "I may be free to devote myself to divine obedience more eagerly"). Heloise boldly states that Abelard's restored presence through letters will allow her to devote herself to "divine obedience." Abelard still has the ability to arouse her, she states, though now he can arouse her for God. Heloise's first letter ends on an appeal to Abelard for an erotic friendship based on shared will and reciprocal indebtedness.

THE DEFIANT INNOCENCE OF THE AMICA

Heloise expresses her desire to participate in an ongoing eroticized *amicitia* and in an exchange of *epistolae ad amicum* in which she occupies the position of the *amicus*, both as addressee and writer. Abelard's response to Heloise strategically deflects her desire, and he avoids acknowledging her main requests by stepping into another genre. Abelard does provide a letter, and, by responding to Heloise's desire for letters, a form of consolation, but he does not reply by matching Heloise's *epistola ad amicum*, the genre of his first letter to an unnamed friend. His model for writing to Heloise is Jerome, whose letters to religious women were well known in the twelfth century.[50] In his second letter to Heloise (letter 5 in the whole collection), Abelard explicitly quotes Jerome's famous letter 22 (to Eustochium) twice,[51] and all of his letters to Heloise contain Jeromian gestures. As Jerome de-eroticized his relationships with Paula and Eustochium by negating their sexuality through an obsession with their daughterly virginity, Abelard attempted to de-eroticize his relationship with Heloise by addressing her as sister, abbess, and bride of Christ in the context of their shared monastic vocation. His letters, though not entirely lacking in personal intimacy, work to position her as the addressee of a Jeromian letter of direction, not as the *amicus* and *amica* she clearly defines for herself in her first letter.

Abelard's forms of address to Heloise in his first reply are telling. His salutation at the beginning reads, "Heloisae, dilectissimae sorori suae in Christo, Abaelardus, frater eius in ipso" ("To Heloise, his most dearly beloved sister in Christ, Abelard, her brother in Christ.")[52] She is "my sister once dear in the world now dearest in Christ,"[53] and he concludes the letter with a hexameter couplet addressing her and her sisters.[54] But this deflection of desire on to a love triangle formed of Abelard, Christ, and Heloise, part of Abelard's strategy of de-eroticizing their letter-writing, actually succeeds in maintaining or continuing their desire. A third party, which is named either Christ, the Spirit, or the church in their letters, mediates their desire by outwardly legitimizing their continued intimate exchange. The discourse that mediates their desire also represents it. The strategy to de-eroticize their epistolary conversation, of course, has precisely the reverse effect: their desire becomes the ultimate signified since it is repressed and thus explicitly acknowledged in the strategies taken to avoid it.[55]

Abelard praises Heloise's *prudentia*, her wisdom and accomplishments as leader of the Paraclete community. He writes to her in the vocational mode, asks for her prayers, and, fearing bodily harm from his enemies, he asks her to bury him at the Paraclete if he should die or be killed. He encourages her life of prayer and praises the role of women in the church, concluding with a request that she pray for his soul and not be concerned for danger to his body. By positioning himself in another way through a letter of direction, he has strategically rejected taking up the position of the *amicus* and avoided the main requests of Heloise's letter.

Heloise's second letter reveals a resisting reader and continued negotiations of identity in the form of a dialogic response to Abelard's letter.

Rather than accepting Abelard's construction of her subjectivity as that of the addressee in a Jeromian letter of direction – with the erasure of both her sexual identity and the new position that she negotiated for herself as a literate woman – she replies again as Abelard's *amica* and *amicus*, but she readjusts her rhetorical form by writing a hybrid letter fashioned by merging the *epistola ad amicum* and the vocational letter. She begins her second letter by repositioning herself as a writer in full possession of that very masculine knowledge, rhetoric: she opens by questioning the formal regularity of Abelard's prior salutation, in which, contrary to dictamenal practice and "the natural order,"[56] Abelard put her name first.[57] Her salutation places him first, "Unico suo post Christum unica sua in Christo"[58] ("To her one and only after Christ, his one and only in Christ,") and continues the blending of *amor* and devotion while gesturing to the triangulation of love through Christ that Abelard sets up in his prior letter. She complains to Abelard that he has not written the *consolatio* that she requested; indeed, he wrote a letter that increased the desolation of her and her sisters by requesting that they take responsibility for his funeral and tomb if his enemies should prevail over him. She continues her heavy use of the ethical appeal, focusing on her identity and character.

When read in the dialogical context, it is quite clear that Abelard's deflection of her desire, his genre switching, and his refusal to answer Heloise as a partner in *amicitia* and *amor* occasion Heloise's further resistance to being defined and positioned by Abelard's discourse. The main body of her second letter begins with a strong Boethian lament against fortune and against God's sense of justice, in which she sees that they were punished for *fornicatio* after their marriage, Abelard paying for them both in his body and she being banished to the repressive life of the convent.[59] Throughout this letter, however, she uses Abelard's language without embracing it: she believes that Abelard believes they were justly punished by God, but she maintains her innocence as strongly as she did in her first letter.[60]

Heloise thus strongly resists accepting that Abelard's castration, their separation, and taking monastic vows were God's just punishment for their love affair. Much of the argument of her first letter was based on the contrasting terms *amor* versus *conjugium* and *amica* versus *uxor*, and in her argument against God's justice in her second letter she contrasts *fornicatio* with *conjugium*, fornication and marriage, terms established by the church. She asserts that she will always blame God for the greatest cruelty[61] in bringing on punishment after they had an honorable marriage: "the Lord in His anger laid his hand heavily upon us and would not endure a clean marriage bed [*immaculatum. . .thorum*] though he had long tolerated a defiled one [*pollutum*]."[62]

The word *torus* or *thorus* (mount or bed) squints in two directions like the term *amica*: parallel to *thalamus*, another classical term that Heloise uses in her first letter, *torus* is used metaphorically for "(bridal) bed" or "marriage," but it can also have the sense of "lovers' bed" or the bed of any sexual union.[63] Heloise uses the same word, *thorus*, with her two adjectives, clean and undefiled, implying that she is referring to their shared bed and relationship both before and after marriage. She asserts that, as far as she is concerned, nothing changed in their sexual union but the perception of God's judgment. Furthermore, her repeated use of moral terms is done in part ironically, since at this point in the letter she is working with Abelard's premises about the cause of their misfortunes but blaming God for the terms of their moral dilemma in the first place. This ironizing of the terms in which they are forced to view the story of their lives is parallel to her strategy of defiant submission in letter 1, a strategy she uses later in this letter.

After a rhetorical lament on the nature of women and their tendency to bring great men to ruin, Heloise returns to the dilemma of her desire, her sense of being innocent when judged according to their ethic of pure intention, and therefore her inability to find repentence. Heloise's first letter builds to the rhetorical crescendo containing her argument about preferring the freedom of love to the bonds of marriage, and her second letter follows a similar structure: the rhetorical climax is her highly charged argument about the state of her own desires, her sense of being a hypocrite in the convent, and her renewed eroticizing of their mutual religious commitments.[64] The rhetorical crescendo begins with a confession:

In tantum vero ille quas pariter exercuimus amantium voluptates dulces mihi fuerunt ut nec displicere mihi nec vix a memoria labi possint. Quocumque loco me vertam, semper se oculis meis cum suis ingerunt desideriis, nec etiam dormienti suis illusionibus parcunt. Inter ipsa missarum sollempnia, ubi purior esse debet oratio, obscena earum voluptatum phantasmata ita sibi penitus miserrimam captivant animam ut turpitudinibus illis magis quam orationi vacem; que cum ingemiscere debeam de commissis, suspiro potius de amissis. Nec solum que egimus sed loca pariter et tempora in quibus hec egimus ita tecum nostro infixa sunt animo. ut in ipsis omnia tecum agam nec dormiens etiam ab his quiescam. Nonumquam etiam ipso motu corporis animi mei cogitationes deprehenduntur, nec a verbis temperant improvisis.[65]

[But the extent to which the lovers' pleasures we engaged in together have been sweet to me, they can never displease me nor scarcely fade from my memory. Whenever I turn, they always rush before my eyes with their longings, and they do not even spare me with their fantasies when I'm sleeping. During the celebration of the mass, when prayer should be purer, indecent fantasies of those pleasures take hold of my most unhappy soul deep within so that I am devoted more to those base fantasies than to prayer. I should groan about what I have done, but instead I sigh for what I have lost. Not only what we did together but also the times and places where we did them are imprinted with you on my mind; in these memories I do everything [again] with you, and even while sleeping I have no rest from them. Sometimes the thoughts of my mind are disclosed by movement in my body itself, and they [the thoughts] do not abstain from unexpected words.]

This extraordinary confession is followed by a gesture toward the asceticism that she should be espousing – quoting Romans 7.24, "unhappy man that I am, who will free me from the body of this death," one of Jerome's favorite verses – and she even affirms that Abelard's wound to his body has spared him the pangs of desire and even healed many wounds in his soul.[66] She concludes this part of the argument with a description of the pain of her unfulfilled desire and its justification in the traditional terms of female weakness:

Hos autem in me stimulos carnis, hec incentiva libidinis, ipse juvenilis fervor etatis et jocundissimarum experientia voluptatum plurimum accendunt, et tanto amplius sua me impugnatione opprimunt quanto infirmior est natura quam impugnant.[67]

[But the passion of youth and the experience of the most delightful pleasures greatly inflame the pangs of the flesh and incentives of desire within me, and they oppress me with their assault so much more as the nature they attack is weaker.]

Heloise concludes the central confession with an acknowledgment of hypocrisy, which she says she feels strongly in an age when hypocrisy abounds in the church. Rather than being encouraged from Abelard's praise, she complains that she needs his prayers and understanding for her emotional and moral condition, which she attributes to following Abelard's command as his lover: "in every stage of my life up to now, God knows, I feared to offend you more than God, and tried to please you more than him. It was your command, not divine love, that pulled me to the religious life." Here again she sets up rhetorical oppositions through syntax and end rhyme: "your command" (*tua. . .jussio*) contrasts with "divine love" (*divina. . .dilectio*).[68] This statement continues the defiant submission of her first letter, but Heloise registers another conflict here at the close of her second letter: she longs for Abelard's praise because she wishes to please him in all things (*tibi per omnia placere studeo*), but she also appeals to Abelard by confessing her weakness. She is again writing as a friend, but a friend in need, and as his *amica* who cannot deny or erase her continued desire for him alone.

Time, obsecro, semper de me potius quam confidas, ut tua semper sollicitudine adjuver. Nunc vero precipue timendum est, ubi nullum incontinentie mee superest in te remedium.[69]

[Be fearful for me always, I beg you, rather than having confidence in me, so that I may always be helped through your concern. But now you should especially fear, where there is no longer a remedy in you for my unrestrained sexual desire.]

Heloise is still appealing to Abelard as his *amica*, and confesses that her sexual frustration is incurable since Abelard, who was her only outlet for her *incontinentia*, will always be her lover by definition even though no longer in practice. The disarming honesty that accompanies the confessional mode is part of the ethical appeal in this rhetorical performance, which seeks to win over the reader's acceptance through the integrity of the writer's character.

Heloise's first two letters reveal that she defines a new space for herself through strategies of resistance, negotiation, appropriation, and accommodation. She constructs a new identity within literate culture through the conventions of genre and rhetoric, a new form of friendship in which she defines herself as both *amica* and *amicus*, and a position within monastic culture where her erotic bond leads to defiant submission. These strategies lead to larger conclusions about the gendered dialogism on which the letters of Abelard and Heloise are based. As statements in a dialogic series, the letters reveal that they are written to desire, invoke, and construct a certain kind of reader. Writer and addressee switch roles at the level of letter writing, but they do not seek to occupy the same positions or the identities created for them: Abelard does not take up the position desired by Heloise in her first two letters, and Heloise resists becoming simply the spiritualized receiver of authoritative counsel that Abelard's letters construct for her.

Heloise thus refuses to be a mere addressee/reader, the silent receiver lacking authorization to speak or write. What we see emerging in the vacillations between the poles or fields of gender forces in these letters is a momentary emergence of a feminine subject position in Latin prose, a fully empowered feminine *litteratus* – as grammatically impossible as that phrase may seem – who constructs a voice from the kinds of gendered subjectivity provided by medieval discourse. Heloise both accepts her social position as a woman under male authority (as Abbess of the Paraclete) and finds a way to negotiate her own identity in writing, resisting being the *subject of* the masculine writer's voice.

The Abelard–Heloise correspondence thus discloses that masculinity and femininity as positions in literate subjectivity were not pure, absolute states but rather formed from ongoing negotiations among various kinds of (already) mixed subject positions. For twelfth-century *litterati*, gender classes seemed to be natural categories mirrored in language,[70] and maleness and femaleness would have been understood as both natural and social identities. But a close reading of these letters reveals that gendered subjectivity seldom appears as a fixed, one-dimensional identity. Abelard's letters alone disclose that there was no easy equation between social sex identity and gendered subjectivity; indeed, the Abelard–Heloise correspondence reveals a play or drift away from a sense of fixed or essential gender identity and creates an image of an alternating or ever-vacillating current through which literate subjectivity was constructed. Heloise's strategy of negotiation and new self-definition utilized the gender categories of the twelfth century and resisted the totalizing or essentializing functions that these categories often served.

Notes

1   The masculine position, assumed to be taken up by men, is clearly
    indicated in Martianus Capella's definition of *grammatica*, which is stated in
    a string of cognates of *littera* (letter, writing): "my art has four parts: letters/
    writing (*litterae*), the discipline of the written (*litteratura*), the man of letters
    (*litteratus*), and skill in writing (*litterate*). *Litterae* are what I teach, *litteratura*
    is I myself who teach, the *litteratus* is he whom I have taught, and *litterate* is
    what he whom I form practices expertly." (*De nuptiis Philologiae et Mercurii*

3.231, ed. James Willis [Lepizig: Teubner, 1983], p. 62). Peter Helias, a contemporary of Abelard, is also explicit about the gender of the *litteratus* formed through *grammatica*. The literate subject is defined as a masculine agent (*artifex*) who both practices a special form of knowledge and is empowered by it: "grammatica, quod ipsa est literalis scientia, eo, scilicet, quod litteratum efficit. Litteratum vero dicimus illum qui litteras. . .Est igitur artifex huius artis litteratus vel potius litterator." (Petrus Helias, *Summa super Priscianum*, ed. Leo Reilly, 2 vols. [Toronto: Pontifical Institute, 1993], 1: 61–64). On the history of the term *litteratus*, see H. Grundmann, "Litteratus-illiteratus: Der Wandel einer Bildungsnorm von Altertum zum Mittelalter," *Archive für Kulturgeschichte* 40 (1958): 1–65.

2 Scholarly and critical work on women writers in the Middle Ages has expanded greatly since the mid-1980s, and I cannot cite all the relevant studies here. For an orientation, see: Peter Dronke, *Women Writers of the Middle Ages: A Critical Study of Texts from Perpetua to Marguerite* (Cambridge: Cambridge University Press, 1984); Katharina M. Wilson, ed., *Medieval Women Writers* (Athens, Ga.: University of Georgia Press, 1984); Barbara Newman, *Sister of Wisdom: St. Hildegard's Theology of the Feminine* (Berkeley: University of California Press, 1987); and Karen Cherewatuk and Ulrike Wiethaus, *Dear Sister: Medieval Women and the Epistolary Genre* (Philadelphia: University of Pennsylvania Press, 1993).

3 My reading of Heloise's letters has been informed by the work of several scholars, but I would like to point out the following studies that I've found most useful: Peter Dronke, *Abelard and Heloise in Medieval Testimonies* (Glasgow: University of Glasgow Press, 1976) and *Women Writers of the Middle Ages*, pp. 107–43; D. E. Luscombe, "From Paris to the Paraclete: The Correspondence of Abelard and Heloise," *Proceedings of the British Academy* 74 (1988): 247–83; Barbara Newman, "Authority, Authenticity, and the Repression of Heloise," *Journal of Medieval and Renaissance Studies* 22/2 (1992): 121–57.

4 Generated by bogus medievalism and rank prejudice, a hermeneutics of suspicion was applied to the letters in the second half of the nineteenth century. In the first half of this century, a full assault on the authenticity of the letters was waged both by scholars who never studied a single manuscript of the letters and by others like John Benton, who at first claimed to find enough inconsistencies in the documentary record to support radical doubts about authenticity and then recanted to a more moderate position. For a history of the authenticity debate and recent opinion as the letters, see especially J. T. Muckle, "The Personal Letters Between Abelard and Heloise," *Medieval Studies* 15 (1953): 48–67; Jacques Monfrin, "Le problème de l'authenticité de la correspondance d'Abélard et

d'Heloise," in *Pierre Abélard – Pierre le Vénérable: les courants philosophiques, littéraires et artistiques en Occident au milieu du XIIe siècle* (Colloques internationaux du Centre National de la Recherches Scientifiques, 1975) (Paris: CNRS, 1975), pp. 409–24; Peter von Moos, "Le silence d'Heloïse et les idéologies modernes," in *Pierre Abélard – Pierre le Vénérable*, pp. 425–68 and "Post festum – Was kommt nach der Authentizitätsdebatte über die Briefe Abaelards und Heloises?" in Rudolf Thomas, ed., *Petrus Abaelardus, Trierer Theologische Studien*, Band 38 (Trier: Paulinus, 1980), pp. 75–100; D. E. Luscombe, "The Letters of Heloise and Abelard since 'Cluny 1972,'" in Rudolf Thomas, ed. *Petrus Abaelardus*, pp. 19–39; and the studies cited in n. 3 above.

5   The main pre-fifteenth-century manuscripts are: Troyes, BM 802 (s.xiii ex./ s.xiv in., prob. convent of the Paraclete); Paris, BN lat. 2923 (s.xiii ex.) (which belonged to Petrarch by 1344); Paris, BN lat. 2544 (s.xiii ex./xiv in.) (belonged to James of Ghent, master at Paris, *c.* 1330); Reims, BM 872 (s.xiii ex./s.xiv in.); Oxford, Bodleian Library, Add.C.271 (29565) (s.xiv 2/ 2) (letters 1–5; 5 in part). Most manuscripts contain letters 1–7 and the preface to 8, which seems to be the canonical version known to most readers. The Troyes manuscript alone contains a complete copy of letter 8, *De regula sanctimonialium*, Abelard's rule for nuns. For a complete description of the manuscripts, and an account of some known but lost copies, see the edition by Jacques Monfrin, *Abélard: Historia Calamitatum* (Paris: J. Vrin, 1959), pp. 9–46, and J. Barrow, C. Burnet, and D. Luscombe, "A Checklist of the Manuscripts Containing the Writings of Peter Abelard and Heloise," *Revue d'histoire des textes* 14–15 (1984–85): 183–302.

6   I follow Luscombe's conclusions in "From Paris to the Paraclete"; see especially 270–71, where Luscombe argues for the Paraclete origin of Troyes manuscript, BM 802, considered the best surviving manuscript of the letters as well as other documents pertaining to religious life at the Paraclete.

7   On the historical background of the letters, see Luscombe, "From Paris to the Paraclete."

8   I'd like to thank Deborah Everhart for sharing her research on Heloise and the Paraclete and for pointing out the importance of viewing the Paraclete in this way.

9   In the *Historia calamitatum*, Abelard states that they exchanged love letters to enjoy each other's conversation even while absent: "nosque etiam absentes scriptis internuntiis invicem liceret presentare et pleraque audacius scribere quam colloqui, et sic semper jocundis interesse colloquiis" (Monfrin, *Abélard*, p. 71, 296–99). Heloise in her first letter confirms that

Abelard wrote her frequent letters during the time of their love affair in Paris: "cum me ad turpes olim voluptates expeteres, crebris me epistolis visitabas" (Monfrin, *Abélard*, p. 117, 269–270). The collected correspondence is thus a continuation of their letter writing.

10 References to the collected letters of Abelard and Heloise are from the following editions: letters 1, 2, and 4 (Abelard's *Epistola ad amicum pro consolatione* or *Historia calamitatum*, and Heloise's first and second letters) are from the edition of Monfrin, *Abélard*, and the other letters of the collected correspondence are from the edition of Muckle, "The Personal Letters Between Heloise and Abelard," *Medieval Studies* 15 (1953): 47–94, and "The Letter of Heloise on Religious Life and Abelard's First Reply," *Medieval Studies* 17 (1955): 240–81. The collected correspondence (letters 1–8) is also in J.-P. Migne, ed., *Patrologia latina*, (Paris, 1844–55), 178: 113–326. (I will use the abbreviation *PL* in subsequent references.) References to Monfrin's edition or *Abélard*: Historia calamitatum (n.5) will include page and line numbers. Translations throughout are my own. I will supply the Latin original with a translation when the Latin text is needed for close reading and an English translation alone when my argument requires only the sense of a passage.

11 *Peter Abelard: Letters IX–XIV*, ed. E. R. Smits (Groningen: Rijksuniversiteit, 1983), pp. 219–37. Also *PL* 178: 325–36.

12 *PL* 178: 677–78.

13 *Ibid.*, 731–32.

14 *Ibid.*, 379–380.

15 *Ibid.*, 1771–72. Abelard's collection of hymns for the Paraclete (*PL* 178: 1771–816) also contains prefaces to each section written for Heloise and her community.

16 My thinking on the historically dynamic, as opposed to static or essentialist, approach to gender and subjectivity has been informed by several recent articulations of theory and historical research, of which I consider the following to be exemplary: Judith Butler, *Gender Trouble: Feminism and the Subversion of Identity* (New York: Routledge, 1990) and *Bodies that Matter: On the Discursive Limits of "Sex"* (New York: Routledge, 1993); Joan Scott, "Gender: A Useful Category of Historical Analysis," in *Gender and the Politics of History* (New York: Columbia University Press, 1988); Michel Foucault, *The History of Sexuality: An Introduction* (New York: Vintage Books, 1978); and Thomas Laqueur, *Making Sex: The Body and Gender from the Greeks to Freud* (Cambridge, Mass.: Harvard University Press, 1990). A full bibliography on gender and sexuality can be found in Jonathan Dollimore, *Sexual Dissidence: Augustine to Wilde, Freud to Foucault* (Oxford: Clarendon, 1991).

17 The literature on twelfth-century monasticism and the Cistercian order is
    vast, but I can recommend the following for general background: Jean
    Leclercq, *The Love of Learning and the Desire for God*, trans. C. Misrahi (New
    York: Fordham University Press, 1974); and Louis Lekai, *The Cistercians:
    Ideals and Reality* (Kent, Ohio: Kent State University Press, 1977).

18 On monastic friendship, see Brian Patrick McGuire, *Friendship and
    Community: The Monastic Experience, 350–1250* (Kalamazoo, Mich.:
    Cistercian Publications, 1988), especially, ch. 6, "The Age of Friendships:
    Networks of Friends, *c.* 1120–*c.* 1180," pp. 231–95; Jean Leclercq, *Monks
    and Love In Twelfth-Century France* (Oxford: Clarendon, 1979); Adele Fiske,
    "Paradisus Homo Amicus," *Speculum* 40 (1965): 436–59; G.
    Vansteenberghe, "Deux théoriciens de l'amitié au XII siècle: Pierre de Blois
    et Aelred de Riéval," *Revue des sciences religieuses* 12 (1932): 572–88. For a
    useful account of the literary uses of monastic treatments of *amor* and
    amicitia, see Lee Patterson, *Negotiating the Past: The Historical Understanding
    of Medieval Literature* (Madison: University of Wisconsin Press, 1987), pp.
    115–53.

19 On monastic letters, see McGuire, *Friendship and Community*, pp. 164–70,
    231–34, and Jean Leclercq, "L'amité dans les lettres au moyen-âge," *Revue
    du moyen âge latin* 1 (1945): 391–410 and "Le genre épistolaire au moyen-
    âge" *Revue du moyen âge latin* 2 (1946): 63–70.

20 On the homoerotic expression of friendship, see McGuire, *ibid.*, 244–51,
    pp. 327–33, and John Boswell, *Christianity, Social Tolerance, and
    Homosexuality* (Chicago: University of Chicago Press, 1980), pp. 244–48 (on
    Baudri) and pp. 221–26 (on Aelred). On the eroticized poetic epistles of
    Baudri and Constance, a nun at Angers, see Dronke, *Women Writers of the
    Middle Ages*, pp. 848–91.

21 On medieval letters and letter collections, see Giles Constable,
    "Introduction" to Constable, ed. *The Letters of Peter the Venerable*, 2 vols.
    (Cambridge, Mass.: Harvard University Press, 1967), 2: 1–44 and *Letters
    and Letter-Collections*, Typologie des sources du moyen âge occidental, fasc.
    17 (Turnhout: Brepols, 1976).

22 For an overview, see James J. Murphy, *Rhetoric in the Middle Ages* (Berkeley:
    University of California Press, 1974), pp. 194–268, and Martin Camargo,
    Ars dictaminis, ars dictandi, Typologie des sources du moyen âge occidental,
    fasc. 60 (Turnhout: Brepols, 1991). The relationship between Heloise's
    letters and the *ars dictaminis* was also suggested by Muckle, "The Personal
    Letters," 50–51. The collected correspondence of Abelard and Heloise was
    probably written between 1132 and 1136. The rules for *dictamen* were
    widely known in Italy and France shortly after Alberic of Monte Cassino
    wrote his *Flores rhetorici* or *Dictaminum radii* around 1087. By 1135, the year

the Anonymous of Bologna wrote the *Rationes dictandi*, the *ars dictaminis* was already a genre in its own right; see James J. Murphy, ed., *Three Medieval Rhetorical Arts* (Berkeley: University of California Press, 1971), pp. 3–4, and the translation of the *Rationes dictandi*, pp. 5–25.

23 See Constable, *Letters and Letter-Collections*, pp. 11–26, and McGuire, *Friendship and Community*, pp. 232–34.

24 See Patterson, *Negotiating the Past*, pp. 115–41.

25 See John W. Baldwin, *The Language of Sex: Five Voices from Northern France Around 1200* (Chicago: University of Chicago Press, 1994).

26 Heloise's concern with *amicitia* was noted by Dronke (*Women Writers of the Middle Ages*, pp. 112–20), but he did not consider the larger context of gender and subjectivity which frames the genre and the rhetoric of Heloise's letters.

27 Monfrin, *Abélard*, p. 111, 4–5.

28 Heloise repeats this "title" later in the letter as *ad amicum epistola pro consolatione* (Monfrin, *ibid.*, p. 114, 153).

29 See Monfrin, *ibid.*, p. 112, 40, and p. 117, 270.

30 *Ibid.*, p. 112, 40.

31 References to Seneca's letters are from *Seneca: Ad Lucilium Epistulae morales*, ed. Richard M. Gummere, 3 vols., Loeb Classical Library (Cambridge, Mass.: Harvard University Press, 1917).

32 Monfrin, ed., p. 112, 49–61.

33 Ed. Gummere, *Epist.* 40.1, I: 264.

34 *absentium littere amicorum* (Monfrin, *Abélard*, p. 112, 50); *presentiam tuam* (*ibid.*, p. 112, 58–59); *vel sermone presentem vel epistola absentem consolari tentaveris* (*ibid.*, p. 114, 121–23); *non concupiscebat absentem et non exardebat in presentem* (*ibid.*, p. 115, 190–91); *nec colloquio presentis recreer nec absentis epistola consoler* (*ibid.*, p. 116, 219–20); *tui presentia fraudor, verborum saltem votis, quorum tibi copia est, tue mihi imaginis presenta dulcedinem* (*ibid.*); *tuam mihi presentiam reddas* (*ibid.*, p. 117, 266–67).

35 On this manuscript, see Monfrin, *Abélard*, pp. 20–22. I found that the manuscript divides into separable booklets of Senecan material and the letters of Abelard and Heloise, but each unit was copied by the same scribe and prepared in the same workshop, most likely at Reims itself.

36 Monfrin, *ibid.*, p. 112, 69–73.

37 *amicus*, s.v., *A Latin Dictionary*, eds. Lewis and Short (Oxford: Clarendon, 1879) and the *Oxford Latin Dictionary*, ed. P. G. W. Glare (Oxford: Clarendon, 1982).

38 See McGuire, *Friendship and Community*, pp. 40–42, 89–90, and *passim*.

39 Monfrin, *Abélard*, p. 113, 76–80.

40 *Ibid.*, p. 113, 92–99.

41 The comparison with the *Heroides* was made by Dronke, *Women Writers of the Middle Ages*, p. 107; on the *Heroides* and verse epistles by women in the eleventh and twelfth centuries, see also pp. 84–106. On *declamatio*, see Murphy, *Rhetoric in the Middle Ages*, pp. 38–42.

42 "Et quod maius est dictuque mirabile, in tantum versus est amor insaniam. . ." (Monfrin, *Abélard*, p. 114, 138–39).

43 See Monfrin, *ibid.*, pp. 75–79.

44 *Ibid.*, p. 75, 425–26.

45 *Ibid.*, p. 78, 545–49.

46 *Ibid.*, p. 114, 147–61.

47 *Ibid.*, p. 123, 239–49, and *passim*.

48 *Ibid.*, p. 116, 217–24.

49 *Ibid.*, p.117, 257–60, 265–75.

50 On Jerome's letters and the aristocratic women in the community he directed, see J. N. D. Kelly, *Jerome: His Life, Writings, and Controversies* (New York: Harper and Row, 1975), pp. 91–103. A convenient collection of representative letters, including the famous letter 22 to Eustochium, is found in F. A. Wright, ed and trans., *Select Letters of St. Jerome*, Loeb Classical Library (New York: G. P. Putnam's Sons, 1933).

51 See Muckle, ed., "The Personal Letters," pp. 83, 87.

52 *Ibid.*, p. 73.

53 *Ibid.*

54   Vive, vale, vivantque tuae valeantque sorores
        Vivite, sed Christo; quaeso, mei memores.   (Muckle, *ibid.*, p. 77)

55 The nature of this repression and its effects on their language are matters that I intend to treat more fully in my book-length study of the letters of Abelard and Heloise.

56 "preter consuetudinem epistolarum, immo contra ipsum ordinem naturalem rerum" (Monfrin, p. 117, 2–3).

57 For background on dictaminal practice for salutations, see n. 22 above.

58 Monfrin, *Abélard*, p. 117, 1.

59 See *ibid.*, pp. 119, 67–121, 152.

60 "Sed et si purget animum meum innocentia nec huius reatum sceleris consensus incurrat. . ." (*ibid.*, p. 121, 155–58).

61 "Deum. . .quem super hac semper injuria summe crudelitatis arguo" (*ibid.*, p. 121, 171–72).

62 *Ibid.*, p. 120, 102–05.

63 See *Oxford Latin Dictionary*, ed. Glare, sv. "torus," sense 5, and *A Latin Dictionary*, eds. Lewis and Short, sv. "torus."

64 Monfrin, *Abélard*, pp. 122, 193 and p. 124, 281.

65 *Ibid.*, p. 122, 193–207.

66 *Ibid.*, p. 122, 207–16.

67 *Ibid.*, p. 122, 216–20.

68 *Ibid.*, p. 123, 239–42.

69 *Ibid.*, p. 124, 2278–81.

70 See Petrus Helias, *Summa super Priscianum, De genere*, ed. Reilly, 1: 322–27.

4

The dissenting image: a postcard from Matthew Paris

MICHAEL CAMILLE

. . .have you seen this card, the image on the back of this card? I stumbled across it yesterday, in the Bodleian (the famous Oxford library), I'll tell you about it. I stopped dead, with a feeling of hallucination (is he crazy or what? he has the names mixed up!) and of revelation at the same time, an apocalyptic revelation: Socrates writing, writing in front of Plato, I always knew it, it had remained like the negative of a photograph to be developed for twenty-five centuries – in me of course. Sufficient to write it in broad daylight. The revelation is there, unless I can't yet decipher anything in this picture, which is what is most probable in effect. Socrates, the one who writes – seated, bent over, a scribe or docile copyist. Plato's secretary, no? He is in front of Plato, no, Plato is behind him, smaller (why smaller), but standing up. With his outstretched finger he looks like he is indicating something, designating, showing the way or giving an order – or dictating, authoritarian, masterly, imperious. Almost wicked, don't you think, and voluntarily. I bought a whole supply of them.[1]

The revelation unto Jacques Derrida began on June 4, 1977 when, in the bookshop of Oxford's Bodleian Library, he came across a postcard reproducing a drawing of Socrates and Plato, from a manuscript in the collection (fig. 4.1). It is not difficult to appreciate why this image struck the contemporary thinker with a belated sense of recognition. In his earlier influential work *Of Grammatology*, Socrates and Plato were described as the mythical originators of Western philosophy and as fundamental to its prioritization of speech over writing. From the self-presence of the Socratic

4.1 The postcard: Socrates and Plato

voice to the orality implicit in Saussure's system of signs, the spoken word, Derrida argued, has always been valued above the written. For Socrates, speaking in Plato's *Phaedrus*, writing was not only secondary, it also always lay open to the dangers of unauthorized duplication and citation. Citing Nietzsche's description of philosophical origins: "Socrates, he who does not write," Derrida's own effort was to invert this traditional logocentric prejudice by showing how writing can be understood as prior to, if not contiguous with speech.[2] And now, suddenly, he had come across an image which seemed to parallel his own quest to deconstruct two thousand years of philosophical talk – an image in which Socrates writes. The image so fascinated the contemporary philosopher that a whole book emerged, as it were, on its back, published in English in 1987 as *The Post Card: From Socrates to Freud and Beyond.* Here the scene of writing is described again and again, especially that reversal by which "Socrates turns his back to plato, who has made him write whatever he wanted while pretending to receive it from him. This reproduction is sold here as a post card. Socrates writing, do you realize, and on a post card."[3] Plato is seen as getting an erection in Socrates' back, the diagonal object jutting from Socrates' thigh (probably his scabbard) becomes "the insane hubris of his prick." Is he riding a skateboard or pushing a baby carriage? Derrida's delirious designations focus however on the inversion of that myth of philosophical origins on which is built "everything in our bildopeic culture, in our politics of the encyclopedic, in our telecommunications of all genres, in our library, for example, the marvelous Bodleian, everything is constructed on the protocolary axiom. . .Socrates comes before Plato."[4]

But is this actually the case? Does Plato come *before* Socrates in this picture? Because today we continue to prioritize the oral source of language, Plato's figure and gestures would seem at first to put him first. But looked at in terms of written language, this relationship is not so simple, for as Derrida himself notices, an inverse power relation is expressed in the two labeling inscriptions, the capitalization of "S" but not "p," a relationship only possible to articulate in the visual form of writing and in which Socrates definitely has priority over his small p partner. Moreover, looked at as a system of pictorial components read from left to right like script, it is also worth noting that the traditional gesture that signals speech in this image, Plato's extended left hand with its pointing finger, actually comes after Socrates' head. Although "before" the other's eyes, the speaking hand follows his face in the sequence. Plato's right hand, similarly pointing, seems to finger Socrates in the back, as if urging him on. But does this come before the dictating hand or is it simultaneous with it? From the perspective, neither of speech, nor of writing, but of painting, the two figures are, like their names, spatially differentiated on the parchment page but apprehended together as a unity. The designer has done everything he can to overlap and bring together their bodies in the act of producing discourse. With his smaller hat, more diminutive body and his elbow ruptured by the frame, "plato" here too seems to be designated as lesser than "Socrates." But this does not locate him as either first or second. What this preliminary analysis is meant to suggest is that, while in the temporality trajectory of verbal/textual discourse one can think of something coming "before" and "after," in the complex simultaneity of the visual realm such relations are far less secure.

The postcard is reproduced four times in Derrida's book; in black and white on the cover, in a tiny version on the spine, in color on page 251 of the text, and finally in a fold-out at the very end, the exact size of the "original postcard" (4 inches by 6 inches). This allows it to be kept in view on the right of the open pages while reading the rapturous dated messages of the text, which were inscribed upon the back. This strategy of redeployment, displacing and multiplying the image from its original context, is decidedly Derridian, emphasizing the indeterminacy of writing which "can be cited, put between quotation marks. . .engendering an infinity of new contexts in a manner which is absolutely illimitable."[5] The postcard is not in fact an image but a detail. It reproduces only part of the actual page of the manuscript, Oxford Bodleian Library, MS Ashmole 304 folio 31 verso. Outside the double, ruled frame, are inches of parchment and an added inscription. Likewise its surface is not a flat two-sided piece of thick paper with "Post Card. Printed in England by Waterlow Ltd." printed on its back alongside a blank frame for a stamp. It is the verso of a parchment folio which wrinkles and curves slightly inwards at the outer corners, being the flesh side of an animal skin, also bending over as it comes close to the inner edge and binding. Most crucial of all, the image is not seen in isolation but springs outwards as the left hand side of a diptych-like double-page opening (fig. 4.2). Just as Derrida never reproduces the other side of the postcard, the obverse and as it were crucial side (remember he describes the picture as being on the back (. . . [*dos*] . . . of the card), he does not mention the crucial facing page of the manuscript. Derrida never reproduces the thirteenth-century drawing in this actual

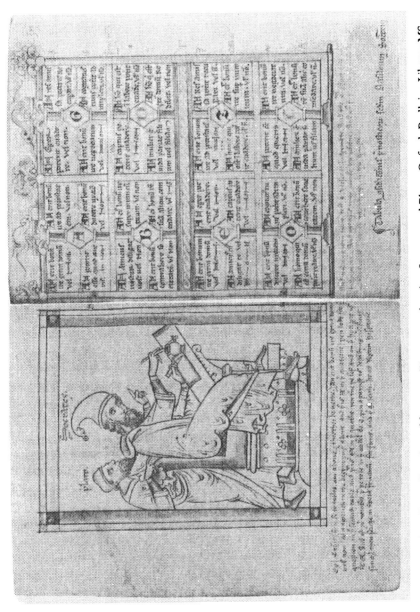

4.2 Matthew Paris: Opening of fortune-telling tract, showing Socrates and Plato. Oxford, Bodleian Library MS Ashmole 304, fols. 31v and 32r

locus, where its function is to preface a sequence of diagrams of a complex fortune-telling system. Although he finally examines the manuscript himself, two years later on July 20, 1979, the historical object was less important to the philosopher than its contemporary reproduction. This is borne out by a number of subsequent philosophical and critical discussions of the *The Post Card*, where the picture is repeatedly and mistakenly referred to as "an engraving."[6]

In this essay I am less interested in the postcard recently sent by Derrida and its philosophical play than the one sent by Matthew Paris, seven centuries ago, in front of a game which told the future. Although I contrasted the two at the outset, in other respects a manuscript is not all that different from a postcard. On parchment rather than paper it is likewise a communicative event – a combination of marks, traces, texts, and images that can be turned, looked-at, and read, recto and verso, and carried through time and space on a flat surface. That message, in both textual and visual form, is encoded and its decipherment is dependent upon the addresser and addressee sharing the same code. My own historical interpretation, conscious of its provisional nature and unwilling to assign one single "truth" or meaning to this unusual depiction of the two philosophers, although shaped and stimulated by Derrida's analysis far more than by paleographical or art historical research, will differ markedly from his. Seeing this image in historical terms means viewing it, not as a reflection or a representation of a pre-existent, universal set of various theories of language, but as the articulation and performance of theories of language in a very specific time and place and even as a reaction *against* them. This capacity of an image to call into question and interrogate rather than simply replicate verbal ideas, or even worse to "illustrate" them (a concept that did not exist during the Middle Ages), will be crucial to my discussion of this "dissenting" image; dissenting not only in its refusal to follow the patterns of textuality inscribed in various thirteenth-century learned culture and institutions, but in its very status as an image within that culture. My analysis differs most radically from Derrida's in giving priority neither to writing, nor to the speaking Logos, but rather to the painting hand of Matthew Paris as its author. At a moment when cultural studies, in general, and medieval studies, in particular, are witnessing a "visual turn," I want to ask whether we can interrogate speaking, reading, and writing during the Middle Ages through the process of picturing.[7]

Most discussions of this image not only take its representation of reading and writing, but also its status as a picture totally for granted. In January, 1979 Derrida contacted an art historian, what he calls a "kunstgeschichte specialist," in order to show him "how to read the card" and received the following letter:

Dear Sir, your question can be answered quite simply. One has but to read the miniature verbally. Socrates is in the course of writing. Plato is beside him, but is not dictating. He is showing, with his index finger pointed towards Socrates: Here is the great man. With the left index finger he is drawing the attention of the spectators, who must be imagined more to the right toward the philosopher who is writing. Therefore he is rather subordinate, of lesser site and with a more modest headpiece. Please accept my kindest regards.[8]

This anonymous "expert" interpretation seems to me no more accurate than its Derridian deconstruction. An overtly literal account of the picture with its imaginary audiences outside the frame, it is just as influenced by post-medieval, illusionistic paradigms as the post-modern philosopher's imagined skateboard. Moreover, the art historian in his authoritative rhetoric of declarative statements sees the image as a self-sustaining representation, a miniature which can quite easily be "read." The alterity of the image, its absolute disjunction from our own practices of "writing," "dictating," or "reading," is here glossed over.

This is in keeping with an earlier opinion by the medieval manuscript expert Francis Wormald who, in 1942, when publishing the drawing for the first time, stated that "The iconography. . .does not seem to raise any special problems beyond those general to such representations."[9] Iconographic interpretation is a means of decoding the message of an image as though it were a text. In terms of manuscript illustration this method too has a strong positivist thrust, being based on nineteenth-century philology with its emphasis on creating genealogies and stemmata. Kurt Weitzmann's influential book on methods of studying medieval illustrations states that "iconographic study. . .has to precede stylistic analysis."[10] His system is based entirely upon the notion that pictures work just like texts, are copied like texts are miscopied, so that one has to re-create archetypal cycles, lost models from which later medieval picture cycles stem. Matthew Paris certainly copied the fortune-telling tract from an earlier Latin prototype, itself based ultimately on an Arabic original, so there is nothing to prevent this image being a direct copy of an earlier, lost frontispiece, although, as I shall argue later, I think this unlikely. This need to root the image in a linear succession of duplication with products stretching back to a privileged original, and locating meaning in some anterior space to the signs which actually convey it, is again something that Derrida has consistently refuted in his work on Rousseau and the myths of the origins of language. Perhaps Derrida's greatest contribution has been to highlight the limits and the false claims of philosophical systems that are allied to these art historical methods of closed-off and inherited meaning.

In all these publications the image is of interest not because of its supposed content, but because it is a work in the style of Matthew Paris and can be added to the list of drawings by his hand. As a monk at the Benedictine Abbey of St. Albans from 1217 to 1259, Matthew spent most of his life translating Latin saints' lives into the vernacular and illustrating them as well as composing a vast illustrated chronicle of world history in Latin, the *Chronica majora*. In old French the word *"histoire"* meant picture as well as story, and Matthew was the first and perhaps the last English historian to make full use of *"histoires"* in both senses of the word. His connections at court and with some of the leading scholars of the day perhaps explain his writing and illustrating the Oxford manuscript with its collection of unusual pseudo-scientific treatises. Another art-historical exegesis of the image, by A. G. and W. O. Hassall, goes as far as to link the expressions on the faces of the figures with Matthew Paris himself. The "excited and alarmed" face of Plato is, according to these scholars, "a rather comic effect" which "is surely no accident, but reflects Matthew Paris's alert personality."[11] One can immediately see how Derrida would wholly disagree with this myth of origins in this scenario, constructing coherence, completeness, and even a self, merely through the power of the proper name. But Derrida's discussion of the visual arts, collected in *The Truth in Painting*, does not provide an alternative strategy for exploring the drawing because his interest is not as much in paintings themselves, but, as in *The Post Card*, in the framing, positioning, margins, edges of works.[12] From now on my own analysis has to leave Derrida behind, not because I think he is totally wrong about the image, but because he does not actually see this drawing as an image at all but only as a series of displacements. As Alan Bass notes, "the word *poste* derives from the Latin *ponere*, to put, to place. It is therefore linked to position."[13] If I am to negotiate Matthew Paris' drawing as it was seen in the thirteenth century, I must begin with its place as a site of representation and inscription.

The image appears in a manuscript containing the *Liber experimentarius* of Bernardus Silvestris and other fortune-telling tracts, as one of a group of four author pictures (there were originally at last two more in this manuscript), each prefacing a work of arcane astronomical or prophetical knowledge, including texts ascribed not only to Bernardus Silvestris but to Euclid, the Arabic scholar Hermannus Contractus of Reichenau, and, of course, to Socrates. The latter along with Plato introduces the fortune-telling system of a type known as the *Sortes* or "Book of Fate."[14] The method of obtaining one's fortune was by geomancy, using numbers and thirteen diagrams which follow on subsequent pages. The title of the tract is written across the bottom of the opposite page beneath the opening diagram, "*Prognostica Socratis Basilei*," or "The Prognostications of Socrates the King" (fig. 4.2). At the bottom of the picture a later, perhaps of fourteenth-century, hand has added a text in English directing the reader to the diagram opposite, where there are thirty-two boxes, containing two sets of sixteen questions. These words are worth quoting in full because they represent an early reader's response to, and clarification of, the opening:

Here be to tables, oon above and the other benethe. An erit bonum ire extra domum vel non as it apperith in the begynnyng aboue and there is A in the quaterne then loke for the question in the second table and ther is E in that quaterne then turn the lef and on the hyer parte is AE. And if your number that ye toke in the cerkel be 9 than agaynst is descendying ys ficus fructus. Then serche in Spera fructus for ficus and there he seith Ite ad Regem Hispanie.

What this rather cryptic passage indicates is how a reader uses the system. To find the answer to a question such as "is it good to go outside the house or not?" he should look for the question on the page opposite in the box marked A at the top and E at the bottom. If the number then obtained by chance is nine, he should then look in the ninth section from the top on the next page in the column marked AE. This refers him to another diagram called the "Sphere of Fruit" which refers him to various prophecies at the end of the treatise under the names of various kings.

Matthew Paris is not the author of the fortune-telling tract, only its transmitter, although he probably came up with the idea for this image since he was often the first to add pictorial narratives and frontispieces to previously unillustrated works, such as saints' lives. This primary act of drawing a prefatory image to introduce the treatise negates the absence that is normally associated with writing. If the origin of a text is always at a distance from the copyist's pen, displaced by it, the origin of the image is always present and self-evident as a practice and performance. These lines embody the trace of Matthew's arm, his curved movements inscribed upon the flesh. There can be no closer relation between body and text than in the marks of such a drawing, except that is, for speaking with the body's breath. Nonetheless, the authority of this image does not lie in its "originality." It is, like all representations, based on other representations and does not constitute some primal statement about writing on the part of the monastic scribe/artist. Another reason why I believe that Matthew was the author of this prefatory author-portrait is that it is unique except for a subsequent fourteenth-century copy, also made at St. Albans (fig 4.3).[15] This later copy of the whole manuscript contains a fascinating first reproduction of Matthew's image. Long before the Bodleian Library sold postcards, his picture was deemed worthy of duplication, of course along with the text and diagrams of the fortune-telling system. The copyist had no problem with Plato seeming to dictate to Socrates. He did not "correct" the image by switching the two labels. This perhaps suggests that during the Middle Ages the scene was not seen to represent dictation, or perhaps even writing at all. But as well as placing his image in a subsequent genealogy of later copies, the best way to grasp its valences and associations is by understanding that upon which it was itself modeled. Matthew is well known in other contexts for adapting and combining pictorial conventions in new ways and, when devising illustrations for his *Chronica*, often appropriating sacred models to depict secular events. What "stands behind" Socrates' writing in this image is not the voice of Plato but numerous earlier images that Matthew and his monastic audience would have known. Rather than hiding under erasure as a secret, as in modern images, these models were, during the Middle Ages, part of the hermeneutic experience of their interpretation.

The fundamental model "behind" the Socrates and Plato image is the Evangelist portrait in which the inspiring man-angel symbol stands behind St. Matthew as he writes at his lectern (fig. 4.4). Details like dipping the pen in the inkwell are also based upon earlier Anglo-Saxon holy writers. Even these are not "original" but based upon ancient representations of the poet inspired by his muse. Unlike the components of language, every image is shot through, not only with reference to an

4.3 Fourteenth-century copy of the Socrates and Plato image. Oxford, Bodleian Library MS Digby 46, fol. 41v

4.4 Evangelist with inspiring angel. Besançon, Bibliothèque municipale MS 14, fol. 58v

external world, but also to other images. But although modeled on the ubiquitous Evangelist type, Socrates is not producing "The Word." Matthew Paris is careful to delineate him as a pagan, not a Christian author, not as "Matthew-like," i.e. a monastic writer like himself, working to God's dictation, but as other. How is the other or alien aspect of this writing made manifest? Most strikingly the strange curled "eastern-looking" hat, used for Jews and unbelievers like heretics elsewhere in this artist's repertoire, signals the dubious pagan status of Socrates. In a scene of Bishops disputing with the Pelagians in Matthew's *Life of Saint Alban*, it is the learned but heretical astronomers with their instruments who have the same kind of headgear (fig. 4.5). Moreover, the inspiring angel figure standing behind the scribe in Matthew's picture is not the divine inspiration coming to the writer, but just another man, as earth-bound as Socrates. It is as though Matthew Paris used the image of Matthew the Evangelist as a model, solely in order to reverse its divine dynamic, to refuse, rather than refer to the sacred signification of his prototype. Such is the power of images to argue among themselves, to undermine through association and not just reaffirm the truth of the text.

Another of Matthew's often-used visual tropes at play here helps us see why so many commentators, including Derrida, see Plato, standing behind the chair, as "wicked-looking." This is because Matthew Paris has appropriated the evil counselor or whispering devil topos here. It appears, for example, in Matthew's drawing in the *Chronica majora* depicting the Council of Lyons. Here the enthroned figure of Pope Innocent excommunicating Frederick Barbarrossa is accompanied by a conniving counselor, Master Martin, who hovers behind the throne, his pointing hand touching the papal throne in the same way that Plato's hand scrapes the back of Socrates (fig. 4.6). Throughout the *Chronica majora* in both words and pictures, Matthew was distinctly anti-papal and critical of the vice and corruption of the *Curia*.[16] The image of the evil advisor also appears in Matthew's *Life of Saint Alban* and in the Anglo-Norman Apocalypse manuscripts which have also been linked to Matthew's modelbooks.[17] The notion that Socrates was a king explains the use of this trope from a courtly context and the relevance of Plato as the "follower" or courtier figure. If the man behind the chair is the duplicitous dictator behind a powerful speaker in these examples, the question is, has Matthew, in utilizing the pattern, meant to suggest that Plato is similarly flattering or negatively influencing his supposed teacher? If we examine the image as a whole, in

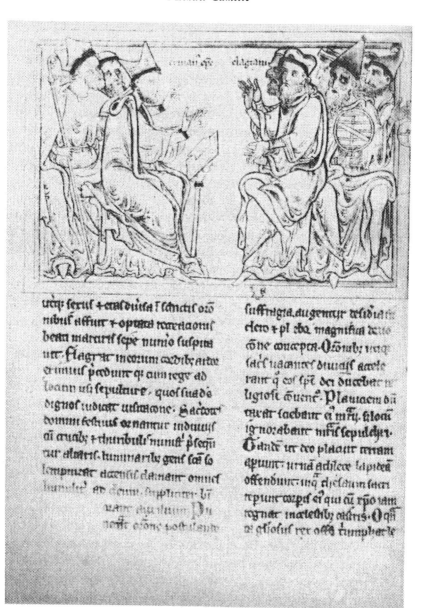

4.5 Matthew Paris: *Life of Saint Alban*, Bishops dispute with Pelagians. Dublin, Trinity College MS 177 (E. I. 40), fol. 54v

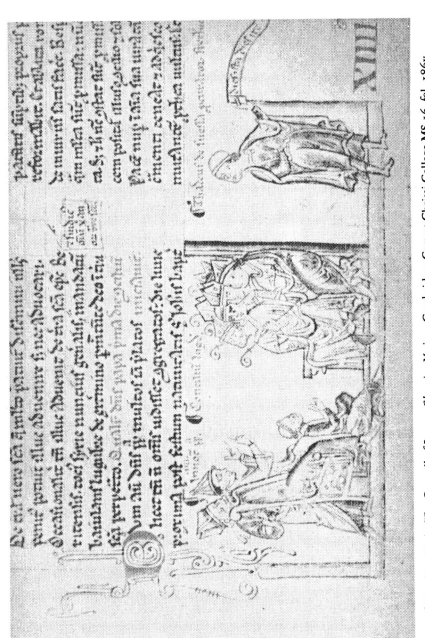

4.6 Matthew Paris: The Council of Lyons, *Chronica Majora*. Cambridge, Corpus Christi College MS 16, fol. 186v

terms of the spatial configurations of the represented court hierarchy, either papal or royal, to be *behind* the throne is a lesser position and situates "plato" as a follower of "King" Socrates. Once again an understanding of the visual language with which Matthew created his image explains aspects which might bewilder the modern viewer. These signs have lost their readability in the way Derrida describes in another essay on the relationship between speech and writing, "Signature, Event, Context":

> For the written to be written it must continue to "act" and to be legible even if what is called the author of the writing no longer answers for what he has written, for what he seems to have signed. . .The situation of the scribe and of the subscriber, as concerns the written, is fundamentally the same as that of the reader. This essential drifting due to writing as an iterative structure, cut off from all absolute responsibility, is indeed what Plato condemned in the *Phaedrus*.[18]

This gap between author and reader was especially felt during the Middle Ages when foundational authority was so crucial to the legitimation of texts. Matthew's picture plays a role in this legitimation process, preventing the text's drifting away from responsibility by presenting its origins in these two philosophers. But what does the image tell us about how these ancient author-figures were viewed and understood by the monastic community of St Albans?

During the thirteenth century most of Plato's writings were as yet unavailable in the West and the interlocutor Socrates, as he appears in the *Dialogues*, was unknown. The Plato and Socrates we see in Matthew's image are not *our* Plato and Socrates (philosophers) or *the* Plato and Socrates (historical characters), but *his* Plato and Socrates. In the Middle Ages these two names were called to mind, often without reference to their specific place in history, in grammatical and dialectical contexts. For example, they were commonly referred to by medieval teachers in academic exercises as part of the much repeated proposition "Socrates is a man." Abelard's commentary on Aristotle's *De interpretatione* analyzes how a statement such as "Socrates is a man" works, by us having two images in our minds, one of Socrates, and another of man in general. Through an amalgam of these the intellect turns up with one single image of it, in which the whole thought can be contemplated.[19] Our post-medieval perceptions tend to relate names to personalities and the individuality of authorship just as we think of Matthew's drawing as a "portrait" of the two historical characters.

In fact, the picture is more a logical proposition, except that it says, not "Socrates was a man" but "Socrates was a king and a magician."

Famous classical figures cut off from the iterative authority of texts they had actually written or inspired, Plato and Socrates were reinvented and reinscribed during the Middle Ages. Like Virgil they were often transformed into arcane magicians or soothsayers, which is what happened to the two philosophers here. The text of the *Sortes* was ultimately based on Arabic divination treatises. Part of the function of these author-images, like that of Pythagoras prefacing his *Prognostics* on folio 42 recto, was to legitimize these dubious texts which many churchmen condemned as geomancy and the work of the devil. On folio 52 verso the twelve Jewish Patriarchs of the Old Testament are pictured for similar purposes. The image thus serves to display the importance and primacy of authorship – the fact that these strange texts and magical visual systems were made by human hands. During the Middle Ages the author or *auctor* did not signify the writer of a text so much as its originator, the one who gives it authority, just as God is sometimes labeled *auctor* of the universe. Matthew Paris would not have called himself an *auctor* but more probably a *scriptor* or perhaps *compilator*. It appears that he had little knowledge of classical writings; in fact the only other place where he mentions Plato is in his Anglo-Norman narrative, the *Life of Saint Edmund*, where he tells us that the young Saint in accepting Christianity gave up the study of the classical philosophers, leaving the "vainglory of Plato for Augustine and Gregory and all philosophy for the evangelists and prophets."[20] Ancient learning was still viewed with distrust, especially in monastic circles, which explains why Matthew presents his pagan king and a magician through the inversed visual tropes of orthodox holy "writers." From the writings of St. Augustine, which St. Edmund embraced after rejecting those of Plato, the monks of St. Albans would have learned most about Socrates and Plato, especially from his great diatribe against classical culture, *The City of God*, copies of which were in the library at St. Albans Abbey.

In book 8 Augustine discusses the natural philosophers of antiquity and the role played by these founding fathers of the pagan tradition. A twelfth-century initial opening this book in a copy of Augustine's text made at the Cistercian abbey of Heiligenkreuz, Austria, provides an interesting comparison with Matthew's image and is one of the few other representations of Socrates and Plato together in medieval art that I have been able to find (fig. 4.7).[21] It represents Augustine's claim that Socrates had been

4.7 Augustine, *City of God*, book 8: Socrates and Plato. Heiligenkreuz, MS 24, fol. 63r

"the first to channel the whole of philosophy into an ethical system" and that his pupil Plato had such affection for his old master that "in practically all the Dialogues he makes Socrates, with all his charm, the mouthpiece not only of his own moral arguments but of all that Plato learned from others or managed to discover himself."[22] This artist, like Matthew Paris, is representing how we know Socrates only through Plato's words, thus investing Plato with his master's absent voice. Both images refer to the textual tradition of the two philosophers in dialogue, interjecting a residue of orality within a scene of scribal authority. However, in the twelfth-century initial, Socrates, wearing a similar "orientalizing" cap as in Matthew's image, does not write (fig. 4.7). Under an archway he holds a closed book and with his other pointing or "speaking" finger is engaged in vocalization. As a dictator he is not that far removed from images of St. Jerome verbally transmitting the Vulgate Verbum to a scribe, common in Ottonian manuscripts (fig. 4.8). The diagonal arm of the "N" separates him from his pupil Plato who is writing on a long unfurling scroll "One Two Three," as if directly relaying the points heard from his teacher. Their separate spatial configuration is perhaps meant to indicate the continuation of Socrates' ideas in Plato's writings after the former's death. But there is another presence in this initial, a spirit missing entirely from the English monk's visual version of their relationship. The swirling cloud forms hovering above Plato's head are based on Christian prototypes of Divine inspiration. But instead of the *manus Dei*, the Evangelist's symbol, or the Holy Spirit thrusting out of the clouds to inspire the earthly writer, as in an Evangelist portrait, an ugly bearded head protrudes from the top corner of the letter. This is the "demon of Socrates" mentioned by Augustine later in book 8, in his attack upon the idolatry of the ancients. The corkscrew nose is reminiscent of Alan of Lille's famous remark alluding to Plato's *Phaedrus*, that "authority has a waxen nose that can be bent in different ways."[23] The writing within this initial letter helps articulate the dubious status of the characters, identifying Socrates and Plato like the *tituli* in Matthew Paris' page. The letters identifying the demon are upside down and straggle from the grotesque nose of the *daemonas Socrates*. Unlike this bad writing which is readable only from the demon's point of view, the written numbers on Plato's scroll are upright from our viewpoint and show the directional flow, left to right of writing. These three words might also indicate the imperfection and partiality of pagan knowledge. In Plato's *Phaedrus* it is

4.8 St. Jerome and scribe, *Gospels*, Bamberg, Staatsbibliothek MS 94 (A. II. 18), fol. 1v

Socrates who is given the famous lines attacking the "forgetfulness" induced by writing. He goes on to compare writing to painting:

The painter's products stand before us as though they were alive, but if you question them they maintain a most majestic silence. It is the same with written words; they seem to talk to you as though they were intelligent, but if you ask them anything about what they say, from a desire to be instructed, they go on telling you just the same thing forever. And once a thing is put in writing, the composition, whatever it may be, drifts all over the place, getting into the hands not only of those who understand it but equally of those who have no business with it.[24]

This Platonic distrust of the written signifier was not lost upon Augustine whose theology of the spoken Logos was influential throughout the Middle Ages. This twelfth-century initial to Augustine's work represents the secondariness and emptiness of writing in this sense, since the numbers on Plato's scroll refer to sequential points of argument rather than the unknowable mystery of the Word.

Writing is often disassociated from the Divine in this way in medieval art. This can also be seen in the traditional iconography of St. Gregory inspired by the Holy Spirit, where the Word is transmitted to and from the mouth of the Pope and only written down by his eavesdropping secretary.[25] Images of divinely inspired speech, like those pictured in the manuscripts of the important female mystic and author, Hildegarde of Bingen (also in the twelfth century), always show her inscribing her visions on wax tablets (a form of writing which was seen as more spontaneous and closer to the springs of speech) separate from their being written down permanently by a male scribe.[26] Derrida's description of writing as a "radical absence" was an opinion shared by most medieval philosophers. As John of Salisbury put it in the twelfth century, "letters are shapes indicating voices. Ceaselessly they speak voicelessly the utterances of the absent."[27] Visual representation was a means of filling-out this absence, since it reintroduced the speaker or writer as the source of his words and also, as we have seen in Matthew Paris' image, his body into the site of authority. But to depict the Socratic voice using the tropes of Divine inspiration, even inverted and demonized, as did the artist of the twelfth-century Heiligenkreuz initial, would have been far too radical for the conservative English monk.

If we can understand why Socrates does *not* write in the Heiligenkreuz initial does this help explain why he *does* write in Matthew Paris' drawing?

Is there here also a distrust of the written signifier? The word for composition in the Middle Ages was *dictare* – to dictate, whereas *scribere* was generally indicative of the slavish copying of script on to parchment. A simpler explanation of the Socrates and Plato image is that Matthew just got the inscriptions muddled. Should Socrates be the dictator and the larger figure be his pupil and scribe, Plato about to write down his master's words as in the Heiligenkreuz initial? This is unlikely, for then the *auctor* would be smaller and less significant than his scribe. In contemporary representations of dictation the scribe is a diminutive, often a tiny figure, in relation to the gigantic authority of the speaking voice. In Matthew's picture that inferiority of writing relative to the power of speech, articulated in secular as well as sacred writers well into the fourteenth century, is in fact reversed. The dictator usually stands in front of the scribe, showing him by gesture and sometimes with the visible signs of words, what he should write down. Josephus, in one twelfth-century English manuscript of his works, holds open his text for the scribe Samuel to copy (fig. 4.9). Note that here real words, words which we can read, are located at the site of authorship, the locus of the speaking voice, whereas the scribe/copyist produces only squiggly lines that visually "stand for" writing.

The text of the *Prognostics* in this manuscript includes the phrase "*Socrates dicitur*" suggesting the oral rather than written composition of the tract, and yet Socrates does not seem involved, even in the subvocalization, or murmuring of his text. Images of philosophers traditionally depict them, not as writers, but as teachers, orally presenting their ideas. But here both have shut their mouths rather solemnly: almost emphatically they are *not* speaking. In medieval art people often speak who have their mouths closed. It is the hand that utters. In another twelfth-century drawing, this time from the schools of Paris, Socrates and Plato appear as speakers, their extended fingers signaling their *disputatio* symbolized in the center of the page in the personification of Dialectic (fig. 4.10). The unfinished hand of Socrates at the bottom left, that below the "speaking hand," reminds us that in Matthew Paris' drawing the alignment of speaking over writing interjects a gap or space between the word and its inscription. In the twelfth-century page Socrates does not write, his hand being literally unfinished while in Matthew's drawing Socrates has not yet even started let alone finished. His erasing hand, which holds the scraper, rests on the desk, as if holding the empty page steady, while his writing hand dips the

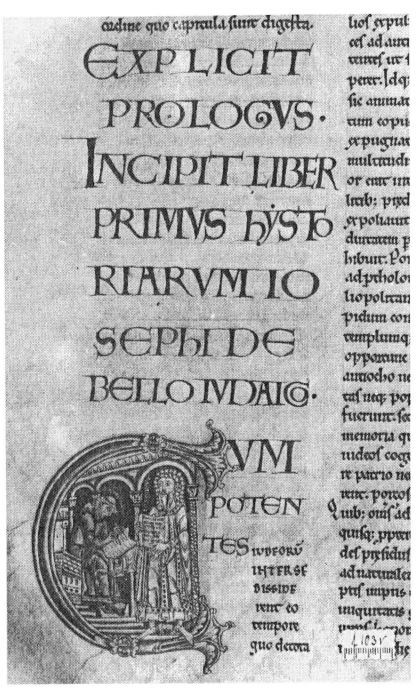

ordine quo capitula sunt digesta.

EXPLICIT
PROLOGVS·
INCIPIT LIBER
PRIMVS hySTO
RIARVM IO
SEPhI DE
BELLO IVDAIC○·
VM
POTEN
TES

4.9 Historiated initial C with Josephus with the scribe Samuel: Josephus, *Antiquities*, Cambridge, St. Johns College MS A 8, fol. 103v

137

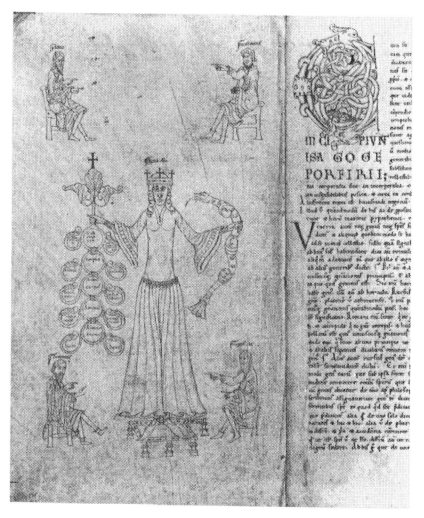

4.10 Dialectic and four philosophers. Darmstadt Bibliothek MS 2282, fol. 1v

pen into the inkwell. The same is true of other pagan writers drawn in the manuscript, for example, Pythagoras who has even more of a disjunction between his writing and his erasing hand across the space of the frame.[28] Significantly, there is nothing written on the square sheet which represents the space of writing in this picture. This may indicate that what Socrates is producing is not a text but a visual diagram like the one opposite and which, as a fortune-telling system points to a future still unwritten. But in many medieval images of writers at work the writing-field is itself blank, signaling the always deferred moment of speech about to become writing, the Word about to become flesh. Just as the unopen mouth can produce speech, the unwritten page is the site of the potential production of writing.

Can Plato's gesture be related to the prognostication process itself? Just as the reader had to "ask the question" aloud to the image alongside and choose a particular square, Plato's gesture "indicates" (from *indicare*, to point out), guides our eyes across the page to the functional squares of the fortune-telling diagram opposite. Thus, perhaps, he is pointing, not to the "author" but to the author's work. Such gestures, situated within the habits and ideologies of readers and manuscript makers in mid-thirteenth-century England, suggests that the "ready to write" gesture of Socrates helps signal the beginning. In the thirteenth century the idea that "beginnings" should be signaled by writing was a rather new notion. In the beginning was the spoken, not the written word. The opening of Vulgate Bibles, the first page, often showed a writer at a lectern, St. Jerome, translator of the Word. But Jerome is not the real beginning, the *In principio* "In the beginning God created the heaven and the earth." This follows folios later in the great "I" initial where the Logos-Creator speaks the universe with the universal talking gesture. I know of no Latin Bible which opens with an image of writing, which is always only the medium of transmission, not the repository of the Truth. The place where we begin to see writing as an autonomous act of human production is in the author-portraits in secular works, by vernacular poets like the thirteenth-century trouvère Adam de la Halle, and the two authors of the *Roman de la Rose*.[29]

Attitudes to writing were, however, changing at exactly the time Matthew penned his picture. In the previous century producers of Holy Writ had still been considered *tuba Spiritus sancti* – the passive channels through which God communicated to people. But new attitudes to knowledge in the thirteenth century gave the human identity of the writer as self-sustained *auctor* a different, no longer necessarily divinely inspired importance. Whereas the author more or less disappears in authorial prologues of the twelfth century, in the thirteenth century, as Alastair Minnis has shown, there was new concern with the active mediating role of the author and his intentions in dealing with the biblical text, and distinctions were made by Bonaventure, for example, between a hierarchy of text producers, from scribe, to compiler, to commentator, and finally to author.[30] Moreover the author was less closely aligned with the manual writer since his thoughts came directly from himself rather than from God. Matthew Paris was a manual writer, whose handwriting has been the object of much study, yet he never represented himself as a scribe in the guise of his egotistical countryman, "Eadwine prince of Scribes" who wrote the famous Psalter at Canterbury a century before and who had himself pictured seated at a lectern like a pseudo-Evangelist. Matthew's only known self-portrait shows him as a monk kneeling as a diminutive donor figure outside the frame of the page in which is placed a monumental enthroned Virgin and Child.[31] Unlike Eadwine or the Alexis master who had produced the *St. Albans Psalter* for the anchoress Christina of Markyate at the abbey a century before, Matthew's manuscripted discourse was not sacred. Penning French saints' lives and chronicles of worldly gossip, he must have been fully aware of the secondariness of his scribal words. Yet Matthew, like all medieval compilers, did take responsibility for what he had written. His *Chronica majora*, for example, which he worked on over decades, ends with a colophon by the scribe who will work on its continu- ation, praising Matthew's abilities as a writer: "Thus far wrote [*perscripsit*] the venerable man, the brother Matthew Paris: and though the hand on the pen may vary, nevertheless, as the same method of composition is maintained throughout, the whole is ascribed to him."[32] This reference to the pen, as a metonym for Matthew's writing, further materializes his function as scribe, and in the abstracting of utterance away from the spoken word it is typical of the communications revolution of the thirteenth century which gave new priority to writing as a form of legal power and authorial autonomy, especially, as Michael Clanchy has shown, in England.[33] It also links authorship to style. Matthew Paris' script and drawing style have allowed historians to construct an *œuvre* for this new kind of author-artist.

Matthew's drawing is fraught with contradictions precisely because it was made at a time when certain oral practices in literate culture were being eroded by the new literacy nascent in the schools and universities. Matthew, as every historian knows, was rapaciously conservative in everything, including his clinging on to older monastic traditions. The various Arabic treatises that Matthew copies here however, are not those analytic commentaries and translations of natural science and astronomy that are part of the contemporary Aristotelian revolution, but arcane tracts of an older tradition that Latin scholasticism would appreciate only partially. He depicts Euclid holding the new astronomical instruments in this same manuscript, emphasizing the increasing role played by the visual and the diagrammatic in thirteenth-century learning. However by the middle of the thirteenth century the legal, scholastic, and theological power of writing was on the rise, in scholastic centers like Oxford where masters of the sacred page focused not on *meditatio* upon the Word, but on the glosses, layout, and *lectio* of the written text. In opposition to this, the work of Socrates and Plato takes place in traditional oral culture rather than in book culture. Matthew Paris rather than Matthew the Evangelist circumscribes his picture of pagan writing within the traditional notions of writing as utterance before it was displaced from its vocal source. It was also increasingly the image of how knowledge was passed in medieval pedagogical systems, in universities where oral abilities continued to be far more important than mere writing. Another "properly" configured image of Socrates and Plato I have found was made by an urban lay professional illuminator in the late fourteenth century who worked for the university of Paris. Illustrating Nicole Oresme's French translation of Aristotle's *Politics*, he pictured Socrates, the scholarly *magister* dictating to his pupil Plato from his professorial chair, a conventional scene of the transmission of knowledge which makes Matthew's of a century before all the more unusual (fig. 4.11).[34] Transformed into good tonsured clerics, this illuminator's Socrates and Plato inhabit the new but more rigidly hierarchical world of the scholastic university, a world which disassociated itself from the body and which was in many ways in direct opposition to Matthew's magical, erotically-charged somatic monastic manuscript-making.

Rather than prioritizing writing over speech, his picture of Socrates about to write works against writing. It is not a dissenting image in terms of the history of Western philosophy. It is, however, a dissenting image in terms of attitudes to writing in thirteenth-century England. Prefacing a tract for telling the future, this image, as I have suggested, looks forward

4.11 Socrates and Plato: Nicole Oresme's translation of Aristotle's *Politics*. Paris, Bibliothèque nationale MS fr. 9106, fol. 311

142

in its priorization of the visual, but backwards in its unashamed orality, resisting change and newer modes of Latin literacy within its particular textual community. This may also have been something of a dubious text, perhaps even an illicit one for the monks, which they might have guardedly regarded as a dangerous innovation and as "other." Yet it was precisely this danger that made it necessary for Matthew to provide author "portraits" here. The whole point about the tradition of the author-portrait in which the Plato and Socrates image must be placed, is to anchor utterance and to fulfill the demand that someone stand behind discourse. Words in medieval culture did not float in an abstract electronic sense as they do in today's information technology – indeed, as Walter J. Ong argues texts only travel in this way after the invention of printing.[35] The postcard – the free-floating traveling text inscribed upon an image – is impossible to conceive in medieval culture where messages were sent, even when written down, by human carriers who would often deliver the words aloud. Derrida's account resonates in our culture, bound up as it is with issues of reproduction, replication, and simulacra.

By contrast, Matthew Paris aimed his picture at an audience taught to think of both language and representation problematically, but always in relation to a sender. The critical diminution or rather the "death of the author" in literary theory over the past decades has only had a confusing effect upon medieval studies where authors are nearly always dead, but also nearly always the foundational force of discourse. As Sean Burke has pointed out in his admirable study of the recent repression and reinvention of authorship, "the process of intention, influence and revision, the interfertility of life and work, autobiography and the autobiographical, author-functions, signature-effects, the proper name in general, the author-ity and creativity of the critic, all these are points at which the question of the author exerts its pressure on the textual enclosure."[36] Poised between orality and literacy, ambivalent toward human and especially pagan knowledge, and crucially concerned with the power and status of writing, thirteenth-century readers/viewers of this image were attuned to these very issues of visual, verbal, and textual authority. Socrates sits on the writing throne not only as King but as author of what follows. An image which Derrida thought emblematized the power of writing over speech is, I hope I have shown, just as much tied up with the obsession with the living voice and the very secondariness of writing that Derrida typifies as the ruling ideology of the Western tradition.

In today's world of e-mail and increasingly rapid and instantaneous electronic communication, Derrida's postcard has itself become rather anachronistic and is as "dead" a form of discourse as ink upon medieval parchment. Matthew Paris' message, by contrast, in its nexus of ambivalent negotiations between the old and the new, interrogates the authenticity of *both* speaking and writing as only the image can. It seems to me, as a picture, to hold far more possibilities for the powers of interactive discourse and the future of communication than does the postcard. Most importantly, it raises the crucial issue of the status of visual art in philosophical debate and in language. It would strike us as odd today to think of illustrating a philosophical text. From Plato to Heidegger the metaphysical tradition has been avowedly anti-iconic, distrusting all representation as false. Yet during the Middle Ages many of the set philosophical texts used at the universities of Paris, Oxford, and Bologna, were illustrated, especially works by Aristotle and his Arabic commentators. The image, which in the Neoplatonic system had been distrusted as a "phantasm," became, in the Aristotelian cosmos, the means of perception and the only source of understanding.[37] At the same time, however, the very indeterminacy and fluidity of meaning in images that makes pictures attractive to post-modern philosophers, like Derrida (in his very visual texts like *The Post Card* and *Glas*) was the main reason for their long exclusion from the medieval intellectual tradition of the seven liberal arts. In the scholastic world images would always have this ambiguous position, being both useful tools of pedagogical practice in logical diagrams and astronomical and geometrical calculations but also false simulacra that led the mind away from truth. As soon as they left the diagrammatic or the discursive for the figurative, that is, as soon as they began to be mimetic of things and objects in the world, centuries of Augustinian anti-image mistrust clouded their capacity to inform and instruct.

Medievalists in all disciplines have often failed to see this dangerously disruptive but fertile power of the visual. For too many literary scholars of the Middle Ages images are still often the iconographic "proof" of textual truth, as they were for D. W. Roberston as well as many of those practicing exegesis under the banner of the "new medievalism" – points of closure and stasis rather than the subversive code-collapsers they actually are. For too many historians of the Middle Ages images are more often used as the distant "mirrors" of medieval reality as though an "everyday life" that escapes textuality can innocently be inscribed by miniaturists, sculptors, and painters without any ideology or critique. And for too many art historians of the Middle Ages, images are discrete, non-verbal expressions of ideas, politics, or patronage, embodying the progress of an autonomous individual visual style. In all these models pictures serve as postcards for arguments written on their backs and sometimes, even inscribed over them obliterating the image altogether.[38] In these many medievalisms visual art is viewed as lesser than and in opposition to writing, when it is usually in the dynamic intersection of the two discourses, as in Matthew Paris' picture of Socrates and Plato, that things happen. This difference – that images are nothing like texts but speak atemporally, silently, and simultaneously both from outside and within them, gives pictures their uniquely liminal status, both in medieval and post-modern culture, an ability to destabilize and critique the system they supposedly are meant to affirm.

Because images are iconic and thus tend to be interpreted in relation to structures in our world, their capacity to outlive texts is extraordinary, but so is their capacity to be reread in relation to the wrong objects or the wrong world, which is some of the fun that Derrida has in *The Post Card*. If in closing, I might be allowed to play a similar game, as a medievalist interested in modes of communication, I would want to make Matthew's image even more significant a sign in the history of human discourse. Socrates is not writing in Matthew's image but is about to activate the grids of the fortune-telling tract that appears opposite. His performance under Matthew Paris' pen is that he is about to draw, to make, to picture. This picture-making capacity will, in future communications systems, overtake all previous discursive strategies. Medievalists are in a better position than most humanists in the university to deal with the current transformation of writing into imaging, because we are so involved in the historical process whereby writing and imaging first became so central in Western culture during the twelfth and thirteenth centuries. The book has been our basis but are we prepared for its end? Matthew Paris' image and the postcard reproducing it will be entirely transformed by new digital and electronic information systems which leave the Middle Ages, the era of writing, behind. In the visual realm, past and future, forwards and backwards, are not the crucial temporal demarcators they are under the thralldom of texts. As a number of recent theorists of the cultural impact of computer-literacy have suggested, the screen is far more like the medieval manuscript in its hypertextual, glossing, rapid scrolling, and iconic-cueing techniques than the isolated frames of the modern printed book. In Jay David Bolter's words "only in the medieval codex were words and pictures as unified as they are on the computer screen."[39] Nothing is more interactive than the medieval book, as on this page of the Bodleian manuscript where a fifteenth-century reader/user decided to write down the instructions below the picture. This writer did not inscribe on its back, as with a postcard, but transformed the space of inscription itself with his gloss. Today Derrida's postcard is, as I have suggested, already defunct as a medium for sending messages, or at least it is a rather quaint, nostalgic mode of communication, depending as it does upon the post office, upon "snail mail" to reach its addressee (fig. 4.1). Matthew Paris' image, by contrast, is instantaneous in its communication, and entertains a future of manic manuscripting, that is, direct hand-controlled manipulations of text and image which integrates writer and reader, picture and viewer, software and user. Nothing could be more post-modern than this medieval image. A ten-year-old friend to whom I recently showed Matthew's picture interpreted the two figures as sharing a computer terminal. Looking at the screen Plato and Socrates can be seen as simultaneously speaking, writing, and drawing. Whereas Derrida's hermetic and individually inscribed postcard (fig. 4.1) can, like his book, be seen as the last gasp of the traditional, two-dimensional, and nostalgic, romantic discourse of a still-text-bound philosophy, Matthew Paris' more open opening of the *Sortes* (fig. 4.2) can, like many medieval works, look toward the iconic discourse of our own tomorrow. Its diagrammatic, almost digitalized, mapping allows the interaction of a viewer/reader who points (clicks) on a particular icon in order to move through this program, and presents its authors as dynamic actors or interactors within their text in the new age of the image. Although when Matthew Paris sent his message in the midst of one communications revolution, he could not have known it, his *Sortes* image also reveals our fate, or at least the fate of writing in the wake of yet another transformation in the human sensorium.

Notes

1 Jacques Derrida, *The Post Card: From Socrates to Freud and Beyond* (Chicago: University of Chicago Press, 1987), pp. 9–10, originally published as *La Carte Postale: de Socrate à Freud et au-delà* (Paris: Flammarion, 1980), pp. 13–14.

2 *Ibid.*, *Of Grammatology*, trans. Gayatri Chakravorty Spivak (Baltimore: Johns

Hopkins University Press, 1974), p. 6. See also his discussion of "Plato's Pharmacy" in *Dissemination*, trans. Barbara Johnson, (London: Athlone Press, 1981), pp. 61–171.

3 Derrida, *The Post Card*, p. 12.

4 *Ibid.*, p. 18.

5 *Ibid.*, "Signature Event Context" in *Margins of Philosophy*, trans. Alan Bass (Brighton: Harvester Press, 1982), pp. 15–18.

6 It is referred to as an engraving throughout the influential study by Gregory L. Ulmer, *Applied Grammatology: Poste-Pedagogy from Jacques Derrida to Joseph Beuys* (Baltimore: Johns Hopkins University Press, 1985) and by Christopher Norris, *Derrida* (Cambridge Mass.: Harvard University Press, 1989), p. 187. Ned Lukacher, *Primal Scenes: Literature, Philosophy, Psychoanalysis* (Ithaca and London, Cornell University Press, 1986), p. 73, also describes Derrida's discovery of "Matthew Paris's engraving in a thirteenth-century fortunetelling book. . .that depicts Plato standing behind the seated Socrates, who is writing at Plato's immediate and urgent dictation." A more careful evaluation of the image in this philosophical matrix is J. Neel, *Plato, Derrida and Writing* (Carbondale: Southern Illinois University Press, 1992), pp. 16–17, although this author captions the image "Plato watching Socrates read."

7 For the new priority of the image in general see W. J. T. Mitchell, "The Pictorial Turn," *Artforum* 31 (March, 1993): 89–94; J. Hillis Miller, *Illustration* (Cambridge, Mass.: Harvard University Press, 1992); Barbara Maria Stafford, *Body Criticism: Imaging the Unseen in Enlightenment Art and Medicine* (Cambridge, Mass.: MIT Press, 1992), pp. 465–75; and for medieval studies in particular, Michael Camille, "Art History in the Past and Future of Medieval Studies," in John van Engen, ed., *The Past and Future of Medieval Studies* (Notre Dame: Notre Dame University Press, 1994), pp. 362–82.

8 Derrida, *The Post Card*, pp. 172–73.

9 F. Wormald, "More Matthew Paris Drawings," *The Walpole Society* 31 (1942–43): 109–12. The first scholarly corpus of Matthew's drawings was made by M. R. James, "The Drawings of Matthew Paris," *The Walpole Society* 14 (1925–26): 1–26.

10 K. Weitzmann, *Illustrations in Roll and Codex: A Study of the Origin and Methods of Text Illustration*, revised edn. (Princeton: Princeton University Press, 1970), p. 205. For recent critical reappraisals of iconography within art history see the various essays collected in B. Cassidy, ed., *Iconography at the Crossroads* (Princeton: Princeton University Press, 1993) and the useful study from outside the discipline by W. J. T. Mitchell, *Iconology: Text, Image, Ideology* (Chicago: University of Chicago Press, 1986).

11 A. G. and W. O. Hassall, *Treasures from the Bodleian Library* (London: Gordon Fraser Gallery, 1976), pp. 73–76, plate 16.

12 See Jacques Derrida, "Restitutions of the Truth in Painting," in *The Truth in Painting*, trans. G. Bennington and Ian McLeod (Chicago: University of Chicago Press, 1987), pp. 256–382.

13 Alan Bass, "Translator's Introduction: L before K," in Derrida, *The Post Card*, p. xxv.

14 The complete visual contents of the manuscript are described in N. Morgan, *Early Gothic Manuscripts (1190–1250)* (London: Harvey Millar, 1982), number 89, p. 40 and its textual contents discussed in L. Brandin, "Les prognostica du manuscrit Ms Ashmole 304," in M. Williams and J. A. de Rothschild, eds., *Studies in Romance Languages Presented to L. E. Kastner* (Cambridge: Cambridge University Press, 1932), pp. 60–67 and T. C. Skeat, "An Early Medieval Book of Fate, the Sortes XII Patriarchium," *Medieval and Renaissance Studies* 3 (1954): 5, plate 2a. Surveys of divination which mention books of fate include Lynn Thorndike, *A History of Magic and Experimental Science* (New York: Macmillan, 1923), II: 10–123 and more recently T. Charmasson, *Recherches sur une technique divinatoire: la géomancie dans l'occident médiévale* (Geneva: Droz, 1980), p. 222.

15 For this copy, MS Digby 45, which allows us to reconstruct the two missing author portraits in Matthew's manuscript, see O. Pächt and J. J. G. Alexander, *Illuminated Manuscripts in the Bodleian Library, Oxford*, III (Oxford: Oxford University Press, 1973): 60, number 659.

16 Suzanne Lewis, *The Art of Matthew Paris in the* Chronica Majora (Berkeley: University of California Press, 1987), pp. 263–64.

17 For the evil advisor topos in the Antichrist scene in an English Apocalypse, Bod. Auct. D. IV 17 see Pächt and Alexander, *Illuminated Manuscripts*, III, plate 39.

18 Derrida, "Signature, Event, Context," p. 17. Derrida's searching analysis of the power of writing in *Of Grammatology*, indebted to E. R. Curtius' brilliant discussion of the metaphor in *European Literature and the Latin Middle Ages* (Princeton: Princeton University Press, 1953) is of great importance in understanding the problematization of language in the Middle Ages.

19 See J. Marenbon, *Early Medieval Philosophy 480–1150: An Introduction* (London: Routledge and Kegan Paul, 1983), p. 137.

20   De Platun lest la veine gloire
            Pur Augustin et pur Gregoire
            Et tute la philosophie
            Fut euangel et prophecie.

    See A. T. Baker, "La vie de Saint Edmond," *Romania* 55 (1929): 350–51.

21 Franz Walliser, *Cistercienser Buchkunst: Heiligenkreuzer Skriptorium in seinem ersten Jahrhundert 1133–1230* (Heiligenkreuz: Vienna, 1969), p. 33, Abb. 46.

22 Augustine, *City of God* book 8, ch. 4, trans. G. G. Walsh and G. Monahan (Washington: Catholic University of America Press, 1952), p. 21.

23 The demon of Socrates is discussed in Augustine, *ibid.*, p. 47; and for Alan of Lille's statement see Peter Dronke, ed., *A History of Twelfth Century Philosophy* (Cambridge: Cambridge University Press, 1988), p. 7.

24 *The Collected Dialoguer of Plato*, eds. E. Hamilton and H. Cairns (Princeton: Princeton University Press, 1961), p. 521.

25 For the image of the inspired St. Gregory, see J. Croquison, "Les origines de l'iconographie gregorienne," *Cahiers Archéologique* 12 (1962) and M. Camille, "Word, Text and Image in the Early Church Fathers," in *Testo e immagine nell'alto medioevo* (Spoleto: Settimane di studio, 1994), pp. 65–92.

26 For illustrations of Hildegarde as author, see K. Clausberg, *Kosmische Visionen: Mystische Weltbilder von Hildegarde von Bingen* (Cologne: Dumont, 1980).

27 John of Salisbury, *Metalogicon*, trans. D. D. McGarry (Berkeley: University of California Press, 1962), p. 38 and M. Camille, "Seeing and Reading: Some Visual Implications of Medieval Literacy and Illiteracy," *Art History*, 8 (1985): 26–49.

28 Oxford, Bodleian Library MS Ashmole 304 fol. 42v., reproduced in Wormald "More Matthew Paris Drawings," plate 28. For the portrait of Euclid and Hermanus see Morgan, *Early Gothic Manuscripts*, fig. 299.

29 For vernacular author portraits in the thirteenth century see Sylvia Huot, *From Song to Book: The Poetics of Writing in Old French Lyric and Lyric Narrative Poetry* (Ithaca: Cornell University Press, 1987).

30 A. J. Minnis, *Medieval Theory of Authorship: Scholastic Literary Attitudes in the Later Middle Ages* (London: Scolar Press, 1984). Another useful discussion is Neil Hathaway, "*Compilatio*: From Plagiarism to Compiling", *Viator* 20 (1988): 18–42.

31 Margaret Gibson, T. A. Heslop, and Richard W. Pfaff, eds., *The Eadwine Psalter: Text, Image and Monastic Culture in Twelfth-Century Canterbury* (London: Humanities Research Association; University Park: Pennsylvania State University Press, 1992), pp. 178–85. For other self-images by Matthew see fol. 6r. of British Library, MS Royal 14.C.vii, reproduced in James, "The Drawings of Matthew Paris," p. 18, and Brian J. Levy, "Autoportrait d'artiste, figure de poète: le cas de Matthieu Paris," in Danielle Buschinger, ed., *Figures de l'écrivain au moyen âge* (Göttingen: Kümmerle, 1991), pp. 193–206.

32 See Lewis, *The Art of Matthew Paris*, p. 43.

33 M. T. Clanchy, *From Memory to Written Record: England 1066–1307* (London: Edward Arnold, 1979). For the autograph hand of Matthew himself see Richard Vaughan, "The Handwriting of Matthew Paris," *Transactions of the Cambridge Bibliographical Society* 1 (1953): 376–94 and S. Patterson, "An Attempt to Identify Matthew Paris as a Flourisher," *The Library* 32 (1977): 367–70.

34 For the translation of Aristotelian concepts into visual signs in this vernacular translation see C. R. Sherman, "Some Visual Definitions in the Illustrations of Aristotle's *Nichomachean Ethics* and *Politics* in the French Translations of Nicole Oresme," *Art Bulletin* 59 (1977): 320–30.

35 W. J. Ong, *Orality and literacy: The Technologizing of the Word* (London: Methuen, 1982), pp. 117–38.

36 Sean Burke, *The Death and Return of the Author: Criticism and Subjectivity in Barthes, Foucault and Derrida* (Edinburgh: Edinburgh University Press, 1992), p. 173.

37 M. Camille, "Illustrations in Harley MS 3487 and the Perception of Aristotle's *Libri Naturales* in Thirteenth-Century England," in W. M. Ormond, ed., *England in the Thirteenth Century*, Proceedings of the 1984 Harlaxton Symposium (Grantham: Harlaxton College, 1985), pp. 31–44. I am at present working on a larger study, *Illuminating Philosophy*, which will explore in depth the status of visual images as pedagogical devices within medieval universities and especially in the classroom.

38 For more detailed critiques of literary and historical uses of illustrations see M. Camille, "Art History in the Past and Future of Medieval Studies" in *The Past and Future of Medieval Studies* (note 7 above).

39 See J. David Bolter, *Writing Space: The Computer, Hypertext and the History of Writing* (Hillsdale N.J.: L. Erlbaum Associates, 1991), p. 74 and the essays in Richard A. Lanham, *The Electronic Word: Democracy, Technology and the Arts* (Chicago: University of Chicago Press, 1993), especially "Digital Rhetoric and the Digital Arts," where he notes that "the struggle between icon and alphabet is not, to be sure, anything new, as the history of illuminated manuscripts attests" (p. 34).

5

The schools give a license to poets

NICOLETTE ZEEMAN

A number of early French romances make substantial claims for their originality. But they also work in interaction with and (re)write narratives apparently already in existence. The prologue to *Erec et Enide* alludes to an intertextual *mouvance* which is both rhetorical and glossatory:[1]

> dist Crestiens de Troies
> que reisons est que totevoies
> doit chascuns panser et antandre
> a bien dire et a bien aprandre;
> et tret d'un conte d'avanture
> une molt bele conjointure.

[Chrétien de Troyes says it is right for everybody always to devote their thoughts and efforts to speaking well and learning well; and from a tale of adventure he fashions a very elegant composition.][2]

Romance composition is a creative reworking of other materials, "a progression and a *dépassement* within a particular continuity" (Freeman, *The Poetics of* Translatio studii, p. 81). This process assumes that language is opaque and figured. So Wace observes that exegetico-rhetorical invention shapes narrative truth and fiction:

> Ne tut mençunge, ne tut veir,
> Tut folie ne tut saveir.
> Tant unt li cunteür cunté
> E li fableür tant flablé
> Pur lur cuntes enbeleter,
> Que tut unt fait fable sembler.

[Not all lies, not all truth, not all foolishness, not all wisdom. To embellish their tales, the story-tellers have so storied, and the inventors of fables have so fabled, that they have made everything appear fabulous.][3]

Marie de France famously sites linguistic obscurity at the center of romance composition:

> Custume fu as anciens,
> Ceo testimoine Preciens,
> Es livres ke jadis feseient,
> Assez oscurement diseient
> Pur ceus ki a venir esteient
> E ki aprendre les deveient,
> K'i peüssent gloser la lettre
> E de lur sen le surplus mettre.
> Li philesophe le saveient,
> Par eus meïsmes entendeient,
> Cum plus trespassereit li tens,
> Plus serreient sutil de sens.

[The custom among the ancients – as Priscian testifies – was to speak quite obscurely in the books they wrote, so that those who were to come after and study them might gloss the letter and supply its significance from their own wisdom. Philosophers knew this, they understood among themselves that the more time they spent, the more subtle their minds would become.][4]

The compositions of the ancients are valued because their strangeness necessitates writerly reading, an inventive hermeneutics. But there may here be an implicit imperative toward rhetorical difficulty as well as clarification, toward figuration as well as toward its unraveling. Marie may even acknowledge that glossing "covers" and obscures prior texts in its own act of unraveling them. This preoccupation with figural obscurity, and its *surplus*, may be replicated in the narrative obscurities or "marvels" of the *Lais* and other romance texts.[5] As in Occitan and Old French lyric, in these narratives an interest in linguistic figuration seems to be a part of a general interest in semiotics.[6]

This may have been encouraged by the reading of "poetry" – classical and classically inspired medieval Latin verse[7] – which took place within the disciplines of medieval grammar and rhetoric. If literacy was available only through these elementary disciplines, anyone who could read and write would have come into contact with them. This would have been true even if these pupils subsequently used their skills in vernacular contexts.[8] Scholars have argued for the influence of textual commentary – the primary vehicle of medieval grammar as of much medieval learning – in the rewriterly aspects of vernacular composition.[9] Others have identified in vernacular compositions assumptions and techniques found in late classical and medieval handbooks of rhetoric. The relation of Latin rhetoric to other vernacular traditions was one of dynamic and constructive opposition, its hold over vernacular composition variable but "profonde et durable."[10]

In the light of this, it seems surprising that the definitions of *poetria* which modern critics have seen to be most prevalent in the schools bear only a limited relation to romance composition. These definitions present *poetria* as either entirely fictitious or a mixture of the fictitious with the true. Its defining features are the elements which are *ficta*, "untrue," "feigned"; *poetria* is *fabula*, *res ficta*, the story of events which did not occur or which could not occur.[11] Here *poetria* is seen in relation to discourses to which the schools attribute a higher degree of "truth" – the languages of history, natural science, philosophy, ethics, or theology. This view is inherited from the classical *scholia* on the poets, which argue that poets may use historical material but that fiction is a characteristic mode of poetry. This is exemplified in the view that the poets have a "license" to alter the truth. This is what they did in composing the myths of the gods, supposedly a central subject for poetry; the "truths" which underlie these myths are historical events which occurred among human beings. Myths are thus a prime instance of poetic fiction. According to the *scholia*, poets also change the narratives they inherit or choose the one that best suits their purposes. They often distance themselves from the notion of truth, claiming ignorance or agnosticism about the historical or mythical narrative that they do not wish to tell.[12]

The view that poetry is untrue feeds, however, into the various recuperative activities practiced in classical and medieval commentary. In the Middle Ages poetry is justified on grounds of aesthetics and ethics: it is pleasurable, affective, persuasive, or exemplary.[13] But commentators also argue that poetry, perhaps because it is at one level "untrue," has a relation to "truer" discourses other than ethics. Poetry alludes directly or indirectly to the phenomena elsewhere described in medieval history, in the arts, natural science, and philosophy. Poetic allusions may be overt and illustrative or they may be oblique and figural – extreme cases are designated, by modern critics at least, as "allegorical." The medieval grammatical commentary "provide[s] a reader with sufficient information – such as history, mythology, geography, and grammar – to understand a work in the context of the historical and social realities of its author's own time."[14] But this glossing also has a more assertive project of epistemological control. The rhetorical and inventive nature of commentary observed by Rita Copeland (see n. 9) often serves to support this project. Indeed, the commentary assumes that it possesses knowledge of truths anterior to the poetic text, truths of which the poetry provides only a partial, figured, allegorical, or fictive version.[15] Notions about poetic fiction evolve, in other words, in close conjunction with notions about the truer discourses which are used both to condemn and recuperate it.

Mark Chinca and others have argued that schools theories of poetic fiction may have influenced romance narrative. Schools notions of poetic *fabula*, *res ficta*, or the lifelike but still fictive *argumentum*, may reappear in these vernacular texts, now no longer constrained by the schools' orientation to their own notions of truth.[16] Nevertheless, to describe romance in these terms may be to regard only one aspect of romance refiguration.

There is another view of poetry attributed to the medieval schools by modern scholars. This is a consequence of the commentary practices mentioned above. According to this view, poetry is a highly troped text whose real but hidden significance can be identified in another, purportedly less troped, language. M.-D. Chenu and Winthrop Wetherbee link *poetria* with medieval theories of allegorical *fabula*, *involucrum*, and *integumentum*.[17] The high profile which modern scholars accord to medieval "allegorizing" commentators and versifiers may be due to a modern preoccupation with allegory; it may also be due to the belief of modern critics that some of these "allegorizing" medieval writers valued poetry unusually highly.[18] However, although the identification and decipherment of strongly metaphorical or "allegorical" features is an essential technique in the reading of the poets, it does not dominate medieval "humanizing" grammatical commentaries on the poets, the number of which, as Baswell notes, vastly outweighs the number of the "allegorizing" commentaries ("'Figures of Olde Werke,'" p. 47). Moreover, even in "allegorizing" commentaries, *poetria* is only one of a range of associated terms used to refer to the allegorical text. Writers are equally – if not more – likely to use the terms which relate either to the untruth of the narrative, *res ficta*, *fabula*, or to the "covering" of the text, *integumentum*, *involucrum*, or *cortex*. *Poetria* can be, but does not have to be, a decodable integument.

More important still, it is not clear that such an allegorical poetic with its assumptions about decipherability is especially relevant to romance narrative. While parts of certain romance texts can undoubtedly be read in these terms, many others cannot, especially in the early French texts.[19]

The term allegory can of course be understood to refer to something less recuperable. Here it foregrounds the irreducibly figurative nature of language, the generative nature of that figuration and its primarily exegetical relation to other discourses. This version of allegory can no doubt be seen in some of the integumental theory and grammatical commentary of the schools;[20] it can also be seen in the rhetorico-exegetical notion of romance assumed by this essay.

It is to this that we shall now turn. For in the grammatical commentaries we can also find descriptions of *poetria* which relate to this notion of romance. According to these descriptions, *poetria* is "licensed" to figure its materials "in other terms." We noted above the long-standing idea that poets change the narratives which they inherit, a view which presents poetry as both inventive and exegetical. But in this context, the poets' "changing" of narrative becomes an index of the degree to which a poetic license to "change terms" impinges on the text. Poetry is here a highly figured language. Its figures are described in terms such as Greek τρόπος (*tropos*), a "turning away," a "deviation" from notionally less figured discourse; or Greek μεταφορά (*metaphora*) and its Latin equivalent *translatio*, a "carrying over," a substituting of one term or discourse for another. Although the description of poetry as figured language could describe all language, here the foregrounding of figuration distinguishes poetry in terms of a special potential for obliquity, inexplicitness, evasiveness, and even obscurity.

Like the other views of *poetria* we have looked at, the description of poetry as licensed figuration often involves a contrast with the hypothetically truer discourses of history, natural science, philosophy, and ethics. But here the contrast between poetry and truer discourse is much less oppositional and for that reason possibly less hierarchized. The assumption that the poet is a changer of discourse places the poet in the role of exegete upon the discourses of the schools. Now poetry may offer a means of evading the requirements of truth or falsehood. As against the notionally more "proper," definitional, dialectical, and closured learned discourses of the schools, poetry is cast as overtly figural, sometimes open, sometimes difficult. As against historical narrative, poetry may be metamorphic rather than factual, "artful" rather than "natural," oblique rather than "direct." As against the languages of natural science, philosophy, or ethics, poetry may be mediating rather than transparent, insinuating rather than defining, opining rather than knowing, descriptive rather than argumentative, exemplary rather than prescriptive, suggestive rather than categorical.

The evasiveness of this notion of poetry certainly means that poetry cannot be so easily condemned according to schools' notions of truth. Whatever the purposes for which this description of poetry was formulated within the schools – and it does not necessarily involve a particularly high valuation of poetry – it represents a potentially desirable and highly appropriable alternative model of writing. Elsewhere I have argued that a similar view conditions Averroes' commentary on Aristotle's *Poetics* in the Latin version of Hermannus Alemannus.[21] Here I shall argue that this version of poetry is powerfully formulated and widely available in late classical and medieval grammatical commentaries on the poets. It describes poetry in terms which may have been highly suggestive for those composing in vernacular contexts outside the schools. The schools may have evolved for their own purposes of epistemological control propositions and theories about poetry which made it possible for writers outside the schools to evade those very purposes of control.

The theories of poetry which modern commentators have understood to refer to poetic fiction-making or poetic allegory can of course be seen as subcategories of this description of poetry as licensed refiguration.[22]

Indeed, a text which can be read according to both these theories of poetry is Lactantius' description of the "officium poetae." Composed in the early fourth century, this passage becomes a commonplace of the Middle Ages, repeated across the centuries by Isidore of Seville, Rhabanus Maurus, Vincent of Beauvais, and Pierre Bersuire:[23] "officium poetae [est] in eo, ut ea, quae gesta sunt vere, in alias species obliquis figurationibus cum decore aliquo conversa traducant" ("it is the business of poets elegantly and with oblique figures to turn and transfer things which have really occurred into other representations.")[24] Here we see the poet as the producer of fictions out of history, and the familiar contrast between poetry and truer discourses, "things which have really occurred." Elsewhere Lactantius reveals himself to be *au fait* with the usual methods of recovering poetic "fiction" (including the "allegorical") in terms of history, philosophy, natural science, or ethics (see col. 172). But these theories, which present poetry as a textuality of change both in the myths of its origin and in the narratives of its process, can also be read to foreground poetic refiguration. Fiction may be an extension of refiguration. According to Lactantius, poets reshape whole historical narratives. Poets do not merely replace a historical language with a figured and "poetic" one, however; they "turn about" and "carry over" (*convertere, traducere*) historical event "into other forms" or "appearances" ("in alias species"). Historical narrative itself is changed. Lactantius' use of the word *obliquus* to describe poetic figuration further suggests the "slantwise," "indirect," or "tangential" modes by which this change occurs. Poetry may or may not directly oppose the truths of history, philosophy, physics, and ethics; but it may evade them by "turning" in some other direction.

Lactantius denies that poetry is falsehood, trying to prevent the contrast between history and poetry from becoming an opposition of truth and poetic lies. His attempt mainly illustrates the lability of poetry. Those who think the poets are liars, he says, "nesciunt enim, qui sit poeticae licentiae modus; quousque progredi fingendo liceat" ("do not know what is the limit of poetic license, how far it is permitted to proceed by fictive methods" [1.11 [col. 171]]). Lactantius reveals a sliding scale of like functions between poetry and lying. Both are modes of "license"; both proceed by "fictive methods." Lactantius' positioning of poetry in relation to untruth is as slippery as his positioning of poetry in relation to truth. When he finally offers what appears to be a hard and fast distinction between poetry and lying, it is by attributing a foolish or pointless (*ineptus*) total invention to lying: "totum autem, quod referas, fingere, id est ineptum esse, et mendacem potius quam poetam" ("but to feign all that you relate is to be a fool and a liar rather than a poet" [1.11 [cols. 171–72]]). To describe lying as total feigning and as unrelated to any other (prior) discourse may be a way of affirming the traditional view that poetry mixes the true with the untrue. But it also points to the relational nature of poetry.

Later, he comments: "nihil igitur a poetis in totum fictum est: aliquid fortasse traductum, et obliqua figuratione obscuratum, quo veritas involuta tegeretur" ("nothing, therefore, is totally made up by the poets; perhaps something is carried over and obscured by the indirections of tropology so that the truth can be wrapped up and enmeshed" [1.11 [cols. 171–72]]). If poetry is fictive, this fiction arises through figuration; if the truth is "wrapped up" (*tegeretur*), it is also "enmeshed," "involved" (*involuta*).

Turning now to the figural view of poetry which underlies this passage, I shall look first at classical and medieval rhetorical theories of figuration; then I shall look at some grammatical commentaries discussing figuration in the poets: Servius on Virgil and later medieval commentators on Lucan. From an early period figuration is seen as especially characteristic of poetry. Aristotle classifies figuration in the category of "unfamiliar" (ξενικός) language, without which poetry will be "mean" (ἰδιωτικός). Quintilian remarks that figuration has a place in both oratory and poetry, but that it is more common in poetry. Servius' commentary on the *Aeneid* documents encyclopedically how the teaching of tropes and figures was linked to the reading of the poets.[25] In the classical period the study of figuration was supposed to be the job of the rhetoricians, but the grammarians in charge of the *enarratio poetarum* tended to appropriate it. This was formally acknowledged in Donatus' fourth-century *Ars major*, a grammatical treatise whose third book was devoted almost entirely to tropology.[26] But classical views on figuration already reflect a grammatical emphasis on "correctness."

Classical rhetoric defines the figure against what it describes as less figured or unfigured language. The Greek word "trope" (τρόπος) signifies a "turn," and implies a "turning away" from and a substitution for such a language; the trope represents "a different 'way' of saying something, a turn of expression which involved a transference from a commonly accepted norm of meaning or usage."[27] In the *Poetics*, Aristotle uses the term "metaphor" (μεταφορά) for all figuration and defines it along with "unfamiliar" or "strange" (ξενικός) language against that which is "clear" (σαφής) or "standard" (κύριος). According to Aristotle, figured and strange languages are desirable in poetry; they merely run the risk of incomprehensibility.[28]

In later rhetorical tradition, however, figuration is contrasted with a different notion of unmediated language – natural or "proper" language. So Quintilian remarks, "propria sunt verba, cum id significant, in quod primo denominata sunt; translata, cum alium natura intellectum alium loco praebent" ("words are *proper* when they refer to the thing for which they were first coined; *metaphorical*, when they are used in a sense different from their natural meaning"). And Donatus, "tropus est dictio translata a propria significatione ad non propriam similitudinem ornatus necessitativve causa" ("a trope is a word carried away from its proper signification to make a likeness, not a proper reference, either for ornament or through necessity").[29] Like Aristotle, later writers such as Quintilian affirm the need to limit figuration for purposes of clarity (for instance, *Institutio oratoria* 8. prologue. 22–28). But, as Kaster observes, because later writers contrast figuration with "natural" or "proper" language, the figure is also for them a deviation from such language. It is close to grammatical incorrectness (*Guardians of Language*, p. 175). This view of figuration assumes an essentially grammatical perspective, according to which all figures tend in the direction of linguistic misuse or error. They are justified by the ancient and authoritative usage of the great poets. They are further justified with an equivocating mixture of positive reasons and excuses: like Donatus above, Quintilian says that they are decorative and pleasing but also necessitated by the requirements of meter (*Institutio oratoria* 1.6.1–2; 1.8.14; 8.3.5).

The most extreme instances of this ambivalence toward figuration are *barbarismus* and *soloecismus*, both in themselves regarded as grammatical errors, although many of them are found in the poetic authorities. Here, they are "licensed."[30] Quintilian states:

> Quaedam tamen et faciem soloecismi habent et dici vitiosa non possunt. . .Schemata igitur nominabuntur, frequentiora quidem apud poetas sed oratoribus quoque permissa. Verum schema fere habebit rationem. . .Sed id quoque, quod schema vocatur, si ab aliquo per imprudentiam factum erit, soloecismi vitio non carebit.

> [Some phrases have all the appearance of a *solecism* and yet cannot be called faulty. . .We will therefore style them *figures*; in fact their use is more frequent among poets, but they have also been allowed to orators. Figures, however, will have some justification. . .I must however point out that what is called a figure will also, if used unwittingly, not lack the flaw of solecism.][31]

Quintilian uses for these the traditional defenses for figuration. Such dubious usages are allowed "poetico iure" ("according to the rule of poetry" [*Institutio oratoria* 1.5.13]). Donatus confirms this view: "barbarismus est una pars orationis vitiosa in communi sermone. in poemate metaplasmus" ("a barbarism is a part of speech which would be faulty in social discourse; in poetry it is a metaplasm" [*Ars major*, p. 392; also p. 393]). Here the genre of the poetic text decides whether or not the variant is an error or a figure. In his commentary on Donatus, Servius shares the view of Quintilian cited above that poetic intention decides the status of the variant; the grammarian Consentius, on the other hand, claims the crucial factor is skilful use and authoritative precedent.[32]

But this extreme version of tropology cannot be confined to the problematic figures of barbarism and solecism. It infiltrates the grammarians' view of all formal tropology. The third book of the *Ars major* treats figuration. In this book, known in the Middle Ages as the *Barbarismus* (from its first word), barbarism and solecism (poetic metaplasm and schema) are treated first, before all the other figures. This order becomes standard for the later Middle Ages.[33] Indeed, all tropology is seen through a lens provided by these particular "vices" of figuration.

Definitions of the figures are also affected. We have already seen that Donatus' definition of *tropus* involves a defense. But Donatus' definition and defense are remarkably similar to those which he uses for metaplasm: "metaplasmus est transformatio quaedam recti solutique sermonis in alteram speciem metri ornatusve causa" ("metaplasmus is a certain transformation of straightforward prose into another shape for reasons of meter or decoration" [*Ars major*, p. 395]). The acknowledgment that *translatio* is sometimes used to avoid repeating a term, on the other hand, means that it sounds more than a little like barbarism/metaplasm, the refusal to replicate a term properly or exactly: "translatio, quae fit quotiens vel deest verborum proprietas, vel vitatur iteratio" ("figuration, which occurs whenever signification is not proper or repetition is being avoided" [Servius, *Commentarii* 1.435]). This overt connection between non-repetition (impaired repetition?) and figuration indicates vividly how notions of identity, substitution, and change underlie this description of figuration. It is a description which continues to be found in the high Middle Ages. John of Salisbury, for instance, speaks of the rules and errors of grammar, continuing:

Figura vero medium tenet locum; et dum aliquatenus recedit ab utroque, non cadit in alterutrius rationem. Omnes. . .declinant vitium, quia prohibetur; sed nonnulli figuris utuntur, quia permittitur. Nam inter vitia, barbarismum scilicet et soloecismum, et artem, que virtus eloquii est et norma, figure et scemata sunt; metaplasmus. . .scema. . .Est enim, teste Isidoro, figura vitium cum ratione.

[The figure, however, occupies an intermediate position, and while it differs to some extent from both, it falls into neither category. All. . .shun grammatical error, since this is prohibited; but many use figures, since this is permitted. For between errors, that is to say barbarism and solecism, and the art of grammar, which is the excellence and rule of good speech, stand figures and schemata;. . .metaplasm. . .schema. . .According to Isidore, a figure is "an error with a reasonable cause."][34]

Here, according to a variant citation from Isidore, all figures have become "errors" or "vices," only modified by their individual justification or *ratio*. They occupy a middle ground between correct and incorrect usage and are "permitted." Metaplasmus and schema are paradigmatic.

Howard Bloch rightly comments, "the idea of metaphor connotes alien-
ation, denaturalization, translocation, or usurpation of linguistic property."
More reductively, however, Bloch associates this with a "nominalist or
modal grammar," "disruptive of any naturalized attachment of word to
physical property (and tending, therefore, toward a supplemental play of
substitutions)." He contrasts this "nominalist" version of language with an
"early medieval grammar" of "proper" signification and goes on influen-
tially to argue that such a nominalist perspective is characteristic of the
troubadour lyric and, partially at least, of Old French romance.[35] But it is
not necessary to read classical and medieval theories of figuration – or
Derridean "supplemental substitution" – exclusively in terms of the
disjuncture between sign and signified. Reiterating and supplanting, they
undoubtedly constitute the "subversive movement of replacement," but
they are also constantly generative of language and its provisional claims to
meaning.

Nor, in these theories of figuration, are "proper" and "figured" language
so categorically opposed as Bloch suggests. The "proper" and the "figured"
here represent different degrees of linguistic marking and are inevitably
formulated and defined in negotiation with each other. Indeed, if these
theories of figuration are suggestive it may be because they define
figuration in relation to several differently marked categories of medieval
grammar and philosophy, of which proper signification is only one.
Figuration is sited in an unstable relation both to "correct" and "incorrect"
usage. It can substitute for either of them. Potentially identified with each,
it can also be differentiated from each of them, and is thus always
potentially a "deviation" which turns away from both. In a remarkable
passage, Kaster proposes that, for the commentators on the poets, figures
exist in a "no-man's-land" between several opposed notions: figures
"commonly mark the boundary between two opposing ideas ... but at the
same time leave it porous or vague" (*Guardians of Language*, p. 175). Kaster
has in mind oppositions such as that between commentary and prescription, rhetoric and grammar, but also *antiqui* and *nos*, authority and correct
usage. Implicit in these last is the opposition error and proper speech,
perhaps even lies and truth. Figuration, then, is the unstable site where the
grammarians negotiate and hold in play a series of extreme polarizations.
The figure itself cannot be exclusively characterized in terms of any one of
these polarizations.

And, in this respect, figuration seems to act much like poetry. Poetry too slips uneasily between the disciplines of grammar and rhetoric, between authority and correct usage, between error and "proper" speech, between lies and truth. Its figures provide, as Kaster says, "buffer zones" at the meeting point of opposing impulses (p. 175). The uncertain space between the grammatical error and the figure is a main site at which rhetorical notions of poetic license evolve. Sometimes formal necessities such as meter are adduced to excuse the use of figures. But sometimes poetic license seems to require no such justification.

In the influential fourth-century commentary on the *Aeneid* attributed to Servius, the author acknowledges as a matter of course "frequenter. . . variant fabulas poetae" ("frequently the poets vary fables").[36] His use of the verb *variare*, to "diversify, variegate, change," argues for an intentionalized exegetical relation between poets and their predecessors or poetic materials.[37] Poetic invention always has a relational dimension. Homer "suppresses" or "remains silent" about things which do not accord with his version of the tale's heroism (1.487; 1.490); elsewhere he asserts something that others consider a lie (6.484). Similarly, when Virgil describes the gate of Dis, Servius comments, "in this place, however, he has followed Homer; only in this he differs, that Homer. . .whereas he. . ." (6.893). Virgil also changes the story of Achilles: "the poet changed this as unworthy of a heroic poem" (1.474).

These narrative changes cannot be separated from more localized forms of poetic change. At 2.268 Servius comments that Virgil refers to the beginning of the night, although later, at 4.522, when Dido cannot sleep, Virgil will refer to the whole of the night: "descriptiones sane pro rerum qualitate vel tenduntur vel corripiuntur: illo enim loco protentio ad invidiam pertinet Didonis vigiliarum" ("descriptions are undoubtedly drawn out or abbreviated according to the nature of the event; in this place the length of the night relates to Dido's reluctance to lie awake" [2.268]). When Venus orders an unpropitious sea voyage, she is called the "daughter of Dione," but when the poet associates her with a fortunate one, "Virgil says that she was engendered out of the sea" (3.19; reference to *Aeneid* 5.801). Narratives of the gods are, after all, an important site for poetic license; when Jupiter is escorted out of the palace of Olympus, *Servius Danielis* remarks, *"poetice mores hominum ad deos refert: ut magistratum deducant"* ("in the poetic manner, he applies human conduct to the gods, so that they escort him like a magistrate").[38] Such mutations of story and descriptive technique are what constitute writing *poetice*.

Figuration, oblique and hidden methods of signification, are all part of this process. When Virgil describes the evening sky as *clausus* ("closed"), Servius extends the figure: it is "more poetico, qui dicunt caelum per noctem claudi et aperiri per diem" ("in the poetic manner, [for] the poets speak of the sky being closed by the night and being opened by the day" [1.374]). Elsewhere he remarks on the animate agencies implied by this figure, "poetarum enim est elementorum habitum dare numinibus" ("it is the practice of poets to attribute the condition of the elements to the gods [1.254]). The cave in which Aeolus encloses the winds is doubly figured, also in a manner which anthropomorphizes the winds. The cave is a *carcer* ("prison"): "translatio est per poeticam licentiam facta. *carcer* autem est undecumque prohibemur exire" ("this is a metaphor according to poetic license. A *prison* is a place from which we cannot depart"). But he notes that, used in the plural, this word also refers to the barriers which hold back chariots at the races. Although Virgil has used the singular form, Servius implies that he alludes by license to this second meaning, likening the winds to chariots or charioteers at the arena: "licet plerumque usurpet poeta" ("it is often permitted for the poet to break the rules" [1.54]).

Servius uses a range of vocabulary to allude to the figural or indirect manner in which the poet writes. When Juno "strives for and cherishes [a hope]," the poet "figurate dixit" ("spoke figuratively" [1.18]; an allusion to Phoebus at *Aeneid* 3.251), "colorate tangit historiam" ("alludes by a figure to the myth" [of the harpies]).[39] Connected to this is "hidden" allusion, so when Anchises refers to "the cradle of our race" on Mount Ida, "latenter dat gloriam Troianis dicens, eos a diis originem ducere" ("in a veiled manner he glorifies the Trojans by saying that their origins were divine" [3.105; also 9.76]). All these allusions involve obliquity or indirection: Turnus says he will fight alone, telling the weary Latins they can watch, and Servius comments "latenter eos ignaviae arguit" ("in a hidden manner he accuses them of cowardice" [12.15]); later on *Servius Danielis* describes Turnus' speech as spoken *oblique* ("obliquely" [12.229]). When Achaemenides claims that it would have been better to be killed by men than the Cyclops, "oblique loquitur: nam vult ostendere, hominum hanc non esse crudelitatem" ("he speaks indirectly: for he wants to show that this was not the cruelty of men" [3.606]). Similarly, *Servius Danielis* uses the term *figurate* when he discusses Anchises' use of horses instead of oxen as an omen of war, and *oblique* for Virgil's use of a term such as *armenta* ("herds") to avoid saying *boves* ("oxen" [*Servius Danielis* 3.537]).

Linked to these ideas is that of brief allusion, "per transitum" ("in passing"). When Aeolus "soothes" the passions of the winds, he does so "ut per transitum ostenderet" ("to show in passing") that the vices of nature can only be modified, not changed (1.57). Such reference "per transitum" is often extremely oblique: when Virgil remarks that "neither two bulls' hides nor the trusty corselet with double scales of gold" could prevent a pike from killing Bitias (*Aeneid* 9.706–07), Servius adds, "bene autem per transitum eius arma descripsit" ("in passing he has described his armor well" [9.703]). Like amplification, abbreviation may also be a means of poetic indirection or obscurity.

One verb which recurs in these contexts is *tangere*. This verb can mean to "touch upon," "mention," "refer to"; it has connotations of lightness, brevity, and indirection.[40] Servius uses *tangere* to describe poetic reference to fables as well as to history, natural science, or philosophy. It always seems to indicate the poet's distance, detachment, even his power to choose, from these various materials or discourses without any obligation to employ them as they are customarily used in their original contexts – so the text *"latenter tangit,"* "clam tangit" ("alludes in a hidden manner," "secretly alludes" [*Servius Danielis* 1.41; Servius 1.363]). Such allusions may be read as purposely ambiguous, as when Virgil "aut latenter proditionem tangit. . .aut virtutem eius vult ostendere" ("either he touches in a hidden manner on the treachery of Aeneas. . .or he wants to show his virtue" [1.488]). "Touching upon" is a characteristically inexplicit, suggestive, or insinuating mode. Of the Palladium, "Vergilius ex parte tangit" ("Virgil in part alludes to it") but "Varro plenissime dicit" ("Varro speaks most fully about it" [2.166]). Elsewhere, for Virgil to "touch on a history in passing" is to write "more suo" ("in his [characteristic] manner" [1.443]). Figural obliquity or obscurity are expected of the poet. So when Aeneas' mother "shows the way" over the sea:

hoc loco per transitum tangit historiam, quam per legem artis poeticae aperte non potest ponere. nam Varro in secundo divinarum dicit ["]ex quo de [ ]Troia est egressus Aeneas, Veneris eum per diem cotidie stellam vidisse."

[In this place Virgil touches in passing on a story which, according to the law of poetry, he cannot write openly. For Varro in the second book of *Human and Divine Antiquities* says that "from the time that Aeneas left Troy, he saw the star of Venus throughout each day."]   (1.382)

"By the law of poetry," poets cannot write in the "open" manner (*aperte*) implicitly here attributed to other writers such as historians (or mythographers; see n. 39).

Such remarks on poetic figuration can be read in relation to overtly allegorizing interpretations of passages of the poem.[41] After all, at 3.349 *Servius Danielis* remarks effusively *"unde apparet divinum poetam aliud agentem verum semper attingere"* ("from which it transpires that, while doing something else, the divine Virgil always touches on the truth"). This apparent claim for the universality of decipherable allegory in the *Aeneid* is, however, contradicted at other points in Servius and *Servius Danielis* (see below). Here I wish to foreground the observation that it is characteristic of poetry to "do something else," especially in contrast to truer languages. Sometimes this means reading poetry as an extended recuperable allegory. But sometimes this means reading poetry in ways not constrained by truth requirements.

So the "tacita luna" of 2.255 "aut more poetico noctem significat, aut physicam rationem dixit" ("either signifies night in the poetic manner, or it has described a natural phenomenon"). It may refer to the astrological *ratio* that the moon is the quietest of all the sounding spheres, or it may be a poetic figure for night, by which, as Servius says later, the sky "is silenced" (*tacetur* [3.515]). Later Servius asks why Jupiter holds up scales during the last fight of Aeneas and Turnus, since he cannot but know the outcome; he offers a possible philosophical explanation, but admits the possibility that "poetice dictum est et ratione caret" ("it is said poetically and has no philosophical cause"). He concludes by noting that the detail is *translatum* ("carried over") from another who has poetic license, Homer (12.725).

When Virgil describes the underworld and its doors open to allow spirits to return to the upper air, Servius explains that some readers understand Virgil's underworld to be the earth under the planets and read it allegorically. "According to the high knowledge of the philosophers" the open doors of Dis signify the possibility of souls returning to the higher spheres. But there is an alternative: "aut poetice dictum est" ("or it is said poetically"), for Lucretius teaches that the underworld does not exist (6.127). Later Servius will make it clear that in this license Virgil is following Homer (6.893). When Aeneas asks if many do return "to the sky," Servius adds:

Miscet philosophiae figmenta poetica et ostendit tam quod est vulgare, quam quod continet veritas et ratio naturalis. nam secundum poetas hoc dicit: credendum est animas ab inferis posse ad corpora? ut *caelum* superos intellegamus, id est nostram vitam. secundum philosophos vero hoc dicit: credendum est animas corporis contagione pollutas ad caelum reverti?

[He mingles poetical fictions with philosophy and offers as many popular views as to what is provided by truth and the natural order. For according to the poets, Aeneas says: "can it be believed that souls can return from the underworld to their bodies?" By *sky* we understand the people above, that is, human life. According to the philosophers, he says this: "can it be believed that souls contaminated by the corruption of the body can return to the heavens?"] (6.719)

Alongside these allegorizing glosses in the language of ethics and philosophy, then, there is a "poetic" and "popular" *figmentum*, indifferent to its truth status, unrepentantly figurative and narrative.

At other points the commentary observes without any apparent condemnation how Virgil's text differs unrecuperably from truer discourses or the *"res vera"* (*Servius Danielis* 1.651; Servius, 6.288; 6.770). On Juno's "sorrow," *Servius Danielis* recalls an earlier writer on the impassability of the gods: "bene philosophice dubitavit" ("from a philosophical point of view [the commentator] has doubted this" [1.9]). Elsewhere, commenting on Virgil's anthropomorphic Jupiter "pondering human cares in his heart," Servius notes that either he speaks according to Stoic views about the caring gods, or he is exploiting *"poetica licentia"* in contradicting the Epicureans (1.227; also 2.689). Even if the poet is repeating a philosophical truth, after all, it is in the context of myths about the gods which were by and large understood not to accord overtly with philosophical truths. When repeating the teachings of philosophy, in other words, the poet does not have to treat them according to philosophical criteria.

The same can be said for Virgil's *ad hoc* use of geographical and historical truths. When Virgil appropriates a true geographical description to describe the port of Carthage, for instance, he is doing it to disguise his own inventive "feigning":

Topothesia est, id est fictus secundum poeticam licentiam locus. ne autem videatur penitus a veritate discedere, Hispaniensis Carthaginis portum descripsit.

[This is *topothesia*, that is, a place feigned/refigured according to poetic license. So that he should not appear to have utterly left the truth, however, he has described the port of the Spanish Carthage.] (1.159)

Here certain "truths" are employed to obscure the swerve from the truth implicit in the figure of *topothesia*. Elsewhere, referring to the historical explanations for Ascanius' cognomen, Servius says:

ab hac autem historia ita discedit Vergilius, ut aliquibus locis ostendat, non se per ignorantiam, sed per artem poeticam hoc fecisse. . .sic autem omnia contra hanc historiam ficta sunt, ut illud ubi dicitur Aeneas vidisse Carthagin[e]m, cum eam constet ante LXX annos urbis Romae conditam. inter excidium vero Troiae et ortum urbis Romae anni inveniuntur CCCXL.

[Now, Virgil departs from this history in such a way as to show in several places that he has done so not through ignorance but according to poetic art. . .in the same way all [these] things have been devised in opposition to this history: such as where Aeneas is said to have seen Carthage, when it is agreed that Carthage was established seventy years before [the founding] of the city of Rome. In fact 340 years intervene between the destruction of Troy and the rise of the city of Rome.] (1.267)

Virgil "turns away," "departs," from Cato's history, though when it is to his purpose later on, he will cite the history that he suppresses here. Virgil's relation to history is itself changeable, sometimes deferring it, sometimes endorsing it, constantly reshaping it. This could well illustrate the traditional view that poetry mixes truth and fiction; but it also describes an endemically refigural poetic practice.

Servius can use notions of truth to highlight Virgil's poetic license. When Venus talks to herself, he comments, "hoc fictum est. . .unde sciret poeta?" ("this is feigned. . .how could the poet know it?" [1.86]). Here he appeals to a historical notion of really observed event and yet he does so in the context of a mythic – and hence unobservable – narrative. Here Servius too is playing poetic games with notions of truth, in which the figure of observed history appears only to assert the figurally inventive nature of Virgil's narrative. It is scarcely surprising that the *Servius Danielis* contradicts its own remark about Virgil's constant reference to the truth: *"in carminibus quaedam nec ad subtilitatem nec ad veritatem exigenda sunt"* ("in poems certain things are not to be made to conform to strict interpretation or truth").[42]

One aspect of the poet's right to choose between different versions is the right not to choose at all (see n. 12 above). The view that poetry is open-ended and polysemous is implicit in the commentators' multiple glosses on single texts, and the notion of poetic agnosticism intentionalizes this polysemy within the poet. Sometimes Servius attributes some innuendo to

Virgil's agnosticism, remarking of Anius and Anchises, "the poet does not say openly [*palam*] in what manner they were friends" (3.82). Often, however, Virgil's agnosticism is read as suggestive but evasive. To speak of Crete as "medio ponto" at 3.104 may mean "far from the land," but as Crete stands at the meeting point of four seas, it may also mean *"medio pontorum*, quod Latinitas non recepit ("*in the middle of the seas*, which was not acceptable Latin" [3.104]). When Virgil refers to the "longa oblivia" imbibed from Lethe before the spirit leaves the underworld, Servius comments that, according to the poets, the spirit forgets things past and, according to the philosophers, the future; "medium tenet dicendo 'oblivia'" ("Virgil takes the middle position by [just] saying 'forgetfulness'" [6.714]).

The notion of uncertain knowledge or opinion is integrally associated with poetic license. Servius replies to critics of the passage where Jupiter changes the Trojan fleet into sea nymphs, and comments, "figmentum hoc licet poeticum sit" ("it is acceptable for this to be a poetic fiction"). Of the word *fertur* ("it is said") used at 9.82, *Servius Danielis* adds: *"sane quidam 'fertur' reprehendunt, quod dicendo auctoritatem rei detraxerit. alii laudant, quod dicendo 'fertur' incredibili rei auctoritatem dare noluit"* ("doubtless some criticize *it is said*, because by saying this the poet has undermined the authority of the event; others praise it, because by saying it he has refused to attribute authority to this unbelievable event" [9.81]). Right at the beginning of the commentary, however, Servius himself makes the connection between uncertain opinion and poetry: Juno's love "is said" to be for Carthage, *fertur*:

et ingenti arte vergilius, ne in rebus fabulosis aperte utatur poetarum licentia, quasi opinionem sequitur et per transitum poetico utitur more.

[and, so that he should not openly use poetic license in matters of myth, Virgil [speaks] with great art as if he follows opinion and [only] in passing uses the poetic mode.] (1.15)

Uncertain knowledge is here an artful figure of poetic license.

This rewriterliness is remarkably akin to that attributed to Sinon deceiving the Trojans. On the one hand, he mingles true and false narratives: "praemitt[i]t vera et sic falsa subiung[i]t" ("he first speaks truths and in this way he tacks on lies" [2.81]). He speaks "sub falso crimine proditionis. et rem notam per transitum dicit" ("under a false accusation of treachery; and yet he touches in passing on a known fact" [2.83]). This "good art of lying," as Servius calls it, is already reminiscent of traditionally recognized descriptions of poetry. On the other hand, Sinon's speech can also be seen as an exercise in uncertainty: "et sciendum ex hac historia partem dici, partem supprimi" ("it should be noted that part of this story is told, part suppressed" [2.81]). Sinon "medium se praebet: nam nec negat, nec confirmat eos navigasse" ("places himself in the middle, neither denying nor confirming that they have sailed" [2.136]). When Servius concludes "artis est in argumentorum angustia incertis uti sermonibus" ("it is artful to use ambiguous language at the awkward moments of narrative" [2.136]) he could be describing a Servian poetics of refiguration and evasion.

These views are also available in later medieval commentaries on Lucan's *Pharsalia*. The underlying assumption of all these glosses is that the poets say things in ways "other" than commentators. A typical passage from the widely disseminated twelfth-century commentator Arnulf of Orleans illustrates the degree to which paraphrase dominates his gloss: "as if he should say. . .And so, therefore, construe. . .he says *iacent* because. . .that is. . .that is. . .this is to say briefly. . ."; elsewhere Arnulf introduces a gloss with the words "si aperte dicat. . ." ("if he were to speak openly. . .").[43]

This poetic other-speaking is both figured and licensed. The *Commenta Bernensia*, preserved in a tenth-century manuscript, notes how Lucan calls the North wind by the name of the South and says that water is "punished"; such refiguring is by *"poetica licentia."*[44] Another commentary, partly transcribed by Karl Weber, says, "per poeticam phantasiam dat sensum inanimatae rei" ("through poetic imagination he animates an inanimate object").[45] And a twelfth-century commentary, also transcribed by Weber, sometimes attributed to Anselm of Laon, remarks: "in descriptionibus locorum fingit, inde vocatus est poeta" ("he invents in descriptions of places, and from this he is called a poet"); "loquitur de praeteritis quasi futura essent; ita enim solent loqui poetae" ("he speaks about past things as if they were in the future; poets usually speak in this way").[46] According to Arnulf of Orléans in the twelfth century, to speak of the trees touching the sky is "poetica yperbole" (3.246). Arnulf also notes other indirect poetic modes. When Lucan refers to Nero's coming as a wonderful thing, "hoc dicit oblique et derisorie" ("he says this indirectly and scornfully" [1.33; also 1.35]). Lucan's mention of the grand funeral that Pompey did not have incites the comment, "more suo per remotionem ostendit Lucanus que solent fieri in potentum funeribus" ("in his [usual] manner, Lucan shows by negation what usually occurs at the funerals of the powerful").[47]

According to Arnulf, Lucan is always "touching upon" truer discourses: "astronomiam tangit," "morem tangit," "physicam tangit," "causas tangit," "hec similitudo tangit Cesarem" ("this similitude alludes to Caesar" [in order: 1.641; 5.49; 8.108; 9.1040; 3.318]). And yet, unlike these other languages, poetry is characterized by its instability in relation to categories of truth. Arnulf cites Macrobius to the effect that if Lucan had said shadows "never" (*numquam*) leaned sideways at Syene, this would be incorrect; "poeticum sit et non philosophicum" ("this would be poetic and not philosophical" [2.587]). Again, it is not quite true to say that when Saturn is at the high point of the zodiac this causes floods:

Ut dicit Macrobius rem quidem tetigit sed veritatem perturbavit. Rem quidem tetigit quia ad hoc ut diluvium sit, necesse est quod Saturnus sit in summitate celi; veritatem autem non dixit quia non ideo quod est in summo celi est diluvium.

[As Macrobius says, he has indeed touched on the matter but distorted the truth. He has indeed touched on the matter because in order that there should be a flood Saturn has to be high in the sky; he has not spoken the truth, however, because it does not follow that because he is high in the sky there is a flood.][48]

Poetry effects a "distortion," a "perturbation" of the truth. Although it can be read in accordance with truer discourses, its terms are different. Sometimes it "hides" the truth: "rem tangit sed veritatem occulit" ("he touches on the matter but hides the truth" [3.247]); "hic breviter tangit unde contingat et quando exustio. Tangit autem rem sed veritatem abscondit" ("here he touches briefly on where and when a fire may catch. He touches on this but hides the truth" [1.655]). In the same line, we might note, Arnulf also notes that poets "touch" in the same allusive manner on fables or myths. Although Arnulf takes a darker view of fantastical poetic inventions than Servius – *"licentia* ideo dicit quia talis scientia potius est abusio quam usus, unde abusiones poetarum licentie dicuntur" ("Lucan calls this *licentia* because such 'knowledge' is more an abuse than a proper use, for which reason the abuses of the poets are called licenses" [6.436; also 9.623; 10.282]) – his view and that of the other medieval Lucan commentators echoes that of the Servian commentary.

And, as in Servius, there are also more non-committal, open aspects to this poetry. When two interpretations of a fable are possible, Arnulf instructs the reader to choose between them, for "the poet touches upon both possibilities of these fables" (2.716). If the mode of more truth-oriented discourses is to "affirm" (*affirmare*), then Arnulf agrees with Philip Sidney that the poet "nothing affirms": Lucan mentions a *fabula* and Arnulf comments "non affirmat verum esse ut historiographus sed tangit ut poeta de sororibus Phetontis que ibi fuerunt mutate in populos, alii dicunt in alnos" ("he does not, like a historian, affirm it to be true, but like a poet he touches on [the fable] of the sisters of Phaethon who were changed into poplars there, some say alders").[49] Even the *historiographus* of myths is more concerned with questions of truth than the *poeta*. "Ponit tres opiniones more philosophi sed nullam solvit aut affirmat more poete" ("he offers three opinions in the manner of the philosopher but in the manner of the poet he neither resolves nor affirms any of them" [1.412; also 1.417–19; 9.619]). Opinion is a central version of the uncertain knowledge which characterizes this poetry, as one of the commentaries published by Weber remarks: "proprium est poetarum, ut non unam sectam solummodo, sed diversorum opiniones suo carmini inserant" ("it is typical of poets not to hold to one school of thought only but to insert the opinions of many schools into their poem").[50] For Arnulf of Orléans as for Servius, moreover, opinion is a rhetorical stratagem integrally associated with poetic license: "nam si aliquid ficticii inducit, non ex sua parte sed ex aliorum hoc inducit, apponit enim vel ut perhibent, vel ut dicunt, vel ut memorant" ("for if he introduces anything fictitious, he introduces it not on his own word but on the word of others and says 'as they assert' or 'as they say' or 'as they relate'" [*accessus* p. 4]).

All these descriptions present poetry in relational terms, as highly inventive, but in interaction with real or hypothetical anterior materials. This interaction is a rhetorical and figural process, frequently tending toward the indirect, oblique, and obscure. Even elucidatory commentary, after all, "covers" over texts even as it clarifies them.

I shall conclude with the example of Hugh of St. Victor. Although he does not approve of poetry, he better represents the view of poetry discussed here than a contemporary of his who has been praised by modern critics for his approval of poetry, the commentator on the *Aeneid* once known as Bernardus Silvestris.[51] Hugh seems to illustrate particularly well how views formulated in one context and according to one ideological project can be appropriated in other contexts and as a part of even ideologically opposed projects.

In the *Didascalicon* Hugh of St. Victor condemns poetry as an "appendage" to the arts of Christian philosophy.[52] But his description of poetry is ambivalent. He claims that nothing to be learned from the songs of the poets is not also available in the arts, which suggests that the relation of poetry to the arts is one of continuity as well as difference.

Quicumque ad scientiam pertingere cupit, si relicta veritate artium reliquis se implicare voluerit, materiam laboris, ut non dicam infinitam, plurimam inveniat et fructum exiguum.

[Whoever wishes to attain knowledge but, abandoning the truth of the arts, chooses to get involved in those fields that are left, will find great – not to say infinite – labor and very little reward.]   (3.4 [p. 55]; my translation)

Here the verb "se implicare" can signify "to be perplexed, confounded," but also "to be entangled, involved." Ostensibly a condemnation, it also describes how the reader of poetry is imbricated in the complexities of the poetic text. Similarly, the criticism implied in "materiam laboris, ut non dicam infinitam, plurimam" is undermined by the high value accorded elsewhere in this work to the labor of learning and, indeed, to the textual imbrication of the Bible: "thus also is honey more pleasing because enclosed in the comb, and whatever is sought with greater effort (*exercitio*) is also found with greater desire."[53]

The notion of poetry as bearing an oblique relation to the discourses of truth, as figural, entangling, labor-intensive, and sometimes obscure is supported by the rhetorical view of poetry we have found expressed in Hugh. Poets:

et brevem materiam longis verborum ambagibus extendere consueverunt, et facilem sensum perplexis sermonibus obscurare. vel etiam diversa simul compilantes, quasi de multis coloribus et formis, unam picturam facere.

[often used to draw out a brief matter with extended verbal digressions and darken easy meanings with intricate speeches, compiling even opposite things together to make one picture out of many figures and shapes.]

(3.4 [p. 54]; my translation)

Poetry mutates all that it touches. These lines argue for linguistic opacity and polysemy as the defining feature of poetry. Poetry is *perplexus* – "ambiguous," "obscure," but only because it is "involved," "intricate." Poets make one "picture," but by compiling diversity. "Compilation" may imply a forceful "grabbing together,"[54] but it may also imply a degree of detachment: "compilers" can incorporate texts and opinions into poetry with or without making them their own. Poetry and the appendage arts "quaedam ab artibus discerpta sparsim et confuse attingunt" ("touch on certain things torn from the arts, in a scatter, higgledy-piggledy"). Like *tangere*, of which it is a derivative, *attingere* can denote "to deal with," "take on," and again "to touch upon in speaking," "mention lightly"; it also has physical dimensions, meaning "to touch."[55] *Servius Danielis* uses it in place of *tangere* (3.133; 3.349). Hugh's *attingere* may invoke notions of physical "touch" – a contact that is particular, imagistic, impactive, appropriative ("ab artibus discerpta"). But it may also denote the brevity, lack of systematics, or conceptual remove with which the poet alludes to phenomena ("sparsim et confuse"). When Hugh cites Virgil to argue that poetry is as far from philosophy "Lenta salix quantum pallenti cedit olivae" ("as the bending willow gives way to the pale olive" [3.4 [p. 54]]), he may, in the mobility and evasiveness of the willow, figure those of poetry.

Against Hugh we could cite Petrarch and Boccaccio. In the defense of poetic "obscurity" they use all the biblical material whose status is so ambiguous in the *Didascalicon*. Although Boccaccio's case also involves reading poetry as a decodable allegory, he also draws on the views of the grammarians about "figurae dictionum" ("figures of diction") and "peregrina vocabula" ("alien words"). To those who object to such poetic *obscuritas*, he says:

quid aliud dicam, non habeo, nisi ut gramaticales iterum scolas repetant, pedagogi ferulam subeant, studeant, discantque, quid veterum auctoritate circa talia poetis licentie datum, scrupulosiusque scrutentur, preter vulgaria atque domestica que sint etiam peregrina!

[my only advice is for them to go back to the grammar-schools, bow to the teacher's cane, study, and learn what license ancient authority granted the poets in such matters, and give particular attention to the things that are, besides common and homely, alien to boot.][56]

But Hugh's description of poetry is also interesting because he is opposed to poetry. He illustrates the degree to which the figural view of poetry pervaded medieval clerical culture – indeed, his exclusion of poetry from the canon may actually allow him to describe it more freely.[57] His opposition to poetry as described by the grammarians certainly suggests how views formulated according to one ideology can be read according to another. It may be that in turn Hugh's description of poetry could be appropriated with or without the condemnation he wrote into it.

Although medieval grammatical teaching about poetry was formulated for the purposes of moral and scholarly recuperation, then, it seems to have had a potential significance for those writing according to other agenda – whether against Latin poetry or in favor of vernacular romance.

It was no doubt available to the great part of those vernacular writers who learned to read and write under clerical tuition. This teaching and its theories of poetry instantiate a very fruitful relationship between the medieval schools and vernacular textual culture. It is arguable that romance composition would not have developed in the way it did if it had not been catalyzed by the commentators' notions of *poetria*. Texts such as *Erec et Enide*, the *Brut*, or the *Lais* of Marie de France address secular questions about aristocratic militarism and sexuality, questions almost entirely repressed in the schools. They do so by evading schools categories of correctness and incorrectness, truth and falsehood. Like poetry, they are narratives characterized in terms of rhetorico-exegetical change or refiguration. They work not by overt statement or logical argument but by oblique and frequently intertextual practices of descriptive emphasis, bias, and suggestion.

These academic theories of poetry illustrate the heterogeneity of teaching within the schools and the potential for internal difference within that teaching. It may have taken a forceful vernacular appropriation to render this particular internal difference radical, but the materials here appropriated are firmly written into classical and medieval grammatical teaching. The texts we have looked at represent an all-pervasive body of thought within the schools. And yet their teaching may have had textual consequences which the most ingenious glossator could not have rendered safe.[58]

Notes

1 Paul Zumthor, *Essai de poétique médiévale* (Paris: Seuil, 1972), especially pp. 65–75; Michelle A. Freeman, *The Poetics of* Translatio studii *and* Conjointure: *Chrétien de Troyes's Cligés* (Lexington, Ky.: French Forum, 1979); Matilda Tomaryn Bruckner, "Intertextuality," in Norris J. Lacy, Douglas Kelly, and Keith Busby, eds., *The Legacy of Chrétien de Troyes*, 2 vols (Amsterdam: Rodolpi, 1987–8), 1: 223–65: Douglas Kelly, *The Art of*

Medieval French Romance (Madison: University of Wisconsin Press, 1992), introduction and chs. 1–4.

2 Chrétien de Troyes, *Erec et Enide*, ed. Mario Roques (Paris: Champion, 1973), lines 9–14; translated by D. D. R. Owen, in Chrétien de Troyes, *Arthurian Romances* (London: Dent, 1987), p. 1 (altered).

3 Wace, *Le Roman de Brut*, ed. Ivor Arnold, 2 vols (Paris: Société des anciens textes français, 1938–40), lines 9793–8; my translation.

4 *Les Lais de Marie de France*, ed. Jean Rychner (Paris: Champion, 1971), lines 9–20; translated by Robert Hanning and Joan Ferrante, *The Lais of Marie de France* (Durham, N.C.: Labyrinth Press, 1978), p. 28.

5 Jean Frappier in Hans Robert Jauss and Erich Köhler, eds., *Grundriss der romanischen Literaturen des Mittelalters* (Heidelberg: Carl Winter, 1972–), IV/ 1: 146–47 (henceforth I will refer to *GRLMA*); Kelly, *Medieval French Romance*, chs. 5 and 6.

6 Paul Zumthor in *GRMLA*, IV/1: 72; Peter Haidu, *Lion-queue-coupée. L'écart symbolique chez Chrétien de Troyes* (Geneva: Droz, 1972); Howard Bloch, *Etymologies and Genealogies: A Literary Anthropology of the French Middle Ages* (Chicago: University of Chicago Press, 1983), chs. 5 and 6.

7 Richard Hamilton Green, "Dante's 'Allegory of the Poets' and the Medieval Theory of Poetic Fiction," *Comparative Literature* 9 (1957): 124–25; Glending Olson, "Making and Poetry in the Age of Chaucer," *Comparative Literature* 31 (1979): 272–90. I use Latin *poetria* and English *poetry* interchangeably in this sense.

8 Tony Hunt, "The Rhetorical Background to the Arthurian Prologue: Tradition and the Old French Vernacular Prologues," *Forum for Modern Language Studies* 6 (1970): 6–10; Kelly, *Medieval French Romance*, pp. 68–69.

9 See n. 1; on the rhetorical, contestive nature of exegesis and its implications for vernacular literature, Rita Copeland, *Rhetoric, Hermeneutics, and Translation in the Middle Ages. Academic Traditions and Vernacular Texts* (Cambridge: Cambridge University Press, 1991). On grammatical commentary in the classroom, Gernot R. Wieland, "The Glossed Manuscript: Classbook or Library Book?" *Anglo-Saxon England* 14 (1985): 153–73.

10 Zumthor, *GRLMA*, I: 75; also pp. 61–78; Freeman, *The Poetics of* Translatio studii, introduction; Bruckner, "Intertextuality," 240–45; Kelly, *Medieval French Romance*, ch. 2.

11 R. B. C. Huygens, ed., *Accessus ad auctores. Bernard d'Utrecht. Conrad d'Hirsau, Dialogus super auctores* (Leiden: Brill, 1970), pp. 51, 59, 75, 88; A. J. Minnis and A. B. Scott, eds., with David Wallace, *Medieval Literary Theory and Criticism c. 1100–c. 1375. The Commentary-Tradition* (Oxford: Clarendon, 1988), ch. 4; Mark Chinca, *History, Fiction, Verisimilitude. Studies*

in the Poetics of Gottfried's Tristan (London: Modern Humanities Research Association, 1993), ch. 4.

12 Paule Demats (for whom this is poetic "corruption," "déformation"), *Fabula: Trois études de mythographie antique et médiévale* (Geneva: Droz, 1973), ch. 1 (citations pp. 13, 35); Stanley F. Bonner, *Education in Ancient Rome: From the Elder Cato to the Younger Pliny* (London: Methuen, 1977), p. 237; D. C. Feeney, *The Gods in Epic: Poets and Critics of the Classical Tradition* (Oxford: Clarendon, 1991), ch. 1; Chinca, *History, Fiction, Verisimilitude*, ch. 4.

13 Judson Boyce Allen, *The Ethical Poetic of the Later Middle Ages. A Decorum of Convenient Distinction* (Toronto: University of Toronto Press, 1982); Minnis and Scott, *Medieval Literary Theory*, chs. 1, 2, 4, 7, 8.

14 Christopher C. Baswell, "'Figures of Olde Werk': Visions of Virgil in Later Medieval England," Dissertation, (Yale, 1983), p. 47, on grammatical commentary, ch. 1; Minnis and Scott, *Medieval Literary Theory*, chs. 1, 2, 8. On the identification and decoding of extreme or "allegorical" figuration in the commentaries, see n. 17 below.

15 Martin Irvine, *The Making of Textual Culture. "Grammatica" and Literary Theory, 350–1100* (Cambridge: Cambridge University Press, 1994), pp. 246–47; Copeland, *Rhetoric, Hermeneutics, and Translation*, pp. 81–82. On the classical *scholia*, see Demats, *Fabula*, ch. 1; Feeney, *The Gods in Epic*, ch. 1.

16 Chinca, *History, Fiction, Verisimilitude*, ch. 4.

17 Here the term *poetry* "means the recourse to allegory": Winthrop Wetherbee, *Platonism and Poetry in the Twelfth Century* (Princeton: Princeton University Press, 1972); citation p. 16 (adapted); M.-D. Chenu, "The Symbolist Mentality," in his *Nature, Man and Society in the Twelfth Century*, selected and trans. Jerome Taylor and Lester K. Little (Chicago: University of Chicago Press, 1968), pp. 99–145; also Kelly, *Medieval French Romance*, pp. 255–62; Olson, "Making and Poetry", 278; 282. For medieval allegorizing commentary and theories of *integumentum* see the bibliography in Copeland, *Rhetoric, Hermeneutics, and Translation*, p. 247 (n. 57); also Baswell, "'Figures of Olde Werk,'" chs. 2, 3; Irvine, *Textual Culture*, ch. 6 (in allegory, "one can distinguish the level of expression or rhetorical form from the level of content or additional signification, the signifier and the signified" [p. 248]).

18 See John of Salisbury, *Ioannis Saresberiensis Metalogicon libri IIII*, ed. C. C. J. Webb (Oxford: Clarendon, 1929), 1.5.21–25.

19 Michel Zink, "Héritage rhétorique et nouveauté littéraire dans le 'roman antique' en France au moyen âge: remarques sur l'expression de l'amour dans le roman d'*Eneas*," *Romania* 105 (1984): 261, 268; Nancy Freeman-Regalado, "*La Chevalerie Celestiel*: Spiritual Transformations of Secular

Romance in *La Queste del Saint Graal*," in Kevin Brownlee and Marina Scordilis Brownlee, eds., *Romance. Generic Transformation from Chrétien de Troyes to Cervantes* (Hanover and London: University Press of New England, 1985), pp. 96–101 and references.

20 See Peter Dronke, *Fabula: Explorations into the Uses of Myth in Medieval Platonism* (Leiden: Brill, 1974), ch. 1. Irvine foregrounds the notion of decipherable "allegory" and then elides it with the view that all interpretation is "allegorical" (*Textual Culture*, pp. 121, 133, 245); a brief discussion does not in my view do justice to a complex of very different views of epistemological control which can be implied by these positions (pp. 265–71).

21 Nicolette Zeeman, "Alterations of Language," *Paragraph* 13 (1990): 222–26.

22 Chinca writes of the commentators' "underlying feeling that all figurative language is a form of fiction and appropriate to poetry" (*History, Fiction, Verisimilitude*, p. 73; also pp. 71–76); for a reading of all poetic figuration as fundamentally allegorical, see: Chenu, "The Symbolist Mentality"; Irvine, *Textual Culture*.

23 *Isidori Hispalensis. . .etymologiarum sive originum libri XX*, ed. W. M. Lindsay, 2 vols (Oxford: Clarendon, 1911), 8.7.10; *Rabani Mauri De universo* (*Patrologia latina*, 111: 9–614), XV.ii (col. 419); *Speculum doctrinale Vincentii* [Venice: Hermann Liechtensein, 1494], III.cx (f. 48r); Petrus Berchorius, *De formis figurisque deorum, Reductorium morale, Liber XV, cap. i*, ed. J. Engels, 3 vols (Utrecht: Institut voor Laat Latijn, 1960–66), Prologus (p. 1).

24 *Lucii Caecilii Firmiani Lactantii Divinarum Institutionum septem libri* (PL 6: 111–822), 1.11 (col. 171); my translation; see also the rest of this chapter and 2.11 (cols. 313–14). Chinca comments on Lactantius' "exclusive identification of fiction with ornamental language" (*History, Fiction, Verisimilitude*, p. 75); also Demats, *Fabula*, pp. 50–54; Irvine, *Textual Culture*, pp. 239–40.

25 Aristotle, *The Poetics*, trans. W. Hamilton Fyfe in *Aristotle. The Poetics. "Longinus" on the Sublime. Demetrius on Style*, Loeb Classical Library (Cambridge, Mass.: Harvard University Press, 1982), 22.1–7 (1458a); Quintilian, *Institutio oratoria*, trans. H. E. Butler, Loeb Classical Library, 4 vols (Cambridge, Mass.: Harvard University Press, 1966–69), 1.5.11; 10.1.28–29; Servius, *In Vergilii Aeneidos commentarii* in *Servii grammatici in Vergilii carmina commentarii*, eds. George Thilo and Hermann Hagen, 3 vols (Leipzig: Teubner, 1881–87), I–II (annotation according to *Aeneid* line references in edition), citations at 1.251; 2.18; see also Bonner, *Education*, p. 229. Servius includes further commentary material interpolated in the (?)seventh century (henceforth *Servius Danielis* and presented in italics); on

this text, G. P. Goold, "Servius and the Helen Episode," *Harvard Studies in Classical Philology* 74 (1970): 101–21.

26 Copeland, *Rhetoric, Hermeneutics, and Translation*, pp. 11–21, 55–62.

27 H. G. Liddell and R. Scott, *A Greek-English Dictionary*, rev. H. S. Jones (Oxford: Clarendon, 1968), "τρόπος"; citation from Bonner, *Education*, p. 229. On metaphor and the figure as a substitutive "deviation," Paul Ricoeur, *The Rule of Metaphor. Multi-disciplinary Studies of the Creation of Meaning in Language*, trans. Robert Czerny (London: Routledge and Kegan Paul, 1978), pp. 18–20, 47, and study 5; Ricoeur assumes, surely unnecessarily, that such a figure conveys "no new information" (p. 20); on the notion of "common language," pp. 19–20.

28 Aristotle, *Poetics*, 22.1–7 (1458a); see Liddell and Scott, *A Greek-English Dictionary*, "μεταφορά." On this broad notion of metaphor, see Ricoeur, *The Rule of Metaphor*, p. 17.

29 Quintilian, *Institutio oratoria*, 1.5.71 (translation altered); *Donati ars grammatica* (henceforth *Ars major*) in *Grammatici latini*, ed. Heinrich Keil, 7 vols (Leipzig: Teubner, 1857–80), IV: 399; my translation. On the contrast with "proper" and "natural" language, see Bloch, *Etymologies and Genealogies*, pp. 40–54, 115–19, 159–60; Robert A. Kaster, *Guardians of Language. The Grammarian and Society in Late Antiquity* (Berkeley and Los Angeles: University of California Press, 1988), pp. 176–77.

30 Bonner, *Education*, pp. 200, 204, 228; Bloch, *Etymologies and Genealogies*, p. 116; for a more nuanced version, Kaster, *Guardians of Language*, pp. 173–75. On "poetic license" in general, Feeney, *The Gods in Epic*, ch. 1.

31 Quintilian, *Institutio oratoria*, 1.5.52 (translation altered); on barbarism, 1.5.11–13.

32 Servius on Donatus in *Grammatici Latini*, ed. Keil, IV.447; Consentius in *Grammatici Latini*, ed. Keil, V.396; Servius has a tripartite classification of error/poetic figure/proper speech (*barbarismus/metaplasmus/lexis* and *soloecismus/figura/schema* [*Commentarii*, 5.120]); see Kaster, *Guardians of Language*, pp. 173–74.

33 Donatus, *Ars major*, pp. 392–402; James J. Murphy, *Rhetoric in the Middle Ages: A History of Rhetorical Theory from Saint Augustine to the Renaissance* (Berkeley and Los Angeles: University of California Press, 1974), pp. 32–34. See also Isidore, *Etymologiarum libri XX*, 1.32–37; Martianus Capella, *De nuptiis Philologiae et Mercurii libri VIII*, ed. Adolf Dick, addenda Jean Préaux (Stuttgart: Teubner, 1969), 3.326.

34 John of Salisbury, *Metalogicon*, 1.18 (p. 45); trans. Daniel D. Mcgarry, *The Metalogicon. A Twelfth-Century Defense of the Verbal and Logical Arts of the Trivium* (Berkeley and Los Angeles: University of California Press, 1962), p. 54 (altered).

35 Bloch, *Etymologies and Genealogies*, pp. 118, 160; on early medieval grammar, pp. 34–63; on nominalist grammar, pp. 115–19, 159–60.

36 6.617. On Servius, see Kaster, *Guardians of Language*, pp. 169–97; on the importance and continued availability of Servius and Servian-derived commentaries throughout the Middle Ages, see Baswell, "'Figures of Olde Werk,'" ch. 1, especially pp. 53, 79, and n. 58; "The Medieval Allegorization of the *Aeneid*: MS Cambridge, Peterhouse 158," *Traditio* 41 (1985): 195. In the absence of corroboration from later Virgil manuscripts, later dissemination of the views here documented from Servius and *Servius Danielis* will be illustrated by the continuing presence of the same notions in later medieval commentaries on Lucan (see below).

37 See Demats, *Fabula*, pp. 28–29; in contrast, p. 33.

38 *Servius Danielis*, 10.117; compare the attribution of a body to a spirit (1.582) or the personification of inanimate phenomena (1.291; 1.420); metaphor was classified as it linked categories of the animate and the inanimate, the rational and the irrational (Quintilian, *Institutio oratoria*, 8.6.9–13).

39 3.256. On the use of the term *historia* for myth, see Bonner, *Education*, pp. 219, 261.

40 Charlton T. Lewis and Charles Short, *A Latin Dictionary* (Oxford: Clarendon, 1879), "tango," C.

41 Irvine, *Textual Culture*, p. 135.

42 *Servius Danielis*, 9.74; see Feeney, *The Gods in Epic*, pp. 38–39; also Demats, *Fabula*, p. 33.

43 *Arnulfi Aurelianensis glosule super Lucanum*, ed. B. Marti (Rome: American Academy in Rome, 1958); annotation according to *Pharsalia* line references in edition, as in the commentaries that follow; 4.674–76, 5.279. On Arnulf of Orleans, pp. xv–xxix; on the influence and dissemination of this commentary, pp. liv–lvi, lx–lxxii. On this and the following Lucan commentaries, see Berthe Marie Marti, "Literary Criticism in the Mediaeval Commentaries on Lucan," *Transactions and Proceedings of the American Philological Association* 72 (1941): 245–54; Chinca, *History, Fiction, Verisimilitude*, ch. 4.

44 *Commenta Bernensia, Scholia in Lucani Bellum civile*, ed. Hermann Usener, vol. I (Leipzig: Teubner, 1869), 3.1; 4.143.

45 Transcribed from what was MS Berlin, Königliche Bibliothek 1012 lat. fol. 35 as MS BC in *Scholiastae, Marci Annaei Lucani Pharsalia*, ed. Karl Friedrich Weber, 3 vols (Leipzig: Gerhardus Fleischer, 1828–31), III; citation at 8.197 (also compare 7.451 with Servius, *Commentarii*, 1.235). On the manuscript, see Valentin Rose, *Die Handschriften-*

Verzeichnisse der Königlichen Bibliothek zu Berlin, 2, 3 (Berlin: A. Asher, 1905), pp. 1300–03.

46 Transcribed from what was MS Berlin, Königliche Bibliothek 1016 lat. fol. 34 as MS B in *Scholiastae*, ed. Weber; citations at 3, prologue; 1.38. On this manuscript and commentary, see Rose, *Handschriften-Verzeichnisse*, pp. 1304–08; Max Manitius, *Geschichte der lateinischen Literatur des Mittelalters*, 3 vols. (Munich: C. H. Beck'sche, 1911–31), p. 238.

47 8.729; see Marti, "Literary Criticism," 248–9.

48 1.651; Macrobius, *Commentarii in somnium Scipionis*, 2.7.16; Arnulf also cites this at *Glosule* 2.587; 3.247.

49 2.410; for *affirmare* associated with *veritas*, also 6.357; compare "poetice dictum est, ne opponatur" (3.253).

50 6.608, MS BC; also Arnulf of Orleans, *Glosule* 9.301–18; 5.133–39; 10.219–58; see Marti, "Literary Criticism," 248.

51 "Bernardus" reads Virgil allegorically; the purposes he attributes to Virgil the poet are clearly identifiable in the language of the schools and, apart from the banal desire to please Caesar, they are as virtuous as those he attributes to Virgil the philosopher (*The Commentary on the First Six Books of the* Aeneid *of Virgil Commonly Attributed to Bernardus Silvestris*, eds. Julian Ward Jones and Elizabeth Frances Jones [Lincoln: University of Nebraska Press, 1977], pp. 1–2).

52 *Hugonis de Sancto Victore Didascalicon de studio legendi*, ed. Charles Henry Buttimer (Washington: Catholic University Press, 1939), 3.4. Jerome Taylor notes that the views of Hugh are opposed to the "school of Chartres" with which the "Bernardus" commentary has been associated (*The Didascalicon of Hugh of St. Victor*, trans. Jerome Taylor [New York: Columbia University Press, 1961], pp. 211–12 [n. 44]).

53 *Didascalicon*, 5.2 (p. 96); trans. Taylor, p. 121; see also *Didascalicon* 3.6; 3.12–17; 5.5; and Chenu, *Nature, Man and Society*, p. 121.

54 Irvine, *Textual Culture*, pp. 241–43.

55 Lewis and Short, *A Latin Dictionary*, "at-tingo."

56 Giovanni Boccaccio, *Genealogie deorum gentilium libri*, ed. Vincenzo Romano, 2 vols (Bari: Gius. Laterza, 1951), 14.12 (p. 716). See also Francesco Petrarca, *Invective contra medicum*, ed. Pier Giorgio Ricci (Rome: Edizioni di storia e letteratura, 1950), pp. 68–71.

57 The exclusion of poetry from the classifications of the arts does not necessarily preclude productive or benevolent views on poetry (see *The Didascalicon of Hugh of St. Victor*, trans. Taylor, p. 212 [n. 44]).

58 For invaluable criticism and advice, I thank John Henderson; also Mark Chinca, Simon Gaunt, Simon Goldhill, and Ian Robbins.

6

The science of politics and late medieval academic debate

JANET COLEMAN

What is currently considered the autonomous discourse of politics is a development of the emergence of the early modern state in Europe. In an important and perhaps surprising sense, the *autonomy* of early modern political discourse developed *outside* the university and in opposition to what the university milieu had become in the early modern period. Hobbes' scorn for the university's slavish attitude to Aristotle and other "authorities" led him to develop a theory of politics, based on human experience, that was meant to be autonomous in the sense that it drew eclectically on past thinking and yet owed nothing to the university as an institution of learning with its settled categories of discourse. But prior to the seventeenth century, politics was not a distinctive discipline with its own subject matter and methodology; it had not yet disengaged itself either from the dominance of practical moral philosophy/theology as studied in medieval universities, or from rhetorical and ethical discourse as studied in humanist schools.

In the humanist schools as in medieval universities, the discussion of the organization of human communities and of behavior considered appropriate within communities of men alongside analyses of moral right, of virtue, and of personal responsibility for one's acts, be they the acts of ruler or ruled, were still tied to ancient authoritative discourses. In the early stages of a student's education, these discourses were first confronted in the process of learning to read and write a foreign language, Latin. Students across Europe were taught to read ancient Latin texts of Holy Scripture, Roman history, Roman moralists, and the Latin Church Fathers. Using the texts of ancient Roman grammarians and rhetoricians (themselves translations and commentaries on ancient Greek theories of grammar and rhetoric), and supplementing these with Latin translations of Aristotle's rhetorical and logical treatises from the later twelfth century onwards, medieval *and* renaissance students absorbed theories about the relation between human thinking and language. They absorbed explicit (and sometimes conflicting) theories concerning the relation between reason and emotion and between persuasive speech and collective action, and they learned how to distinguish between virtuous and vicious behavior and between legitimate governance and its opposite. In this sense, medieval and renaissance students were being prepared for professions in the non-academic world in much the same ways. Education was vocational and for this reason it is appropriate to regard humanist schools as providing a very similar education, but in truncated form, to that received by students in the later medieval university arts course programs. Although we know that fifteenth-century humanists were concerned to divorce themselves from some of the methods of textual analysis of university logicians and theologians, they were still the heirs, as were medieval university students, of ways of speaking about what we would call "the ethical" and "the political" that were inherited from the ancient Roman and Greek worlds and which were transmitted in university arts courses. How they *re-interpreted* and *used* these ancient masters and their "classical" agenda is, in part, what is so significant about the *continuity* of the medieval and renaissance periods across Europe. Latin remained the language of most political theorizing during the later Middle Ages and well into the renaissance. When the vernaculars came into their own, many of the earlier scholarly Latin terms and expressions were "translated" and put to new use. But during the medieval and renaissance periods there was never a wholesale and self-conscious attempt, as there would be in the seventeenth century, to reformulate the ethical and political world from "the begin-ning," as it were, and vernacular texts always related back to the already formulated "languages" of moral discourse that were found in a wide range of authoritative Latin texts. To my mind, Machiavelli was no exception to this.[1]

When present historians of "political ideas" approach the texts of the Middle Ages they tend to study a range of discourses that collectively are called by them "political thought." For the Middle Ages, "political thought" as a category is a messy business, not least because it is everywhere and it invaded all genres. If, for the moment, we exclude those university commentaries and disputes which dealt formally with current political questions, and focus instead on a variety of other genres beyond those studied in that part of the liberal arts called "practical moral philosophy and theology" we can group texts either according to genre, or according to topic. For instance, we have numerous mirrors for princes (*de regimine principi*), numerous tracts on political ecclesiology and on the theory of powers known as *de potestate papae (et regia)*, a corpus of texts dealing with evangelical poverty, political sermons, and other such works. Most of these texts were written by men who had been educated in the university milieu and often to a rather high level, although their texts were not necessarily written for narrowly educational purposes. Rather, university graduates wrote for powerful patrons or as members of a religious order embroiled in partisan debates that were current beyond the walls of the academy. Nonetheless, what we recognize as the "languages" of their ethical and political discourses emerged out of the theoretical and practical concerns that constituted the heart of formal, university study in the fields of theology, canon and civil law, Ciceronian and other Roman rhetorical theories and practices, and Aristotelian philosophy taken in its broadest sense. In other words, ethical and political theories and practices were, in a fundamental and broader sense than we are used to, precisely what the medieval university was instituted to debate. Resultant theories of knowledge, of morals, nature, humanity, society, and the "state" varied according to whether a student or master approached these subjects through the categories of theology, Roman law, canon law, Christian Platonism, Aristotelian or Ciceronian rhetorical and logical tracts, the Latin poets, history as provided by Roman historians or by more recent chroniclers, custom and precedent. Where "ethical" discourse focused on the individual in relation to the communal whole, "political" discourse focused on the collectivity.

As Antony Black has recently observed, educated people employed several distinct "languages," that is, separate vocabularies with their own concepts, prose styles, methods of argument and criteria of judgment, standard texts, and authorities.[2] Starting with their political convictions they then deployed these various languages to bolster what they already believed. They used authorities the way they used "the past," to justify their own already held convictions. But their convictions were not uniform. That is why the various "languages" were of such use. The *theological language* of the Old and New Testaments in Jerome's Latin Vulgate translation along with the writings of the Church Fathers were drawn upon in their discussions about government and social relations, about kingship, obedience, moral responsibility, and the hierarchical relations between ruler and ruled, as well as the moral equality of all humans before God. They used the *language of feudal and customary law* supplemented by the *language of academic civil and canon lawyers* to discuss similar issues concerning government and social relations, group organization and the relation between representative heads and represented members. They used *"Ciceronian"* language (from the *De officiis* and elsewhere) and *Aristotelian language* as found in his rhetorical and logical treatises or as found in early paraphrases of his *Ethics* (Hermannus Alemannus, from Arabic *c.* 1243–44 as well as, by the 1260s, the language of the *Nicomachean Ethics* [in Grosseteste's translation]) and the *Politics* (in Moerbeke's translation) to discuss once again, social relations and government, kingship and other forms of collective rule, best constitutions interpreted in the light of their own experience, custom and precedent, moral responsibility, and the relations between ruler and ruled. And they "mixed" these different languages and cited texts from these different traditions in order to formulate answers to "ethical" and "political" questions that were on the contemporary agenda.

My aim in what follows is to discuss those aspects of the medieval university arts course which would give a student training in ethical and political discourse, and then to see how academic discourse traveled outside the arts course curriculum and was transformed to suit political conditions. Intellectual scholastic freedom of debate was, during the thirteenth and fourteenth centuries *within* academic milieux, quite astonishingly vociferous and often led to the composition of tracts that were much more topical, outspoken, and indeed dangerous than would be the case for theological and political discourse within the university from the fifteenth century onwards. At the end of this essay I shall try to explain why this came to be so, using the history of the University of Oxford as an example.

"Politica" and *"ethica"* in the twelfth-century "schools" and in the thirteenth-century universities were a part of *philosophia/theologia moralis* or *philosophia/theologia practica.*[3] Because *"politica"* did not stand alone, it is misleading to suppose that there was any *disciplinary* debate over the *status* of politics in medieval academic milieux.[4] As we shall see, the really important debate was the one between lawyers, on the one hand, and arts faculty philosophers and theologians, on the other, over who best understood the nature of politics and was, therefore, best able to teach it so that

university students could thereafter take up offices in "state" (*respublica, regnum, civitas*) or church.

In the study of the liberal arts and notably grammar, rhetoric, and logic, "*ethica*" and "*politica*" were simply part of what were called the practical arts or practical virtues. In Boethius' commentary on the school text *In Isagogen Porphyrii commenta*[5] there was already a discussion of *scientia politica* as a "science" and as that part of practical philosophy which aims to treat virtue (*virtus*) and is to be distinguished from theoretical philosophy which treats the truth (*veritas*). We must be careful here not to understand their use of the word "science" in the phrase "political science" in nineteenth- and twentieth-century terms, thereby implying some kind of empirical, objective, universally-applicable, law-bound and value-free method of investigating "facts." To them, rather, "science" meant a way of knowing that emphasized normative, *human ideas* about a distinct subject matter or object of knowledge. When the term "science" was modified by "political" it was taken to be a branch of the wider field of practical moral *philosophy* that was necessarily invaded by value and was concerned with appropriate *human acts* in the world. What they knew about reality was a consequence of what they first knew about human knowing. They focused on mind and language first in order to get at the extra-mental and the extra-linguistic.

Boethius said political "science" belonged to moral philosophy which is divided into ethics, economics, and politics. In this Boethius was followed by Isidore of Seville.[6] We find Hugh of St. Victor speaking unproblemati- cally about the three practical arts – ethics, economics, and politics – in his *Didascalicon de studio legendi*.[7] He places ethics as a part of practical philosophy between logic (grammar, dialectic, and rhetoric) and theore- tical philosophy (theology, physics, and mathematics) (*Disdascalicon* 4.14). William of Conches advised that after the study of eloquence (grammar, dialectic, and rhetoric) a student should study practical philosophy, that is, ethics, economics, and politics before going on to theoretical philosophy (mathematics, physics, and theology).[8] Since the liberal arts were initially based on Roman pedagogy which aimed at producing men of letters and culture, medieval teachers were happy to follow Quintilian's *Institutio oratoria* where they read that a teacher of oratory was concerned with the moral development of his students. Cicero's *De inventione* was also held to be a moral classic, especially for its book 2 where virtue was discussed. Cicero's scheme of the virtues was adapted from his *De officiis* in the florilegium known as the *Moralium dogma philosophorum* (anon.). John of

Salisbury is well known for having been greatly influenced by the Roman moralists, notably Cicero. And when we consider that the *logica vetus* (which included Aristotle's *Categories* [*Praedicamenta*] and the *Perihermenias* [*De interpretatione*]) was intensively studied, we are not surprised that Abelard in his own work called *Scito te ipsum* or *Ethica*, would draw not only on Scripture and the Church Fathers but also on Aristotle's *Categories* for its discussion of virtue as a habit. Abelard notes how Aristotle says that a habit is not simply a disposition of character but a quality acquired by effort. This, he says, is what a virtue is.[9] Hence, classical ethics were central to the arts education from at least the twelfth century.

But because I want to examine the place of ethics and politics in university milieux notably during the later thirteenth century and thereafter, we need to begin the story somewhat later, by which time numerous additional works of antiquity had already found their way into university curricula. As Arabic works in Latin translation were increasingly read, especially the works of Avicenna (*Metaphysica* x.4) who included excerpts from Al-Farabi's *De scienciis*, Latin scholars of the early thirteenth century became more familiar with ancient discourse on the ethical status of the "state" and the degree of human "happiness" achievable through the right relationship between ruler and ruled. With the placing of all the known works of Aristotle on the arts faculty lecture program at the University of Paris in 1255, the study of the "authentic" Aristotle, as translated into Latin, was increasingly pursued by philosophers who were concerned primarily to "read" the texts literally to an audience of scholars most of whom would never proceed to a higher faculty (or even obtain their BA). The aims of arts faculty lecturers were somewhat different from those studying the same works in the theological faculties and in the *studia* of religious orders. The Parisian ruling that no theology should be taught in the arts faculty enabled arts faculty philosophers to read Aristotle "literally" and allow him to speak for himself, as it were, without in the first instance trying to determine whether or not what he said was true. By 1255 the works of Aristotle that were read in lectures were largely the translations of his logical and natural science books that had flooded into Europe from the later twelfth century onwards and that had been added to the *logica vetus*, those Aristotelian and other texts that had already been the set texts of higher education for centuries. To the works of logic and rhetoric were finally added Aristotle's *Nicomachean Ethics* and to a much lesser degree, his *Politics*. It was the *Ethics* rather than the *Politics* which taught arts students of the later thirteenth century and increasingly throughout the fourteenth century what kind of "science" politics was meant to be. It was able to do this because students were already familiar with Aristotle's ethical and political observations in his logical and rhetorical works which they had previously studied. Without getting involved in the arts faculty debates of the 1260s concerning radical Aristotelians like Siger of Brabant (fragments of whose *Liber de felicitate* and *Quaestiones morales* survive)[10] and Boethius of Dacia, it is sufficient to be aware that arts students were able to hear Aristotelian texts read literally by masters and more advanced BAs in their respective lectures, along with the brief magisterial questions arising from this textual exposition which were dictated to them. (By the later fourteenth century, Cambridge University's statutes, MSS Old Proctor-Caius, 54–56, record the texts required for a BA under the general rubric *De modo audiendi textum Aristotelis*.)[11] Masters in the higher faculty of theology were also treating some of these texts, notably those that dealt with the soul/mind and metaphysical issues. The point is that some of Aristotle's works were doubly treated.

The university's vocational course of study was meant to prepare its students for future careers in church or "state." There is ample evidence that the great impetus to scholastic development in the twelfth century, and the emergence of universities in the thirteenth century in which scholasticism flourished, came from a practical need for clear, authoritative solutions to practical questions about collective "governance" relating to things both personal and public: marriage, baptism, authority in secular society and church, the legitimacy of self-founding groups and their autonomous organization within a social hierarchy of organizations like religious orders, guilds, and city governments. Medieval universities like Paris, Oxford, and Bologna, owed their success to their development of *methods* to answer what we would call moral and political questions. They were set up as "think tanks" which serviced church and "state." They developed techniques for accumulating, arranging, reorganizing, interpreting a vast body of written materials from the past and present so that answers could be given to those questions it was thought important to ask, with consequences outside the university itself as well as within it. It is here within what would become a *conservative methodology* for answering questions that scholastic *critical freedom* lay. The wide range of substantive questions and arguments within what undoubtedly became a tight, academic, argumentative format allowed not only for the emergence of numerous personal and regional differences, but also for the growth of "schools" of interpretation or "circles" with recognizably distinct "perspectives" on current issues. All served the same end: to answer questions convincingly and authoritatively from an ever-expanding agenda of practical moral and political issues. That the questions and answers to them kept changing as the agenda in church and "state" changed meant that the universities needed to teach rules of analysis and debate, that is, a *procedure* by which problems could be brought to light and solved. They learned these procedural rules from the ancients and then developed them to serve their own agendas. The scholastic *quaestio*, for instance, posed a problem the solution to which was found in apparently conflicting authorities. Laying out authorities on both sides they distinguished among meanings of terms with the view to discovering how conflicting authorities could be used to bolster one favored position or another, and at the same time do justice to the authorities themselves. As Southern has rightly pointed out with reference to the later twelfth century onwards, "the remarkable developments of this time in government and society in theology and law and in the application of rational discourse to ordinary life would not have taken the form they did if the schools of Paris and Bologna had not existed."[12]

It is no longer thought that European academics were taken by storm when Aristotle's *Nicomachean Ethics* and *Politics* were translated into Latin, the *Ethics* by Grosseteste *c.* 1250 (the *ethica vetus* was available in the twelfth century [books 2 and 3], and the *translatio antiquior* [*ethica nova* which comprised book 1 and a few fragments] was already available in the early thirteenth century),[13] and the *Politics* by William of Moerbeke in 1260 for the *translatio imperfecta* (book 1 and part of book 2), and *c.* 1265 for the *translatio completa*.[14] But the reason that is usually given for the readiness of Christian Europeans to "accept" Aristotle's political observations is that they were, in fact, impervious to his distinctly ancient Greek political convictions and simply "translated" what they saw in the texts to bolster what they already believed in a society that was constructed in very different ways from that of fourth-century BC Greece. We need to realize, however, that what they believed was already in large part Aristotelian. If one looks at the university arts curriculum for the thirteenth century, one finds a student progressing from certain advanced grammatical studies to Aristotelian logic, beginning with the *Praedicamenta (Categories)* and the

Perihermenias (De interpretatione) and, from the middle of the twelfth century, learning the *logica nova* as well, which comprised the *Posterior* and *Prior Analytics*, the *Sophistici elenchi*, and Aristotle's *Topics and Rhetoric.*[15] Grammar as the first subject of the trivium and the prerequisite to all the other liberal arts was, by the thirteenth century, under the control of logic and metaphysics, the rules of grammar being derived and justified by recourse to logic and to metaphysical theories about reality. Grammar became a branch of speculative philosophy.[16] Once allied to dialectic, grammar had become a "science." Aristotle's logical works, and especially the *Posterior Analytics* (translated *c.* 1140 by James of Venice),[17] were undoubtedly difficult, but provided for those who stayed with it a theoretical account of general reasoning based on observation and leading to a body of "scientific" knowledge. In this work students confronted questions concerning the degree of certainty in the acquisition of knowledge, along with principles for the systematic organization of human knowledge. The limits of human knowledge were exposed in the specification of demonstrative knowledge. Here Aristotle discussed the logical structure of argument and proposed rules for studying the data that was available to the human senses. And in the final chapter of the *Posterior Analytics* Aristotle made a very unPlatonic point. He asked: how are humans able to obtain the primary knowledge of principles which are necessary to demonstrative argument? He answered by saying that such principles are not innate nor are they acquired from pre-existing knowledge (*contra* Plato). Rather, first principles must come from some capacity of the soul/ mind for recognizing general truths which then fit the evidence of the senses. As we shall see, when later thirteenth-century scholars had Aristotle's *Ethics* and read book 6 on the nature of "political science" as distinguished from other "sciences" and arts, they were already prepared to interpret Aristotle's distinction between scientific and other kinds of thinking and to accept his classification of political "science" or prudence as distinct from scientific demonstration. By this time they were also familiar with a conception of learning that linked, rather than divorced, the soul and the body so that it was now natural to speak of men learning from the particulars of sense experience from which they generalized to moral rules of behavior. Prudence, or political "science" was a way of thinking, a consequence of experience rather than of a revelation from on high.

Initially, the general question concerning the *object* of "scientific" knowledge, belief, and opinion, was formulated as an *epistemological* problem by men whose learning was sufficiently advanced for them to be recognized as teachers; and what they often taught was grammar. It was debated as far back as the early twelfth century and, indeed, before. The earlier view, a realist position, held that the object of scientific knowledge was an extramental, universal, and separable thing to which common words referred. Realists accepted a *direct relation* between the human mind's logical operations, its concepts, and mental and spoken/written propositions on the one hand and reality on the other. But with the recovery of more of Aristotle's logical works, the object of scientific knowledge came to be the universal that was found inherent in the world of individual things but, as Abelard insisted, was not itself *in* the world *as* a thing. Rather, in talking about objects of thought (what ideas are ideas of) Abelard said that we use words to signify an objective *status* in individual things which share the *status* to which the words refer. Logical dialectic shows us that signs (images, words, ideas) enable natures of things to have meaning for us without extracting the nature or *status* from things as though they were separable somethings. Logic was for Abelard an *ars sermocinalis*, an art concerned with the use of language where the term is the object of analysis as a bearer of meaning. Universality is ascribed only to words and not to things. Universality involves a grammatical concept. Meaning is imposed upon the term by human choice in the establishment of linguistic conventions. And because there are many languages there are many linguistic conventions.[18]

Abelard developed his views on language as a consequence of reading Boethius' commentaries on Aristotle's *logica vetus* along with his own analysis of Aristotle's works. As more of Aristotle's logical works became entrenched in the arts course as the *logica nova*, some went further and maintained that the object of scientific knowledge was nothing other than the *proposition about* extramental reality. Others, who still believed there was a natural grammar which had its basis outside language and in reality, argued for a universal grammar that was dependent on the structure of reality. Grammar for these *modistae* expressed the general essence of reality and language reflected the structure of this reality.[19] But increasingly, this realist perspective was confronted by "nominalism" or "terminism," and by the fourteenth century the object of scientific knowledge was to be acknowledged by some as the mental proposition, the mental language or thought which signified external reality which was itself signifiable as a state of affairs to which spoken or written propositions in a variety of conventionally established languages referred. From the thirteenth to the fourteenth centuries we can observe a continuous methodological shift in the modes of critical analysis of authoritative texts.[20] The linguistic theory of supposition proved to be one of the keystones of the *logica moderna* of the arts faculties in universities of the later thirteenth and fourteenth centuries, focusing on supposition: what entity(ies) does the term in a proposition stand (supposit) for? Across the faculties we observe a tendency to analyze almost every problem metalinguistically where all matters for discussion were to be treated by analyzing the propositions and the terms in propositions *that stood for* events and entities. *Scientia* dealt with propositions in the first place and propositions were the only things that could be said to be true or false. Both in the fields of natural science and in the practical moral sciences as taught in arts faculties, propositional analysis became central to discussions which sought to relate the world of individuals and events by means of a unifying theory. If individuals and events involving individuals are contingent (in that they can be or they can not be, and therefore, are not necessary), then it was asked, how can we have a *scientia*, which proposes stable laws of behavior, that nonetheless deals with possibles or contingencies? The answer was that stability comes from thought and language, from *propositiones* that speak *about* contingencies. Terminists/nominalists like the Oxford Franciscan William of Ockham and others maintained that only individual, particular *res permanentes* exist, that is, only individual substances and instances of qualities exist.[21] *Scientia*, however, deals with propositions which are the means for transmitting knowledge about particulars. By critically examining Aristotle's set texts in the arts course in order to understand his meaning with greater accuracy, and by indicating how others had misinterpreted him, university philosophers and theologians were free to make Aristotle conform to their own interests and attendant methodological demands.

If debates over the *object* of scientific knowledge were central to the arts course curriculum, focused as it was on logic, a related issue was the classification of different kinds of science and their subjects. Amongst the different sciences were those called *practica*, and here *scientia politica* was eventually taken to be, following Aristotle's *Ethics* (I, ii, 4–5, 1094a, 27–29) the most sovereign. I believe it was precisely in the disputes between arts and theology faculty moralists, on the one hand, and the law faculties, on the other, that the real debate was sustained concerning politics as a "science." Already in the thirteenth century civilian lawyers were calling themselves *politici*, but philosophers who dealt with the *ars politica* as practical moral philosophy insisted that lawyers knew nothing of the moral virtues and hence, were no more than sophists.[22] Hence, they argued that the appropriate place to study practical moral philosophy, divided into *solitarium/monasticum, privatam/oeconomicam, et publicam/politicam /civilem* was, in the first instance, in the university's arts course.[23] The arts course taught one to read and analyze the texts of the ancient moralists and the Church Fathers, and from these texts one learned how to rule oneself, one's family, and the city/"state." The academic argument over the "science" of politics that was to have most effect on the future of the university itself was with respect to which expert, in arts or in law, was best able to influence legislators or princes. Who was best able to apply himself to the primary significations of events as written down in authoritative texts from the past in order to render such texts of use to the present? Academic philosophers and theologians joined forces especially against the civilian (Roman) lawyers in a battle for power inside and outside the university that would run from the thirteenth to sixteenth centuries with increasing virulence. The lawyers won as the early modern state came into being.

What was distinctive about an arts course education? When we speak about the arts course curriculum and its requirements for the BA and then MA, we are dealing with those students who stayed the course and went on to do advanced studies. We are looking at bachelors who were a distinct class of students, that is, advanced scholars who were accredited assistant lecturers to masters and on their way to becoming regent masters themselves. They had a recognized status above ordinary scholars. (In Cambridge, for instance, their functions were similar to Paris bachelors in 1245.)

There is still a tremendous resistance to examine the content of the arts course seriously on the part of historians whose interests lie elsewhere than in intellectual history. Because *we* are not educated in the intricacies of ancient logic and rhetoric there is an implicit resistance to accept the considerable sophistication of advanced university students. We must bear in mind, however, that the students who were able to stay the course were the ones who got the high placements in medieval bureaucracies. Hence, it is argued here that medievalists ought to become more familiar with the substance of a medieval university education. It would also be of benefit to historians who treat the fifteenth-century renaissance and its educational ideals and practices in humanist schools and in universities. This is because most students went to university in order to qualify for lucrative employment within the established orders of church, government service, or one of the organized professions. Their skills were meant to be utilitarian, not least in the production of propaganda on behalf of papal, imperial, or royal and civic patrons and their respective ideologies. Alan Cobban has rightly pointed out that at the university stage, the world of an average student was dominated by a conservative mode of thought based on an agreed core of authorized texts.[24] The hallmark of a university education was the mastery of digested and approved texts, expounded logically, where questioning was encouraged as a form of training. Rigorous training in the logical analysis of texts and argument underlay all the university disciplines and the adversarial technique of disputation was taken to be foundational for later occupations, not least for those allied to the law. If the average undergraduate was not an independent inquirer, some of his more advanced teachers certainly were and it was these men, from arts and theology faculties, who were subsequently employed to write ideological tracts which would constitute some of the most radical thinking on politics, taken in its broadest sense, that is known from the medieval period. One thinks here of Marsilius of Padua, of John of Paris, of William of Ockham, of Nicole Oresme, and of John Wyclif among many others. Within the walls of the university the communal life of disputation and the exposition of pagan and Christian texts were held to be necessary activities of an autonomous guild of masters and/or students being trained in utilitarian skills. Of course, universities, especially in northern Europe, were foundations tied to ecclesiastical and episcopal domination and hence, were observed and from time to time chastised for curricular developments that looked dangerous to church authorities which saw themselves as responsible for a universal Christendom. But by the fifteenth century, when cities, princes, and kings took over as founders and protectors, universities would become increasingly allied to national or civic perspectives.[25] In becoming national institutions their intellectual autonomy would shrink in ways earlier medieval academics could not have imagined.

During the fourteenth century the arts faculty at Oxford exercised more influence than any other single faculty. So far as we can tell there were no formal qualifications for admission of undergraduates to Oxford. Most arts faculty students were scholars in their middle to late teens. Oxford scholars preparing for the BA "determination" spent around five to six years listening to unpretentious readings and paraphrasings of set texts. In the fifteenth century the course was reduced to four years. They attended ordinary and cursory lectures. Concessions for not following some pre-scribed course of instruction were made, but attendance at ordinary lectures was compulsory and a student supplicating for a degree had to confirm he had heard all of them (in Latin). Some of the set texts were supposed to be heard twice *ordinarie* and others at least once *cursorie*. Ordinary lectures were delivered at a set time in the morning by a master lecturing magisterially. A BA who had "determined" after a minimum of five years could not deliver ordinary lecture and normally lectured *cursorie* in the late afternoon. But both kinds of lectures, whether given by a BA on his way to "inception" as an MA, or by a master, were in the form of detailed readings and paraphrases of a set text and a brief discussion of selected problems – *quaestiones* – arising from the text just expounded. The morning questions were dictated by the master as part of his exposition of the text and students developed techniques of rapid handwriting (tachy-graphy rather than shorthand). Afternoon cursory lectures by a BA were given under the direction of a master who assigned specific books to his BA for him to lecture on for the year. The choice of texts was from the list of old and new logic and from the *libri naturales*. An undergraduate scholar, therefore, heard older students who had already "determined" as BAs as well as MAs reading and briefly commenting on set books of the trivium, quadrivium, and the three philosophies (natural, moral, and metaphysics). In addition, undergraduates had to attend disputations, respond *de sophismatibus* and *de quaestione*. Prior to determining as a BA, the scholar was mainly involved in hearing lectures on the old and new logic and the books of natural science, most of which, but not all, were by Aristotle.[26]

If a student proceeded to the higher faculty of theology he would find that the analytical benefits of logic and the problems and examples drawn from the arts course study of natural philosophy held a central place to such a degree that the boundary between philosophical and theological methods and concerns had, by the middle of the fourteenth century, become almost non-existent. This was the kind of theology that appealed to continental scholars and, as Courtney has shown, had a revolutionary impact on the curriculum of continental universities and *studia* between

1340 and 1420.[27] Indeed, during the fourteenth century Oxford theology developed its own independence and character and this was then assimilated by Parisian theologians with an impact *in Paris* that was to last until the early sixteenth century.

Peculiar to this period in Oxford was the lack of any allegiance to particular schools of thought: aspects of Thomist, Scotist, and Ockhamist ways of thinking survived together and spawned followers who simultaneously adopted and rejected arguments of their respective "masters." Courtenay believes this was due, in part, to the relatively weak ideological ties between a master and those who attended his lectures.[28] Masters exercised little more than administrative control over students and the very choice to follow a particular master on some specific issue was largely a matter of a student's personal decision. It also seems that the university authorities exercised little control over what went on in the lectures of masters. The peculiar situation in which the Franciscan theologian William of Ockham found himself when the Thomist university chancellor Lutterel took a complaint about his theological positions to the papacy in Avignon neither prevented his revisionary thinking on logic, language, and his interpretation of Aristotle's categories from being disputed by his contemporaries in Oxford, nor were his theological views formally condemned. Another story can be told about how Ockham left Oxford for Avignon in order to defend himself and then joined the imperial court of Louis of Bavaria from which he wrote his political tracts against the contemporary papacy. But that story would tell us nothing about a university or any other authoritative clamp-down on the views he expressed in his lectures and commentaries. Before 1325 Ockham had devoted himself entirely to academic studies and especially to writing what would be considered immensely influential commentaries on Aristotelian logic for students, either in his own Franciscan *studium* in Oxford or elsewhere, or to be used more widely (for example, the *Summa totius logicae*). At the university of Paris (1339), the ruling that Ockham's works were not to be lectured on[29] appears to be no more than a statement that his texts had not (yet) been accepted as part of the standard core course despite the tremendous interest they appear to have awakened. Ockham manuscripts are very well represented in France and Italy.[30]

If we know more or less what constituted the core texts to be lectured on in the arts course treatment of logic and natural science, there is more of a debate over whether the translations of Aristotle's *Ethics* and *Politics* were similarly absorbed into the curriculum. From an examination of university statutes (for Oxford, Paris, Cambridge, and Toulouse) it seems clear that from the later thirteenth century and during the fourteenth century familiarity with Aristotle's *Ethics* was increasingly required for bachelors who had already determined and who proceeded as more advanced students, lecturing to younger undergraduates but also going to lectures of their masters. In other words, it came to be required that the ten books of Aristotle's *Ethics* had been heard as ordinary lectures by an advanced student who wished to become a master (MA).[31] Aristotle's *Politics*, however, only appears in the early fourteenth-century Oxford statutes and there it is listed as an acceptable course which may be chosen by inceptors from among others whereas the *Ethics* is required. What would a student learn about the "science" of politics if he attended lectures where Aristotle's *Ethics* was read and briefly expounded in the form of magisterial questions?

In book 6 of the *Ethics* (iii–viii, 1139b14–1142a31) Aristotle discusses five different "states of mind/soul" by which the soul arrives at truth "by affirmation and denial." These "states of mind" are art, science, prudence, wisdom, and intuition. My focus here will be mainly on the differences he sees between the different states of mind called *technē* (art), *episteme* (science), and *phronesis* (prudence). Aristotle classifies each mind-state in relation to the kind of truth each may attain. What kind of mind-state is political thinking? It is important for us to become accustomed to his way of speaking about political "science" as a kind of *thinking* about a certain class of objects. Medieval students had no difficulty with this. We saw that earlier discussions of *scientia* had dealt with questions concerning the objects of scientific knowledge in more advanced grammar and logic courses. As we shall see, each state of mind has a different mode of proceeding and a different object.

The third state of soul/mind, that is, the third mode of thinking, Aristotle calls prudence (*phronesis*). He says that we call someone prudent if he is able to deliberate rightly about what is good and advantageous for himself, not in particular respects as, for instance, what is good for health or physical strength, but what is conducive to the good life (for man) generally. A prudent person calculates successfully with a view to some serious end and since one deliberates about variable things and about things that can be done by oneself, (this is what deliberation is), one is not in the sphere of "scientific" thinking *per se* which deals in the realm of the necessary. Aristotle had already discussed how scientific knowledge (*episteme*) implies the ability to *demonstrate* and he referred back to his treatment in the *Posterior Analytics*. Since it is impossible to deliberate about things that are necessarily so, prudence is not a science. Nor is it an art. An art (*technē*) was already defined as that mode of thinking concerned with production rather than action. Production aims at an end other than itself. But prudence is concerned with action whose end is doing well. Prudence, then, is a reasoned state of mind that is capable of action with regard to things that are good or bad for man. Aristotle says that nobody deliberates about things that cannot be otherwise than they are (i.e., the necessary). And nobody deliberates about ends, only about means to ends. The prudent man, then, deliberates about means to an end, and the end is itself a practical good that can be attained in action; he calculates about means to the best of goods attainable by man. Prudence is then, a *quality* that belongs to those who can envisage what is good for themselves and for people in general. One is not born with this quality but acquires it from experience. Prudence is a *virtue* rather than an art. It is the virtue of that part of the soul that is susceptible to reason and there are two parts of the soul so susceptible. It is the virtue of that part of the soul that deals with the variable and the contingent; but there is also a part of the soul that deals with the necessary – and that part of the mind/soul is engaged in "scientific" thinking, or demonstrative reasoning. Prudence, however, is the virtue of that part of soul that forms opinions. Opinions are formed with regard to the sphere of possibles or variables where something can be or cannot be, can be done or not be done. Although prudence *is* concerned with universals, that is, the principle that the end of all deliberation is the good for man, prudence *as a virtue* takes cognizance of particulars. It is practical: a prudent man needs to have some theoretical knowledge but to be effective in action he needs experience and practical knowledge. Hence, prudence as a virtue is concerned with conduct whose sphere is particular circumstances.

Aristotle goes on to say that the "science" that *coordinates* prudence is the "science of politics." Why call politics a "science" if we have been told that prudence is not one? Aristotle says that political "science" and prudence are the same *state of mind* but are different in essence. Aristotle has already said that *scientific thinking* deals with the necessary and operates by demonstrative reasoning; prudence, because it deals with the contingent and particular, is not a "science" but a virtue. Students would have understood the difference because they had already covered logical, demonstrative reasoning when they studied the *logica nova*. Prudence, however, mostly deals with the particular in conduct and operates in the sphere of possibles, contingencies, and variables. The kind of prudence that is confined to the daily administration of public affairs and deals with particular circumstances is practical and deliberative. It is called deliberative because it considers a course of action that is not yet decided and, therefore, is not necessary. A prudent man acts as the result of the deliberating process. Therefore, politics cannot be a demonstrative "science." It is, nonetheless, a kind of thinking, a state of mind. Aristotle then implies that to be involved in deliberating for the *collective good* of men is a different species of knowledge from that deployed in deliberating about one's *own* good. Then he says something crucial to link an individual's prudence with a kind of collective prudence or political "science." Although people tend to call prudent those men who are concerned only with the self and the individual and therefore seek their own good, he says it is impossible to secure one's own good independently of domestic and political "science" which seek the collective good, in family and in the state. Politics, that is, political thinking about the *collective* human good, is then the full realization of prudence, the latter being found also at the levels of household and individual.

Aristotle mentions how people tend to speak of prudence when they discuss the collective entity "the state"; the implication is that men tend to generalize in speech from personal prudence to deliberation about collective well-being. Hence, one aspect of "generalized" prudence or political "science" is controlling and directive, and is called legislative science. But the other (indeed, primary) aspect of prudence deals with particular circumstances and, he says, bears the name that properly belongs to both aspects: "political science." This is because, without the virtue of deliberative reasoning about particular circumstances and conduct, a virtue learned from experience and with a moral end in view (the good for man), the controlling and directive aspect of political "science," legislating, would be inadequately carried out. You cannot legislate for a collectivity unless you have first developed virtues and learnt to be prudent from experience of particulars and deliberation on these with a moral end in view. Arts faculty philosophers would be only too aware how this reinforced their view that lawyers and legislators needed to be trained first in the difference between demonstrative reasoning and deliberative reasoning with a moral end in view before they took up roles as law makers. Aristotle goes on to say that people tend to use the term "prudence" primarily for acts that result from deliberation concerning self-interest. But, he says, prudence is wider in application and rightly belongs to all the forms called domestic, legislative, and political "science" (and he divides the latter into deliberative and juridical/judicial "science"). However divided, prudence (when applied to individuals as means [acts] to their particular good on the one hand, and on the other, applied to means [acts] to the collective good of a community of men and otherwise called legislative and political "science"), is *not* scientific knowledge *per se*. "Science" modified by "political" is a *kind* of "science," a *kind* of *deliberative* thinking that is distinct from that kind of thinking that is truly "scientific" for Aristotle, *episteme*, which is a kind of *demonstrative* reasoning that deals with the necessary. Prudence deals with enactments, the last step done as a consequence of deliberation in particular and variable circumstances. Prudence, he says, apprehends the ultimate *particular* which cannot be apprehended by scientific knowledge.

Once again, we note that the object of prudence is the good for man. But since man is not the highest being in the world, political "science" or prudence is not the most important mode of thinking by which the soul arrives at truth. "It is extraordinary that anyone should regard political science or prudence as most important, unless man is the highest being in the world" (*Ethics*, vii 1141a19 ff.). But Aristotle says that there are other beings far more divine in nature than man (the visible heavenly bodies and invisible God, the first mover). Hence, *sophia* which he defines as a scientific *and* intuitive knowledge of what is by nature most precious, is the highest mode of thinking, higher than prudence/political "science" *and* higher than demonstrative "science."

Prudence or political "science" then, in its wide application belongs to individual, domestic, legislative, and political (in the sense of collective) "science." It moves from being applicable to individual well-being to the well-being of the collectivity. And the mind-state leading to acts appropriate for the individual is related to the mind-state that leads to acts appropriate for the collectivity. This repeats the familiar categories of twelfth- and thirteenth-century moralists who divided practical moral philosophy in the arts course into *solitarium, privatam et publicam vel aliter in ethicam, oeconomicam et politicam vel aliter in moralem et dispensativam et civilem*. The emphasis is on the development of moral habits, virtues as qualities built up from an individual's experience of particulars in the realm of contingencies and then applied to the collective whole. It is a distinctive kind of "science," a mode of thinking about what is good and advantageous for oneself and for man generally. There is a practical part of the soul/mind which forms opinions about possible and contingent things, about conduct and behavior, and which deliberates about the means to man's practical end or good. Political "science," because it deals with the public good, is divided into legislative and juridical/judicial "science."

A student who had previously studied Aristotle's logic, including rhetoric and topics along with Boethius' commentaries, would already be familiar with the different forms of argument appropriate to *scientiae* with different objects. A student would especially be familiar with special topics useful for logical argument in deliberative, judicial, and epideictic rhetoric,[32] that is, with a species of plausible oratory and its categories which enables public opinion to be swayed. He would know that rhetoric was defined as a "science" of discourse which moves both the intellect and the emotions but is distinct in aim from dialectic which moves only the intellect. He would know that rhetoric had its own subject matter dealing with the particular circumstances of human affairs and allowing for judgment between the more or less good in contingent circumstances. He would know that dialectic, on the other hand, deals with all being and, by means of the syllogism, treats the truth *simpliciter*.[33] From at least the late thirteenth century (*c.* 1270) when Moerbeke's translation of Aristotle's *Rhetoric* replaced that prepared by Hermannus Alemannus from Arabic (*c.* 1256)[34] he would have known that rhetoric was a *kind* of *dialectica moralis*, a *kind* of "science" whose conclusions were true in *most* cases. He would now see not only that the rules of rhetoric he had spent so much time on were tightly allied to the kind of "science" Aristotle understood politics to be in the *Nicomachean Ethics*; he would also be told that if he followed a career in the "state" or church bureaucracy and hence, deliberated about means to the general, collective human good, he would find his rhetorical training useful especially if his audience were educated men in *parlement* or the papal *curia*. If they were uneducated and vulgar he would be told that experience would count more than ornate and closely argued syllogisms because such an audience would want to know the consequences of actions rather than the cause of things.[35] Most of all he would know that a student who had not studied university "logic" in this wide sense with its moral underpinnings would not be suitably trained to advise legislators or be able to take up judicial posts in church or "state" hierarchies.

Thus far, my argument has been that Aristotelian discourse concerning the nature of "scientific" thought and the place of ethics and politics within an intellectual frame of practical moral philosophy was already known from the study of Aristotle's works on logic and rhetoric, so that lectures on the *Ethics* would have seemed like a furthering of a perspective which students had already adopted. If Buridan's fourteenth-century arts faculty *quaestiones* on Aristotle's *Rhetoric* are anything to go by, it is obvious that a student would ostensibly be hearing lectures on rhetoric but would actually be hearing the lecturer spend an inordinate amount of time on discussions of ethical, political, and psychological issues.[36]

Recently, some important research has been done to discover just how much the translations of Aristotle's *Politics* actually influenced arts courses in universities of the later thirteenth and fourteenth centuries.[37] The influence of Aristotle's *Politics* appears to have had a somewhat different history from the influence of the *Ethics*. In the 1270s the major commentator on the *Politics* in the arts faculty at Paris was Peter of Auvergne (Petrus de Alvernia). He is usually known as the continuator of Thomas Aquinas' literal commentary on the *Politics* (Aquinas only completed up to iii.8, 1280a6), but recent research shows Peter to have been less of a disciple of Aquinas than was previously thought. He was not a Dominican but probably attended Aquinas' lectures. Peter delivered a still unedited commentary on the *Politics* in *quaestio* form (MS. Paris Bibl. nat. lat. 16089 fols. 274r–319r) in addition to a literal commentary (*scriptum*). Although familiar with Aquinas' perspective he elaborated on a number of issues in his own way. Peter says in his introduction to his commentary on the *Politics* in *quaestio* form that he wishes to distinguish his reading of Aristotle from the way "others" read him in order to provide political "science" with a philosophical basis. Flüeler believes this refers to a wish to distinguish an arts from a theology faculty reading.[38] I would think the distinction highlighted is also the one between the arts faculty's understanding of political "science" as practical moral philosophy and that of the law faculty and practicing Roman lawyers. Furthermore, to read Aristotle as an arts faculty lecturer methodologically meant something quite specific; Peter's statement has much in common with that expressed by the radical Aristotelian arts faculty lecturer Siger of Brabant when commenting on Aristotle's *De Anima*: "our principle aim is not to inquire whether Aristotle spoke the truth about the soul but rather to discover what the philosopher's opinion was on this matter."[39] Peter's 126 *quaestiones* cover *Politics* books 1–7, focusing most on books 1 and 3 and, using the tight syllogistic form, he applies material from other works by Aristotle to elucidate the text. Jean Dunbabin has provided an interesting discussion of some of the issues Peter treated with originality.[40] Other than the works of Peter of Auvergne, however, there are very few mentions or surviving manuscripts of commentaries from arts faculties on Aristotle's *Politics* until the late fourteenth and the fifteenth centuries.[41] (We have little information about which of the commentaries mentioned by contemporaries were ever actually published. We simply know that lectures were delivered as *scriptum et quaestiones super libros politicorum.*) Although early fourteenth-century Oxford statutes speak of the *Politics* as part of the teaching program, students could choose between it and the *De animalibus* and they then spent only six weeks studying either! In Paris it was lectured on but only "extraordinarie," and it is from Paris (and Prague) that we have surviving arts commentaries.[42] Whereas universities of the fourteenth and fifteenth centuries in Prague, Vienna, Cologne, Heidelberg, Cracow, Leipzig, Erfurt, and Basel spent four to six months reading the *Politics*, Flüeler believes there are *no* important Oxford commentaries for the corresponding period (for example, *anon.* Balliol College Cod. 146A and Bodleian 292 fols. 180va–219ra) aside from the very famous one by Walter Burley (*c.* 1338–39) who also wrote a university "textbook" *expositio* on the *Ethics*. The *Politics* commentary, however, was dedicated to the Bishop of Durham, Richard de Bury and then was presented to Clement VI in Avignon.[43] From here it became very popular in Italy and to judge from surviving manuscripts it was the most widespread commentary on the *Politics* that was read both within universities and outside.

But if we look elsewhere, notably to thirteenth-century Dominican *studia* and in university theology faculties where the mendicant orders had numerous distinguished masters, we see a much greater influence of Aristotle's ethical *and* political discussions penetrating treatises that compared the organization of secular society with that of the church. In their *studia* Dominicans produced literal commentaries on the *Ethics* and *Politics* as soon as these works appeared. Indeed, even before Moerbeke had translated the entire *Politics*, Dominicans seemed interested in its analysis and evaluation of different constitutions (monarchies/tyrannies, popular versus aristocratic constitutions), its discussion of citizenship, and its emphasis on political agency. When Aquinas returned as a master in theology to the University of Paris in 1269, he not only worked on part II of his *Summa theologiae* but he also wrote his literal commentaries on Aristotle's *Ethics* and *Politics*.[44] Albertus, Aquinas' teacher, had previously lectured at the Dominican house in Cologne on Aristotle's *Ethics* and Aquinas' notes and questions on these lectures have survived. But it is thought that Aquinas was not much influenced by Albertus when he came to write his own commentaries on the *Ethics* and *Politics*. It was in many of his other *theological* works, for example, *Summa contra gentiles* and his commentary on the arts faculty core text *De praedicamentis*, that Aquinas refers to Aristotle's *Politics* from either the *translatio imperfecta* of Moerbeke (book 1 and part of book 2 – *c.* 1260) or from the *translatio completa* (*c.* 1265 – whole work translation). Many other citations from Aristotle's *Politics* appear in the *Summa theologiae* and in his only strictly political work, the *De regimine principum (de regno)* written for the young king of Cyprus.[45] Aquinas was able to cite from books 1–3 of the complete translation in *c.* 1268 and from books 5–8 by 1271.

By the last three decades of the thirteenth century and during the first decades of the fourteenth century Aristotle's *Politics* was beginning to be cited in a variety of mirrors for princes, tracts *de potestate regia et papale*, and in occasional extra-university philosophical and theological literature written for one "ideological" cause or another. Miethke has recently emphasized that the well-known publicist debates of the fourteenth century were essentially academic debates within royal or imperial party circles.[46] One thinks here of John of Paris' *De potestate regia et papali*,[47] of Giles of Rome's *De regimine principum* and his *De ecclesiastica potestate*, of Ockham's various political tracts, and even of Dante's *Monarchia*. The audience for these works comprised learned, university men who, like Marsilius and Ockham, were adopted by extra-university political circles and courts. All the political theory of the fourteenth century, in fact, belongs to a learned tradition which originated in the university and all of the authors knew scholastic formulations of the "science" of politics as this was part of ethics or practical moral philosophy. A fourteenth-century publicist did not have a *general public* for his writings. This was a period in which manuscripts rather than printed texts were the only ways in which disputants could get to know conflicting political positions and, therefore, we should not imagine a "free market" but rather what Miethke calls a "geschlossenen Offentlichkeiten" ("restricted general public") for these texts.[48] During the fourteenth century many of these scholastic Latin tracts began to appear in vernacular translations (for instance, Marsilius of Padua's *Defensor pacis* [1324] appeared in a French translation in Paris [1375] and in a Florentine translation [in 1363]).[49] While often drawing on canon and Roman law, most of these publicist tracts, including those by Ockham and especially his *Dialogus*,[50] emerged from the university treatment of Aristotelian philosophy married to the values found in the texts of Roman moralists prescribed for the arts course. What many of them produced was an Aristotelian ecclesiology as well as a theory of governance in secular society founded on Aristotelian philosophical principles applied to contemporary political fact. Giles of Rome's *De regimine principum* blended Cicero, Aristotle, and Roman law, but when he described the relation of the king to law, he described him as a judge dealing with particulars who must tailor the law to meet the circumstances and act with equity (III, ii, 29 fol. 314v [Rome, 1556]). His ideal king is a mixture of the Roman law's "public person" and Aristotle's supremely virtuous ruler whose activities are those of the outstandingly prudent man as described in the *Ethics* books 6 and 5 (V, 10, 1137b on equity [*epieikeia*]) respectively. He makes the point that civil lawyers are not to be trusted. They are to be considered ignorant of politics (*De regimine* II, ii, c.8 . . .*legistae. . .appellari possunt idiotae politici*). In the France of Philippe IV and at a time when so much publicist literature in support of either king/ emperor or papacy was being composed, lawyers were said to have lost their moral sense, their chivalric values, and to have upset the system of orders.[51] As Miethke has observed, the real rivals of the arts and theology faculties' approach to ethics and politics were the jurists who also studied texts on political and social ordering.[52] Canon lawyers focused on church "politics" and civil lawyers defined *politica* as the *scientia civilis* as it was to be found in Roman law – the *Corpus iuris civilis*. The contrast with arts faculty expositions of political "science" as moral philosophy is striking. In Ockham's university publication, the *Quodlibeta septem*,[53] he took up the familiar question of the nature of moral "science" and presented the following extraordinary, revolutionary interpretation of Aristotelian ethics, turning the "science" of prudence (*phronesis*) into a demonstrative "science" (*episteme*) which Aristotle, in *Ethics* book 6, (as we have seen), claimed it was not. At the same time, Ockham insisted that juristic "science" was not a demonstrative "science":

In so far as we can define morality in its large sense as "human acts subject absolutely to the will" then the *scientia moralis*, when considered as a nonpositive science is that which directs human acts without any superior precepts. The precepts known by all men are *per se nota vel nota per experientiam* (self-evident or known through experience) and this is how any man can determine what is honest. The moral science called positive or *scientia iuristarum* is not a demonstrative science because juristic rules are founded on human positive laws which are not propositions that are evidently known [but rather are the result of convention]. The *disciplina moralis non positiva* is, however, a *scientia demonstativa* because we deduce conclusions syllogistically from principles that are either self-evident or evident through experience.

In Ockham's opinion, non-positive morality is known most certainly by any and every human experiencer of the world. This can be shown to be the case by logicians engaged in an analysis of moral behavior as represented by propositions (in thoughts and in conventional language). Non-positive morality is a higher, demonstrative "science" than is juristic positive "science." And Ockham believes that anyone with sufficient literacy who has been trained to read texts, and most notably Scripture, will find there descriptions of the way men live and have always lived in the world. The non-positive moral "science" which Ockham defines as those precepts known by all men enables anyone literate to judge the truths communicated by Scripture! Implied here is that jurists have no privileged access to the truth of experience as expressed in moral philosophy and known by all men.

The rivalry between philosophers/theologians and jurists appears even more clearly in Nicole Oresme's French translation and commentary on Aristotle's *Politics*, a work undertaken at the request of king Charles V of France and dedicated to him.[54] Oresme, a master in theology and a student of Buridan, observed that the lawyers who circled round Charles V were bad counselors. They were capable of having a vast influence on public policy through flattery. He said that lawyers treated Roman law as dogma rather than interpreting law in relation to the common good. Not having studied philosophy, lawyers were incapable of understanding the principles behind the law; "ceulz qui apprennent premierement les lays ne pevent apres aprendre philosophie."[55] Lawyers were the ones who led states into tyrannies by attributing to princes a *plenitudo potestatis (plenitude de poste)*. According to Oresme, they favored absolutism: he believed that the fourteenth-century Italian civil jurists Baldus and Bartolus had turned the *princeps* into a *Deus in terris*.[56] To their presumed absolutism, Oresme opposed the Aristotelian "poste moderée" or temperate monarchy.

Krynen has shown how this anti-jurist opprobium among philosophers and theologians continued into the fifteenth century when it was argued by Jean Gerson and Pierre d'Ailly that the major science of society and its values should be the preserve of philosophers and theologians. The codes of Roman law must have lesser authority than moral philosophy and Scripture. Increasingly, however, sovereigns across Europe were choosing the jurists to constitute the "think tanks" of future states. The history of the University of Oxford in the fifteenth century provides a case-study of this tendency.[57]

We know that university claims to privileges like intellectual freedom have always depended on the conditions of founding. Oxford's immunities from secular jurisdictions were authorized by royal charters. The university attempted to obtain further exemptions from external interference from episcopal jurisdiction and visitation, but to no avail. By the end of the fourteenth century, Oxford's privileges were puny when compared with the organs of church and state. The university was consulted as a learned, corporate body on a variety of issues, not least, ecclesiastical questions following the Great Schism and during the period of ecclesiastical councils, but the limits of university autonomy were increasingly emphasized by a government that made certain that academics supplied the answers it desired and which were then circulated as independent opinions. At the beginning of the fifteenth century, intellectual freedom was hedged round by the kind of society in which the university was situated. Social cohesion increasingly depended on a public religion, conformity to whose orthodoxy was seen to be the precondition of social harmony. Like Cambridge, Oxford was becoming a national university. Together, these two universities maintained their monopoly of higher education in England and were integrated into the workings of the fifteenth-century state. They depended more and more on benefactors and patrons. Increasingly throughout the fifteenth century, men trained in the Oxford faculty of canon and civil law appear to have called the shots, if not always successfully within the university itself then certainly outside it in the episcopacy, in royal diplomacy, and in chancery.

The enormous intellectual vigour and influence of Oxford logicians, natural philosophers, and theologians on European learning reached its peak in the fourteenth century. The logic that was developed and explored within the prevailing theological context reached a level of sophistication that was not attained again anywhere until Leibniz in the seventeenth century. But with the Hundred Years War, the Schism, the conciliar period, the heresy of Wyclif and government response to it, Oxford began to close in on itself in a manner that allows us to draw conclusions about the nature of the conservative response to its home-grown "premature reformation." Theological and logical originality, along with the moral and political discussions that often followed from *quaestiones* on theological and logical set texts were shifted off the agenda.

In this milieu the recognizable system of autonomous colleges was developed where private study could be fostered within an increasingly "casual" relationship between colleges and university faculties. But that peculiarly open form of scholastic argument, defended as a right to debate *probabiles opiniones*, where one could put forward views with which one did not necessarily agree and which one had no intention of asserting as necessarily true, was being checked by those who feared the inevitable escape of such ideas beyond university walls into wider society. As the fifteenth century began, Oxford had the dubious distinction of having produced the first doctor of theology to be named a recalcitrant heretic, John Wyclif. Where the university's earlier exercise of discipline over its members had run to fines, suspensions, even imprisonment, and certainly expulsion, by the fifteenth century changes to the statutes were not only motivated by a need to maintain law and order but by a general concern to check the tendency toward heretical views. Academic lawyers, aggrieved by the dominance in university administration of masters of arts and theologians, were quick to stir up feelings against them. They reported to ecclesiastical authorities that certain artists and theologians supported Wyclif. The external authorities of church and state stepped in.

Wyclif and his intellectual contemporaries belonged to a new elite whose knowledge was accessible to an increasingly educated laity. Some of his followers eventually abandoned the schools for the pulpit to broaden their critique of contemporary religious and social ills. Out of this movement came translations of the Bible in English. The deliberate dissemination of this vernacular text well beyond Wyclif's followers proved immensely influential. And this literary achievement along with Lollard sermon cycles were products of Oxford scholarship, of trained academic minds whose projects were carried through, at least in some of their stages, within Oxford colleges themselves. With Wyclif and the perceived need to "purify the infected waters" of the university at the turn into the fifteenth century, Oxford became a national concern. The tremendous response of church and state to these affairs gradually convinced university masters that it was safer to become enrolled in the propagation of established orthodoxy than to engage in originality of mind.

Lawyers came to be more numerous than theologians and physicians in the university and their prospects for worldly advancement were much better than those pursuing the liberal arts. Newly arrived law students were not required to study the arts at all. They argued that on-the-job training in, for instance, ecclesiastical courts should exempt them from the normal academic exercises and lectures. They complained that university statutes insisted that no one could receive a degree unless he swore he had heard every word of every chapter of set texts. They supplicated for numerous exemptions (graces) from fulfilling standard requirements. The predominance of Oxford graduates appointed to episcopal sees or as deans of cathedrals grew to a monopoly between 1216 and 1499 and nearly half of those appointed to the episcopate were lawyers of civil, canon, or both laws. Academic lawyers served the crown in diplomacy and in the courts of admiralty and chivalry. Chancellors and Masters of the Rolls were academic lawyers. The wealth they accumulated was often bequeathed for educational purposes and the university benefited. But as the university scholars who were once the sons of yeomen and husbandmen came to be replaced by sons of gentlemen or higher during the sixteenth century, other changes took place in the university system. By the early sixteenth century neither students nor university authorities appear to have thought that lectures needed to be attended to receive one's degree. One John Farre, a bachelor of civil law was, in 1527, given a grace to vary the time and place of his lectures so long as he lectured for at least a quarter of an hour! A bachelor of law could be granted a grace to deliver lectures in vacation suggesting that it was not thought important whether there were any scholars present to hear him!

Doubtless, this is evidence of Oxford's burgeoning collegiate structure which increasingly provided colleges with a freedom to shape their own destinies and that of those in their charge. The university gave way to spaces of private study, college communities, which provided a variety of short-lived associations of ambitious minds. But the parallels with continental descriptions of the fate of independent thought that had previously been sustained by the university milieu, are striking. On the continent, the intellectual's freedom of thought and personal moral integrity were played out behind the closed doors of his private chamber or in the depoliticized "academies." These "private" recesses were contrasted with courts and public places in which political dissembling had become the norm. The new technical skill of "politics," a new "science" of politics *divorced* from practical philosophical/theological morality, was now only to be deployed for "reasons of state."

Notes

1 Janet Coleman, *Ancient and Medieval Memories: Studies in the Reconstruction of the Past* (Cambridge: Cambridge University Press, 1992), pp. 538–99, and Coleman, "Machiavelli's *via moderna:* Medieval and Renaissance Attitudes to the Past," in Martin Coyle, ed., *The Prince as Cultural Text* (Manchester: Manchester University Press, 1995).

2 Antony Black, *Political Thought in Europe 1250–1450* (Cambridge: Cambridge University Press, 1992), pp. 7–12.

3 Peter Abelard, *Ethics*, ed. and trans. D. E. Luscombe (Oxford: Clarendon, 1971) p. xv: "Ethical thought was promoted in the 12th century by theologians who were usually monks or canons or schoolmen (*scholastici*) and by teachers and students of the liberal arts." Abelard was a theologian, a logician, and a monk.

4 But see Rita Copeland, *Rhetoric, Hermeneutics, and Translation in the Middle Ages: Academic Traditions and Vernacular Texts* (Cambridge: Cambridge University Press, 1991) for a discussion of the reclassification of the sciences in the wake of Aristotle's organon entering the curriculum and where poetic and rhetoric came to be classified as part of logic after the middle of the twelfth century, p. 160. Also, Karen Fredborg, "Buridan's *Quaestiones super Rhetoricam Aristotelis*," in J. Pinborg, ed., *The Logic of John Buridan* (Copenhagen: Museum Tusculanum, 1976) pp. 47–58, who notes a shift in the thirteenth century from interest in the Ciceronian–Boethian to the Aristotelian doctrine of the art of rhetoric (p. 50).

5 Boethius, *In Isagogen Porphyrii commenta*, eds. G. Schepes and S. Brand (Corpus Scriptorum Ecclesiasticorum Latinorum 48, Vienna: Tempsky, 1906), pp. 7–9.

6 Isidore of Seville, *Etymologiarum libri XX*, ed. W. M. Lindsay (Oxford: Clarendon, 1911), 2.24.16.

7 Hugh of St. Victor, *Didascalicon de studio legendi*, ed. C. Buttimer (Washington, D.C.: Catholic University of America Press, 1939), 2.19,

pp. 37–38: "Practica [ars] dividitur in solitarium, privatam et publicam; vel aliter in ethicam, oeconomicam et politicam; vel aliter in moralem et dispensativam et civilem." Hugh equates *publica* with *politica atque civilis* and says *polis Graece, Latine civitas dicitur.*

8   Cited in Abelard, *Ethics,* ed. Luscombe, p. xviii.

9   *Ibid.,* book 2 on prudence and virtues, pp. 128–29.

10   Georg Wieland, "The reception and interpretation of Aristotle's *Ethics,"* in Norman Kretzmann, Anthony Kenny, and Jan Pinborg, eds., *The Cambridge History of Later Medieval Philosophy* (Cambridge: Cambridge University Press, 1982), pp. 657–72, 662.

11   M. B. Hackett, *The Original Statutes of Cambridge University: The Text and its History* (Cambridge: Cambridge University Press, 1970), pp. 297–99.

12   R. W. Southern, *Robert Grosseteste: The Growth of an English Mind in Medieval Europe* (Oxford: Clarendon, 1986), p. 50.

13   Aristotle, *Ethica Nicomachea,* ed. R. A. Gauthier (Aristoteles Latinus XXVI. 1–3 fasc. 2, Leiden/Brussels: Brill/Desclée de Brouwer, 1972).

14   Aristotle, *Politica: translatio imperfecta,* ed. P. Michaud-Quantin (Aristoteles Latinus XXIX. 1, Bruges/Paris: Desclée de Brouwer, 1961) and Aristotle, *Politicorum libri octo cum vetusta translatione Guilelmi de Moerbeka,* ed. F. Susemihl (Leipzig: Teubner, 1872).

15   Hackett, *The Original Statutes of Cambridge University,* pp. 298–300; J. A. Weisheipl, "The Curriculum of the Faculty of Arts at Oxford in the Early Fourteenth Century," *Mediaeval Studies* 26 (1964): 143–85.

16   *Grammatica Speculativa of Thomas of Erfurt,* ed. and trans. G. L. Bursill-Hall (Longman, 1972), introduction, pp. 1–126.

17   Aristotle, *Analytica Posteriora,* ed. L. Minio-Paluello and B. G. Dod (Aristoteles Latinus, IV.1–4. Paris/Bruges: Desclée de Brouwer, 1968).

18   Coleman, *Ancient and Medieval Memories,* pp. 233–73.

19   Bursill-Hall, *Grammatica Speculativa,* pp. 20–26.

20   John Murdoch, "The Development of a Critical Temper: New Approaches and Modes of Analysis in Fourteenth-Century Philosophy, Science and Theology," *Medieval and Renaissance Studies* 7 (1978): 51–79, 59.

21   Lorenzo Valla in the fifteenth century would adapt this theory.

22   Albertus Magnus, *Super Ethica,* lib. x, iii, c.3 in *Opera omnia,* ed. A. Borgnet, vol. VII (Paris, 1891): 639:
Politica autem repromittunt quidam sophistice dicere, cum tamen nullus eorum per doctrinam suam aliquid politicorum possit agere. . .Sophistas autem hic vocamus, non qui decipiunt locis sophisticis, sed ab imitatione sophistarum copiose ab apparente sapientia, qui seipsos vocant politicos, cum nesciant quae sit ars politica. . .et repromittunt docere politica, cum artis et virtutis politicae penitus sunt expertes.

23 Hugh of St Victor (above n. 7). Vincent of Beauvais, *Speculum doctrinale* (1244–59), I. 18 (Douai, 1624, repr. Graz, 1965) col. 17:

> Haec dividitur in theoricam et practicam. Practica est moralis philosophia. . .quae ab antiquis solet dividi in monasticam, oeconomicam et politicam; quae divisio penes habitus diversos, quibus mediantibus homo regit seipsum, vel propriam familiam, vel civitatem totam.

24 Alan B. Cobban, "Reflections on the Role of Medieval Universities in Contemporary Society," in Lesley Smith and Benedicta Ward, eds., *Intellectual Life in the Middle Ages: Essays Presented to Margaret Gibson* (London: Hambledon Press, 1992), pp. 227–41, 229.

25 *Ibid.*, pp. 234–35.

26 Hackett, *The Original Statutes of Cambridge University*, pp. 125, 277, 300; Wiesheipl, "Curriculum of the Faculty of Arts at Oxford," 143–85; J. M. Fletcher, "The faculty of arts," in J. I. Catto and T. A. R. Evans, eds., *The Early Oxford Schools* (The History of the University of Oxford, vol. I, Oxford: Clarendon, 1984): 370 ff.

27 W. J. Courtenay, "Theology and Theologians from Ockham to Wyclif," in J. I. Catto and T. A. R. Evans, eds., *Late Medieval Oxford* (The History of the University of Oxford, II [Oxford: Clarendon, 1992]): 1–34; see p. 7.

28 *Ibid.*, p. 11.

29 *Chartularium Universitatis Parisiensis*, eds. H. Denifle and E. Chatelain, 4 vols. (Paris, 1889–97), 2: 485 (n. 1023). This refers to his teaching on logic and natural science. See Coleman, *Ancient and Medieval Memories*, pp. 500–37, 536 (n. 90).

30 Jean-Philippe Genet, "The Dissemination of Manuscripts Relating to English Political Thought in the Fourteenth Century," in Michael Jones and Malcolm Vale, eds., *England and Her Neighbours, 1066–1453: Essays in Honour of Pierre Chaplais* (London: Hambledon Press, 1989), pp. 217–37, 230.

31 Wieland, in *The Cambridge History of Later Medieval Philosophy*, p. 657 believes that it was only in the second half of the fourteenth century that the *Ethics* was adopted as a regular textbook in arts faculties and it came to be intensively studied during the fifteenth century; this may be an underestimation. Cambridge MSS Old Proctor-Caius statute 83, *c.* 1385+ but deriving from the thirteenth century (Hackett, *The Original Statutes of Cambridge University*, p. 276 [n. 5]): "quod in universitate rite audierit in scolis libros aristotelis. . .et omnes libros ethicorum. . .audiat ordinarie." There is further reference to *moralia per terminum* (Hackett, *ibid.*, p. 277); Hackett reconstructs the four years of study placing *Ethica* in the summer

terms of both the third and fourth years, p. 299. The faculty of arts at the University of Toulouse (1309) refers to the first five books of *Ethics* read during the first year and the last five during the second year: M. Fournier, *Les Statuts et privilèges des universités francaises depuis leur fondation jusqu'en 1789* (Paris, 1890–92), I: 465 (n. 542). For Oxford, there is an early fourteenth-century statute which refers to the possibility of choosing Aristotle's *Politics* but requires *Ethics* for inception; see *Statuta Antiqua Universitatis Oxoniensis*, ed. S. Gibson (Oxford: Clarendon, 1931), pp. 32–33. See R. A. Gauthier, "Les *Quaestiones super Librum Ethicorum* de Pierre d'Auvergne," *Revue du moyen âge latin* 20 (1964): 233–60. Gerard d'Abbatsville (d. 1271) stipulated in his will that theology students in Paris should have access to an alphabetical index of the *corpus vetustius* of Aristotle's writings and the *Ethics, Politics*, and the *Rhetoric* (MS Paris, B.N. lat. 16147 (AL 678). For Paris, 1366, we have a requirement that MA candidates attend lectures on the *Ethics*, in *Chartularium Universitatis Parisiensis*, III: n. 319.

32 In his *Quaestiones super Rhetoricam Aristotelis*, Buridan calls these *deliberativum, disceptivum*, and *exclamativum*, I.3, q. 19: "utrum species rhetoricae sunt tres et non plures scilicet deliberativum, disceptivum, exclamativum," cited in Fredborg, "Buridan's *Quaestiones*," p. 55.

33 All of these issues follow the thirteenth-century commentary by Nicolas of Paris on Boethius' *De differentiis topicis*, book 4, from MS Munich clm. 14460 fols. 161r–166v as discussed by Fredborg, "Buridan's *Quaestiones*," pp. 49–50.

34 W. F. Bogess, "Hermannus Alemannus's Rhetorical Translations," *Viator* 2 (1971): 227–50.

35 Fredborg, "Buridan's *Quaestiones*," p. 53.

36 Buridan's commentary deals with *Rhetoric* i–ii, 22 (1395b 28) in MS Erfurt Ampl. q. 319 and MS Leipzig U.B. 1246. Some of the following relevant ethical subjects are drawn from the list of extant *quaestiones* as transcribed from the manuscripts in Fredborg, "Buridan's Quaestiones," pp. 55–58: i, 4, q. 22 "utrum omnes civilitates praeter optimam intensae et remissae corrumpantur"; i, 5, q. 23, "utrum nobilitas, amici, divitiae et alia quae enumerat Aristoteles sint partes felicitatis"; i, 5, q. 25, "utrum divitem esse magis consistat in usus divitiarum quam in possessione"; i, 5, q. 26, "utrum honorantur iuste quidem maxime qui beneficia praestiterunt et utrum etiam honorari debeat qui potest beneficiari'; i, 5, q. 28, "utrum robur sit pars felicitatis, id est utrum exigatur ad perfectissimum et decoratissimum statum quem homo potest habere in politia"; i, 5, q. 31, "utrum bona fortuna sit pars felicitatis, hoc est utrum requiratur ad perfectissimum statum quem homo potest habere in politia"; i, 6, q. 35,

"utrum contrarium [malo] eius in quo inimici civitatis gaudent sit bonum civibus"; i, 7, q. 47, "utrum melius sit iniuriam pati quam iniuriam facere"; i, 7, q. 49, "utrum quod plures eligunt sit melius eo, quod pauciores"; i, 7, q. 54, "utrum melius sit quod ad multa est utilissimum"; i, 9, q. 56, "post hoc autem utrum in solum virtute iustitia contingat inhoneste pati"; i, 9, q. 59, "utrum virtutes virorum sint honestiores et per consequens meliores virtutibus mulierum" (!); i, 9, q. 61 "utrum virtus sit operum principaliter iv virtutes"; etc.

37 Christoph Flüeler, "Die Rezeption der 'Politica' des Aristoteles an der Pariser Artistenfakultät im 13. und 14. Jahrhundert," in Jürgen Miethke, ed., *Das Publikum politischer Theorie im 14. Jahrhundert*, Schriften des Historischen Kollegs, München 21 (Munich: Oldenbourg, 1992), pp. 127–38; Christoph Flüeler, *Rezeption und Interpretation der Aristotelischen Politica im späten Mittelalter*, 2 vols. Bochumer Studien zur Philosophie 19.1 and 2 (Amsterdam/Philadelphia: B. R. Grüner, 1992).

38 Flüeler in Miethke, ed., *Das Publikum*, p. 134.

39 Siger de Brabant, *Quaestiones de anima intellectiva*, ed. B. Bazan (Louvain/Paris: Publications Universitaires [Louvain], 1972), c. 6, p. 99: "quod nostra principalis non est inquirere qualiter se habeat veritas de anima sed quae fuerit opinio philosophi de ea."

40 Jean Dunbabin, "The Reception and Interpretation of Aristotle's *Politics*," in Kretzmann, Kenny, and Pinborg, eds., *The Cambridge History of Later Medieval Philosophy*, pp. 723–37. Also see her discussion in "Government," in J. H. Burns, ed., *The Cambridge History of Medieval Political Thought* (Cambridge: Cambridge University Press, 1988), pp. 477–519. On Peter of Auvergne see James M. Blythe, *Ideal Government and the Mixed Constitution in the Middle Ages* (Princeton: Princeton Unviersity Press, 1992), pp. 77–91.

41 Flüeler has discussed the arts faculty compositions of Peter of Auvergne, Siger of Brabant, an anonymous Milan commentator, Petrus de Casis (1300), John of Jandun, Nicolas of Autrecourt (1330), Albert of Saxony (1358 – read "extraordinarie,") Henry Totting de Oyta, and Nicolas de Vaudemont (1379–98) in *Rezeption und Interpretation*.

42 Flüeler, *ibid.*, pp. 33–34.

43 *Ibid.*, p. 34 (n. 131).

44 Wieland in *The Cambridge History of Later Medieval Philosophy*, p. 662 says he wrote these for himself and not for lectures, but Flüeler in Miethke, ed., *Das Publikum*, p. 129 and *Rezeption und Interpretation*, p. 30 thinks they were for his lectures at the Dominican *studium* in Paris, at St. Jacques.

45 Flüeler dates the *De regno* at 1273 and not 1265. He thinks it was dedicated to Hugh III of Cyprus rather than Hugh II, see *Rezeption und Interpretation*, p. 28.

46 Jürgen Miethke, "Das Publikum politischer Theorie im 14. Jahrhundert. Zur Einfuhrung," in J. Miethke, ed., *Das Publikum*, pp. 1–24.

47 Janet Coleman, "The Intellectual Milieu of John of Paris O. P.," in Miethke, ed., *Das Publikum*, pp. 173–206.

48 Miethke, ed., *Das Publikum*, p. 11.

49 Marsilius of Padua, *"Defensor Pacis" nella traduzione in volgare fiorentino del 1363*, ed. Carlo Pincin (Turin: Luigi Einaudi, 1966).

50 Roberto Lambertini, "Wilhelm von Ockham als Leser der 'Politica'. Zur Rezeption der politischen Theorie des Aristoteles in der Ekklesiologie Ockhams," in Miethke, ed., *Das Publikum*, pp. 207–24, 219.

51 Jacques Krynen, "Les legistes 'idiots politiques'. Sur l'hostilité des théologiens à l'égard des juristes, en France, au temps de Charles V," in *Théologie et droit dans la science politique de l'état moderne*. Actes de la table ronde de l'Ecole française de Rome 147 (Rome: Ecole Française de Rome, Palais Farnèse, 1991), pp. 171–98, 172.

52 Miethke, ed., *Das Publikum*, p. 14.

53 William of Ockham, *Quodlibeta septem*, ed. J. C. Wey in *Opera Theologica* IX (St. Bonaventure, New York: St Bonaventure University, 1980), Quodlibet II, q. 14, pp. 176–78: "utrum de moralibus possit esse scientia demonstrativa." See Janet Coleman, "The Relation between Ockham's Intuitive Cognition and His Political Science," in *Theologie et droit dans la science politique de l'état moderne*, pp. 71–88.

54 Nicole Oresme, *Le livre de politiques*, ed. A. D. Menut (Philadelphia: University of Philadelphia Press, 1970).

55 Krynen, "Les legistes 'idiots politiques,'" p. 184 (n. 49).

56 *Ibid.*, p. 186.

57 In what follows, I have drawn on the material presented in Catto and Evans, eds., *History of the University of Oxford*, II, to highlight the general trends from the fourteenth through to the early sixteenth centuries.

7

Desire and the scriptural text: Will as reader in *Piers Plowman*

JAMES SIMPSON

In Passus 18 of the B-text of *Piers Plowman* (written after 1377), Will (the poem's narrator) describes how he descended to Hell to witness the liberation of imprisoned souls by Christ. He recounts his vision in this way:

> What for feere of this ferly and of the false Jewes,
> I drow me in that derknesse to *descendit ad inferna*,
> And there I saugh soothly, *secundum scripturas*,
> Out of the west coste, a wenche, as me thoughte,
> Cam walkynge in the wey; to helleward she loked.
> Mercy highte that mayde, a meke thyng with alle,
> A ful benigne burde, and buxom of speche.   (B.18.110–16)[1]

Many aspects of this passage suggest an "experiential" narration – a narration, that is, in which the reader is expected to believe that the experience described actually happened to the narrator. Will is unquestionably the "I" around which the syntax of the passage is organized, and he goes so far as almost to promise us that he witnessed what he describes – "I saugh soothly," he says, which might remind us of Dante's astonishing oath in *Inferno* 16.127 that he, too, *really* saw what he relates about Hell ("*per le note / di questa comedia, lettor, ti giuro, / . . .ch'i vidi.*") And like the narrator of the "General Prologue" to the *Canterbury Tales*, he claims no absolute knowledge of what he relates – both narrators qualify their account with warnings about the limitations of their knowledge: "as me thoughte" (line 13), "so as it semed me" ("General Prologue," line 39).

We seem to have a narrative in which the narrator's knowledge is limited to what he saw. But if certain aspects of the passage point to that kind of narrative, other features of this little scene point in different directions. Despite the qualification "as me thoughte" Will does in fact

215

have complete knowledge – he simply tells us what Mercy's name is, without thinking to give any account of how he discovered the name. He seems, that is, to see the scene before him both as a first-person participant recounting what he experienced from within the scene, and as an impersonal, omniscient narrator, who sees the whole scene from outside.[2]

But even more troubling for a reading of this passage as realism authenticated by narratorial experience are the Latin insertions. The fact that there are two languages need be no problem for a "realistic" narration in itself – many multilingual speakers will pepper discourse in one language with phrases from another. But when we reflect that these phrases are drawn from the same text, the Apostles' Creed, which itself recounts in summary form the experience Will lays claim to here, then our confidence in Will's posture of personal authentication cannot help but suffer. If the vernacular lays claim to the experiential, the new, the contingent (the *seen*), it does so only in the shadow of a different kind of narrative, the sonorous, immutable, impersonal discourse of the Latin Creed – a text which is *read*.

Two kinds of narration seem to be rubbing shoulders here, one which (like the *Canterbury Tales*) authenticates itself by reference to the narrator's experience, while the authenticity of the other is derived (like, say, *Troilus and Criseyde*) from texts. The juxtaposition of these two, quite distinct (and normally exclusive) narrative modes is strikingly evident in the single line: "And there I saugh soothly, *secundum scripturas*" (line 112). The sense of each half line here pulls in different directions: as I have already suggested, the first half declares the narrative conditions of "realistic," first-person narrative; the second, by contrast, appeals to an entirely different source for narrative matter, something *read* rather than seen. Langland certainly takes care to insert the Latin into the syntax of an English sentence; equally, the Latin contributes to a perfectly regular metrical pattern in English alliterative verse (aa/aa). But no amount of syntactic and metrical regularity can disguise the conceptual oddity here of claiming authority for a narrative from two sources which are, on the face of it, logically opposed.

Line 112, then, hovers between two narratorial modes, one claiming authenticity by reference to experience, the other by reference to books. The previous line is poised between the same possibilities: "I drow me in that derknesse to *descendit ad inferna*." Here the Latin conforms metrically, but the syntax is broken: we expect a prepositional phrase from the run of the English, but the Latin offers us a main clause. Perhaps the best sense we can make of this line is to insert quotation marks around the Latin – Will, as reader (or his eye), "moves to" the passage *"descendit ad inferna."* But this is clearly unsatisfying, since there is an obvious parallelism of *experience* between the English and the Latin: it is not entirely possible to retain the image of Will as reader "moving to" a given passage which he then cites, since Will is himself in darkness – in *that* darkness indeed – which can only be the darkness of Hell, to which Christ, the implicit subject of *"descendit,"* himself also withdraws. Neither sense is perfect, and so neither gives way to the other.

In short, we are presented with two narrative sources built into the same short narrative: that of the first-person narrator's contingent, "realistic" experience, on the one hand, and that of a text, on the other. In the one case Will is an active participant, in the other he is a reader. The immediate purpose of this essay is to make sense of the copresence of two apparently exclusive narrative modes. But before I do, I would like to set my argument in a slightly broader frame.

"Will as reader": this formulation might strike us as odd, since we are so accustomed to think of Will as one who experiences action (or who debates about the nature of experience), rather than as one who reads texts. The very concept of "will" evokes the discourses of experience and morality, since, after all, it is through experience that a Christian rectifies his or her will.[3] In Christian discourse the notion of will, or desire, immediately evokes the dangers of wilfulness in experience, on the one hand, and the moral ideal of conforming one's will to the will of God, on the other. The "will," translating both *sensualitas* and *voluntas* – both wayward desire and a rational appetite – is the moral focus of personal experience, the locus in which the self either pulls away from, or conforms itself to, the will of God.[4] As such, it inevitably evokes narratives to do with personal moral experience. And no one would deny for a moment that the discourse of personal morality is central to *Piers Plowman*. Just as the narrative of individual episodes in the poem is determined by the semantic range of a word ("mede," for example), so too, it could be argued, does the whole narrative of *Piers Plowman* explore the semantic range of the word "will." The poem charts, that is, the effort of a proper noun ("Will,") to which attach negative senses of will (both wilfulness and sensuality), to become a genuinely common noun, to be absorbed in a charitable church, where "alle kyne cristene" are "cleuynge on o will" (C.17.128).[5] "Will" is the ground of Christian biography and autobiography.

But given the intensely moral bent of much literature and "literary theory" in the later medieval period,[6] it is not surprising to observe that the notion of the will evokes subsidiary discourses to do with the writing, recitation, and reading of texts. Observe the way in which Chaucer's "Squire's Tale" is generated out of a mutual desire in teller and audience (represented here by the Host):

> "Squier, com neer, if it youre wille be,
> And sey somwhat of love; for certes ye
> Konnen theron as muche as any man."
> "Nay sire," quod he, "but I wol sey as I kan
> With hertly wyl; for I wol nat rebelle
> Agayn youre lust; a tale wol I telle.
> Have me excused if I speke amys;
> My wyl is good, and lo, my tale is this."[7]

The goodness of a teller's will is here invoked as the grounds by which he be excused if his tale falls short of its mark (as indeed the "Squire's Tale" does, in my view). But the passage reveals how the will, or desire, is the very condition out of which the story's production and reception arises in the first place: the Squire desires to tell the story, "with hertly wyl," in response, he says, to the Host's "lust."

The Squire's reference to his own good will as a teller here is, I think, born of a growing concern with the moral status of authors in the later medieval period.[8] But just as medieval "literary theory" has a good deal to say about *authorial* will and intention, so too does it focus on psychological and moral categories (and especially the will) with respect to *readers*. Thirteenth-century scholastic thinkers, for example, gave subtle accounts of the ways in which different scriptural styles were designed to move different aspects of the reader's soul. Some books of the Bible had a disputative mode (the Book of Job, for example), and were designed to appeal to the reason; other rhetorical modes used in the Bible were designed to appeal to, and to move, the will.[9] These modes were variously defined as preceptive, exhortative, prophetic, and prayerful.

For theologians in an Augustinian, Franciscan tradition, it is especially through the will's correction that humans are saved;[10] accordingly, such theologians stress the importance and superiority of literary modes in the Bible designed to appeal to the will. St. Bonaventura, for example, writing about 1258 in his *Breviloquium*, says this about the doctrine by which Christians might be saved:

. . .Quia enim haec doctrina est, ut boni fiamus et salvemur; et hoc non fit per nudam considerationem, sed potius per inclinationem voluntatis: ideo Scriptura divina eo modo debuit tradi, quo modo magis possemus inclinari. Et quia magis movetur affectus ad exempla quam ad argumenta, magis ad promissiones quam ad rationcinationes, magis per devotiones quam per definitiones, ideo Scriptura ista non debuit habere modum definitivum, divisivum, et collectivum.[11]

[This doctrine exists in order that we should become good and be redeemed, and this is not achieved by deliberation alone, but rather by a disposition of the will. Therefore, Holy Scripture had to be handed down to us in whatever way would dispose us best [to goodness]. Our affections are moved more strongly by examples than by arguments, by promises than by logical reasonings, by devotions than by definitions. Scripture, therefore, had to avoid the mode of proceeding by definition, division, and inferring. . .][12]

In an earlier article, I tried to show how these discussions about the intended psychological effect of writing might apply to the intended effect of *Piers Plowman* on its own readership.[13] I argued that the poem moves from an argumentative mode, appealing to the reason, to a series of literary modes designed to appeal to the will. I think I was correct to make this connection between literary and psychological categories, but in looking at Langland's attempt to move the will of his readers, I was missing something quite startling in the text itself. For if we are making connections between the correction of the will and the experience of reading, then surely we should look to models of reading from within the poem itself, and particularly to the representation of Will himself as a reader. Just as Langland intends that the will of his readers be moved by his text, so too does he often represent Will, as the human will, as a readerly model being moved from within the text, and being moved through his encounter with scriptural texts. We have had many excellent studies of *Langland* as a reader, but none of Will as reader.[14]

Will's "reading" of Scripture is necessarily provoked by desire (that is an important aspect of what his name means, after all).[15] Will, as the locus of human desire, produces the most startling interpretations of Scripture, and the measure of whether or not these interpretations are "right" is itself determined by the degree to which the will is rectified by them. Moments of breakthrough in the poem are moments of desire-inspired reading by Will. Such, at any rate, will be the larger argumentative goal of this essay. In section I I will simply outline the case that Will is effectively represented as a reader – that a critical part of Will's moral experience is his experience as a reader. In the following section I will define the characteristic (and startling) hermeneutic turn of Will as reader.

But if Will's moral history is in part the history of his reading experience, then I also want to propose here that Langland builds into his poem a polemic about reading: Will's reading changes across the poem, and these changes have radical implications for the institutional, academic treatment of texts. Will's moral history necessarily involves his history as a reader; but this history itself has implications for what might be called the politics of culture. I will briefly explicate these implications in section III.

To summarize the foregoing remarks, we can say that medieval "literary" theory certainly developed ideas concerning the Will with regard to writing and reading. The notion of Will as a kind of personified authorial *intentio* is a rich and so far unexplored one; but in this essay I will rather look at the equally unexplored idea of Will as *reader*. He is, at certain critical moments, a representation of the reading will, as it confronts the text of Scripture.

I

But, a skeptic among my readers might reply, Will is not actually represented as a reader in *Piers Plowman* – we have no scenes in the poem where Will sits and reads. There is no scene comparable to those fascinating moments in, for example, Chaucer's poetry, where Chaucer represents himself as an absorbed reader, sitting "domb as any stoon," reading "at another book / Tyl," as the Eagle says to Geoffrey, "fully dawsed is thy look" (*House of Fame*; lines 656–58).[16] That is almost true (though Will does read both the Pardon at B.7.108, and the writ of Moses at B.17.9–14a), but in the present section of this chapter I will survey some encounters between Will and Scripture. When we "unpack" them, what we observe is an increasingly unmediated, and increasingly affective relationship between Will and Scripture. The subject of Will as reader will emerge in this chapter as a very large one.[17] All I can hope to do here is to take a series of "snapshots," as it were, by way of preparing the ground for a much fuller study.

(i)

In Passus 1 Will encounters not a text, but an institution: Holy Church. But texts are not, of course, far away, since Holy Church adduces scriptural authority for what she says. She descends from the Tower of Truth, and she insistently recalls the textual source of her truthfulness by appealing to Scripture – "by the Gospel" (B.1.90), "by Seint Lukes wordes" (B.1.91), "by sighte of thise textes" (B.1.134): qualifiers of this kind thread the texture of her sermon. Will even characterizes her speech as a kind of biblical talking – he says that he is perplexed as to what woman it was "That swiche wise wordes of Holy Writ shewed" (B.1.72). Let us observe a small example of her speech to Will, to observe how scriptural texts are mediated to Will by the institution, and how they are deployed consistently for moralizing effect. In her address to Will, Holy Church is encouraging the rich to give alms:

> For though ye be trewe of youre tonge and treweliche wynne,
> And as chaste as a child that in chirche wepeth,
> But if ye loven lelly and lene the povere
> Of swich good as God sent, goodliche parteth,
> Ye ne have na moore merite in Masse ne in houres
> Than Malkyn of hire maydenhede, that no man desireth.
> For James the gentile jugged in hise bokes
> That feith withouten feet is [feblere] than nought,
> And as deed as a dorenail but if the dedes folwe:
> *Fides sine operibus mortua est &c.*   (B.1.179–87a)

Here, certainly, there is an implication that the will is to be corrected by authoritative texts: Holy Church is addressing Will, and instructing him in matters of moral action. But the encounter, I agree, can hardly be described as one of reading.

In the first place, it is not an individual experience: Holy Church uses the "ye" form, and this is no politeness to Will (whom she addresses in the singular). Instead she capitalizes on this apparently individual encounter for a more general homiletic address, to the rich in this case, or more specifically to "the will" of the rich. As we might expect in discourse of this kind, the keynote is struck in the citation of the scriptural text. But the rhetorical lead-up to that climax is very skilful, built around the central moral opposition of "treuthe" and love, and embroidered with some witty word play. The full staves of line 182 ("good," "God," "goodliche") do not merely alliterate, but also imply a rather profound sense of the derivation and distribution of private property. Holy Church puns, too, on "feet": the primary meaning must be "deeds" (French *faites*), but in the context of the next line, which refers to deeds "following," the English sense of "feet" is activated retrospectively. And, finally, she brings the distant Latin down to earth with the colloquialism "deed as a dorenail" (with the further phonic play of "deed" and "dedes.")[18]

So the scriptural text is mediated to Will through skilful rhetoric; the Latin is presented as immutable, while the English plays brilliantly around it. But however lively the vernacular, it is effectively designed to mediate and illuminate the Latin text. What Langland presents to us here is the public dissemination of Scripture by the Church – Will's reception of the Bible here can in no way be described as an act of private reading and reflection.

(ii)

Will falls out of participating directly in the action until Passus 8. When he re-enters the narrative, we observe the deployment of scriptural texts, but the nature of this use has changed entirely from Passus 1. Holy Church used Scripture to assert moral truths; in Passus 8 it is Will who deploys Scripture, and he puts his reading to the ends of theological argument.

In Passus 8, before he falls asleep, Will encounters a pair of friars, "maistres of the Menors," whom he asks, with perhaps exaggerated courtesy (*"pur charite,"*) the question which is to preoccupy him until Passus 13, as to "where that Dowel dwelleth" (B.8.13). The friars, characteristically confident, effortlessly claim that "dowel" dwells among the friars themselves. Will's courtesy begins to look disingenuous, a trap deliberately set for his interlocutors, as he unhesitatingly pounces on them with an apparently prepared answer:

> "*Contra!*" quod I as a clerc, and comsed to disputen,
> And seide, "Soothly, *Sepcies in die cadit iustus.*
> Sevene sithes, seith the Book, synneth the rightfulle,
> And whoso synneth," I seide, "[certes] dooth yvele, as me thynketh,
> And Dowel and Do-yvele mowe noght dwelle togideres.
> *Ergo* he nys noght alwey at hoom amonges yow freres:
> He is outherwhile elliswhere to wisse the peple."   (B.8.20–26)

Will names his own procedure here – he adopts an academic discourse of formal disputation, "as a clerc," and so deploys a syllogistic reasoning to counter the friars.[19] As in Passus 1, scriptural texts, in Latin, are used here in a vernacular speech, but they contribute to quite different discursive ends: in Passus 1, as we have seen, the biblical text is produced by the institution, and designed to serve morally persuasive ends to a generalized public. Here, instead, it is the non-academic who turns a biblical text against the academic representatives of the Church. And Will produces the scriptural citation for the purposes of rational demonstration rather than moral persuasion. Scripture is used as a counter in academic debate. Will may not be represented as reading here, but he certainly is represented as *having read*. And he is represented as having assimilated his reading by a rigorously rational, scholastic procedure, applying the strictures of human logic to the scriptural text. This is the kind of reading characterized and condemned by Wyclif as producing "contentiones. . .sophisticas."[20]

But Will's use of his reading in this section of the poem, so far from moving and exciting his will (himself), depresses it. Despite the fact that he presents himself as humbly searching for "dowel," Will's answer to the friars about the impossibility of finding moral probity amongst the righteous is ready-made. It could presumably have been used in reply to anyone who had tried to tell Will where "dowel" was to be found. And repeatedly in these passus (up to the inner dream of Passus 11, at least), Will turns his reading against the moral purpose of reading. His encounter with the figures in the dream here (and particularly with Study and Clergy) recalls and replays an educational *cursus* in which Will is first taught to read (by Study), and then to read theology (by Clergy).[21] All this is the preparation for encountering Scripture itself, but when this happens, it turns out to be a dispiriting experience. Will repeatedly turns his reading against the value of reading. To Scripture he recalls what he has read in Augustine about the uselessness of reading:

> The doughtieste doctour and devinour of the Trinitee,
> Was Austyn the olde, and heighest of the foure,
> Seide thus in a sermon – I seighe it writen ones –
> *"Ecce idiote rapiunt celum ubi nos sapientes in inferno mergimur"*
> And is to mene to Englissh men, moore ne lesse,
> Arn none rather yravysshed fro the righte bileve
> Than are thise konnynge clerkes that konne manye bokes. . .
> (B.10.450–55)[22]

And why should reading be useless? Mainly because, as Will himself says to Scripture, there is one book Will *cannot* read; in reply to Scripture's first speech to Will, he replies dismissively:

> "This is a long lesson," quod I, "and litel am I the wiser!
> Where Dowel is or Dobet derkliche ye shewen.

Manye tales ye tellen that Theologie lerneth,
And that I man maad was, and my name yentred
In the legende of lif longe er I were,
Or ellis unwriten for som wikkednesse, as Holy Writ witnesseth:
Nemo ascendit ad celum nisi qui de celo descendit.
And I leve it wel, by Oure Lord, and on no lettrure bettre." (B.10.369–75)

The Book of Life is closed to Will; and if the one text that Will believes
more than any other concerns God's predestination of souls, then that
seems to negate the value of reading any other texts: there is only one book
that matters, and that cannot be read. Moral improvement through
reading will not, according to the doctrine of predestination, affect Will's
chances of being written into the Book of Life one way or the other. And
neither will it help him to read the Book of Life itself. All Will's reading
here, then, serves only to neutralize the moral purpose of reading.[23]

(iii)

My third example reveals a total change in Will's reception of scriptural
texts. In Passus 11 Will experiences an inner dream. In this heightened
state, he re-experiences the issues of salvation he had debated from the
beginning of Passus 8; but here the issues are broached in intensely personal
terms, whereas they had earlier been handled as matters of academic
dispute. In the inner dream of Passus 11 Will, as the central locus of action,
does generate the discourses of personal experience and moral action which
we normally associate with the will as a potentially wayward desire. For
here Will is led astray by meretricious desire. But part of this concentrated
replay of his moral life, in fact the decisive part, is an encounter with the
text of Scripture. Not only do we have the experiential, biographical Will
here, then, but we are also presented with the will as reader.

As Will has been abandoned by the friars in his search for salvation, he
suddenly hears a sermon by Scripture:

This was hir teme and hir text – I took ful good hede:
"*Multi* to a mangerie and to the mete were sompned;
And whan the peple was plener comen, the porter unpynned the yate
And plukked in *Pauci* pryveliche and leet the remenaunt go rome."
(B.11.111–14)

When Holy Church had given a sermon in Passus 1, we read, and Will
listened to, the homily in its entirety. Here, on the contrary, the "sermon"

stops after the statement of its theme, an elaboration of the austere conclusion to the Parable of the Wedding Feast: "Multi enim sunt vocati, pauci vero electi" (Matt. 22.14). And what eclipses the sermon is Will's intensely personal reflection on it; the text is displaced by its "reader":

> Al for tene of hir text trembled myn herte,
> And in a weer gan I wexe, and with myself to dispute
> Wheither I were chose or noght chose. . .   (B.11.115–17)

Will is disputing here, but the manner of the dispute is not at all academic. He is not using scriptural citations as counters in impersonal, theological arguments about salvation; instead his dispute is rather with himself, and it is more informed by acute anxiety than by the subtle exercise of intellectual skill.[24]

I began section 1 by remarking that we have no scene in *Piers Plowman* where Will reads privately. But what does this scene between Will and Scripture really represent? Will confronts Scripture; no institution mediates this encounter, as Holy Church had mediated Will's reception of Scripture in Passus 1. And there is, accordingly, no elaboration of the scriptural text: Will confronts the stark oppositions of *multi* and *pauci* alone. It seems to me that the real event of this personification allegory can only be described as one of reading: Will has been taught to read by Study; taught to argue theology by Clergy; and here he exercises the highest point of his education by reading Scripture alone, in an intensely personal way. What else could we mean when we say "Will confronts Scripture" than, in effect, "Will reads Scripture"? Will reads alone, his experience unmediated by any institution. And he reads very much according to the pleasure of the text, a point I elaborate in the following section.

(iv)

Let us look, finally, at the scene in Passus 13 which I take to be a representation of an academic feast, where Conscience is the master of the college and Clergy and the Doctor of Divinity his guests on high table, while Patience and Will sit on the side-tables in the body of the hall. This is a critical and explosive scene in the poem as a whole. I shall return to its institutional implications in the final section of this chapter, but for the moment I would like simply to make the point that Will's experience in this academic context is in part a reading experience.

Scripture serves all the guests. How else can we interpret the following action except as the representation of an act of reading?:

> Conscience ful curteisly tho commaunded Scripture
> Bifore Pacience breed to brynge and me that was his mette.
> He sette a sour loof toforn us and seide, "*Agite penitenciam,*"
> And siththe he drough us drynke: "*Dia perseverans* –
> As longe," quod he, "as lif and lycame may dure."
> "Here is propre service," quod Pacience, "ther fareth no prince bettre!"
> And he broughte us of *Beati quorum* of *Beatus vir*res makyng,
> And thanne he broughte us forth a mees of oother mete, of *Miserere mei,*
>   *Deus Et quorum tecta sunt peccata*
> In a dissh of derne shrifte, *Dixi et confitebor tibi.*   (B.13.46–54)

If Will digests scriptural texts here, with Patience as his companion, this can effectively mean nothing else than that Will is reading patiently: provoked by Conscience, Will desires patiently to ingest texts of Scripture which promote penitential reflection. A new practice of reading is being evoked in the poem, whereby a reader chews on, and ruminates on, the "food" of Scripture. Whereas Will's reading had seemed a sterile and morally useless activity in Passus 10, here Scripture, patiently attended to, re-enters the living current of moral experience. But it does so only as Will reads in a personal, affective way, where Scripture is mediated to him by nothing but his own conscience. He reads in the manner indicated by Augustine; addressing those who convert, Augustine says this:

Nos autem qui conuenimus, pascamur epulis Dei, et sit gaudium nostrum sermo ipsius. Inuitauit enim nos ad euangelium suum, et ipse cibus noster est, quo nihil dulcius, sed si quis habet palatum sanum in corde.[25]

[We, however, who gather, let us feed on the feasts of God, and let his words be our delight. For he invited us to his Gospel, and he is our food, than which there is none sweeter for him whose heart's palate is healthy.]

This tradition of digesting scriptural texts is richly represented in twelfth-century monastic exegesis;[26] the experiential, tactile quality of this "edible" reading is also adduced in thirteenth-century scholastic contexts, where it is deployed by way of confirming the certainty (and, therefore, the disciplinary superiority) of theology as a science. Thus Alexander of Hales, for example, argues that the mode of Scripture (which he equates with theology as a science) is certain by virtue of its grounding in the "taste" of the will:

Est certitudo speculationis et est certitudo experientiae; praeterea est certitudo
secundum intellectum et est certitudo secundum affectum. . .Dico ergo quod
modus theologicus est certior certitudine experientiae, certitudine quoad
affectum, quae est per modum gustus, in Psalmo [118.103] "Quam dulcia
faucibus meis eloquia tua. . ."[27]

[There is certainty bred of investigation and certainty bred of experience.
Besides, there is certainty according to the intellect, and certainty according to
the will. . .I say, therefore, that the theological mode is more certain in terms of
the certainty that comes from experience; and in terms of the certainty that
relates to the will, which operates through taste, as in the Psalm, "How sweet is
your eloquence to my taste."][28]

We could, of course, go on observing moments where Will is effectively
represented as a reader: the meetings with Abraham, Moses, and the
Samaritan in Passus 16 and 17, for example, seem to me to represent
Will's reading of the Old Testament (for Langland, in a long tradition of
exegesis, the Samaritan is equivalent to an Old Testament type).[29] Will
reads the Old Testament as dynamically pointing forward to the Christian
dispensation, and his reading of these figures propels him, along with the
figures themselves, to Jerusalem, where he both witnesses Christ and reads
about Christ (the acts are indistinguishable) in the way we observed in our
introduction. But from the four "snapshots" of Will receiving scriptural
texts considered so far, we can conclude this section by remarking that
these passages, taken in sequence, trace the growth of a reader: from
passively receiving texts mediated by the institution of the Church, Will
passes to an academic, rational deployment of Scripture. And from here he
moves (after a period of profound and radical disillusion with scriptural
reading) to an affective, dynamic, and sophisticated practice of biblical
reflection.

II

It may be that I have convinced my readers of one half of my title, "Will as
Reader in *Piers Plowman*," and equally, it may be that we are better placed
to understand the apparently contradictory narrative projections of the
small passage from Passus 18 with which we began: for Langland,
particular kinds of reading are experience. "Experience" and "auctoritee"
are not ultimately exclusive sources of knowledge in *Piers Plowman*:
particular kinds of reading themselves produce experience. But what of the

first half of my title, "Desire and the scriptural text"? In this penultimate section, beyond suggesting that Will's attraction to Scripture is fundamentally a matter of desire, I want to elucidate Will's hermeneutic bent. What kind of interpretations does the will produce?

In Passus 3 Conscience, a reader well versed in scriptural texts, seems to imply that Mede has not read those parts of the Bible which contradict her own economic practice (B.3.259–79). Mede, like some of the women in Chaucer's poetry (for example, the Wife of Bath, and Proserpine), clearly knows her Bible well. She replies indignantly:

> "I kan no Latyn?" quod she. "Clerkes wite the sothe!
> Se what Salomon seith in Sapience bokes:
> That thei that yyven yiftes the victorie wynneth,
> And muche worshipe have therwith, as Holy Writ telleth –
> *Honorem adquiret qui dat munera, &c.*" (B.3.332–36a)

At an equivalent moment in Chaucer's poetry (Proserpine disputing with Pluto, for example), it is the woman whose hermeneutic skill, and whose sheer breadth of reading, defeats the ostensibly learned male opponent. In *Piers Plowman*, however, Conscience turns out to have been a more scrupulous reader than Mede; he insists on clerkly and male prerogatives in the matter of reading, for he is not taken in by that casual "*&c.*" Mede, he says, is like a lady who read the text "omnia probate" at the end of a page, and, much pleased with this ("and that plesed her herte,") failed to turn the folio, where she would have found the further, qualifying injunction, "Quod bonum est tenete":

> And so [mys]ferde ye, madame – ye kouthe na moore fynde
> Tho ye loked on Sapience, sittynge in youre studie.
> This text that ye han told were [tidy] for lordes,
> Ac yow failed a konnynge clerk that couthe the leef han torned.
> And if ye seche Sapience eft, fynde shul ye that folweth,
> A ful teneful text to hem that taketh mede:
> And that is *Animam autem aufert accipientium &c.*
> And that is the tail of the text of that tale ye shewed. (B.3.345–51)

The lay reader Mede, whose interpretations satisfy lordly greed, is checked here by Conscience's imagined cleric, who will insist on reading the whole text, however unpalatable, or "teneful" it might be. What characterizes Conscience's reading is its completeness, its determination to grasp the full sense of a scriptural text, not just those parts which might please a reader.

Conscience's is a "truthful" reading: once he has established the whole sense, he appeals to "Truth" – "truthe that text made," he says (line 343), and his point could equally apply to his own reading, since it is designed to get at the rationally perceptible truth of texts.

Conscience, then, would seem to be hostile to an affective hermeneutics: Mede and Conscience's imagined woman reader both read according to the "pleasure of the text," according to what they desire from the text to suit their own interests, rather than according to what the text means.[30] By contrast with this affective reading, Conscience's might look like a stable and morally persuasive hermeneutic position. But in fact, I want now to argue, Conscience's model of reading turns out to be radically inadequate. What Langland works toward in *Piers Plowman* is a reading model in which texts must bend to the *best* desires of their readers. What turns out to be wrong with Mede's reading is not that it satisfies readerly desire; it is rather that Mede's desire is egoistic, a "propyr" rather than a "comone" will, to use Walter Hilton's Bernadine terms.[31]

The biblical text "Animam autem aufert accipientium" is not the only "ful teneful text" in *Piers Plowman*. The Pardon received by Piers in Passus 7 provokes "pure tene" in him, and well it might. Read literally (and how else could we read it, sent as it is from Truthe?), the "pardon" demolishes the premises of pardon by insisting on strict payment by God. It is a text ironic with respect to its formal designation ("pardon,") but that irony serves only to insist on the inescapably literal force of what it actually does say. And just as the text Mede has not read threatens to damn the soul, so too does the "pardon"; Will reads it along with Piers:

> And I bihynde hem bothe biheld al the bulle.
> In two lynes it lay, and noght a le[ttre] moore,
> And was writen right thus in witnesse of truthe:
> *Et qui bona egerunt ibunt in vitam eternam;*
> *Qui vero mala, in ignem eternum.*　　　　　(B.7.108–110b)

This might sound equitable, but Will's experience up to this point has suggested that humans are simply incapable of doing well. Piers' own response to this text is to refute it, and his refutation is not simply implicit in his tearing of the document, but also in the text he cites from the Psalms:

> And Piers for pure tene pulled it atweyne
> And seide, "*Si ambulavero in medio umbre mortis*
> *Non timebo mala, quoniam tu mecum es.*"　　　(B.7.115–17)

The text of the Pardon itself seems to allow for no escape: it is sent by Truth, and its terms are relentlessly literal, disallowing the escape route of allegoresis. In the face of this austere, impersonal, and apparently absolute statement, Piers nevertheless has recourse to a biblical text which formulates an intimate relationship to God in terms of personal faith; the Pardon poses itself very much as a document, as "auctoritee," whereas Piers' text from Psalm 22 effaces its textuality by speaking *for* Piers in a moment of extreme anxiety. Despite his not knowing *how* the pardon is wrong, Piers does not believe it. It is a "teneful text," but Piers, despite his evident anguish, is able to read beyond it. His reading is quite different from Mede's (Piers reads to the end, and does not read simply to satisfy desire), but it resembles Mede's insofar as neither read according to the letter of "truthe."

Will, on the contrary, does read as Conscience would have him do so; he respects the Pardon as the document sent by, and written by, "Truthe." And in the passus that follow he repeatedly cites, Bunyan-like, biblical texts which imply his deeply pessimistic, literalist reading of the Pardon:

> . . . Soothly, *Sepcies in die cadit iustus*   (B.8.21)

> *Nemo ascendit ad celum nisi qui de celo descendit*
> And I leve it wel, by Oure Lord, and on no lettrure bettre.
>   (B.10.374a–75)

> For sothest word that ever God seide was tho he seide *Nemo bonus.*
>   (B.10.438)

Almost the entire burden of Will's arguments in these disputative passus points in the same direction as Truthe's Pardon: that all will be damned, since, as Will insists by reference to Scripture, "Nemo bonus." The best we can hope for is predestination, whereby God saves whomsoever he will, regardless of moral effort. But can Will, as the will, be satisfied with this? The very word "will," as I mentioned earlier, designates that part of the soul which desires. Can human desire be wholly satisfied with the strictures of reason and justice, especially when those strictures determine that humans can do nothing toward their own salvation?

If the will *were* satisfied with the strictures of Truthe, then the poem would, presumably, stop at Will's predestination speech, where Will glimpses the one possibility of salvation. But the poem does not in fact stop here (not in the B- and C-texts, at any rate), and the fact that it does not implies Will's dissatisfaction. It is Will, as desire, who generates the forward movement of this section of the poem, even out of the despair to which belief in predestination seems inevitably to lead. The turning point out of despair is a moment of reading, in the encounter with Scripture in the inner dream of Passus 11, which I discussed briefly in section 1. As I said earlier, Will encounters Scripture in a moment of profound and personal anxiety: here, too, we have a figure trembling before another "teneful text," questioning the possibility of his own salvation in the face of a text which would seem to minimize that possibility ("Many are called but few are chosen.") We should now pause over the nature of Will's "reading" of this text, since it reveals the startling quality of what may be called Langland's voluntarist hermeneutics.

Scripture's text would seem to offer no serious hope to Will of salvation – any literal reading of it would confirm Will's pessimistic reading of the Pardon. Curiously, however, Will turns this negative and pessimistic text to extraordinarily hopeful ends. He thinks on his baptism, and on the open welcome of God made in Isaiah 55.1: "O vos omnes sicientes, venite [ad aquas]"; he cites the resurrected Christ's own words (Mark 16.16) about the salvific power of baptism and belief: "Qui crediderit, et baptizatus fuerit, salvus erit." Will, as human desire, responds to Scripture's apparently damning text by citing other texts from Scripture that point in quite different (more hopeful) directions. Like Piers earlier (also responding to a "teneful text") Will refuses to read literally here, according to the apparent, rationally clear sense of the text.

Will's speech is not, however, one of unchecked optimism: his reference to the legal claims his baptism allows, provokes recognition of the legal responsibilities of that baptism: the Christian, like the serf, cannot disclaim the legal constraints which bind him to his lord. Should he do so, and run "recchelesly" about (like the "recheless" Will himself in Passus 10 and early in Passus 11), the lord has the right to put him in prison, where (and here the spiritual tenor of the legal comparison becomes its vehicle) Conscience will

> . . .acounte with hym and casten hym in arerage,
> And putten hym after in prison in purgatorie to brenne,
> For his arerages rewarden hym there right to the day of dome,
> But if Contricion wol come and crye by his lyve
> Mercy for his mysdedes with mouthe or with herte.   (B.11.132–36)

Will is not only a reader of the Bible; he is also familiar with manorial legal and bureaucratic procedures. But in this argument, although both sets of texts (the biblical and the legal) admit of the possibility of punishment, neither, in Will's reading, damn strictly: both allow for forgiveness, or at least (in the matter of a runaway serf) for legal repayment. Both allow for the possibility of escape from legal liability through compensation to the wronged party.

I have argued elsewhere that this speech is the turning point of the Third Vision, and, effectively, of the whole poem, since this affirmation of the possibility of God's mercy, made for the first time in the depressive aftermath of the so-called "Pardon," allows a way out of Will's overwhelming sense of the inescapability of God's absolute justice.[32] The comparison with statuted law allows for the importance of legal constraint, while equally recognizing that law need not be absolute. The modification of strict justice built into the statuted law offers a way of correlating the pessimistic and the optimistic texts of Scripture.

In the context of the present article, however, the essential point is not so much to understand the theological argument Will makes, as to observe that Will makes it. Will "reads" Scripture by answering back to it, not only with other scriptural texts with a very different, more optimistic, import, but also by reference to contemporary law. And Will's reply to the austere text of Scripture is born out of his own dissatisfaction with it: as the will, the locus of human desire, Will cannot "read" Scripture in passive, rational acceptance of texts which ignore human desire. He arrives at a reading, that is, which satisfies, and is measured to, the will of the reader, and to his contemporary experience. And despite the fact that his reading seems totally at odds with the austere, exclusive thrust of the text offered him by Scripture ("many are called. . .,") by the time he has finished, the text of Scripture is agreeing with him:

> "That is sooth," seide Scripture; "may no synne lette
> Mercy al to amende, and mekenesse hir folwe;
> For thei beth, as oure bokes telleth, above Goddes werkes:
> *Misericordia eius super omnia opera eius."* (B.11.137–39a)

Langland represents a dynamic reading process here, whereby reader and text interact, and whereby the reader's own desires and contemporary experience contribute substantially to the reading arrived at. The "normal" directions of text informing reader are here reversed: it is Will who reads a hopeful message into Scripture's austere text, at which point Scripture agrees. He reads in the manner of St. Bernard, as described by a contemporary:

Utebatur Scripturis tam libere commodeque ut non tam sequi illas quam praecedere crederetur et ducere ipse quo vellet, auctorem earum ducem Spiritum sequens.[33]

[He used the Scriptures so freely and skilfully that he seemed less to follow than to precede them, and to lead wheresoever he would, following their author, the Holy Spirit.]

The measure of success for Will's reading is not its philological accuracy in unpicking the meaning of the biblical text; the reading arrived at is justified rather by the effect it has on its reader: Will not only makes the reading here, but is himself dignified by it. From this point on in the poem, Will can see a place for human effort, both moral and intellectual, in the economy of salvation.[34]

So it is a long way from Scripture's austere text to Will's hopeful response, and a way characterized, apparently, by contradiction. But the poem as a whole gives authority to Will's reading: from this point on, the poem confirms the value of good works, and the existence of God's mercy above his justice. The rest of the poem confirms the rereading of the pardon proposed here by Will: that "dowel" does not mean "doing well" by the standards of God's absolute justice; "dowel" instead means doing well, or doing one's best, within the standards of God's mitigated justice, through penance. And not only does the poem authorize Will's voluntarist hermeneusis – Will's reading also has a very long and authoritative tradition behind it. In the *De doctrina christiana*, for example, Augustine says this:

Sic euersa tyrannide cupiditatis caritas regnat iustissimis legibus dilectionis dei propter deum, sui et proximi propter deum. Seruabitur ergo in locutionibus figuratis regula huiusmodi, ut tam diu uersetur diligenti consideratione quod legitur, donec ad regnum caritatis interpretatio perducatur. Si autem hoc iam proprie sonat, nulla putetur figuratur locutio.[35]

[Thus when the tyranny of cupidity has been overthrown, charity reigns with its most just laws of love for God for the sake of God and of one's self and of one's neighbour for the sake of God. Therefore in consideration of figurative expressions a rule such as this will serve, that what is read should be subjected to loving scrutiny until an interpretation contributing to the reign of charity is produced. If this result appears literally in the text, the expression being considered is not figurative.][36]

The pardon's injunction to "Dowel" in order to be saved had seemed inescapably literal and relentlessly threatening. Will's reading of this injunction finally produces an understanding of it which contributes to the "reign of charity," precisely by recognizing that liberating ambiguities may lie within even the most apparently literal and legalistic of documents.

III

Is it significant that Augustine's account of interpretive practice in the previous citation should be so insistently political in its metaphors? In literate societies the connection between reading practice and politics (broadly understood) is often very close. Modes of reading Scripture are, of course, near the heart of the Reformation in the sixteenth century; and for confirmation that kinds of reading provoke "political" (or at least ecclesiological) questions in the late fourteenth and early fifteenth centuries, one need only think of, say, Wyclif's *De veritate sacrae scripturae* (1377–78), or of Arundel's *Constitutions* (drafted in 1407). Wyclif's tract about biblical hermeneutics turns to radical ecclesiological questions concerning disendowment.[37] Arundel's *Constitutions* prohibit, among other things, the reading of any tract by Wyclif in the schools or anywhere else without authoritative permission; the translation of Scripture into English; and the ownership of any translation of the Bible made in Wyclif's time without permission.[38]

Where do the "affective hermeneutics" of *Piers Plowman* stand in this "political" spectrum? This is a much larger question than can be answered in the brief span that still remains of this essay. In what follows I sketch the argument that Langland's representation of Will as reader contains a polemic about reading; as for Augustine, so too for Langland: a charitable hermeneutics involves a political overturning of sorts ("sic euersa tyrannide cupiditatis caritas regnat iustissimis legibus dilectionis"). Will's reading only comes to fruition in an entirely reformed Church; for Will to be reformed as a reader, so too must the Church be reformed.

On the face of it, however, Langland's hermeneutics, as I have described them, look very conservative: Will moves from scholastic to monastic habits of reading, and this move is squarely within an Augustinian tradition. And within the spectrum of readerly practice in the twenty or so years after *Piers Plowman*, it would seem to fall more on the conservative than the radical, Wycliffite side. In Nicholas Love's early fifteenth-century *Mirrour of the Blessed Lyf of Jesu Christ* (a text licensed by Archbishop

234

Arundel in 1410),[39] we find reading directions which square, by and large, with the phenomena we have observed in Langland's poem. In a long tradition of devotional piety,[40] Love encourages his readers to make themselves "present to thoo thinges that bene here writen seyd or done of oure lord Jesu";[41] and he also encourages his readers imaginatively to embroider the biblical text for themselves, with the sole restriction that the imaginative reading be devout, "not by errour affermyng,"[42] and that it be an imagination "by resoun."[43] This interpretive freedom allows for a very personal reading: with regard to the Lord's Prayer, for example, Love says that "there is non other prayer made of man that schall be to hym so sauery and so effectuele"; when God will give the person who reflects on this text grace, the reader will find "with gret likyng diuerse vndurstandyng therof most pertynent to his desire and that othere than is writen in the comune exposicion therof."[44]

The conservative position is, therefore, paradoxically liberal, allowing as it does readerly desire to appropriate the text of Scripture. Certainly there are discreet bounds placed on the reader's freedom, bounds marked by the term "reason." Love never explicitly says what he means by this term, but one may assume that he means something like "what the Church teaches." And the freedom he encourages is imaginative and affective rather than ratiocinative – the reader is never encouraged to follow this imaginative freedom through to ecclesiological questions. Within these bounds, however, the reader is permitted a good deal of scope for enlarging and personalizing the text.

By contrast, Wyclif's hermeneutics seem sternly restrictive on the face of it. Wyclif's *De veritate sacrae scripturae* (the text on which my discussion of Wyclif's hermeneutics is based) expresses anxieties about readers interpreting the equivocations of Scripture "ad votum," according to their desire.[45] Likewise, he insists that Scripture is distinct from interpretations given it by readers.[46] And, correlative with the previous two points, he insists that the reader respect the authorial intention of Scripture.[47] All this would seem to make Wyclif a genuine precursor of Protestant hermeneusis. But before we accept this, we should observe the peculiarity of his ultra-realist position.

Wyclif's main polemic in the *De veritate sacrae scripturae* is against academic readers of Scripture who question its truthfulness on account of its often figurative literary mode. But Wyclif's own response to academic questioning of Scripture is to affirm an academic principle, that arguments can be drawn only from the literal sense of the Bible.[48] Where Wyclif differs from his academic opponents is in his astonishing move to claim that (from God's perspective) the *whole* of Scripture is literal, the whole of Scripture employs "proper," non-figurative language.[49] For Wyclif Scripture is essentially an idea in the mind of God, which does not stand or fall by its material instantiations in the letters and parchment of books.[50] So far from leading to a Protestant philology, Wyclif's theoretical position (as distinct from the practice of his followers translating the Bible) leads away from codicological and philological investigation of Scripture. His position ostensibly claims respect for the text above the reader, whereas in fact he has merely heightened the power of the reader, by allowing him or her to claim (a purely ideological) access to authorial intention, without any extra philological equipment. The position is, of course, ideal for a polemicist, but the real knowledge of Wyclif's reader remains pretty much identical with the "affective" reader of Scripture, given that both are faced with the text from a human, not divine point of view. It is for this reason that Wyclif also demands that the reader interpret until he or she find an interpretation consonant with charity;[51] and it is for this reason that Wycliffite exegesis often looks identical in practice to standard fourfold exegesis. Wyclif's reader stands in exactly the same position as any reader in the past, with the exception of being able to base arguments on any passage of Scripture (regardless of its figurative language), in the confidence that this was God's intended meaning.

If my analysis is correct, what drives Wyclif's exegetical theory is his acceptance of the academic principle that arguments can only be based on the literal sense. However much Wyclif might seem to be attacking academic practice, the most startling feature of his theory (that the whole Bible is literal) is determined by his acceptance of this academic principle. When we return to Langland's "voluntarist hermeneutics," we may conclude by observing that he spectacularly distinguishes it from an academic literalism. And however much Will's reading might seem to conform with Love's conservative practice, Langland takes care to register its radical, ecclesiological implications.

Let me end, then, with some remarks on the feast scene of Passus B.13. In section I we saw how Will's "food" in this scene is constituted by texts, and that Will's "reading" here is best understood by reference to monastic habits of exegesis. This might seem a conservative posture, but in the context of the scene as a whole, this kind of reading turns out to be profoundly disruptive. Conscience, represented as the master of an academic hall, subtly questions his guests about the nature of Dowel – first the obese Doctor of Divinity, then the theologian Clergy, and finally the eremitic figure on the side-table, Patience. I have no wish to repeat what I have said elsewhere about this scene;[52] here I simply remark that Conscience's decision to abandon his position at the head of the college and to follow Patience out into the street (B.13.180–201) could not be more spectacular as an act of social and institutional disruption. Clergy, astonished and offended, insists on the power of academic hermeneusis, by parading his knowledge of the literal sense of Scripture, against a fragile, poetic, figurative mode:

> "What!" quod Clergie to Conscience, "are ye coveitous nouthe
> After yeresyeves or yiftes, or yernen to rede redels?
> I shal brynge yow a Bible, a book of the olde lawe,
> And lere yow, if you like, the leeste point to knowe,
> That Pacience the pilgrym parfitly knew nevere." (B.13.183–87)

But Conscience, in this representation of an academic dispute about modes of reading, is unpersuaded by academic exegesis. What does move Conscience (the very model of a "truthful" reader in Passus 3) is the will of Pacience:

> "Nay, by Crist!" quod Conscience to Clergie, "God thee foryelde.
> For al that Pacience me profreth, proud am I litel;
> Ac the wil of the wye and the wil of folk here
> Hath meved by mood to moorne for my synnes.
> The goode wil of a wight was nevere bought to the fulle:
> For ther nys no tresour therto to a trewe wille." (B.13.188–93)

As the poem approaches Christ's loving act of redemption, so too does it plumb the human capacity to love. It is only by modeling themselves on the measureless capacity of the divine will that humans find satisfaction and dignity before God. But at this moment in the poem the impulse to meet the measure of the will provokes both a hermeneutic and an institutional *transitus*. And, although I do not have space to argue the case here, it seems to me that the desires of Will as reader are not satisfied by leaving the academic establishment; they remain unfulfilled as long as the Church itself is unreformed until Passus B.19. The fulfilment of Will as reader requires nothing less than the reformation of the Church.

Notes

1 All citations from the B-Text of *Piers Plowman* (the version discussed in this article) are from *William Langland, The Vision of Piers Plowman*, ed. A. V. C. Schmidt, revised edn. (London and Melbourne: Dent, 1987). Citations from the C-Text are from *Piers Plowman by William Langland*, ed. Derek Pearsall, York Medieval Texts, second series (London: Edward Arnold, 1978).

2 For a wider discussion of the narratological distinctions I make here, see J. A. Burrow, *Langland's Fictions* (Oxford: Clarendon, 1993), ch. 3.

3 For the history of the idea of the "will," see especially Albrecht Dihle, *The Theory of Will in Classical Antiquity*, Sather Classical Lectures 48 (Berkeley and Los Angeles: University of California Press, 1982). For the renewed importance of the will in fourteenth-century theology, see J. B. Korolec, "Free Will and Free Choice," in Norman Kretzmann, Anthony Kenny, and Jan Pinborg, eds., *The Cambridge History of Later Medieval Philosophy* (Cambridge: Cambridge University Press, 1982), pp. 629–641. John Bowers, *The Crisis of Will in* Piers Plowman: (Washington, D.C.: Catholic University of America Press, 1986), discusses the relevance of fourteenth-century developments for the notion of "will" in Langland's poem (pp. 41–60).

4 Among the senses of "will" (as noun) given by *The Oxford English Dictionary*, second edn., the following are relevant to Langland's usage: I.1.a, "desire, wish, longing"; I.2, "carnal desire, or appetite"; II.5.a, "the action of willing or choosing to do something"; II.6.a, "the power or capacity of willing; that faculty or function which is directed to conscious and intentional action"; II.9.a, "undue assertion of one's own will; wilfulness, self-will."

5 For subtle (and complementary) accounts of the way in which the poem's "subject" is Will/the will, see David Lawton, "The Subject of *Piers Plowman*," *Yearbook of Langland Studies* 1 (1987): 1–30, and Anne Middleton, "William Langland's 'Kynde Name': Authorial Signature and Social Identity in Late Fourteenth-Century England," in Lee Patterson, ed., *Literary Practice and Social Change in Britain, 1380–1530* (Berkeley and Los Angeles: University of California Press, 1990), pp. 14–82.

6 See, for example, Judson Boyce Allen, *The Ethical Poetic of the Later Middle Ages: a Decorum of Convenient Distinction* (Toronto, Buffalo, and London: University of Toronto Press, 1982), pp. 3–66.

7 *Canterbury Tales*, 5.1–8. Citations of Chaucer's works are from *The Riverside Chaucer*, third edn., ed. Larry D. Benson (Oxford: Oxford University Press, 1988).

8 For which see especially A. J. Minnis, *Medieval Theory of Authorship: Scholastic Literary Attitudes in the Later Middle Ages* (London: Scolar Press, 1984).

9 For discussions of the *formae tractandi* of Scripture, see especially Minnis, *ibid.*, pp. 119–45.

10 The voluntarist/intellectualist divide in thirteenth-century scholastic theology is treated concisely by Ulrich Kopf, *Die Anfänge der theologischen Wissenschaftstheorie im 13 Jahrhundert*, Beiträge zur historischen Theologie 49 (Tübingen: J. C. B. Mohr, 1974), pp. 198–210. For accounts of how differing conceptions of theology might influence writers in the vernacular, see A. J. Minnis, "Affection and Imagination in *The Cloud of Unknowing* and Hilton's *Scale of Perfection*," *Traditio* 39 (1983): 323–66.

11 *Breviloquium*, in *S. Bonaventurae opera omnia*, ed. The College of S. Bonaventure, 11 vols (Quaracchi, 1882–1902), v: 206 (prologue, paragraph 5).

12 The translation is drawn from A. J. Minnis, A. B. Scott, with David Wallace, eds., *Medieval Literary Theory and Criticism, c. 1100–c. 1375: The Commentary Tradition* (Oxford: Clarendon, 1988), pp. 235–36.

13 James Simpson, "From Reason to Affective Knowledge: Modes of Thought and Poetic Form in *Piers Plowman*," *Medium Aevum* 55 (1986): 1–23.

14 The main studies here are: D. W. Robertson and Bernard F. Huppé, *Piers Plowman and Scriptural Tradition* (Princeton: Princeton University Press, 1951); Ben H. Smith, *Traditional Imagery of Charity in* Piers Plowman (The Hague and Paris: Mouton, 1966); Stephen A. Barney, "The Plowshare of the Tongue: The Progress of a Symbol from the Bible to *Piers Plowman*," *Mediaeval Studies* 35 (1973): 261–93; David Aers, *Piers Plowman and Christian Allegory* (London: Edward Arnold, 1975); John A. Alford, "The Role of Quotations in *Piers Plowman*," *Speculum* 52 (1977): 80–99; Helen Barr, "The Use of Latin Quotations in *Piers Plowman* with Special Reference to Passus XVIII of the 'B' Text," *Notes and Queries*, new series 33 (1986): 440–48; Steven Justice, "The Genres of *Piers Plowman*," *Viator* 19 (1988): 291–306; John A. Alford, Piers Plowman: *A Guide to the Quotations*, Medieval and Renaissance Texts and Studies 77 (New York: Center for Medieval and Early Renaissance Studies, SUNY Binghampton Press, 1992).

15 *Oxford English Dictionary*, second edn. sense 1.1.a, "desire, wish, longing."

16 For further examples of Chaucer as a fictionalized reader, see Jill Mann, "The Authority of the Audience in Chaucer," in Piero Boitani and Anna Torti, eds., *Poetics: Theory and Practice in Medieval English Literature*, The J. A. W. Bennett Memorial Lectures, seventh series (Cambridge: D. S. Brewer, 1991), pp. 1–12.

17 Victoria Sellar, to whom I am grateful for many conversations on this topic, is currently preparing a Cambridge M.Litt. on it.

18 See Mary Clemente Davlin, *A Game of Heuene: Word Play and the Meaning of* Piers Plowman, Piers Plowman Studies 7 (Cambridge: D. S. Brewer, 1989), pp. 41–42 for further word play in this passage.

19 For further discussion of the scholastic style used here, see James Simpson, Piers Plowman: *An Introduction to the B-Text* (London and New York: Longman, 1990), pp. 107–10.

20 Wyclif, *De veritate sacrae scripturae*, ed. Rudolf Buddensieg, 3 vols (London: Wyclif Society, 1905–7), 1:29, line 2. Needless to say, Wyclif's comment about the sterility of scholastic dispute is part of a huge tradition of opposition to scholastic treatment of Scripture. For some twelfth-century examples, and further references, see James Simpson, "The Role of *Scientia* in *Piers Plowman*," in Gregory Kratzmann and James Simpson, eds., *Medieval English Religious and Ethical Literature: Essays in Honour of G. H. Russell* (Cambridge: D. S. Brewer, 1986), pp. 49–65.

21 I argue that this is the educational cursus followed by Will in Kratzmann and Simpson, *ibid.*

22 For a short but far-reaching discussion of this passage, see C. David Benson, "An Augustinian Irony in *Piers Plowman*," *Notes and Queries*, new series 23 (1976): 51–54. See n. 24 below. See Alford, *A Guide to the Quotations*, p. 70 for other contexts in which quotation of Augustine, *Confessions*, 8.8 ("surgunt indocti et caelum rapiunt. . .") appears.

23 Wyclif himself seems to have undergone a conversion from scholastic treatment of texts to a form of reading more responsive to God's grammar. See *De veritate sacrae scripturae*, ed. Buddensieg, 1:23, 100.

24 Will's response to Scripture's text here has resonances with the reading experience which converted Augustine, as related in the *Confessions* (translated by William Watts, 2 vols [Loeb Classical Library, London and Cambridge, Mass.: Harvard University Press, 1912]). The relevant chapters are 8.8–12. Augustine goes into the garden in despair at the carnality of the learned beside the spirituality of the unlearned: "Surgunt indocti et caelum rapiunt," he despairingly comments (8.8, volume 1:422). He disputes with himself- "mecum contendebam," (8.10, p. 450), analyzing the doubleness of human will. He hears the child's accidentally providential song, "tolle lege," before remembering St. Anthony, who came by chance upon a Gospel text by which he was converted. Augustine returns to his friend reading the Gospel, snatches the book, and, reading it at random, is converted by a passage from Romans, after which he needs read no more: "nec ultra volui legere, nec opus erat," (8.12, p. 464).

25 *Sancti Aurelii Augustini in Iohannis euangelium tractatus 124*, ed. D. R.

Wellems, *Corpus Christianorum series latina* 36 (Turnholt: Brepols, 1954), 7.2, lines 20–24, p. 62.

26 See Jean Leclerq, *The Love of Learning and the Desire for God*, trans. C. Misrahi (London: SPCK, 1974), pp. 89–90; and his *Un maitre de la vie spirituelle au xie siècle: Jean de Fécamp*, Etudes de théologie et d'histoire de la spiritualité 9 (Paris: Vrin, 1946), pp. 98–99. For examples of the topos in monastic writing, see William of St. Thierry, *Tractatus de natura et dignitate amoris, Patrologia latina* 184: 379–408 (at col. 399); Bernard of Clairvaux, *Sermones in cantica canticorum, Patrologia latina* 183: 779–1198, Sermon 85.8 (at cols. 1191–92), and 85.9 (at col. 1192). For monastic exegesis generally (with reference to this topos), see Henri de Lubac, *Exégèse médiévale: les quatre sens de l'écriture, Théologie*, 2 vols. in 4 (Paris: Faculté de Théologie S.J. de Lyon-Fourvière, 1959–64), II:582–620. See also Klaus Lange, "Geistliche Speise," *Zeitschrift für Deutsches Altertum* 95 (1966): 81–122. For Langland's use of the topos, see Jill Mann, "Eating and Drinking in *Piers Plowman*," *Essays and Studies* 32 (1979): 26–43 (37–38).

27 *Doctoris irrefragabilis Alexandri de Hales summa theologica*, 4 vols (Quaracchi, 1924–48), question 1, article 2, response, p. 9. See Elisabeth Gossmann, *Metaphysik und Heilsgeschichte: Eine theologische Untersuchung der Summa Halensis* (Munich: Max Huber, 1964), pp. 32–36, for Alexander's use of the concepts *"gustum," "experientia."* Kopf, *Die Anfänge der theologischen Wissenschaftstheorie*, pp. 211–17 surveys the question about the certainty of theology as a discipline.

28 Translation (slightly modified) from Minnis and Scott, eds., *Medieval Literary Theory and Criticism*, p. 216.

29 See Smith, *Traditional Imagery of Charity in "Piers Plowman,"* pp. 74–93.

30 Chaucer's works provide many examples of such readers: the Wife of Bath and Pluto, for example. I have argued at length that Gower's Amans also provides a model of such a reader (*Sciences and the Self in Medieval Poetry: Alan of Lille's* Anticlaudianus *and John Gower's* Confessio Amantis [Cambridge: Cambridge University Press, 1995], ch. 8). Perhaps the model of this cupidinous reading in Middle English vernacular writing is the God of Love (very much a reader) in Chaucer's prologue to the *Legend of Good Women*.

31 The relevant Bernardine background of this concept is discussed in Etienne Gilson, *La théologie mystique de saint Bernard*, Etudes de philosophie médiévale 20 (Paris: Vrin, 1934), pp. 73–74. For an example, see Bernard of Clairvaux, *De diligendo deo, Patrologia latina* 182:973–1000, ch. 13.36 (at cols. 996–97). The concept can also be found in Augustine: see *De libero arbitrio*, in *Sancti Aurelii Augustini contra academicos, de beata vita, de ordine, de magistro, de libero arbitrio*, ed. W. M. Green, *Corpus Christianorum series latina*

29 (Turnholt: Brepols, 1970), 11.53.199, p. 272. Walter Hilton draws on the tradition in his tract *Propyr Wille*, in C. Horstman, ed., *Yorkshire Writers: Richard Rolle of Hampole and his Followers*, 2 vols (London: Swan Sonnenschein, 1895–6), 1:173–75.

32 James Simpson, *An Introduction*, pp. 118–26.

33 Cited from de Lubac, *Exégèse médiévale*, 11:585 (n. 7).

34 My account of Will's reading squares with Davlin's account of Pees as a reader in Passus B.18 (*A Game of Heuene*, p. 99).

35 *Sancti Aurelii Augustini de doctrina christiana, libri IV*, ed. Joseph Martin, *Corpus Christianorum series latina* 32 (Turnholt: Brepols, 1962), 3.15.23, p. 91. See also 1.35.39, p. 29, and 1.40.44, pp. 31–32. For a lucid account of Augustine's project in the *De doctrina christiana*, see Rita Copeland, *Rhetoric, Hermeneutics, and Translation in the Middle Ages: Academic Traditions and Vernacular Texts* (Cambridge: Cambridge University Press, 1991), pp. 154–58, especially p. 158: "This program gives the reader power of invention. It gives reading and interpretation. . .a new status, as textual power shifts from authorial intention to 'affective stylistics,' to what the reader can do with the text."

36 *Saint Augustine, On Christian Doctrine*, trans. D. W. Robertson (Indianapolis: Bobbs-Merrill, 1958), book 3.15, p. 93. I have altered Robertson's translation of "diligent" to "loving" in the phrase "diligenti consideratione."

37 See, for example, chs. 25–27 of *De veritate sacrae scripturae*. For Wyclif's preparedness to use Scripture for polemical purposes, see Michael J. Hurley, S. J., " 'Scriptura Sola': Wyclif and his Critics," *Traditio* 16 (1960): 275– 352. I am very much indebted to Kantik Ghosh for discussion of Wyclif's hermeneutics.

38 The constitutions cited here are the sixth and seventh. See Anne Hudson, "Lollardy: the English Heresy?" *Studies in Church History* 18 (1982): 261–83, rpt. in Anne Hudson, *Lollards and Their Books* (London and Ronceverte: Hambledon Press, 1985), pp. 141–63 (pp. 147–38 for discussion of these constitutions). For the Oxford context of Arundel's *Constitutions*, see Anne Hudson, *The Premature Reformation: Wycliffite Texts and Lollard History* (Oxford: Clarendon, 1988), pp. 82–103. For the use of English in theological matters, see Hudson, "Lollardy: the English Heresy?" and Margaret Aston, "Wyclif and the Vernacular," in Anne Hudson and Michael Wilks, eds., *From Ockham to Wyclif, Studies in Church History* subsidia 5 (Oxford: Blackwell, 1987), pp. 281–330.

39 For the text of Arundel's license of Love's translation, see Elizabeth Salter, *Nicholas Love's* Mirrour of the Blessed Lyf of Jesu Christ, *Analecta Cartusiana* 10 (Salzburg: Institut für Englische Sprache und Literatur, 1974), pp. 1–2.

For the consistently anti-Lollard position of Love's work, see *Nicholas Love's Mirror of the Blessed Life of Jesus Christ*, ed. Michael G. Sargent, Garland Medieval Texts (New York and London: Garland, 1992), pp. xliv–lviii.

40 For this tradition, see Salter, *ibid.*, pp. ix–xx.

41 *Nicholas Love's* Mirror, ed. Sargent, Proheme, p. 13, lines 1–2.

42 *Ibid.*, Die Mercurii, ch. 15, p. 74, line 42. See also Proheme, p. 11, line 1.

43 *Ibid.*, Die Mercurii, ch. 15, p. 74, line 41.

44 *Ibid.*, Die Mercurii, ch. 18, p. 86, lines 38–41.

45 For example, Wyclif, *De veritate*, 1:28, lines 3–7, 101, lines 2–3.

46 For example, *ibid.*, 1:61, lines 11–14, 386, lines 15–18.

47 For example, *ibid.*, 1:125, lines 21–126, line 7.

48 See A. J. Minnis, "'Authorial Intention' and the 'Literal Sense' in the Exegetical Theories of Richard Fitzralph and John Wyclif," *Proceedings of the Royal Irish Academy* 75 (1975) 1–31, for the history of this academic stricture.

49 For Wyclif's striking appropriation of the whole of Scripture for the literal sense, see: Minnis, *ibid.*; G. R. Evans "Wyclif on Literal and Metaphorical," in Hudson and Wilks, eds., *From Ockham to Wyclif*, pp. 259–66; and Rita Copeland, "Rhetoric and the Politics of the Literal Sense in Medieval Literary Theory: Aquinas, Wyclif and the Lollards," in Piero Boitani and Anna Torti, eds., *Interpretation: Medieval and Modern*, The J. A. W. Bennett Memorial Lectures, eighth series (Cambridge: D. S. Brewer, 1993), pp. 1–23.

50 For example, Wyclif, *De veritate*, 1:108, line 2–109, line 24; 1:114, line 1–115, line 1. For Langland, by contrast, the reality of Scripture is very much dependent on its material realization: in Passus 10 he introduces Scripture's comments thus: "'I nel noght scorne,' quod Scripture; 'but if scryveynes lye. . .'" (line 329).

51 Wyclif, *De veritate*, vol. 1:156, line 21–157, line 15.

52 See Simpson, *An Introduction*, ch. 5.

8

"Vae octuplex," Lollard socio-textual ideology, and Ricardian–Lancastrian prose translation

RALPH HANNA III

Early in "A Dialogue between a Lord and a Clerk on Translation," the beleaguered Clerk, a self-dramatization of the author-translator John Trevisa, once more attempts to evade his Lord's command to translate Ranulph Higden's *Polychronicon*. He argues that his interlocutor, the Lord, needs no such translation because he can already speak, read, and understand Latin. The Lord, ostensibly a version of Trevisa's patron Sir Thomas Berkeley, shreds this argument – just as he demolishes the Clerk's other evasions – by replying, "þer ys moche Latyn in þeus bokes of cronyks þat Y can noȝt vnderstonde, noþer þou." And Berkeley continues, "noþer þou, wiþoute studyinge and auysement and lokyng of oþer bokes."[1]

The Lord here directs attention to an important aspect of medieval Latinity. Like everyone else in the Middle Ages, he *learned* his Latin: it was not his, nor anyone else's mother tongue, but, as the Lord notes at the head of the "Dialogue" (p. 290/20–26), an acquired *lingua franca*, useful for a variety of purposes. Yet Berkeley sees clearly that his form of Latin literacy, however well developed, differs from that of his interlocutor. The Clerk acquired Latin in another manner altogether, one which makes his Latin not simply "a learned language" but a "learnéd" one.

For the Clerk's language acquisition is imbricated in a textual system. In addition to studying a language, he has been exposed to techniques for reading and has gained along with a language a bibliography, explanatory volumes disposed in clear intertextual patterns. Berkeley claims Trevisa can cope with Higden because he knows how to resolve textual difficulties, because he has been trained in reference scholarship, a range of authoritative sources, and because he knows appropriate ways of bringing them to bear on a text. As Clerk, his learning of Latin, his language acquisition, is the simultaneous acquisition of a panoply of aids to learning itself. Clerical linguistic skills include, as a part of "language," interpretative aids; for this reason, clerical Latinity constitutes an extensive licensing system. Unlike other groups, clerics learn not just a language but a mode of visualizing the entire world as a textual system. Like London cab-drivers, possessors of that licensed skill colloquially known as "The Knowledge," clerics can identify their linguistic training as learning itself, a claim to which Trevisa's Lord, I suspect, would probably accede.

Lollard writings form a particularly interesting piece of medieval textual production because they de-dialogize Trevisa's "Dialogue" and manage simultaneously to voice both Trevisa and Berkeley. Production of such texts as the Lollard Bible couples the linguistic/textual apparatus which Trevisa's Lord invokes as a property of clericism, the identification of language learning with what Dan Jenkins would probably call "learning its own self," its secret textual operations shut off even from highly sophisticated Latin users, with a second, and radical agenda. This second agenda is at least analogous to the ethic of socially dispersed knowledge for which the Lord speaks in Trevisa's "Dialogue," but it constitutes a more pressing program because it addresses salvation, rather than mere information. The result is an amalgam peculiar, although far from unique, in Ricardian–Lancastrian England.

Certainly, contemporary analogies to Lollard textual behavior are easy to find. For example, in *Boece*, Chaucer did not translate simply the "naked text" but conflated with his Latin version both Jean de Meun's French and substantial detail from the commentary tradition which rendered Boethius "legible" to sophisticated Latin literates. (And Chaucer's behavior was extended by the Augustinian canon John Walton's derivative verse rendition, which infuses vastly more of Nicholas Trivet's explanation, in this case with gender-bending implications not so far removed from the gender-neutrality of Lollardy: Walton's patron was Trevisa's Lord's daughter, now Countess of Warwick.) Similarly, in the alliterative *Siege of Jerusalem*, the author, an Augustinian canon of Bolton (West Yorkshire), undertook a definitive history of the Roman sack of 70 AD. He used standard clerical reference skills to access and integrate at least four separate sources, three of them learned texts (and two of these not of especially extensive English circulation): the apocryphal "Vindicta salvatoris," Ranulf Higden's *Polychronicon*, and Josephus's *Bellum Iudaicum*.

Yet whatever the analogies, Lollardy remains unique in its explicit understanding of what such procedures mean. For in the work of the sect, a textual ideology predicated on specialized training, and thus special restriction, is appropriated for purposes which destroy the very presumptions of that ideology. The exclusions built into the clerical ideal of learning, that one must be educated in Latinity in a specific way to understand texts properly, are undone. For this ideology now serves vernacularity, and Lollard writers attempt acts of textual propagation which would give this now vernacularized ideology universal social currency.[2]

Such appropriated clerical activity serves radical ends. The Englishness of Lollard texts exists after all, as Trevisa's Lord argues of his projected Higden translation in the "Dialogue," to destroy the very nature of clericism itself, its claim to be an exclusive form of knowledge and its effort to constitute that exclusivity both linguistically, as Latin itself, and spatially, as a property of the organized learned library. The English of the translations reconstitutes learnedness as potentially available to every person, regardless of gender (another form of clerical exclusiveness). Such an audience includes aural literates, persons who absorb the text through the ear and who would be deemed illiterate in any clerical circle.[3] In this process of dissemination, the Lollard Bible, of course, responds to imperatives written within the text of Scripture itself, imperatives which Lollard clerics see as largely ignored in the panoply of learning with which the text has in the past been invested. The Oxford research library, the post-biblical encrustation on the text, has become more valuable to orthodox clericism than the bare message of that salvation Jesus promised all believers, now available for a suitably universal social use.

Lollardy has some very powerful deconstructive ways of conceiving this problematic, ways of placing and obliterating clerical conservatism. For example, the author of the Lollard Old Testament prologue claims that "þe comune Latyn biblis han more nede to be correctid, as manie as I haue seen in my lif, þan haþ þe English bible late translatid."[4] For him, the very scholarly operations involved in translation have created a text more perfect than that in clerical circulation. For example, the prologue describes (lines 25–35) collation of copies and emendation of the Latin text on the basis both of standard exegesis and ancient sources (lemmata in the Church Fathers and Nicholas of Lyre's report of the Hebrew).[5] Heretical activity parasitic upon clerical textual ideology has superseded the ideology by which it may be branded as heretical. However, this supersession itself deserves analysis: implicitly, it makes an anti-clerical claim against an indifference to the central clerical text by those who should have done most to preserve (if not disseminate) it. Established clericism bespeaks a slackness which has apparently found other activities of greater use and moment than textual attention. The renegade clerics who open the text out to vernacular use are thus truer to it than its Latinate protectors.

Such an account of Lollardy strikes a note revolutionary and democratic – and certainly attractive to moderns for just those reasons. But I want to consider here an instance, perhaps unique in Lollard writing, in which, implicitly, the voices of Trevisa and Berkeley, Latinate clerk and intellectually eager secular audience, part company again. I think this offers telling commentary on the difficulties of appropriating learned texts in late fourteenth-century England.

Because "Vae octuplex" is obviously not a well-known work, it deserves something more than a passing introduction.[6] Its title identifies its subject: the work, a sermon, explicates Jesus' eightfold "woe," his curse in Matthew 23.13–33 – "Vae vobis, scribe et Pharisei, ypocrite." The exegesis in this sermon, which concentrates upon only one of the groups which Jesus curses, the Pharisees, locates the work within a nearly ubiquitous genre, Lollard anti-mendicant satire. The author identifies the Pharisees directly with the friars, on the basis of those orders' claim to a life of special spiritual excellence:

. . .þese pharisees. . .lyuon ypocrytes lyf þat hemself haþ fownden, and þei maken oþre men conformen hem þerto, for þei seyn þat þis ly3f is þe beste of alle; and so lif þat Crist ordeynede is al put obac.   (22–25)[7]

And the text, although recognizing the other groups Jesus curses and occasionally (for example, at 83–86) directing its attention to them, concentrates upon these figures because they clearly stand as a recent distraction of clerical attention:

Crist bydduþ us be war wiþ þese false prophetis þat comen in cloþing of schep and ben wolues of raueyne. And þese ben specially men of þese newe ordres, and moste þese frerys þat laste comen in.   (1–4)

In this rendition of hypocritical modern Phariseeism, friars always direct their activities toward *mundana*, toward piling up things of this world: they are exclusively interested in behaviors that profit them financially, whatever more august claims they may make for their orders – "þei louen erþe and erþely þingus" (13).

Beyond its subject matter, the work reflects other common Lollard concerns. "Vae octuplex" appropriates and transforms a piece of academic discourse: such vernacularization of the learned Latinate tradition is endemic everywhere in Lollardy, not simply in its wresting of the Bible from ecclesiastical control. In this case, the author adapts one of Wyclif's own works and is thus engaged in a total popularization: he detaches the piece not simply from its original linguistic setting but from the discursive context within that language as well.

The text appropriated from Wyclif, "Exposicio textus Matthei xxiii" (called in every manuscript "De vae octuplici," even though it treats more of the biblical text, all of Matthew 23, than the English does) is a bit of polemical exegesis (perhaps composed in 1381). In its Latin manuscript circulation, it has a ubiquitous companion, a similar exegesis applied to Matthew 24. But the two texts address different problems: the exegesis of Matthew 24 is primarily anti-papal, and not nearly so academic in method as Wyclif's "Vae octuplex." Indeed, Wyclif shapes three early chapters of "Vae octuplex," on the value of clerical learning, as a quodlibetal question (they explain "rabbi"/"magister" in Matt. 23.7); this portion of his text occasionally circulated separately as such a *quaestio*.[8] The identification of Pharisees and friars, as well as the virtually total concentration upon only this group, the English writer inherits from his learned source, the *doctor evangelicus*.[9]

But this exegetical text is not only freed from its Latinate circulation for more general use: its generic affiliations have changed as well. The English author produces a typical Lollard sermon, with a sequential explanation of the (in this case, unlike most of the sermons, divided) biblical text followed by general moral exhortation. And the English work most typically circulated in a fashion appropriate to this generic transformation – twelve of the fourteen surviving manuscript copies insert "Vae octuplex" into the Lollard sermon cycle. Although individual manuscripts show various placements, "Vae octuplex" most usually is appended to those sermons which explicate the dominical gospels. And, although Wyclif's Matthew 24 exegesis also occurs in Lollard translation ("Of Ministers in the Church"), any yoking of the two (as occurs ubiquitously in the Latin) is generally absent in English manuscripts.[10] This manuscript presentation resuscitates a biblical text which lacks an ecclesiastical occasion, a place in the calendar, but a biblical locus too important to miss out on.[11] Thus "Vae octuplex" comments upon ecclesiastical suppressions of, and deviations from, God's word – those canonical choices inherent in forming a liturgy. This implicit comment dovetails neatly with the author's central (and for me, exceedingly problematic) theme, the friars' deviation from an appropriate Christian worship.

At least in part, what is problematic about "Vae octuplex" depends upon assessing the relationship of English sermon and Latin source-treatise. The English version, while certainly shaped by the arguments of the master, is extremely erratic in its appropriation of its source. At some points, the author seems engaged in reasonably close translation from the Latin; at other times, he shows a thorough independence from Wyclif. At least some odd gestures, for example, the unexpected reference to "þe þrydde cawtel of þe fend" (257) – the first two "cautels" are nowhere explicitly noted [12] – might suggest that English transmission, rather than appropriation from Latin, has been erratic: although usually more concisely detailed than a sermon *reportatio*, the Middle English "Vae" which survives may reflect editing from some more extensive text.

But whether we ascribe its shape to author or redactor, "Vae octuplex" displays an uneasy and unprincipledly erratic relationship to the "Exposicio textus Matthei xxiii." The concluding third of the sermon (from about line 237) introduces homiletics foreign to the academic source,[13] but in addition, the English often ignores Wyclif's precise exegetical distinctions, even where such precision would be helpful to what appears his argument.

Yet such independence from the master is fitful. The English Lollard reproduces an extensive and learnedly logical Wycliffian demolition of ecclesiastical dispensations (lines 94–115).[14] But on other occasions, he intrudes some bits of Wyclif in so attenuated a fashion that they are not readily comprehensible without some reference to the Latin source. For example, after twenty lines which provide a moral reading of Matthew 23.23–24, the preacher suddenly refers to "luytul þing þat saueroþ helþe of mannys body" (lines 170–71). The words return to the *littera* of the biblical text, "mente and anet and comyn" (line 143), words which the English author has not heretofore explained at all. These are surely "little things," not great spiritual matters, but the qualification – that they are all medically useful herbs – depends upon the Latin's elaborate moral *distinctio* based upon the precise medical powers of each spice (OM 344/26–345/13; see n. 6). In contrast, although he elsewhere ignores the sharp distinctions which drive Wyclif's moral exegesis, the preacher adds similar touches to the source; the phrase "person howses" (line 36) adds to the subsequent exegesis of "wydewes housis" (Matt. 23.14), from the Latin, a reference to the anti-mendicant verse 2 Timothy 3.6. The exact shape appropriation takes here seems driven by no very consistent principle.

Further, the sermon does make additions of a sort foreign to the *doctor* and of at least moderate spriteliness. It adduces its own anti-fraternal charges, which then stand as experiential evidence of fraternal behaviors blatantly identifiable with those acts Jesus curses in the text. Thus, lines 65–71 extend the frequent anti-mendicant charge of childstealing and adduce tactile details not in Wyclif. And the author adds a number of purely literary touches to Wyclif's soberly demonstrative argument, for example, "þe laddur. . .to heuene" (lines 19–20) or both the medical and biblical references in lines 237–41. Plainly, the Lollard preacher had sufficient interest and knowledge to acquire, read, and understand the basic thrust of Wyclif's Latin. And his absorption of the text is neither passive nor sequential: the medical metaphor to which I have just alluded in fact rewrites a parallel figure about boiling water in a far removed locus in Wyclif's tract (OM 315/12–17). The preacher desired an academically authoritative reading of scriptural authority and believed this should be translated for public oral dispersal, rather than private consultation in the study. Yet equal to his knowledge and desire is a certain ineptitude, an inability to cope with the text with any consistency.

In form, "Vae octuplex" accords with the nearly three hundred other sermons of the full Lollard cycle. And that form, just as the inclusion of a sermon without an assigned occasion within the dominical cycle, provides a rhetorical counterpoint to the issues addressed. As a *sermo antiquus*, a straightforward explication of the full scriptural text, concluding with moral exhortation,[15] "Vae octuplex" should uniquely fit its subject-matter: the old ways of true, Lollard Christianity as opposed to the behaviors of what the preacher everywhere calls "new sects."[16] This preacher attends directly to the full biblical text and thereby distinguishes himself from the inept preaching of the mendicant orders, the *sermo modernus* with its truncated textual attention and interest in anecdotal amplification which he describes early on:

þei entren not to vndirstondyng [of hooly wryt], ne þei suffren oþre men to vndurstonden hit wel. Somme prechen fables and somme veyne storyes; somme dockon hooly wryt and somme feynon lesyngus; and so lore of Godis lawe is al put obac. (15–19)

Insofar as they have or need a source, the preacher derives these complaints from chapters of Wyclif's "Exposicio" preceding those which deal with the actual "Vae" (OM 319/15–18, 331/5–12 and 33–35, 332/5–8).

Similarly, the preacher on several occasions attacks "new" forms of fraternal exegesis. These hermeneutic methods, he claims, reject the biblical letter for a gloss of human inspiration; he wraps himself in the mantle of an older patristic hermeneutics which he perceives as primarily literal.[17] And finally, although the argument remains largely implicit and inadequately developed in the sermon, he argues that the primary guide to Christian action may be found in God's Law, always in Lollard terms known through preaching like his own:[18] in the new mendicant world, modern Pharisees have replaced that educational mission with their own special institutions. These activities, monetarily more salubrious than mere preaching, they defend through particularistic glosses.

In its double emphasis on the good old ways, articulated in an old-fashioned rhetorical form, and on the heinous modern deviations which oppose them, "Vae octuplex" participates in a commonplace Lollard rhetorical strategy. This typical move belates the opposition and identifies it, and not Lollardy, as heretical innovation. Most particularly if one reads the sermon backwards, through the preacher's exhortations at the end, one must condemn friars as departing from what should be a single Christian way of life. As Pharisees with a unique and special spiritual regimen, friars typify "private religions" and have deserted the single Christian truth (based upon that historical moment which grounds and founds Christianity, the literal truth of the gospel narrative). In the new mendicant world, truth has become multiple, a question of persons and of their later evaluative perceptions imposed upon the gospel: historically placeable human proclamations have overturned the divine word, and the church has become the "synagoge of Sathanas" (294). The preacher, in rejecting such accretions, ascribes to his sect the priority of the originary Christian text and makes of his adversaries heretical latecomers, overly punctilious about non-Christian, non-gospel institutions they have themselves created.

Moreover, he cleverly articulates this view through frequent puns:[19] in the new mendicant world, semantic polyvalence replaces the singularity of "bileeue," the faith, just as potentially variable fraternal glosses and papal decrees have usurped the place of the biblical *littera*. Perhaps most tellingly, the author almost coalesces the strong verb "fynden" with the weak "founden."[20] This particular example of verbal perversion attacks the friars' lack of scriptural grounding for their activity ("founding," compare Wyclif's claim that fraternal institutions are *infundabilis*, for example, OM 340/33–34); simultaneously, the preacher insists that these are newly invented ("founden") behaviors and that they are probably entered for the sake of livelihood (another sense of the verb "fynden").[21] Such verbal perversion, such an indiscriminate mixture of illicit acts, typifies mendicant behavior. The new sects put themselves ahead of the true faith, shoulder it out of the way (even displace God and arrogate to themselves privileges that should be his – dispensation and absolution at confession, lines 120–40).[22] Through such arguments, appropriation from Latin forms an important mode of salvation economy: vernacularism takes over duties ignored by an abusive Latinate ecclesiastical community.

But however powerful the effort to belate mendicant activity, "Vae octuplex" in the long run presents a faulted hermeneutics (which might be alleged, I would suggest, against Wyclif as well – although he's quite conscious of the danger). The preacher can only score his points by reading Matthew 23 as prophetic. For him, the biblical text fulfills itself in time: it can't, in some way, "be about" the actual Pharisees who plagued Jesus but must be construed, in a typically extended Lollard literal reading, as a statement of ecclesiastical history, a hint God left in the text to be actuated at some later time. (In the preacher's source, Wyclif argues this point at some length [OM 336–37], to demonstrate that neither this text nor Matthew 24 can be Jesus' historical statement about evangelical "current events").[23] Reading the text this way, as a Lollard, makes revelation continuous, a product of historical consciousness, yet equally of historical estrangement from the letter. Such a hermeneutic strategy thus undoes its own claims – rather than being at the origin, the adept reader can only be later, only involved in claiming that he recuperates the origin through his reading.

And this view becomes extremely problematic in the face of "Vae octuplex"'s anti-fraternalism. First, the claim that such a Lollard reading actuates the literal "trewþe of þe gospel" should be perceived as highly contentious, in some measure a shredding of the very *sensus litteralis*. The Lollard preacher here must utterly reject the most commonplace sort of literal reading – "Littera gesta docet:" the text as historical narrative. And he must do so in the interests of a prophetic literal sense: like substantial chunks of Scripture, Matthew 23 should be read as symbolic *littera*, as instruction in ecclesiology, Jesus speaking for "The Church." But, in these terms, friars, who presumably read the text as Jesus' comments, at one particular point in his ministry, about a specifically Jewish sectarianism, may in fact claim the high ground of antiquity more readily than the Lollard preacher. For they adopt the old-fashioned, straightforward view that Matthew 23 represents historical narrative, and they bring to the text none of that attenuated textual attention which the preacher would see as signs of their newfangledness, their "fables and. . .veyne storyes."

Secondly, if the preacher believes the mendicant failure to escape the bare reading of Matthew 23 as *gesta* perverse, other problems about reading strategies emerge. For the mendicant effort to create a scriptural basis for their orders rests, just as surely as the Lollard reading, upon a prophetic perception of the biblical *littera* and a belief in continuous revelation. In these terms, friars can scarcely be accused of "docking holy writ," if by that the preacher means that they do not attend to the non-historical *littera* (rather than just commenting on a few verses in their *sermones moderni*). For friars defend themselves and their orders by posing the question "What is the appropriate form Jesus' voluntary poverty should take in the modern world?"

Whatever the claims Wyclif and his Lollard follower advance, both Lollards and friars are fighting over exactly the same grounds, the rights to the same reading strategies. The matter isn't, as the heretical authors here claim, one of hermeneutic principle, but simply of distribution – which loci should have which interpretations? Moreover, this is an issue the English preacher certainly lacks care in expressing: when he makes his strongest anti-fraternal charge, identifies the friars' church as "synagoge of Sathanas," he alludes to the historical Jewish basis of the gospel Pharisees and, in his search for an appropriately polemical insult, risks reduction of the text to a non-prophetic *littera*. (In doing so, he ignores Wyclif's wiser choice – for the *doctor evangelicus*, friars represent the *ecclesia antichristi*, a locution which responds to the biblical *gesta* but is foreign to this English text.)

This battle over textual interpretation has one further complication in "Vae octuplex" – the sermon's resolutely anti-intellectual, yet hortatory, conclusion. If what the preacher venomously calls "þe newe sectis" have shattered the unity of Christian "bileeue," he wishes to regain that unity, to return to "þe hool ordre of Crist" (229–30). But his prescription for such a return to origins is extraordinarily reductive. He asserts what we would expect from his earlier statements, the utter sufficiency of the gospel text for the faith: "Byleue is an hyd trewþe þat God telluþ in his lawe." But on this occasion, he adds a qualifying second clause to the sentence: "and it is declared ynow in comun crede of cristen men" (308–09).

Scriptural text has been reduced to pat statement. The preacher rhetorically establishes this claim for the powers of simplicity by a preceding discussion of competing eucharistic theories (258–79). There the Lollard's simple "Godus body in forme of breed' (261) is opposed to such fraternal academic newfangledness as the formulation from Aristotelian logic "an accident wiþowte suget" (265).[24] But when the preacher offers his formulation, the gospel (God's law) identification of the truth which grounds Christian faith becomes problematic. In the scriptural text such a truth is "hyd," hidden or obscure; the prophetic reading must be unveiled or extracted from narrative events through the kinds of contested hermeneutics I have been discussing. The preacher's injunction to his congregation then becomes far simpler: sufficient grounding in the faith appears in the open proclamations of the Apostles' Creed.[25]

But this conclusion then undermines the presumptions of the preacher's preceding argument, in which gospel truth is the unequivocal source of the faith. If study of Scripture provides the "best evidence" of the mendicants' depravity, both in Jesus' explicit statements and in the absence of any "grounding" for fraternal activities, the preacher plainly settles for an illogical (and presumably inadmissible) second best in his conclusion. Jesus' words as source of belief plainly outrank the Apostles and their creed both temporally and in terms of spiritual power.

Further, one should consider the preacher's rejection of the biblical text as "hyd," too obscure for argumentative purposes, an act of rhetorical bad faith. This move renders the Bible, the standard for measuring the friars' deviation from the law, a text which his audience should heed less than the more available and easily comprehensible creed. The phrasing "[Truth] is declared ynow" implicitly makes the demonstrable equivalent to the pellucid (cf. the derivation of *declare* from Latin *clarus*, contextually opposed to *obscurus*, the preacher's "hyd").

Moreover, the preacher here comprises the very *métier* of his sermon, which presupposes that exegetical interests are proper and relatively unproblematic. In fact, before he has concluded, he even suggests – ironically, just as mendicant opponents of Lollard biblical translation did – that his congregation should avoid precisely difficult textual speculations: "muse not in specialte abowte trewþus þat God wole huyde" (345).[26] Ultimately, the Bible becomes for him just a ready source of pulpit invective, and in his conclusion, the preacher allows silence, the lack of reference to friars in the creed, to overwhelm and replace the Word altogether.

But "Vae octuplex"'s bad faith is not limited simply to the author's use of Scripture to excoriate friars and his subsequent withdrawal from it. Far more troubling to me, he displays an equal bad faith I would identify as intrasectarian (and probably class-marked). One of Lollardy's strongest political attractions is precisely what the preacher identifies as the hallmark of old, true Christianity – the single and ostensibly democratic community of the faithful.[27] And it is precisely this vision which the preacher finds he cannot, in his conclusion, sustain.

This democratic vision inheres everywhere in Lollardy and is centered in the academic scriptural translation which forms the movement's great literary monument. In the unique siting of this heresy, there is an assumed continuity between an Oxford theology master, his university-trained disciples (translators and missionaries), and their public audience (a wide range of, to us, quasi-literate groups dispersed in society at large, from the plough to the urban guildhall). But these diverse constituencies cohere as a movement in their common apprehension of English Scripture and in their eagerness to explicate it and to live by it, regardless of differences in intellectual gifts.

"Vae octuplex" is so troubling – and perhaps uniquely troubling among Lollard documents – precisely because it fractures, just as surely as "þe newe sectis" do, the single community of the Lollard faithful. The author attempts to appropriate academic discourse, Wyclif's exegesis, for a general public: his initial rhetorical stance testifies to the single community one expects. But this preacher finds he cannot fully absorb Wyclif, cannot translate but only adapt him – and an erratic adaptation at that. He consciously recognizes a fissure between the sophisticated academic source and his most willing efforts to appropriate it.

In the conclusion of his sermon, this self-consciousness of the disparity between the preacher's and his master's ability to comprehend is re-enacted as a fissure between his pulpit and the congregation. In this re-enactment, he utterly deserts the gospel accounts and his wiser academician/master – Wyclif's attack on MA mendicant preachers reaffirms the value of the "rudus" or "ydiota" as preacher (see OM 331/9–30). As a result, the preacher resituates his audience – not the eager followers of exegesis presupposed in the first half of the sermon, but a flock of John

Carpenters: "Ye, blessed be alwey a lewed man / That noght but oonly his bileve kan!"[28] For this preacher, at least, the Lollard vision of gospel origins, the historical moment when peasants proved prophets, fails. He inadvertently affirms nothing so much as the divided and polyvocal world he excoriates – and this world is created for him by the very hermeneutic moves through which he seeks to arrest its progress.

In the broadest sense, then, the author of "Vae octuplex" concludes his sermon dialogically – speaking both as Trevisa's Lord, who wants to pass on Latinate learning, and his Clerk, who advocates a restricted text, cloaked from untutored examination. "Vae octuplex" incorporates a powerful "translation ideology," a logic whereby materials traditionally reserved only for clerical scrutiny should be propagated in the vernacular. But whatever the preacher's ideology, his sermon equally incorporates Trevisa's Clerk's more traditional doubts: these appear, not as the Clerk would utter them, but as an implicit "translation practice" a great deal less assured than the author's overt ideological claims. Quite simply, practice must attend to the social insertion of the work, its suitability to a general audience without that training Latinity always conferred in the Middle Ages. And in these terms, "Vae octuplex" vitiates ideological daring into pedestrian withdrawal: the Lollard preacher remains comparably detached from his audience and as protective of the text he provides as one imagines orthodox Latinate clerics to be.

One might then wonder whether the Lollard translation program (along with other Ricardian–Lancastrian efforts) was not, to borrow Anne Hudson's term, "premature." Certainly, at least traces in the works of this preacher's contemporaries testify to analogous difficulties of audience consumption. The development of Lollard biblical translation, for example, involves the rejection of a clerically inspired literalism in favor of greater English accessibility. In the original translation effort, the Lollard clerics adopted an extreme literalism, extending to the retention of Latin syntax and word-order, including subject-object-verb order within clauses: in this procedure, they clearly responded to a widespread belief among learned exegetes that Vulgate word-order had an inherent value in the reading experience – it resolved some textual difficulties. But the text which resulted, illegible in terms of English reading practice, required extensive revision: eventually, as the Later Version prologue records, the text was "opened," put into English idiom for vernacular consumption.[29] But in adopting that procedure, the Wycliffite translation team simultaneously jettisoned the possibility of some sophisticated textual operations the work was initially, in some measure, designed to facilitate.

To offer only a single further example, Chaucer's *Boece* adopts a literalism analogous to that of the Wycliffite Early Version. The result appears less severe than Lollard Scripture because Chaucer frequently relied upon Jean de Meun's already parsed text for much of his word-order, but this he carefully checked (and very frequently corrected, especially for lexis) against the Latin and commentaries on the text. But the use of commentary, which inspired Chaucer to offer some materials of his own, while it imitates Latin textual practice, in its original moments very frequently functions as an anti-Latinate bow to Chaucer's expected vernacular audience. In his insistently exact rendering of the Latin, Chaucer reproduced Boethius' double negatives – in Latin positive statements, in English doubly emphatic negatives – and then had to gloss them to elucidate them for readers. And attention to Latin forms and lexis (with concomitant neologism) necessitated yet further glosses.[30] Like the Latin models they appropriate, these glosses offer explanations of obscurities, but the obscurities are not inherent in the Latin, but in the translator's practice; they express Chaucer's recognition that his readers were incapable of the sophisticated textual recuperation which the translation seems implicitly conceived to facilitate.

Moreover, the visual circulation of *Boece* testifies to the poet's prescience. British Library, MS Additional 16165 was copied by John Shirley, inferentially for the Beauchamp affinity, about as sophisticated a group of vernacular literates as one might hope to find in the 1420s. And at least four copies mentioned in fifteenth-century wills and inventories were at some point in lay hands.[31]

But the most extensive evidence of medieval *Boece* readership involves persons in clerical status. Cambridge University Library, MS ii.3.21, an extensive Boethian anthology with Latin text and commentaries, was donated to the Library before 1424 by John Crowcher, later a Doctor of Theology and Dean of Chichester Cathedral. Thomas Cyrcetur, a canon there, gave the chained library of Salisbury Cathedral what is now Cathedral MS 113 (which includes a start at providing a Latin text).[32] Bodleian Library, MS Bodley 797, where *Boece* appears along with patristics and theology, was owned by the Augustinian friars of Clare (Suffolk), at least two individual Augustinians, and the Carthusians of Sheen. The vernacular Boethius commentary (which uses Chaucer's translation for lemmata) occurs in Bodleian, MS Auctarium F.3.5, with contents similar to those of Bodley 797: it is conceivably the very book ("liber super Boecium in anglicis") which appears in wills of 1457 and 1482 associated with fellows of Lincoln College, Oxford and of Eton College.[33] As Ian Doyle has reported to me in conversation, the hospital at Toddington (Bedfordshire) owned a copy in the late fifteenth century. And John Walton, Augustinian of Oseney, as I have already noted, used both a copy of *Boece* and Trivet's Latin commentary in preparing his verse version.

If Chaucer hoped to popularize Boethius, his efforts were only modestly successful, so far as formal translation is concerned. (The effect of usually exact Boethian appropriation in the poetry is a different issue.) His text was frequently reabsorbed into the literate culture from which the act of translation had sought to extract it: *Boece* appealed primarily to those who already were educated enough to envision an attempt at the Latin original but who may have appreciated vernacular help with some difficulties. The poet's suspicion of his own translation practice, inscribed in his Latin-derived glossing procedures, was in fact justified – whatever ideological claims he may have wished to make for the utility of his literary gesture.[34]

Such contemporary translation experiences support the doubts of "Vae octuplex"'s preacher (and qualify the optimistic ebullience of Trevisa's Lord). However much we are stirred by the claims of the vernacular – which are also the claims of modern secularism[35] and, in Lollard terms, implicitly those of a classless gender-blind society as well – one may overestimate the effectiveness with which translators fulfilled these claims. The audience actually capable of responding with the sophistication demanded by the translators may have been extremely narrow, in fact more exclusive than the Latinate community from which translators claimed they were "freeing" the text. And where that audience may have been more extensive, as is the case with vernacular Wycliffism, the evidence of "Vae octuplex" would suggest that audience limitations might well frustrate the actuation of the translators' most lofty, and most laudable, intentions.[36]

Notes

1 I cite Ronald Waldron, "Trevisa's Original Prefaces on Translation: a Critical Edition," in Edward Donald Kennedy, Ronald Waldron, and Joseph S. Wittig, eds., *Medieval English Studies Presented to George Kane* (Woodbridge: Brewer, 1988), pp. 285-99, here p. 290/57–60.

2 As that of all investigators of Lollardy must be, my thinking about these matters has been thoroughly imbued by the researches of Anne Hudson, especially her magisterial *The Premature Reformation: Wycliffite Texts and Lollard History* (Oxford: Clarendon, 1988). In addition to this work, Hudson has written frequently and provocatively on the linguistic politics of Lollardy; see especially "The Debate on Bible Translation, Oxford 1401" and "Lollardy: The English Heresy?" in *Lollards and Their Books* (London: Hambledon Press, 1985), pp. 67-84 and 140–63, respectively.

3 Cf. my discussions of two such figures: Margery Baxter, in "The Difficulty of Ricardian Prose Translation: The Case of the Lollards," *Modern Language Quarterly* 51 (1990): 319–40, at 331–37, and the forthcoming "Some Norfolk Women and Their Books;" and Chaucer's creation, Alison, in "*Compilatio* and the Wife of Bath: Latin Backgrounds, Ricardian Texts," in Alastair Minnis, ed., *Latin and Vernacular: Studies in Late-Medieval Texts and Manuscripts* (Cambridge: Boydell, 1989), pp. 1–11.

4 I cite Anne Hudson, *Selections from English Wycliffite Writings* (Cambridge: Cambridge University Press, 1978), here p. 69/74–75. Although customarily called "the general prologue" (by Chaucerian analogy?) , it is properly a prologue only to the Old Testament historical and wisdom books, in the later version of the translation. (The prophetic books have a separate prologue, printed in Josiah Forshall and Sir Frederic Madden, eds., *The Holy Bible*, [4 vols. Oxford: Oxford University Press, 1850], III: 225–26.) The author modeled his work upon Latin annotational procedures – the commonplace presentation as a prologue to the Vulgate Old Testament of Jerome's *epistola* 53 "Ad Paulinum" and the "Praefatio in Pentateuchum ad Desiderium," and inserted materials from Nicholas of Lyre's Old Testament prologues. The text, unlike much of the labor which formed the Lollard Bible, may be narrowly datable, February 15, 1395–January 22, 1397; see Hudson, *Selections*, p. 174.

5 See, for example, the clarifying addition "Whi is liȝt ȝouun," inserted into Job 3.23 to indicate that the construction here parallels the preceding question (cf. "Quare. . .data est lux?" in verse 20); or the marginal gloss to Job 3.4, which indicates that one clause is not part of the Hebrew text, or that to Job 20.16, which corrects, on the basis of the Hebrew, a scribal error in some Vulgates (and in the earlier Wycliffite version) and argues that Jerome, in his translation, failed to recognize the multiple senses of a Hebrew word. All these reflect Lyre, *Postilla literalis in totam bibliam*, in *Biblia latina*, 4 vols. (Lyons: Johann Siber, *c.* 1488), vol. II, folios Gg 6va, Gg 6rb, and ii 5rb, respectively.

6 I cite from Pamela Gradon, ed., *English Wycliffite Sermons II* (Oxford: Clarendon, 1988), pp. 366–78, replacing the text of Hudson, *Selections*,

pp. 75–83, but not Hudson's notes, pp. 177–79. For the source, to which I will turn below, see "Exposicio textus Matthei XXIII," ed. Johann Loserth, *Johannis Wyclif Opera Minora*, Wyclif Society (London: Wyclif Society, 1913), pp. 313–53, hereafter OM.

7 Wyclif sees this speciality inherent in the very name; cf. "phariseus interpretatur a populo divisus" (OM 335/19–20).

8 Matthew 23.7 has a venerable history in antimendicant invective and made this chapter a central satirical document; see Penn R. Szittya, "The Antifraternal Tradition in Middle English Literature," *Speculum* 52 (1977): 287–313, especially pp. 294–301. Wyclif's *quaestio* forms chs. 4–6, OM 323–32; on the rubrics of the Latin manuscripts, see OM xxxvi. For further detail concerning the Latin transmission of Wyclif's exegesis of both Matthew 23 and 24, see Williell R. Thomson, *The Latin Writings of John Wyclyf: An Annotated Catalogue* (Toronto: Pontifical Institute, 1983), pp. 215–20.

9 Although the interests of Wyclif's tract are uniformly broader near the beginning of his discussion (for example, OM 315), he also focusses narrowly on the four orders (cf. 334–35).

10 See Anne Hudson, ed., *English Wycliffite Sermons I* (Oxford: Clarendon, 1983), pp. 49–50. The exact placement intended is somewhat unclear and is complicated by "Vae" 's unclear relations to "Of Ministers." In the English sermon cycle, "Of Ministers" usually comes at the end of the sermons for the proper of saints (so in ten of fourteen copies; two others have the work in a booklet capable of such placement). But "Vae" occurs most often (seven times plus one movable booklet) as a pendant to the cycle which explicates the dominical gospels. The six manuscripts with only one of the texts would seem to confirm this separate presentation: four of these lack that set of sermons to which the text there missing is usually appended. I thus remain uncertain that the two texts have in English the same intimate relationship implicit in the Latin presentation (or that *Sermons* properly prints them together): generically, "Of Ministers" appears more overtly tractlike than does "Vae."

11 Cf. "Of Ministers":

> This gospel telluþ muche wysdam, þat is hud to monye men; and specially for þis cause, þat it is not al rad in chyrche. But siþen it is of euene auctorite wiþ oþre gospelis of Crist, and of hud sentence of God þat were profiȝtable to þe chyrche, somme men wolden seyn hit in her modyr language as þei can.
>
> (*Sermons* II: 328/1–5, derived from OM 359/33–35)

Unlike the totally ignored Matthew 24, every bit of Matthew 23, *except* the "eightfold woe," was read in the course of the liturgical year: verses 34–39 on St. Stephen's Day, verses 1–12 on the second Tuesday in Lent. See the translated Sarum lectionary, Forshall and Madden, *Holy Bible*, IV: 684, 685.

12 There is a reference to "þe furste cauteel" at line 38, where it contextually means "the first woe," a sense impossible at line 257. Other uses of the word, of no particular aid in elaborating the distinction, occur at lines 44, 164 (=OM 346/1–2), and 244.

13 Although the writer may have been inspired by Wyclif's ch. 13 (OM 350–53); OM 352/18–37, for example, takes up the topic of the unity of the faith which animates the end of the English sermon.

14 Especially the first half; see Hudson, *Selections*, p. 178, 77 ff. ns.

15 See Th.-M. Charland, *Artes praedicandi: contribution à l'histoire de la rhetorique au moyen age* (Paris: Vrin, 1936), pp. 111–12, 243–7; and Harry Caplan, "A Late Mediaeval Tractate on Preaching," in Harry Caplan, *Of Eloquence: Studies in Ancient and Mediaeval Rhetoric*, eds. Anne King and Helen North (Ithaca: Cornell University Press, 1970), pp. 40–78.

16 See Hudson, *Premature Reformation*, pp. 347–51; on fraternal prayer (mentioned at "Vae," lines 40–42) and preaching, see pp. 195–96.

17 Although in Lollard discussions, this involves a number of moves we would see as frankly allegorical; see the prologue, chs. 12–14, Forshall and Madden, *Holy Bible*, I: 43–56; and cf. Hudson, *Premature Reformation*, especially pp. 271–72.

18 Cf. "Trewþe of þe gospel is cristen mennys byleue, and by þat schulden men stonden" (164–65); or "Trewþe þat God hymself seiþ and techeþ in þe gospel, þat schulde men worsschipon and taken as byleue" (167–69).

19 Cf. Hudson, *Selections*, p. 178, 95 ff. ns.; and the "upsodoun" topos, another example of language losing its plain referent, at lines 284–94.

20 See Hudson's discussion of "ground," in "A Lollard Sect Vocabulary?" in *Lollards and Their Books*, pp. 165–80, at pp. 171–72.

21 Cf. the sneer in lines 203–04, that friars' "ground," the basis for their activity, which should be a precise instruction in Scripture, is worldly goods, identified with an action Scripture finds reprehensible, being filled with dead men's bones (cf. Matt. 23.27).

22 The materials are probably inspired by Wyclif's ch. 2 (OM 317–19); note "blasfemye" (line 122) and OM 317/32. For Lollard attitudes to this sacrament, see Hudson, *Premature Reformation*, pp. 294–99; cf. the conclusion which the preacher ascribes to "somme discrete men:" "hit is ynow to [men] for to ben assoylud of God" (lines 137–38).

23 "Of Ministers" includes a lengthy discussion of the point (lines 109–70), derived from its source in the master.

24 Eucharistic speculations form the aboriginal Lollard heresy; see Hudson,

Premature Reformation, pp. 281–90. The preacher buttresses the Lollard phrasing with a series of exact references to the Church Fathers, who stand for an antique literal reading of Matthew 26.26: these are equally as standard as learnéd, cf. Hudson, *Selections*, p. 178, notes at 238, 241, 244.

25 This documentary source is not chosen simply for its antiquity and proximity to Christian origin. The preacher has good reason for rejecting (lines 301–05) Nicene and Athanasian statements: the former, for example, makes the church apostolic as well as catholic and includes no reference to the communion of saints. However, the preacher's opinion scarcely represents the spectrum of views held by the sect: a Lollard commentary on the Athanasian Creed survives.

26 See my discussion of the mendicant attacks, "Difficulty," pp. 325–28; and cf. Hudson, *Selections*, p. 179, 305 ff. n.

27 See Hudson's discussion of the priesthood of all believers, *Premature Reformation*, pp. 325–27.

28 Chaucer, "The Miller's Tale" 3455–56; see Margaret Aston's trickledown theory of Lollardy, "William White's Lollard Followers," in Aston, *Lollards and Reformers* (London: Hambledon Press, 1984), pp. 70–100 (and "Difficulty," p. 332 [n. 34]).

29 See Hudson, *Selections*, p. 68, lines 36–66.

30 See the notes in Larry D. Benson et al., *The Riverside Chaucer* (Boston: Houghton, 1987), pp. 1019 (5 p 4.36n on double negatives) and 1007 (1 p 4.229–30n), m 5.25–26n on other explanatory glosses).

31 The Additional manuscript contains a strenuously lay-oriented Latin "Regula sacerdotum," testimony to what I take as commonplace magnatial trope linking textual and physical disendowment. In one of the lay testamentary bequests, dated 1420, John Brinchele, tailor of London returned his English *Boece* to a probably Latinate clerical setting, to David Fyvyan, rector of St. Benedict Fynke (*Early English Text Society*, original series 78, p. 136 n.). The manuscript willed by Sir Peter Arderne, Baron of the Exchequer, in 1468, sounds as if it could have been Additional 16165 (*Testamenta Eboracensia* 4: 102 n.).

32 The single leaf that forms University of Missouri, Fragmenta Manuscripta 150 comes from a manuscript which also included the Latin text, perhaps another sign of clerical provenance.

33 See A. B. Emden, *A Biographical Register of the University of Oxford to A.D. 1500*, 3 vols. (Oxford: Clarendon, 1957–59), II: 890 (David Hawkebroke), III: 1662 (John Sedgefelde), III: 1803–04 (William Strete). Auctarium F.3.5, originally seven separate manuscripts, may not have achieved its current form until the late sixteenth century.

34 *Boece* lacks any explanatory preface, and for Chaucer's views on the

usefulness of translation, one must rely on the preface to his piece of "kiddie lit," *The Astrolabe.*

35 Trevisa's "Dialogue," after all, has a not very distant subtext, his translation of an Ockhamesque dialogue advocating magnatial suzerainity in ecclesiastical affairs.

36 This paper incorporates pieces of "The Ideology of Lollard Bible Translation," read for the South Atlantic Modern Language Association, November, 1989; and *"Vae octuplex* and Lollard Social Ideology," read for the Modern Language Association, December 1989. I'm grateful to Lorraine Stock and Martin Irvine, who organized these panels, and to several pointed interlocutors in my audiences, among whom I would especially single out Tony Spearing and Sheila Delany. Rita Copeland has been unfailingly supportive of my work and has made numerous improving suggestions to which I have attempted to respond.

9

Sacrum Signum: sacramentality and dissent in York's theatre of Corpus Christi

SARAH BECKWITH

Quod non capis,
Quod non vides,
Animosa firmat fides
Praeter rerum ordinem.

(Thomas Aquinas)

God does not offer himself for observation.

(Hegel)

I

The difficulty, outrage, and opportunity of a sacrament lies, by common consensus, in the way in which it yokes together the visible and the invisible.[1] Difficulty, because there is nothing self-evident about the form of this relation or the reasons for it; outrage, because divinity is inevitably and necessarily traduced by the limitation in a figure, and opportunity because both the ideological and utopian dimensions that accompany the sacrament as symbol derive from the rupture rather than the continuity of meaning between visible and invisible, from the excess of the signified over the sign. This tension between the seen and the unseen is at its most impossible and contradictory in the central sacrament of the late Middle Ages, the body of Christ; the doctrine of transubstantiation claims the greatest allegiance and the maximum faith from participants in the mass precisely because of its flagrant transgression of the evidence of the senses.[2] This tension between the visible and the invisible, constitutive of the very working of Corpus Christi as a social imaginary, is explored in Corpus Christi theatre wherein it finds an apt and congruent form for elucidating

264

and enacting the symbolic (rather than logical) potentialities of sacrament-ality.[3]

This essay makes a preliminary exploration of the York Corpus Christi cycles' symbolic enactment and investigation of sacramentality. In arguing for the necessity of a hermeneutic and symbolic analysis of sacramentality at the heart of the York plays I hope to show at once the poverty and the impossibility of arguments that define these plays, and by extension other dimensions of a sacramental religious culture, as either merely orthodox or dissentient.[4] I want to show that dissent as critical consciousness is intrinsic to symbolic formation as such, and a component part of the sacramental culture enacted in these plays. To locate narrowly doctrine-driven versions of dissent or defenses of orthodoxy in the plays is to fall prey precisely to what might be termed the inquisitorial fallacy, in which complex practices are deformed through the constricting filter of the ecclesiastical tribunal.[5] Beyond the cruel choice of the increasingly rigid and punitive dogmas surrounding transubstantiation enacted by the ecclesiastical authorities[6] and the positions rendered "heretical" by such strictures then, these plays take up the ethical invitation at the heart of the Augustinian view of the sacrament with all its ambiguities, and they enact it in its most paradoxical and consonant form – in the physical manifesta-tion, the showing forth, of theatre itself.[7] For Augustine, much more interested than his scholastic successors in communion rather than consecration, the Real Presence did not so much inhere in the sacramental object, the fetishized host, but rather in the embodied community of the faithful.[8] It was because he always understood the eucharist in its ecclesial dimensions that salvation had to be social; and insofar as the church for him was not so much the means of salvation as the goal of salvation, the Real Presence was the relation of the community to each other in the presence of God. It is perhaps in the collective, enacted, and embodied form of Corpus Christi theatre that late medieval vernacular theology tests out and explores these possibilities.[9]

When the early Church Fathers wrote about sacramentality, it was baptism that was the paradigmatic form for thinking through the impli-cations of, and rationale for, the relation between outward sign and inward grace. The very wondrousness of baptism, that death, as Tertullian described it, should be washed away in a bath, informed a belief that came to define the very nature of faith.[10] It was the seeming impossibility of this bizarre yet miraculous enactment that meant that skepticism was not so much, as Peter Cramer says in his book on baptism, superseded by faith as its very content. Faith is made and created; it is an ethical act of will and it is the change in the person, not in the ritual object, that is the significant and transformative moment. Meaning is not located in the water of baptism but rather in the strenuous and attentive relation developed toward it. Augustine, whose anti-Donatist writings elaborate a version of faith around the sacrament of baptism, vitally understood our attitude to signs not simply as an intellectual issue – learning to read things in the right way – but rather as learning morally and ethically.[11] Understanding for him was therefore based crucially on love, and it was the very difficulty of belief, the very gap, for example, between words and their meanings, which constructs the possibility for sympathy as an act of attention, will, and love. For Augustine, then, as Cramer stresses, "the power of the sacrament to make visible what is not visible is therefore an ethical question."[12]

Moreover, such an understanding was always a vital and component part of eucharistic thinking and sacramental theology. When considering the question whether the faithful received the body of Christ in mystery or in truth, Ratramnus in his debates with Paschasius Radbertus, made the distinction between reality *in figura* and *in veritate*. The reality in figure is a form of reality that points toward another hidden reality; reality *in veritate* is that form in which its own nature is apparent.[13] For Ratramnus, the eucharist is a reality *in figura*; the reality *in veritate* can be discerned only by faith, and not by means of the evidence of the senses. The central mode of apprehension of the presence of Christ in the eucharist is thus an unsurpassable mystery made necessary at once by the nature of God and by the nature of signification. For Berengar too, in the controversies around which much eucharistic dogma was formed, it could not make sense to assert that Christ was physically present in the sacrament, since no changes in the bread and wine were apparent to the senses.[14] This too is the essentially Anselmian understanding of faith as it is developed in the *Proslogion*, "that I shall not understand unless I believe."[15] Hugh of St. Victor too examines the mysterious aspect of faith in relation to sacrament-ality in some depth and complexity in his book on the sacraments, quoting the famous passage from Hebrews, "faith is the substance of things to be hoped for, the evidence of things that appear not" (Heb. 11.1), thus exemplifying the productive paradox, the essential mystery that had to be at the heart of belief.[16]

And it is this understanding which might gloss a certain flexible and non-dogmatic understanding of the relation between outward form and inner grace in ritual and sacramental action. In this respect (and this is a vital and enduring concern of the Corpus Christi cycles), mere observance of, or obedience to, the law is not sufficient, for faith must come from grace and the sacraments are the complex vehicles of grace. The ethics of sacramentality come from the relation between sacrament and worshiper; they do not automatically reside in the sacrament itself (although naturally, this is a distinction that is often blurred in practice). Indeed a proper understanding of sacramental action might be understood to imply a blurring of ritual object and subject, since sacramental efficacy depends on their momentary indistinguishability.[17]

It is this symbolic understanding of sacramentality that is central to their theatrical elucidation in the York Corpus Christi plays. I intend "symbolic" to stand here at once for an understanding of the sacrament which is not restricted to the dogmatic fetishism of doctrines of transubstantiation as represented in an available tradition of eucharistic controversy, and increasingly insisted upon as axiomatic to clerical Christianity, and for an understanding of the symbol as encountered in modern hermeneutics.[18] For the plays are dense with the opaque signs sent down by God and with the effort to grasp and move through their meaning.[19] In this sense sacramental theatre might be said to offer a richer and newer (and in my view, decidedly and necessarily non-dogmatic) sense of how sacraments cause grace by signifying it.[20] It is in fact in Corpus Christi theatre that the full symbolic complexities and possibilities of sacramentality are explored.[21] Critics drastically reduce their understanding of this theatre when they elucidate it in merely doctrinal terms in relation to Corpus Christi, as if there could be a set of propositions about God to which assent is given or withheld.[22] For Corpus Christi understood as a symbol has no clearcut or simple-minded devotional meaning, nor can it have. This theatre offers a form of the sacramental encounter described by Augustine in his Easter sermon to the newly baptized:

You should know what you have received, what you will receive, what you should receive daily. The bread which you see in the altar, when it has been sanctified by the word of God is the body of Christ. . .If you have received it rightly, you are what you have received.[23]

The very act of receiving rightly is the necessary precondition of the transformative possibilities of the sacrament of the eucharist, and thus meaning is co-created in the *transitus* between recipient and received, constituted through the very structure of address. If we take this August-inian version of sacramentality and read it through the grid of modern hermeneutics, we will see the possibilities of the symbolic dimensions of eucharistic theatre. In this sense the meaning of the symbol of the sacrament is necessarily equivocal, opaque, pointing always and inevitably beyond itself, and so promising plenitude because it is always wanting. As Ricoeur says:

Signification by its very structure makes possible, at the same time both total formalization – that is to say the reduction of signs to characters. . .and the restoration of a full language, heavy with implicit intentionalities and analogical references to something else, which it presents enigmatically.[24]

Since God cannot be understood propositionally, it is in the reach and resource of a symbolic language that he has to be not so much understood, as approached. In his later writings Ricoeur understands ideology and utopia as "imaginative practices" which cohabit in "insuperable tension" the constitutive symbolic dimensions of the social tie. This has important implications for our understanding of dissent in symbolic activity, for if we take Ricoeur's account seriously, the inextricable ideological and utopian dimensions of a culture or a text are formed at the radical level of the social imaginary; they are contemporaneous with the "symbolic constitution of social ties themselves."[25]

What is the importance and significance of this understanding of the symbolism of the sacrament and what distinguishes it from the way Corpus Christi has conventionally been explained? Critics who have explored the relation of the plays to the doctrine of Corpus Christi itself have stressed the plays as an exemplification of doctrine. But little attention here is given to the notion that it is in the sheer opacity of meaning rather than its transparency that the sacramental efficacy of sacramental theatre might lie. It is precisely because meaning cannot be distinguished from sign that the possibilities of meaning are inexhaustible.[26] And it is precisely because the Godhead itself is an inexhaustible mystery that sacraments are the signs of grace.[27] And this inexhaustibility informs both the ethics and the ideology of the symbolic form of this theatre.

2

How do these plays explore and encode sacramentality, then, if we are to reject simplistic, categorical, or merely doctrinal explanations?

The Corpus Christi plays exist in complex relation to the sacrament that they nominally celebrate.[28] As Rosemary Woolf has pointed out, Corpus Christi was unique in the church's calendar because it was outside the commemoration of historical events, the actual event (the Last Supper) having been commemorated on Maundy Thursday. Both the plays and the feast then, as she reminds us, had the "peculiar characteristic of not being tied to historical commemoration."[29] Yet in appearing to rewrite the Christian story in terms of the central sacrament of the church, that sacrament that makes evident, visible, and gracious the dispensation of God's mercy, these plays paradoxically confront that sacrament with its own foundations. These foundations, moreover, appear to exist in a more complex and uneasy relationship than that of mere underwriting or support. In the Christ and the Doctors pageant, for example, Christ discovers the church doctors commenting on their own infallibility:

> We schall ordayne so wele,
> Sen we all clergy knawe,
> Defaute shall no man fele
> Nowdir in dede ne sawe.[30]

"Ordayne" here carries the strict sense of the conferral of authority to celebrate and administer the sacraments, but also the commission to proclaim the word.[31] But it is Christ who has the ultimate authority of teacher:

> The holy gost has on me light
> And has anoynted me as a leche,
> And geven me pleyne poure and myght
> The kyngdom of heuene for to preche.[32]

The doctors discover that Christ, on whom they found their authority, reveals their bookishly blind inadequacy for he "kens more þan we knawes" (line 90), knowing the commandments apparently without any book-learning. And Christ's behests to keep the first two commandments, with their injunction that to love are all the "lawe þat we shall lere" (line 160), is clearly a reproof to the very institution that claims to found itself on the authority of his word, since the doctors have close similarities to medieval clerics. Books are superfluous then to the strenuous but inviting possibility which should be accessible to all:

> The secounde may men preve
> And clerly knawe, wherby
> ʒoure neghbours shall ʒe loue
> Als youreselffe, sekirly.   (lines 153–56)

This confrontation of the authority founded upon Christ with the authority which founds it is a consistent and paradoxical principle of the means of operation of these plays. It is vitally elaborated in the Baptism pageant.

If baptism was the paradigm sacrament used to discuss the relation between form and grace, it was also at the very center of early controversies surrounding sacramentalism.[33] For baptism as a ritual action brings into play the most vital institutional issues of power; without the faith conferred in baptism, all the other sacraments are supposedly annulled, and so baptism alone is necessary for salvation.[34] Issues about the possibility of salvation without baptism were enacted around the sacrament of baptism in the writings of the first formulators of sacramentality, just as they were later to become the focus of Lollard controversy.[35] Indeed the very notion of sacramental objectivity had been first formulated by Augustine in his defense of baptism in response to the claim that the individual evil of an officiating bishop invalidated the sacraments he administered.[36]

But the York pageant of the Baptism opens up the contradiction between authorizing figure and act. Interestingly enough John's act of baptism is preceded by his lament at the insufficiency of mere preaching:

> For yf I preche tham day be day
> And telle tham lorde, of thy comyng
> þat all has wrought
> Men are so dull þat my preching
> Serues of noght.[37]

John ponders the uncanniness of his own baptism of Christ, for if baptism is meant to wash a man clean of sin, to act as a symbolic restoration of and promise of a new life, what can be the point of baptizing the one without sin?

> Bot wele I wote, baptyme is tane
> To wasshe and clense man of synne,
> And wele I wote þat synne is none

> In hym, withoute ne withinne.
> What nedis hym þan
> For to be baptiste more or myne
> Als synfull man?[38]

Christ's answer is that since men cannot go to "endless bliss" unless they
have been baptized and since he is a mirror for man, he must be baptized.
Also the virtue of his baptism will sanctify it. Of course, John still works
away at the contradiction and circularity of this argument:

> þat place þat I yarne moste of all,
> Fro thens come þou lorde, as I gesse.
> How schulde I þan, þat is a thrall,
> Giffe þe baptyme, þat rightwis is
> And has ben euere?[39]

Christ answers enigmatically that righteousness is not only fulfilled in
word but in deed (lines 129–30). It seems that it is vital for the baptism of
Christ not only to be seen to happen but for the institution of baptism to
be seen to be authorized by the very one in whose name it is done.

In exposing the difficulties, rather than the smoothness of institution
and precedent, the play straddles the poles of a debate being reactivated in
the Lollard context. Lollard texts like *The Lanterne of Light*, for example,
stress that John the Baptist would be persecuted as a Lollard were he to
preach in the contemporary world.[40] Contemporary Lollards went back to
the foundations precisely to topple over the ecclesiastical abuse of them,
and as we have seen the plays exacerbate and enact this as a striking
tension.

But of course, in enacting at such length the paradoxes of such an
encounter the plays circle round an impasse that they constantly return to:
the very impossibility of the center of any religious system justifying itself
on historical or indeed ethical grounds.[41] The plays seek to encounter,
describe, enact the sacraments, and part of that project is explaining their
embeddedness, their institution, their inevitable and central justness. But
to explore the origins or the foundations of Christianity is an impossibility,
and all that may finally be discovered is the mystical limit of authority. As
Derrida has recently expressed it:

the law is transcendent and violent, because it depends only on who is before it,
and so prior to it, on who produces it, founds it, authorizes it in an absolute
performative whose presence always escapes him. The law is transcendent and
theological, and so always to come, always promised, because it is immanent,

finite and so already past. Every subject is caught up in this aporetic structure in advance.[42]

The attempt to create a chain of linear causality, the attempt to generate a legitimate lineage for Christian authority, is forced to confront this fundamental rupture. Thus Christ must refer to a time that is both anterior and posterior to present time, and liturgical time, sacramental time, must rediscover the historical memory in the present enactment.[43] But this must always be effected across a gap, in Žižek's terms, and by an aporetic subject. If there is a constant and necessary asymmetry between diachrony and synchrony in any structure, then this is an asymmetry that these plays constantly rehearse.[44] In Žižek's words:

> It is precisely because the chain of linear causality is always broken, because language as synchronous order is caught in a vicious circle, that it attempts to restore "the missing link" by retroactively re-ordering its own past, by reconstituting its origins backwards. In other words, the very fact of incessant rewriting of the past attests to the presence of a certain gap, to the efficacy of a certain traumatic, foreign kernel that the system is trying to re-integrate "after the fact." If the passage from genesis into structure were to be continuous, there would be no inversion of the direction of causality: it is the missing link which opens the space for re-ordering the past.[45]

It is this missing link too that informs the religious subject produced by these plays. The past of recorded Christian history opens up more than it explains in these plays, and in that necessary opacity lies both the transcendence and the ethical possibilities of the religious system as such. If there were not some chronically aporetic gap, as Žižek puts it, we would have not a signifying structure but a "positive network of causes and effects." And a positive network of causes and effects would allow no space for the transcendental.[46] For if God were somehow transparently to disclose himself to us, "our activity would no longer be ethical, since we would do good not because of moral law itself but because of our insight into God's nature."[47]

In the Corpus Christi pageants then, the manifestation of God's message takes the inevitable form of a story, of a narration about God's promise which strives and fails to make prophecy coincide with time, but, of course, it can only do this by imagining a finished world, by projecting the end of this time, and actually in the pageant sequences these two times can never coincide.

In the Chester cycle, for example, the opacity of signs and their temporality are a conscious part of the design of the drama. Miracles (meaning at once God's actions and the performance of plays called miracles) are necessary during the time of Christ to strengthen belief, but such signs actually belong to the historical past in the Chester cycle's understanding, as we see in this passage from "The Last Supper and the Betrayal of Christ":

> for knowe you nowe, the tyme is come
> that sygnes and shadowes be all donne.
> Therfore, make haste, that we maye soone
> all figures cleane rejecte. (lines 69–72)[48]

After Pentecost, God's power is supposed to be manifest in the sacrament and it is the work of the play to persuade its observers to link the redeemed present with the remembered past.[49] The Chester plays make clear the ways in which signs should be interpreted and the danger of the closeness of the relationship between sign and illusion in its very structure, and it makes ample use of expositor figures, setting its action in a very developed framework of exegesis. But the sequence of York's pageants seems to me much more to stress, on the one hand, the incredible juxtaposition and paradox between Christ as instituted in the ecclesiastical structure and the instituting figure himself, and, on the other hand, the sheer difficulty of seeing him even when, perhaps especially when, he has been made manifest. The York pageants make very little use of expositors; they enact themselves much more thoroughly and completely in the murkiness of contingent time, and are content to explore the contradictions and opportunities that emerge out of that juxtaposition.

Let us look at the way in which the sequence of plays from the Crucifixion onwards illuminates the relation between visible and invisible in the sacrament of Christ's body. Many of the pageants explore the difficulty of seeing. The Crucifixion pageants, for example, explore the historically and excruciatingly essential irony that the torturers of Christ do not understand what they are doing. In the York pageant of the Pinners, they are made to construct the central icon of the culture, to make the very sign of crucifixion unwittingly, and one suggested staging is to emphasize this distinction, such that Christ is suddenly elevated to view, so that the audience, having only heard but not seen the pain to which Christ is put, are forced to confront, to see what the soldiers have been doing. Christ's words from the cross invite the audience to match their vision with their feeling:

> Al men þat walkis by waye or strete,
> Takes tente ʒe schalle no trauayle tyne.
> Byholdes myn heede, myn handis, and my feete,
> And fully feele nowe, or ʒe fyne
> Yf any mournyng may be meete,
> Or myscheue mesured vnto myne.[50]

Indeed, here it might be stressed that this is rather different from the meditational traditions precisely because the vision, the sight of Christ is produced, constructed before our very eyes by means of visible social agents, and we are asked to feel, not a simple affective identification with Christ, but an identification that is fully cognizant of the horrors of how it has been produced. The relation between the invisible and the visible is here given a very specific ethical reading.

But the sequence of plays that succeed the death of Christ initiate a time when the very difficulty, the very density of the sign of the risen Christ missed continuously by his disciples and followers, necessitates more and more signs and sights, more and more proofs which themselves often seem to miss their mark. The Resurrection pageant inaugurates a meditation on the difficulty of reading Christ's body by the Centurion's announcement of the "selcouthe sight" (line 47) he has seen.[51] After the announcement of the miraculous sights he has seen, Pilate enjoins the soldiers to "kepis Jesu body / With all youre myghte."[52] The manifestation of Christ's body, its accessibility, presence and absence are a complex metaphor in the pageant as a whole. For as in the "quem quaeritis" trope, the emptiness of the tomb and the absence of the body there paradoxically signifies the fullness of the presence of the Risen Christ. When the two Marys "Come and See" this is the first signification of the resurrection itself. "Sight" is a constant motif in the next sequence of pageants, from Mary Magdalene's "I se hym noght" (line 35), to the replacement of the bread of Christ's body for his resurrected body to the pilgrims at Emmaus, to the productive incredulity of Thomas. We encounter Christ's body then in the confused vision of the others who continually fail to see. Thus Peter in "The Incredulity of Thomas" pageant:

> What was this sight þat we saughe nowe
> Shynand so bright,

> And vanysshed þus and we ne wote how,
> Oute of oure sight?[53]

And the sight of the risen Christ eating a honeycomb is still not enough to convince Thomas who must put his fingers in Christ's side. The Ascension pageant continues the time of signs and wonders showing in a "figure clear" what has not already been made manifest. But as God says at the end of the Thomas pageant, the truly blessed is the one who does not need to see to believe, because only in that way can the essential mystery of the faith be preserved.[54]

What we encounter in this sequence of pageants is a desire for proof to see, and then a series of visions that are always literally too bright to be actually seen as such, constantly disappearing beyond the realms of human vision. Thus again Peter in the Pentecost pageant:

> I myght noȝt loke, so was it light –
> A, loued be þat lorde þat itt vs lente.[55]

Add to this of course, the fact that the artifice, the fabrication, the crude made-ness of the images of Christ descending from the clouds, indicates the mechanical, physically contingent nature of the theatrical exploration of these mysteries.

In the Last Judgment pageant the trajectory of "sight" is all of a sudden reversed. Christ appears again at the very end of time to judge the good and the evil as such, and he appears to us again in his "wounded shirt," but this time the sight to be seen is the judgment itself. The souls are judged on their treatment, after Matthew, of Christ and Christ in man. How have they responded to the thirsty and the hungry? Have they seen the poverty, thirst, and hunger around them? "Whan was it we sawe þe seke, allas?" Because they failed to see, they "schall neuere butt sorowe see / And sitte be Satanas þe fende."[56]

But such a judgment which separates unequivocally the good from the evil, relying on the aptness and inescapable perspicacity of its vision can only be projected into the future time of Last Judgment. Then vision will be transparent and so justice just. But otherwise the signs of this sacramental theatre are regarded as making the necessary concessions to frail man, to quote Pecock's definition of sacrament:

Sacramenting is not ellis þan an holy outwiard worschiping bi outward feleable or sensible signs or tokenes.[57]

Their seeability is a concession to the frailty of mankind:

Mankinde in this lijf is so freel, that forto make into him sufficient remembraunce of thingis to be profitabli of him remembrid he nedith not oonly hereable rememoratif signes. . .but he nedith also therwith and ther to seable rememoratijf signes.[58]

3

Two recent accounts of sacramental culture in the late Middle Ages understand it in reaction formation to Lollardy. Lauren Lepow reads the Towneley Plays as a concerted response to Lollard eucharistic heresy, and Ann Nichols reads the numerous seven sacrament fonts in East Anglia, an area high in Lollardy, as reproofs to heresy and very specific elucidations of Lollard doctrine. In this view, sensible signs, newly material versions of the sacrament in visual and theatrical form were produced, made manifest and "seeable" to counteract Lollard versions of the eucharist, and moreover they were done in a form to which some Lollard versions of representation would in any case take exception. Thus the *sola scriptura* of Lollard versions competed with visual forms of material representation. But for the Lollards and for the Wycliffite realism that underwrote it, such sensible signs could only be a traducement of the logos. These could only be external and superficial, even idolatrous signs without inner substance; in the terms of Wycliffite realism, they would be lacking in reality. Brut, for example, denied that in baptism the sign of water caused what it signified.[59] Thus the very root of sacramental theology, the principle of efficient causality, that signs cause what they signify, was fundamentally denied by the Lollards. For them there was no need of images where knowledge of Scripture would suffice. Wherever possible, the Lollards sought to substitute the clarity of the Scriptures for the idolatrous obscurity of seeable signs. If we compare, for example, the York Corpus Christi plays' transcription of the Ascension pageants with the version we get of this event in the English Wycliffite sermons, we will see that the sermon version is obsessed with seeing through the mistiness of the communication. Whereas the pageants dwell repeatedly on this mistiness,[60] this is triumphantly superseded in this treatment:

And aftur seiþ Crist to hise apostles þat þese þingus he seyde byfore to hem in *prouerbys* and mystily, *but now is come tyme whan he schal not speke þus to hem in*

276

prouerbys, but apertly of his Fadur he schal tellen hem as beste is. . .*And* Cristus *disciplus seydon to hym, "Loo! now þow spekist openly, and þow seist* now *no proverbe, and þerfore we wyton wel þat þow knowest alle þingus.*

The sermon concludes that we should follow the example of the Apostles and

leue þese sensible signes, and taken ensawmple of hooly men, as of Crist and hise apostles, how þei hadde not here þere blisse. But here Crist ordeynede peynes and hate of þe world and pursewyng to men þat he moste louede, to techon vs þat comen after hem. And þus signes of pacience and pursewyng in þis eurþe schulde be tokne of Godus loue and not signes of anticrist.[61]

The Lollard consensus then was to deny the use and mistiness of signs as traducements of the mystery of Christ. They insisted on *sola scriptura* as the legitimate means of access to God and thus they stumbled on the fundamentalist crux: the desire for and impossibility of the eradication of figuration.

But these plays are perhaps best not understood as merely orthodox responses to another developed form of doctrine, understood in as abstract and schematized terms as orthodox clerical culture. For Corpus Christi theatre is at once a verbal and a visual medium and in it the opposition between them is destabilized. They are animated by, and thoughtful about, rather than polarized between these forms.[62] A complex dialectic can be established between word and image on the stage, as in our understanding of the system of representation at work in the plays. They are committed at once to text as a medium, to words, and to actions; they cannot be reduced to either.[63] And I would say that the York plays do this more systematically than the other cycle plays, not by subordinating the difficulty, opportunity, and opacity, the causative mystery of image to the reductive but secure exposition of commentators clerical and otherwise. Rather the clerical commentators are seen as providing a wholly inadequate gloss on the life and body of Christ, and that icon is constantly reconstructed to confront the spectators to match their sight and affect. For it is surely in theatre that the full sacramental definition of signs as sacred things can be most fully exploited, because in theatre iconic identity can be exploited, as can the very tension between outward form and inner thing, between sign and signified, and between the visible and the invisible at the heart of sacramental theology.

In other words, theatre is the perfect form for exploring not what might be unequivocally there, for how in any case could God offer himself for observation, but rather what is signified, and in that complex theatricalization lies new and conflicting meanings. This theatre is neither fully ritualized, nor fully textualized, only being written down and confined to text, a process that involves inaugurating a new regime and understanding, late in its performance history. It is in preserving this essential mystery at the heart of sacramentality, rather than either allegorizing it, subjecting it to scholastic explanation and logic, or doctrinal precision, that these plays may be said to offer up their simultaneously utopian and ideological promise. This utopian promise and ideological function may not be considered separately from each other. For ideology tries to bridge the excess of the demand for legitimacy in relation to the belief held by members of a community, just as utopias "reveal the unstated surplus attaching to authority,"[64] and so neither exist merely in addition to any given social group, but as a constitutive part of the necessary analogies through which any social group represents itself. Dissent within these particular plays at least, does not need to be understood as a purely doctrinally driven set of precepts which exist as a set of merely propositional terms to counter orthodox dogma, but might rather be understood as a component part of a vigorous lay and vernacular religiosity.

Edward Schillebeeckx says that the prime analogue of the sign is human corporeality itself, *in which*, not behind which, the spiritual "interiority" of the person communicates, and it is theatre that can manifest the full sacramental complexity of this signification.[65] Sacraments can be actions and not things in this theatre, and they can be opened out to the audience, to the people who may in this case, as in the Augustinian invitation, become what they receive. Understood within a symbolic regime which will subordinate neither image to text as in later reforming work, or text to image, the full range of this theatre is misunderstood if it is polarized to the doctrinal understandings which reduce the complexity and power at once of orthodoxy as of the dissenting traditions cast in their mould.

The full dialectical complexity of this relation of outward form to inward grace is what is compromised, then, if we try to subordinate the one to the other. For these plays are neither static images, nor rituals which function without a text, though they may partake of either form. They can only be understood as incorporating both. Material and spiritual, external and internal are not then understood as contrasts with each other.[66] And so finally, we might say that the plays themselves treat the relationship between experience and interpretation dialectically, in Nicholas Lash's words, as a matter of "mutually critical correlation," and so they may be said to offer "a sacramental account of the relationship between human experience and a tradition of discourse and behaviour which in interpreting that experience, contributes effectively to its transformation."[67]

Notes

1 There are innumerable definitions of sacraments, some of which will be discussed in this essay, but all agree on the axiom that a sacrament is the "sign of a sacred thing." Most definitions agree on the relation between visibility and invisibility. In Hugh of St. Victor's elaborated definition: "A sacrament is a corporeal or material element set before the senses without, representing by similitude and signifying by institution and containing by sanctification some invisible and spiritual grace" (*On the Sacraments of the Christian Faith*, trans. Roy J. Deferrari [Cambridge, Mass.: Medieval Academy of America, 1951], p. 155).

2 See, for example, Jaroslav Pelikan, *The Christian Tradition: A History of the Development of Doctrine*, III, *The Growth of Medieval Theology (600–1300)* (Chicago and London: University of Chicago Press, 1978): 208: "The requirement that, in order to qualify as a sacrament, a sacred action had to involve the visible 'form' or 'sign' of an invisible reality present there seems to have come from a consideration of the Eucharist, where the notion of 'Presence' was fundamental." The presence was produced through the medium of the crucial priestly blessings of the bread and the wine, and that moment signaled the visual theophany of the mass. As Miri Rubin puts it: "The moment was all-important; before it, gazing and adoring were tantamount to idolatry, after it, spiritual gazing could convey great benefits" (*Corpus Christi: The Eucharist in Late Medieval Culture* ([Cambridge: Cambridge University Press, 1991], p. 54). It was the gesture of elevation that actually signified the moment of consecration, and the doctrine of concomitance meant, as Rubin notes that "by gazing at one species one was in fact viewing the whole body, veiled under the accidents of the host" (p. 55). See also Edouard Dumoutet, *Le désir de voir l'hoste et les origines de la dévotion au saint-sacrement* (Paris: Beauchesne, 1926). As the poem "The Sacrifice of the Mass" in Richard Hill's early sixteenth-century commonplace book suggests, Christ manifests himself in the bread, and it is precisely because this happens without any noticeable change that it can only be seen with the eyes of faith (cited in Rubin, *ibid.*, p. 107). For further consideration on the moment of elevation see Vincent L. Kennedy,

"The Moment of Consecration and the Elevation of the Host," *Medieval Studies* 6 (1944): 121–50. The very difficulty of belief is also an instance of the Catholic understanding of faith as a virtue.

3   The phrase "social imaginary" is explored in Cornelius Castoriadis, *The Imaginary Institution of Society*, trans. Kathleen Blamey (Cambridge, Mass.: The MIT Press, 1987) pp. 133–56.

4   As Steven Justice argues in this volume, and as Gordon Leff argued some time ago, since heresy and orthodoxy exist only in relation to each other we must see beyond the orthodoxy's reduction of reformism and dissent to heresy.

5   For the kinds of questions asked of suspected Lollards, see Anne Hudson, "The Examination of Lollards" in *Lollards and Their Books* (London: Hambledon Press, 1985), pp. 125–39.

6   For the centrality of the eucharist in defining Lollardy as heresy, see Anne Hudson, *The Premature Reformation: Wycliffite Texts and Lollard History* (Oxford: Clarendon, 1988), pp. 281–94.

7   I am not, of course, suggesting that Augustine was an advocate of theatre as such. His comments in book 3 of the *Confessions* and elsewhere make his love of theatre shameful and opaque to himself; see *Confessions*, trans. R. S. Pine-Coffin (Harmondsworth: Penguin, 1961), pp. 55–56. My point is rather that precisely because sacraments must be understood as actions and not things, it is in the theatre of dramatic action that they are best explored and understood. See Joseph M. Powers, *Eucharistic Theology* (New York: Herder and Herder, 1967), p. 151. Powers is influenced by Edward Schillebeeckx, OP; see especially here "Transsubstantiation, Transfinalization, Transfiguration," *Worship* 40 (1966): 324–38. I explore the centrality of the ethical to such an understanding of sacramentality later in this essay.

8   Henri de Lubac defends an Augustinian version of symbolism and the Real Presence in his *Corpus mysticum: l'eucharistie et l'église au moyen âge* (Paris: Aubier, 1949), especially pp. 290 ff.

9   The term "vernacular theology" is one coined by Nicholas Watson in his essay, "Censorship and Cultural Change in Late Medieval England: Vernacular Theology, The Oxford Translation Debate, and Arundel's Constitutions of 1409," *Speculum* 70 (1995): 822–64. I am grateful to Nicholas Watson for sending me a copy of this essay in advance of publication.

10   *De baptismo*, 2.2, cited in Peter Cramer, *Baptism and Change in the Early Middle Ages c. 200–1150* (Cambridge: Cambridge University Press, 1993), p. 54. Tertullian's "Treatise on Baptism" is available in translation in *Baptism: Ancient Liturgies and Patristic Texts*, ed. Andre Hamman (New York: Alba House, 1967), pp. 30–49. The comment about the miraculous

abolition of death in a bath is discussed on p. 31, in the context of a debate about the very difficulty of belief. Citing 1 Corinthians 27 and Matt. 19.26, he states: "Is it not wonderful too, that death should be washed away by bathing? But it is the more to be believed if the wonderfulness be the reason why it is not believed. For what does it behoove divine works to be in their quality, except that they be above all wonder?"

11 Perhaps, as one of the readers of this manuscript hinted, "our attitude to signs" is an outrageous conflation of an Augustinian semiology with our own. But there are many recent critics who have very productively explored the profound and interesting connections between Christian theology and semiology. See, for example, Margaret Ferguson's brilliant essay which links Derridean anti-mimeticism with the Augustinian understanding of all language as metaphorical and sees them both as concerned with "figuration exilée": "Saint Augustine's Region of Unlikeness: The Crossing of Exile and Language," *Georgia Review* 29 (1975): 842–64. See also Kevin Hart's exploration of Christian theology as a semiology, *The Trespass of the Sign* (Cambridge: Cambridge University Press, 1989). Modern hermeneutics are deployed in a tradition of modern Thomism by the Dominican scholar Herbert MacCabe in *God Matters* (London: Geoffrey Chapman, 1987), and investigated by the Catholic theologian Edward Schillebeeckx, especially in his essay "Towards a Catholic Use of Hermeneutics," in his *God the Future of Man* (London: Sheed and Ward, 1969), pp. 1–50. Among more recent studies see Nicholas Lash, *Easter in Ordinary: Reflections on Human Experience and the Knowledge of God* (Charlottesville: University Press of Virginia, 1988), and John Millbank, *Religion and Social Theory: Beyond Secular Reason* (Oxford: Blackwell, 1990).

12 Cramer, *Baptism and Change*, p. 110.

13 For details of these controversies, see Gary Macy, *The Theologies of the Eucharist in the Early Scholastic Period: A Study of the Salvific Function of the Sacrament According to the Theologians c. 1080–1220* (Oxford: Clarendon, 1984), p. 28.

14 The crucial change in the debates surrounding the Berengarian controversy were obviously the introduction of the Aristotelian understanding of *substantia*. For Berengar, if the subjects change, then so must the accidents, and to deny this would be both blasphemy and philosophical inanity, as Macy points out, *The Theologies of the Eucharist in the Early Scholastic Period*, p. 40.

15 Quoted from *Proslogion*, I, in Pelikan, *The Growth of Medieval Theology*, p. 259 (see n. 1 above) and used here specifically in relation to the eucharist. Doubt for Anselm was thus in crucial ways essential to faith. And see Hugh of St. Victor's elegantly complex passages in *On the*

Sacraments, I.10.2, glossing the verse from Hebrews 11.1:

> Faith is the substance of things to be hoped for, the evidence of things
> that appear not: Faith is the substance, that is the subsistence, of things
> to be hoped for, that is of future goods which we hope will come and
> which alone are worthy of our hope and expectation since in them our
> good consists. Faith, therefore, is the substance of things to be hoped for,
> since the invisible goods which are not yet present through [an] act
> presently through faith subsist in our hearts, and faith itself in these
> things is their subsistence in us.

Such things, Hugh specifies, cannot be comprehended either through
likeness, through image, or by that which is felt by us: "Therefore, by faith
alone do they subsist in us, and their substance is the faith in them,
whereby they are believed to be but are not comprehended as to their
nature" (*On the Sacraments*, trans. Deferrari, p. 166).

16 See n.15 above. In Augustine's words: "Mysterium fidei salubriter credi
potest, investigari salubriter non potest," that is, "a mystery of faith can be
profitably believed; it cannot be profitably examined" (quoted in Rubin,
Corpus Christi, p. 22, from Peter Lombard, *Sententiae*, IV.D.11). For
Augustine's commentary on Hebrews 11.1, see *Enchiridion*, ch. 8, in which
he explores the inextricability of the cardinal virtues faith, hope, and love,
all necessitated by the "things not seen" (Philip Schaff, ed., *A Select Library
of the Nicene and Post-Nicene Fathers of the Christian Church* III [Grand Rapids,
Michigan: William B. Eerdmans Publishing Company, 1980]: 239). See
also (in the same volume) Augustine's comments in *De Trinitate* book 13,
ch. 1, p. 167. The loss of this ambiguity central to signification in the
logical precision of scholastic inquiry is a major thesis of de Lubac's *Corpus
mysticum* (n. 8 above), and informs his sense of the possibilities in the
Augustinian tradition:

> . . .si le mystère est essentiellement obscur à nos facultés charnelles, il est
> en lui-même tout rayonnant d'une secrète intelligibilité. S'il constitue
> pour la foi une épreuve, il est en même temps un signe, un appel. Il
> nous invite, il nous stimule à la recherche. Nous devinons qu'il comporte
> un arrière-fond lumineux. C'est une enigme à déchiffrer, c'est une verité
> dont l'expression nous porte au-delà d'elle-même.   (p. 259)

The Victorines pursued an Augustinian genealogy, making the distinction
sacramentum and *res*; for the Victorine school it was the unity of faith and
love that was the *res*. Thus as Macy insists, this view understands salvation
as emerging from a "spiritual, mystical union with Christ rather than
through a natural or substantial union" (*The Theologies of the Eucharist in the
Early Scholastic Period*, p. 103). Such a view is then, in many senses, in the

tradition of Ratramnus and Berengar. For more detail on these
controversies, see Rubin, *Corpus Christi*, pp. 14–21, and A. J. Macdonald,
Berengar and the Reform of Sacramental Doctrine (New York: Richwood
Publishing Co., 1977).

17 Cramer, *Baptism and Change in the Early Middle Ages*, p. 156. As Cramer
    also points out, there is no equation between object and meaning, but a
    bringing out of one from the other. Liturgy might be said to be this
    bringing out (p. 158). Aquinas in his meditations on the sacraments never
    fetishized the host, and always made a clear distinction between sacrament
    as channel, not vessel of grace; see *Summa theologiae*, 3a.62.4: "Grace is not
    said to be in a sacrament as in a subject, nor yet in a vessel inasmuch as a
    vessel is a certain kind of place, but rather inasmuch as a vessel or
    instrument is said to be the tool by means of which some work is
    performed. . ." translation from Blackfriars edition, LVI, *The Sacraments*, ed.
    and trans. David Bourke (London: Eyre and Spottiswoode): 60–61.

18 It need hardly be pointed out that hermeneutics as a tradition is part of,
    and a transformation of, an essentially exegetical tradition. These issues
    remain in modern theology still deeply contested issues; see, for example,
    Lash, *Easter in Ordinary* (n. 11 above).

19 In an unpublished lecture delivered during the York Early Music Festival
    (July 18, 1994), "On Staging the Mysteries," Dick Caws, former founder
    of the "Medieval Players," talked about signs in the York plays as the
    physical form of God's word, and remarked on the remarkably undogmatic
    nature of York's theatrical elucidation of their sheer cumulative density and
    importance in the pageants. My comments are from my own transcription
    of Caws' lecture which has influenced my thinking about the dramaturgy at
    work in sacramental theatre. The notion that sacraments effect what they
    signify is complexly developed by Aquinas in the *Summa theologiae* 3a.62.1.
    The point here, developed out of Aristotelian physics, entails an
    understanding of sacrament as simultaneous cause and sign. In a sacrament
    then, as David Bourke says in his introduction to Aquinas' work on the
    sacraments in the *Summa theologiae*, "the very act of producing meaning and
    the act of causing are one and the same" (Blackfriars edition, LVI: xxi).

20 See Thomas Aquinas, *De veritate* qu. 27 ans. 4 and 13, quoted by Powers,
    Eucharistic Theology, p. 89.

21 I think that the deliberate boldness of this comment can only be read as
    outrageously speculative or utopian on the basis that this theatre must
    enact a narrowly understood doctrine of Corpus Christi, Thomistic or
    otherwise. These plays represent an astonishing vernacular encounter with,
    and appropriation of, the central claims on behalf of the figure at the heart
    of clerical and of Christian culture.

22 See, for example, Jerome Taylor's suggestion that the documents and
liturgical texts of the Feast of Corpus Christi provide "the keys to seeing
that the cycle plays – each cycle in its totality – do indeed possess a
structural or dramatic unity and effectiveness rooted in doctrine" ("The
Dramatic Structure of the Middle English Corpus Christi Cycle of Plays,"
in Jerome Taylor and Alan Nelson, eds., *Medieval English Drama: Essays
Critical and Contextual* [Chicago: University of Chicago Press, 1972],
p. 148). Taylor also describes the Corpus Christi cycles as imitating the
object of Corpus Christi: "I propose that the medieval view of the
significance of the Eucharist, and the themes of the Feast instituted to
remind men of that significance, as we have now seen them, are reflected in
the object imitated by the Corpus Christi cycles in the totality of their
pageants" (pp. 153–54). But this attitude is also prevalent, for example, in
Lauren Lepow's recent book on the Towneley cycle which, lacking a theory
of symbolism, reads the cycle in narrowly theological terms: "My central
interest in this study is the way in which the theology embedded and
dramatized in the Towneley cycle answered the theological stances of
Lollardy" (*Enacting the Sacrament: Counter-Lollardy in the Towneley Cycle*
[London and Toronto: Associated University Presses, 1990], p. 13). Such
views do not appear to have taken into account the concept of "mystery" in
Catholic theology. See, for example, Karl Rahner, "The Concept of Mystery
in Catholic Theology" in *Theological Investigations*, trans. Kevin Smith, IV,
More Recent Writings (Baltimore: Helicon Press, 1966): 36–73. Herbert
MacCabe has a trenchant and lyrical account of the question of God as
mystery in his essay on Creation in *God Matters* (n. 11 above), pp. 5–6; see
also his comments on the "mystery of unity" in his sermon on atonement
written for Holy Week, pp. 76ff. Lash explores the "structural unity of
knowledge and love" implied by the notion of God as mystery in *Easter In
Ordinary*, pp. 238ff.
23 Augustine, sermon 227, *Patrologia latina* 38: 1099–100, quoted in Powers,
Eucharistic Theology, p. 20. See also Augustine's sermon 272 where he
contemplates the mystery of the transformation on the altar:

> How is the bread his body? And the chalice, or rather what the chalice
> contains, how is it his blood? Brethren, these things are called *sacramenta*
> because in them one thing is seen, but something else is understood.
> What is seen has a bodily appearance, but what is understood has a
> spiritual fruitfulness. Thus if you wish to understand the body of Christ,
> listen to the Apostle, who says to the believers: you are the body of
> Christ and his members, it is your mystery which has been placed on the
> altar of the Lord; you receive your own mystery. You answer "Amen" to

what you are, and in answering you accept it. For you hear, "the body of Christ" and you answer "amen." (Quoted in Powers, *ibid.*, p. 21)

It might be argued then that the most important issue about the sacrament for Augustine was precisely not the Real Presence. It was rather the unity and community of the congregation formed through participation in the eucharist. (I am indebted to David Aers for conversation on this point.)

24 Paul Ricoeur, *The Symbolism of Evil*, trans. Emerson Buchanan (New York: Harper and Row, 1967), p. 17.

25 *Ibid.*, "Imagination in Discourse and Action," in Gillian Robinson and John Rundell, eds., *Rethinking Imagination: Culture and Creativity* (London: Routledge, 1994) p. 131. And see his comments on p. 130: "The condition of the production of social messages seems indeed to be a certain kind of non-transparency of our cultural codes."

26 As Ricoeur says in *The Symbolism of Evil*, a symbol is then "that of which enough can never be said and more can always be said" (p. 17).

27 See here, Schillebeeckx, *God the Future of Man* (n. 11 above) p. 41; Lash, *Easter in Ordinary*, p. 231, and MacCabe, *God Matters* (n. 11 above), p. 76.

28 Two recent treatments of the complexity of this relationship are to be found in Steven Justice, *Writing and Rebellion: England in 1381* (Berkeley and Los Angeles: University of California Press, 1994), especially ch. 4, "The Idiom of Rural Politics," and Margaret Aston, "Corpus Christi and Corpus Regni," *Past and Present* 143 (1994): 3–47. Both writers are explicitly interested in the possibilities of dissent within and against the received traditions and understandings of Corpus Christi. For two treatments which explore adjacent issues with more specific relation to Corpus Christi theatre, political order, and ritual form, see my "Making the World in York and the York Cycle," in Miri Rubin and Sarah Kay, eds., *Framing Medieval Bodies* (Manchester: Manchester University Press, 1994), pp. 254–76, and "Ritual, Theatre, and Social Space in the York Corpus Christi Cycle," in Barbara Hanawalt and David Wallace, eds., *Bodies and Disciplines: Intersections of History and Literature in Fifteenth-Century England* (Minneapolis: University of Minnesota Press, forthcoming, 1996).

29 *The English Mystery Plays* (London: Routledge and Kegan Paul, 1972), p. 72.

30 Richard Beadle ed., *The York Plays* (London: Edward Arnold, 1982), p. 175, lines 69–72.

31 Pelikan, *The Growth of Medieval Theology* (n. 2 above), p. 29.

32 Beadle, *The York Plays*, p. 176, lines 101–04.

33 Hudson, *The Premature Reformation*, p. 291. John Tanner of Steventon, for example, considered that baptism in fire and the Holy Ghost was sufficient

without baptism in water; see pp. 279, 292. See also Ann Eljenholm Nichols, *Seeable Signs: The Iconography of the Seven Sacraments 1350–1544* (Woodbridge, Suffolk: The Boydell Press, 1994), p. 98, for William White's lost tract on the baptism.

34 Pelikan, *The Growth of Medieval Theology*, p. 205.

35 See Lepow, *Enacting the Sacrament: Counter-Lollardy in the Towneley Cycle* (note 22 above), p. 98.

36 Pelikan, *The Growth of Medieval Theology*, p. 197.

37 Beadle, *The York Plays*, p. 181, lines 3–7.

38 *Ibid.*, p. 183, lines 77–83.

39 *Ibid.*, p. 184, lines 113–17.

40 *The Lanterne of Light*, ed. L. M. Swenburn, Early English Text Society 151 (London: Oxford University Press, 1917) p. 101. See Lynn Staley's comments on this passage in *Margery Kempe's Dissenting Fictions* (University Park, Pennsylvania: Pennsylvania State University Press, 1994), p. 137. Staley points out that Nicholas Love is anxious to stress the relationship between orthodoxy and order very carefully when he deals with Christ's request that John baptize him, emphasizing with great care the emblematization of humility in an instance which might well "trigger Lollard remarks about the state of the contemporary church" (p. 144).

41 And this is not a preoccupation of the Lollard material which remains finally cornered by its fundamentalist exegetical principles.

42 Jacques Derrida, "The Mystical Foundation of Authority," in David Gray Carlson, Drucilla Cornell, and Michel Rosenfeld, eds., *Deconstruction and the Possibility of Justice* (London: Routledge, 1992), p. 36.

43 That is why Corpus Christi has to be embedded within an account of both the beginning and end of the world. It is also why symbol is always accompanied by narrative.

44 Slavoj Žižek, *For They Know Not What They Do: Enjoyment as a Political Factor* (London: Verso, 1991), p. 198.

45 *Ibid.*, pp. 202–03.

46 As Žižek observes:

> In this precise sense, the notion of transcendental order co-incides with the symbolic: in both cases we have to do with a totality which on the level of ontic enchainment, implies a missing link. Transcendental constitution takes place only within the confines of the ontic finitude – only insofar as the gap separating the phenomenal world of our experience from the suprasensible noumenon persists; only insofar as the Ding-an-Sich remains inaccessible – as soon as this gap is leapt over, as soon as we gain access to the Ding-an-Sich, this means the end of the transcendental signifier. (*For They Know Not What They Do*, p. 217)

47 *Ibid.*, p. 219.

48 Text in R. M. Lumiansky and David Mills, eds., *The Chester Mystery Cycle,* *Early English Text Society* supplementary series 3 (Oxford: Oxford University Press, 1974). See also David Mills, "The Chester Cycle," in Richard Beadle, ed., *The Cambridge Companion to the Medieval English Theatre* (Cambridge: Cambridge University Press, 1994), p. 123.

49 There is an excellent account in Mills, *ibid.*, p. 124. Pentecost, in which the disciples receive the Holy Spirit, is conventionally understood as the precedent for the sacramentality of the priesthood.

50 Beadle, *The York Plays*, p. 321, lines 253–58.

51 See my comments in "Ritual, Theatre, and Social Space in the York Corpus Christi Cycle" (n. 28 above).

52 Beadle, *The York Plays*, p. 348, lines 167–68.

53 *Ibid.*, p. 367, lines 21–24.

54 Cramer, *Baptism and Change in the Early Middle Ages*, p. 171: "It is true of the sacramental vision generally that the more sensible a thing, the more urgent its physical presence, the more possibility it has to be made more-than-physical."

55 Beadle, *The York Plays*, p. 382, lines 111–12.

56 Based on Matthew 25. 35–39; Beadle, *The York Plays*, p. 415, lines 353, 371–72.

57 Reginald Pecock, *The Reule of Crysten Religioun*, ed. William C. Greet, *Early English Text Society* original series 171 (London: Milford, 1927), cited in Nichols, *Seeable Signs: The Iconography of the Seven Sacraments 1350–1544*, p. 159.

58 Pecock, *The Repressor of Over Much Blaming of the Clergy*, ed. C. Babington (London: Rolls Series, 1860), cited Nichols, *ibid.*, p. 159. See also Margaret Aston, *England's Iconoclasts* 1, *Laws Against Images* (Oxford: Clarendon, 1988): 147, for more on Pecock's lost *Book of Worshipping*, a defense of images against Lollard attack.

59 Nichols, *ibid.*, p. 94.

60 See my comments on mistiness of communication in "Ritual, Theatre, and Social Space in the York Corpus Christi Cycle."

61 Anne Hudson, ed., *English Wycliffite Sermons* 1 (Oxford: Clarendon, 1983): 456, 458.

62 This might be understood to be part of the argument pioneered in a forceful and original way by Robert Hanning in his article on the Fall of Angels pageants in the major cycles, " 'Ye Have begun a Parlous Pleye': The Nature and Limits of Dramatic Mimesis as a Theme in Four Middle English 'Fall of Lucifer' Plays," *Comparative Drama* 7 (1973): 22–50. But within this context it is certainly worth thinking about why this theatre as

a form of vernacular theology escaped the scrutiny undergone by so many other forms after the Oxford Constitutions. Perhaps this had to do with the very late commitment of these materials to a form in which they could be easily scrutinized.

63 On devotional imagery and medieval theatre generally see Theresa Coletti, "Spirituality and Devotional Images: The Staging of the Hegge Cycle," Ph.D. dissertation, University of Rochester, 1975; Meg Twycross, "Books for the Unlearned," *Themes in Drama* 5, *Drama and Religion*, ed. James Redmond (Cambridge: Cambridge University Press, 1983), pp. 65–70, and "Beyond the Picture Theory: Image and Activity in Medieval Drama," *Word and Image* 4 (1988): 589–617; and Pamela Sheingorn, "On Using Medieval Art in the Study of Medieval Drama: An Introduction to Methodology," *Research Opportunities in Renaissance Drama* 22 (1979): 101–09.

64 These aspects of utopia and ideology are succinctly explored in Ricoeur's essay "Imagination in Discourse and Action" (n. 25 above), p. 132.

65 Powers, *Eucharistic Theology*, p. 147.

66 As they are in liberal protestantism and its successors. Nicholas Lash meditates in suggestive ways on this theme in his chapter on "Christian Materialism" in *A Matter of Hope: A Theologian's Reflections on the Thoughts of Karl Marx* (Notre Dame: University of Notre Dame Press, 1982), p. 145.

67 Lash, *Easter in Ordinary*, p. 294. In fact one might say that many literary critics have misunderstood and traduced not merely the object of analysis, Corpus Christi as a mystery, but the means of its communication, for they have misconstrued the relation at once between worshiper and object of worship and text and reader, as one of possession and not of donation and interrelationship; see Lash, *Matter of Hope*, pp. 149–50. This is itself a fundamentally idealist error, for it misconstrues the relationship between theory and practice. And as Lash points out in *A Matter for Hope*:

> if the shift from "materialism" to "idealism," in the uses to which theology is put, occurs in the same measure that Christians suppose themselves to be in possession of the truth concerning God, man and society, the circumstances in which such a shift is likely to occur will be those in which theological discourse becomes the ideology of a group wielding social and political power. (p. 150)

I O

Inquisition, speech, and writing: a case from late medieval Norwich[1]

STEVEN JUSTICE

The terms around which a volume like this must arrange itself – orthodoxy and heresy, power and dissent, authority and criticism – almost irresistibly demand of the historian now what they demanded of adherents then: *take sides*. But where, and with whom, does the historian stand?

It is April 18, 1429, and a suspected heretic, John Burell servant of Thomas Mone, appears in the bishop's palace in the city of Norwich, to be examined for heresy in the presence of the bishop, his theologians, and "in mei, Johannis Excestr, clerici, notarii publici. . .presencia,"[2] as the scribe puts it – as he habitually puts it, for this is not a unique occasion. By 1431, he will have recorded sixty such examinations at least; so many records survive of these trials (Foxe mentions twice that number). As a notary, John possesses a battery of formulae that let him record efficiently and then reduce what he has recorded into proper institutional documents. (Back in 1382, when Archbishop Courtenay wanted to record Nicholas Hereford's Ascension Day sermon – he guessed it would be a heretical potboiler, and it was – he sent a notary.) And heresy trials, despite their high stakes, could be deeply formulaic exercises: Lollard suspects in the fifteenth century were often confronted by a set schedule of heretical assertions, which they were to acknowledge or deny and then forswear.[3] The scribe's business began before the suspects appeared, since they were presented with reports of what they had already been heard to say (two cases in the Norwich records preserve depositions taken against the suspects). And his business continued after this preliminary appearance, when the heretics, now confessed as such, were appointed a date to return and abjure the errors they had confessed, and it would seem to have been the scribe's job to draw up the schedule of heresies to be recanted.

So when John Burell appeared in April, 1429, John of Exeter was engaged in business as usual. Burell himself seems unusual only in his eagerness to blame his heresies on others – his brother Thomas, his sister-in-law Matilda, his employer Thomas Mone. They had taught him that confession is to be made only to God; that "it would be better for many priests to take wives and to use them carnally, as many priests do in diverse remote parts"; that no priest has power to make the body of Christ; that the church is the soul of every good Christian; that prayers made in church avail no more than prayers made "in the fields or the forests"; that no one is bound to observe feast days ("Sundays only excepted"); that pilgrimages should not be made to the shrines of Becket or Our Lady of Walsingham ("Mary of Falsyngham," he called her); that no one should swear except when in mortal danger; that tithes should not be made to priests; that prayers and masses do not help the dead; that friars are destroying the world; and – a fascinating piece of apocalypticism, from Matilda – that "no more masses will be celebrated until the end of the world, as is contained in a certain book that has recently come from across the sea into these parts." Whatever John Burell actually said – on this day or before it – this is what John of Exeter wrote.

But is it what John Burell said? While *inquisitio* is what the church called such trials, its attitude toward heresy cannot really be called inquisitive: bishops did not want to know heresy except to recognize it when they found it, did not want to understand the impulse to dissent except as perversity. The inquisitor thought of heresy discovered as lay ignorance confronted by ecclesiastical truth. Recasting the words of the heretics in the language of theological and procedural certainty ought simply to have reproduced the image of heresy that those recording it already entertained. That is why I am interested in one other statement that John of Exeter attributed to John Burell:

Item dicit iste iuratus quod quidam sutor, famulus Thome Mone, docuit istum iuratum quod nullus homo tenetur ieiunare diebus Quadragesimalibus. . ., quia talia ieiunia nunquam erant instituta ex precepto divino sed tantum ex ordinacione presbiterorum, *for every Fryday is fre day* et ideo omni die Veneris quilibet potest indifferenter edere pisses vel carnes secundum sui appetitus desiderium.   (p. 74)

"For every Fryday is fre day." I want to pause and note what seems to have happened. In the massively Latinate record of this inquisition, which not only does not need to allow the accused to speak but barely even offers him the opportunity, the actual words of a Norfolk servant have survived, their vernacular articulation still intact.

So: are these John Burell's words? If not, whose are they? And in any case, why did John of Exeter write them? Why, for that matter, taking Joan Clyfland's deposition against her neighbor Margery Baxter of Martham, did he write this –

informavit istam iuratam et servientes suas predictas quod nullo modo iurarent, dicens in lingua materna: *"dame, bewar of the bee, for every bee wil styngge, and therfor loke that 3e swer nother be Godd ne be Our Ladi ne be non other seynt, and if 3e do the contrarie the be will styngge your tunge and veneme your sowle"* (44)

and this –

lewed wrightes of stokkes hewe and fourme suche crosses and ymages, and after that lewed peyntors glorye thaym with colours, et si vos affectatis videre veram crucem Christi ego volo monstrare eam tibi hic in domo tua propria (44)

After all, vernacular phrases possessed no evidentiary advantage *as* vernacular phrases – no more than they would in Latin. Whatever Bishop Alnwick's interest in maintaining the record of these trials (if he had any; more on this later), it did not rest on the odd English phrase. It is, in fact, unclear what he might need evidence *for*: pious prosecution of his office required evidence only that heretics had confessed themselves heretics, since, that once done, any further conviction for heresy could send them to the stake as "relapses." The minimal importance of the kind of evidence recorded in this book is witnessed most powerfully by its near uniqueness: no record like it survives from the entire fifteenth century or before, despite the many heresy trials in England (which left, at most, laconic entries in episcopal registers); the only similar case is a 1511 record from Bath and Wells. There was no need for any detailed record because there was no court of appeal, no possibility for review, no channel of accountability for which a trial record would ever likely be called.

But if these vernacular phrases served no legal purpose, might they have served the purpose of propaganda, or of ideology? One could argue that John's transcription of vernacular phrases might have been meant to demonstrate or enact the *illiteratura* of the heretics: the cleric found the vernacular quite literally *rustic*, and such phrases might have been thought to demonstrate the stolid rusticity of unorthodoxy.[4] But these notebooks seem not to have been written with an eye to any potential readership,[5] and propaganda assumes an audience. Ideology does not: it does not exist only for other people; it is first of all a way to believe in the reasonableness of one's own assumptions and in the naturalness of one's own authority, if one has any. So John need not have planned for an audience to have preserved these vernacular utterances for ideological purposes. The explanation looks promising, since his position (as I'll suggest) likely bespoke a form of ambition that would want to think episcopal authority a virtuous or at least a desirable thing and challenges to it unwholesome (though I'll also suggest that that position was also capable of leaving him institutionally unanchored). But even on the face of it there are problems: while a stretch of the imagination might conjure up a *reader* who might be reassured by a reminder of the heretics' vernacularity, it is harder to imagine that the scribe, for whom that vernacularity was a present fact at every moment he was making his record, would need that reminder.

These explanations won't do, for the reasons I've listed, and for another reason as well: all of them offer programmatic explanations of what looks very much like a random event. All of them would more easily explain a more consistently macaronic record than John of Exeter's spotty, unpredictable lapses into English. At the same time, these *kinds* of explanation won't do, and how they won't do has something to say about the idiom and formal impulses of what we tend to call "historicist" literary studies – and not just the "New Historicism."

Bishop Alnwick began his prosecutions in September, 1428; at the same time, he instructed the monks of Bury St. Edmunds (a little presumptuously, they might have felt) to be on watch for heresy within their liberty.[6] He was not alone in discovering a new vigor about fighting heresy in this year (Wyclif's grave was solemnly desecrated then), and the reason for this renewed enthusiasm is not hard to infer. Pope Martin V, who had been at odds with the English over the Provisors for years, needed English help in the Hussite crusade, just as the English were coming to need his in their negotiations with France.[7] The sensitive bishop at the end of the 1420s might have felt that a domestic initiative against heresy would sort nicely with the papal campaign, and might have felt called to summon his chancellor, his theologians, and the notary who served as his registrar to ferret out and destroy unorthodoxy within his diocese.

He might particularly feel called to do so if the royal administration had already called him to do it. That is what happened to Bishop Alnwick, and it is of interest because it suggests, here at the beginning of the story, the divided role of the bishop's registrar. Foxe reproduces a patent writ in the king's name dated July 6, 1428, addressed "to *his well-beloved John Exeter*, and Jacolet Germain, keeper of the castle of Colchester," ordering the arrest of "William White, priest" – the revered teacher of the Norfolk Lollards – and other heretics.[8] The royal commission ordering White's arrest set the bishop a task that busied him and his staff through the next three years. "Within short space after," Foxe says, "John Exeter, who was appointed one of the commissioners, attached six persons in the town of Bungay. . .; and committed them to William Day and William Roe, constables of the town of Bungay, to be sent within ten days following, under safe custody, unto the castle of Norwich," where "a great number both of men and women" were tried and punished "by the bishop of the said diocese, called William, and his chancellor, William Bernham, John Exeter being the register therein" (587). The bishop, the chancellor, and the registrar: the chancellor, Bernham, is visibly and unsurprisingly second in command; the surviving records show him regularly conducting trials in the bishop's absence. The pattern suggests that John of Exeter was third in this chain of command, and, in fact, he presided at one of the trials himself, holding it in his own house (89).

So who was he? He was registrar to the bishop of one of England's most prosperous towns, and died in the 1440s a prosperous man;[9] he had enjoyed notarial training (conferring the impressive, continental warrant *auctoritate apostolice sedis*); in Norwich he was John *of Exeter*, suggesting perhaps a careerist mobility; he was married, and in minor orders, which must therefore seem not the start of an ecclesiastical career but a kind of union card; he participated in the episcopal administration as a lower-level administrator; and he was the recipient of a king's writ. This last fact is instructive: this professional administrator, of a sort increasingly important in fifteenth-century royal and ecclesiastical service, was a man of substance in his own right, apt to be summoned to work for the crown in ways that prosperous landholders and citizens often were. That the man ordered to arrest Lollards by the king also recorded their trials for the bishop is not particularly odd: these separate jurisdictions could separately employ the same person. But the different spheres of his activity had their own scales of merit and of prestige: the royal writ bespeaks a position in the country that did not change the scope or prestige of his duties in the bishop's service, and could perhaps even have contrasted pointedly with his usual tasks there. For while John had the education and position that would allow him to serve as judge *pro tem* in the bishop's jurisdiction, and while he had secured for himself an enviable position as registrar, he was still, in his day-to-day duties, a scribe.

How does one describe the class of such a man, and the meritocratic structure by which he might have achieved it? The subtlest sources of class analysis – classical marxist and Althusserian models – are at a loss before the *experience* of class, and before diurnal lives where class is experienced; they tend to treat the choices made, and the sensations felt there, as politically and economically unreal, and therefore unreal *simpliciter*; they can explain revolution, but not doodling. *Who produces?* and *Who profits?* and *Who takes orders?* and *Who gives them?* are questions they can address. *Who gets bored?* is not. And the problem of *interest* – the subjective experience of engagement and curiosity, not the objective quality of material advantage – both marks the experience of meritocratic advancement and displays the fissures in meritocratic faith, in the bureaucratic culture of late medieval England. The quiet complaint of the *House of Fame*, in which Chaucer pretends that someone has to order him to be curious, is that patronage employment, while recognizing and rewarding talent, under-employs it, stupefying the beneficiary. The eagle, taking "Geffrey" by force to where "tidings" might be heard, says that he lacks news even "of thy verray neyghebores, / That duellen almost at thy dores," because

> when thy labour doon al ys,
> And hast mad alle thy rekenynges,
> In stede of reste and newe thynges
> Thou goost hom to thy house anoon,
> And also domb as any stoon,
> Thou sittest at another book
> Tyl dully daswed ys thy look.   (652–58)

The eagle here – on the one occasion Chaucer mentions his everyday duties at the port of London – speaks of recreation as "rest *and newe thynges*," as a revitalizing redirection of attention and interest that Chaucer misses by his lazy recapitulation at home ("*another* book") of the dulling routine of reading and writing at work.

It is the complaint of a man noticed and rewarded for a talent that is stunted by the reward. And it implies a further complaint against the mechanical dispensation of *writing* – copying, reckoning – to one who ought to be *authoring*. The formulaic activity that Chaucer performed at the Port of London as he audited the wool customs lay at the heart of medieval bureaucracies, even marked the most forward-looking ideas of administration. Innocent III could institutionalize reform in part because he commanded a bureaucracy that issued documents in standardized vocabulary and could retrieve and check them once issued; the prelates who returned home from his Lateran Council seem to have brought with them a passion as much for documentary order as for the revitalization of the laity. In English government, the formulaic language of the royal decree allowed the crown to centralize judicial power and produce something that could meaningfully be called a *national* monarchy, and a system of justice that was almost meaningfully *justice* much as it was almost meaningfully *system*: the possibility of appealing to the king's justice required the king's ability to call cases and records forward through a known and established hierarchy and through a standardized set of procedures.[10] Royal revenue depended upon accountable accounting, the sort of thing Chaucer did with the wool customs. This systematization, in other words, multiplied the demands both for and on scribal expertise – on the ability to manipulate this language, to understand its ways, and to reproduce it efficiently – and the proportion of repetitive labor in the scribe's work. Stephen Greenblatt called one of the chapters in *Renaissance Self-Fashioning* "The Word of God in the Age of Mechanical Reproduction." He of course uses Benjamin's phrase to refer to the printing press, but it is worth remembering that the reproduction of texts is always mechanical; before print the mechanical function is performed by people, and precisely by people who might resent it: the nature of writing and the education needed to practice it as a profession meant that one had to prove one's intellectual worth in order to become (so to speak) a typewriter.

That Chaucer was not alone in needing to find and maintain some focus for the mind amid the boredom of textual work is evident in scribes' comments and explicits, in their doodles and marginal drawings. Michael Camille reproduces a picture from a Book of Hours in which words left out of the main text, and added to the margin, are hoisted into place by a rope held in the right hand of a laborer who with his left points to their place in the text.[11] Camille calls such fellows "tiny textual construction workers," but these workers can read Latin well enough to see where the text goes: they are simply the scribe, imagining himself as another sort of menial laborer. The illustration suggests his sense not only of the laboriousness of scribal labor, but also of its humiliating social indecorum, which has given the textually expert a position more like that of a hod-carrier than that of a *litteratus*.

Thomas Hoccleve, poet and Privy Seal clerk, gives a more direct and more plangent voice to the labor of writing than Chaucer does (and his work was more mechanical, his position more commonplace, than Chaucer's). The *Regement of Princes* begins with an account of his melancholy, which (he explains) he suffers because he cannot manage to collect on the annuity the king has granted him. The income left him without the annuity is (he is precise about money) six marks – four pounds – annually, which leads him to cry, "VI marc, yeerly, and no more þan þat."[12] Particularly, as he goes on to say, because other ways of earning are not open to him: "I am nat / In housbondryë worth a myte" (976–77):

> With plow can I nat medlen, ne with harwe,
>   Ne wot nat what lond good is for what corne;
> And for to lade a cart or fille a barwe, –
>   To which I neuer vsed vas to-forne, –
> My bak vnbuxum hath swich thyng forsworne,
>   At instance of writyng, his Werreyour,
>   That stowpyng hath hym spilt with his labour.   (981–87)

Writing reminds Hoccleve of occupations both impossible ("My bak vnbuxum hath swich thyng forsworne") and inappropriate ("To which I neuer vsed vas") to a poet, a man who knew Chaucer, but with this difference: that he has not even the advantages he thinks physical labor brings. One advantage, the one he mentions in this passage, is a putative certainty of livelihood. Another – and this is my point – is variety and interest: on these lines follow six extraordinary stanzas on the pain and boredom of script, work he paints as destitute of the fellowship and cheer that laborers (he imagines) provide for themselves. *Those* workers "talken and syng, and maken game and play, / And forth his labour passith with gladnesse," while the scribes "labour in travuillous stilnesse: / We stowpe and stare vp-on þe shepës skyn, / *And keepë muste our song and wordës in*" (1009–15) amid the silence and labor of copying; the "song and wordes," forcibly contained, emerge only after hours, only in the poetry of complaint.

Which brings me to why I think John of Exeter sometimes substituted for his Latin formulae the English formulae of the accused: *he was bored, he just thought they were interesting.*

I realize that this answer violates what we might call the grammar of interpretation by ignoring the proper predicate of "because." The explanation I have just offered begs for a reduction to motive (Ah, but *why* did he find these phrases interesting? Ah, but why did he find *these* phrases interesting?), to a final cause. The modes of explanation we generally use tacitly prescribe final causes as the only explanatory causes worth naming, and express final causes in discursive terms: one means to mean, when one does things with words.

But what shapes utterances, and where are they shaped? The answers implied by various new literary historicisms are not entirely distinct from those of the formalist criticism under which the new literary historicists were trained. "How is [the critic] to find out what the poet tried to do? If the poet succeeded in doing it, then the poem itself shows what he was trying to do": thus Wimsatt and Beardsley.[13] In this classic statement of Anglo-American formalism, the *agency* of meaning is for the interpreter found, impersonally, in the utterance itself. And since verbal motive can be known only through acts of interpretation, motives are discussable only when they are interpretable. Those two points are implicit in the assertion, and in the critical practice it retrospectively theorized. A third point exists *in potentia*, and is discovered at some point by every successful English major: an assertion that something is without interpretable meaning is a weak assertion: you can always outflank a claim that there are meaningless or uninterpretable or random moments in a work by the simple act of interpreting them, of showing that their apparent purposelessness is only the mask of a plenary meaning awaiting discovery. "New-Critical" exegesis, in other words, drove toward purposeful meaning at the expense precisely of any ability to describe or even imagine the human agency displaying that purpose and the cognitive accidents that can befall human agency.

Now consider David Aers on the Statute of Laborers:

Classifying mobile workers, "wandering labourers" as vagrants, as idle "mendicants and beggars" is an important part of a social and political struggle – as rhetorical classifications always are.[14]

And Paul Strohm on reports of the popularity of Anne of Bohemia, Richard II's queen:

These texts [in praise of Anne] tell us a good deal about contemporary expectations of queenship, and little about Anne herself. In point of fact, rather than hailing Anne as a promised mediatrix, Londoners. . .showed considerable dismay at the time of her arrival over the excessive dowry that Richard was thought to have paid. . .Yet the authority and imaginative centrality of an established interpretative scheme can overrule a good deal of contrary evidence, and so does Anne take her place with such celebrated intercessors as Queen Philippa and Richard's mother Joan of Kent. . .Whatever her inclinations, she seems to have sought earnestly not to disappoint the accompanying political and ethical expectations.[15]

And Susan Crane on monastic chronicle accounts of the English rising of 1381:

That the chronicles of 1381 relegate the rebels to the status of beasts, monstrosities, or misguided fools is a well-known function of the writers' attempts to condemn the revolt and make good sense of its repression.[16]

I cite these not to say that they are wrong, but to suggest that the distinction between their general modes of proceeding and those of Anglo-American formalism lies more in where they look for meaning than in what kind of meaning they look for.

David Aers' designation of the 1388 Statute of Laborers as a "rhetorical" classification puts the issue nicely, and has the advantage for my discussion that I think him quite correct: the "vagrancy" the Statute outlawed had less to do with what laborers did than with landlords' desires to stop them doing it. What I find interesting here is that I cannot tell whether Aers believes he is describing a conscious or an unconscious intention, and – more interesting still – that it does not really matter. "Unconscious intention" is, though unaccustomed, not meaningless: psychoanalysis, for example, offers to interpret the parapraxis to reveal what you *really, though unconsciously*, mean. It seems right to call this a form of intention, since it has structure and purpose very like conscious verbal intention. Ideological critique employs a similar structure: the assumptions about the world that most deeply govern people's articulations are largely unconscious: inconsistencies, contradictions, "fissures" are the parapraxes of hegemonic discourse. But it's not clear who makes the meanings that are thus revealed, or at what level of awareness – or, as I said, how it might matter. Suppose that the element of "struggle" Aers mentions was quite unconscious, "ideological"; suppose then that those who framed the Statute of Laborers were made aware that it would, if enforced, strengthen their position in the extraction of surplus labor value; would we try to imagine that this new awareness would make the Statute seem less attractive or less valid to them, or (therefore) that their class ideology controlled their actions any less completely because they knew what they were doing? Crane would not think so, for she seems to be talking about a deliberate project of obfuscation whose intention is manifest not only to the modern scholar but also to the monastic chroniclers who obfuscated; nevertheless, she implies that it was because they were monastic chroniclers that they needed to see the rebellion condemned. Both these scholars, with their potentially different ways of imagining the authors' relationship to ideologies, nevertheless imagine those ideologies as controlling articulation and supplying its social meaning. Strohm's passage, in fact, implies that the linguistic and social schemata that governed queenship caused the Londoners (or the writers: he is not entirely clear) to perceive Anne as a merciful and intercessory bounty to the king's subjects *despite* their deliberate and conscious attempts to perceive her otherwise on occasions less fully scripted; those schemata ruled them and produced their meanings for them, even in their own despite, and in fact (he concludes) ruled Anne herself. This passage points to another curious aspect of the locutions that Crane and Aers adopt. In Strohm's account, no one in particular thinks these thoughts as meaningfully strategic propositions – purposeful, *motivated* propositions – about queenship, and yet they are meaningful and strategic and they motivate the speech and behavior of everyone. In fact these three passages share very little in the way of assumptions or procedures: Strohm speaks of the ideology of intercessory queenship as something in the air, Crane of the chroniclers' ideology as something deliberately cultivated. And yet we can all recognize in all of them a particular style of historicist criticism. Certainly they share a general attention to the social meaning of language, but this presupposes the most important thing they share: the desire to find in utterances not merely intention, but intention to *mean*, whether or not they can imagine an agency that might have formed the intention.

I wonder whether this deepest imperative of our discursive conventions doesn't coerce our sense of the range of actions that words, spoken or written, might participate in and of the social and institutional relations in which they take place. The equation (often drawn not long ago) between totalizing literary theories and political totalitarianism was obviously glib and malicious word-play, and yet it is hard to explain how, under this régime of interpretation, one can *finally* separate meaning from power: if the making of texts is, severely and always, the making of meaning, then meaning belongs to those who make the texts; if the act of reformulating sayings – which is, in the nature of the case, part of "recording" them – cannot be separated from control of their meaning, then those that control the pen will *ipso facto* generate the meaning. Controlling the pen of course does not always mean working the pen. The bishop's registrar, to call our own John of Exeter as example, only partly controls his pen; the distribution of rewards and sanctions means that John must know as he writes what his employer expects to see. That is the point: the act of verbal production *as an act of meaning* locates itself in the hierarchy that controls meaning as it controls other things. And since, in medieval and early modern studies, at least, no matter whose words we are trying to examine, we receive them through the filter of clerical privilege, imagining that writing always first of all *means* means that we may hear only clerics and their bosses.

I have recently argued that the most tendentiously ideological of hegemonic sources, the most pressured in their need to suppress what they fear, can be useful, even nearly transparent in revealing dissenting thought, precisely because of their tendentiousness.[17] I want now to suggest another, nearly opposite occasion on which sources can reveal what they might want to hide: when authority is so assured that it need not particularly worry about what it hears; or when the person to whom the writing is delegated has one or another reason not to care: when (in either case) the mind is not so much concentrating furiously on something else as concentrating on nothing very intently. This, I am suggesting, is what happened to John of Exeter: a career man, an educated man, in the service of the Bishop of Norwich and executing the mechanical office of transcription, allowed his mind to engage with the words he was hearing, and allowed himself therefore to transcribe them.

Of course, John of Exeter was not ultimately in control of what he wrote; the bishop was. But what did his control amount to? These questions lead us back to the record itself.

It is easy to assume that only the accidents of manuscript preservation prevented other books of trial records like this from surviving.[18] Hudson points out that the Norwich trial codex (bound in modern times into Westminster Diocesan Archives MS B.2) was written on paper rather than on more durable parchment, since (she says) such court records would have no function "beyond the lifetimes of those sentenced within them";[19] other such books, then, may have existed but not survived. The reasoning is solid, but perhaps could go further. For it is not obvious that these documents would have been useful even *during* the lifetimes of the accused, and there is no positive reason to suppose that *even at Norwich* such records were copied or bound in codices for official purposes. The contents of the Westminster manuscript are not the original documents (they are not indentured); but, as Tanner points out, they were copied from loose documents (presumably the originals), not from another codex.[20] Since Tanner and Jacob judge that the manuscript is in John of Exeter's hand, and since Alnwick's register contains no record of the surviving trials, it might be assumed that John was asked to compile this book for the bishop's future reference. But it is a mess, copied haphazardly and with no trace of an intended order, not apparently something set up to enable the retrieval of information, or even with any preliminary arrangement of the exemplars. But while system would matter in a *record*, it would not necessarily matter in a literary compilation, and this book looks altogether like a book compiled after the trials, by snatches and from a mass of unorganized papers; it in fact looks like a miscellany made by John of Exeter for his personal use. (Whether he himself bound the original volume or not is impossible to say, though the foliation goes back at least to the sixteenth century – which means that it was bound by then.)

If my proposal sounds unlikely, it might be observed that there was nothing unusual in the notary's making copies of his own work. Notaries in fact nourished a tradition of self-anthologization. In England, where other, more official records of landholding and agreements made the notaries' legal functions superfluous, practitioners of their trade nevertheless produced artful letter collections that could only priggishly be called formularies. While the *dictamen* remains one of the more puzzling forms of medieval literary art, the pride of its practitioners speaks for itself, and speaks volumes about the compensations and consolations of professionalism.[21] One believes in one's importance as one can: and English notaries, unlike their southern counterparts, had no professional "corporation," no judicial powers, no integral part in public or private litigation. They were not even called "notaries," except by themselves, or by others when they executed some specific notarial function.[22] But they could display their wares: their florid work was not left to blush unseen, but was gathered by the notaries themselves into self-consciously literary garlands.

Even in the north where notaries could hardly think of their work as *publica authentica* in the civilian sense, they nevertheless could hope that their work might find public interest, could launch it as a vehicle of literary ambition or at least of literary self-admiration which in its way is as touching as their other forms of self-importance, adopted so eagerly where they had least external confirmation of it, and in compensation, one suspects, for just that lack.

John of Exeter himself did this at least once: his will mentions "libri mei prapticorum [*sic*] ex labore meo facti et perquisiti."[23] As far as I know, these *libri* have not survived; we cannot know whether the *libri* are separate volumes or the divisions of a volume. And we can have no idea what they might have contained; *unless of course among them were the records of the Norwich trials.*

It feels strangely right that John may have copied these records as samples of his literary art. Taken chronologically, they witness to his fascination with the artfulness of the Lollard speech and of his transcription. His record of their confessions and the recantations – recantations, it must be observed, scripted by himself – show a curious development, one that I believe emerged from nothing more deliberately subversive than an aesthetic preoccupation with rendering the Lollards' energetic vernacular. It can be seen progressing by brief, then by quicker steps. Of John Skilly of Flixton, tried February, 1429, the fifth suspect in the records that survive, John of Exeter records the familiar Lollard assertion of what later centuries would call the "priesthood of the faithful":

Item, quod quilibet homo existens in vera caritate est sacerdos Dei, et quod nullus sacerdos habet maiorem potestatem ad ministranda aliqua sacramenta in Ecclesia quam habet aliquis laicus non ordinatus. (52)

This is subtly different in his English recantation:

Also that Y held and afermed that every trewe man and woman being in charite is a prest, and that no prest hath more poar in mynystryng of the sacramentes that a lewed man hath. (57)

This is an evident rendering of John's own Latin. "Lewed" ("ignorant" or "illiterate") attracts the eye, but we must, reluctantly, admit that it was probably the first synonym for *laicus* to enter his mind. More interesting a phrase is "every trewe man and woman being in charite," and its mobile adjective. In the Latin, "true" modifies "charity" (*in vera caritate*) but in the

English modifies "man and woman." There can be no doubt that Skilly said the latter: "trewe men" and "trewe women" had been Lollard clichés since Wyclif's day.[24] John noted the phrase, but he did not know how to render it in Latin because he did not know what it meant. Writing *vera caritate*, he created a phrase where the actual meaning of "true" did not much matter. Had he placed it where Skilly surely did, he would have had to decide: *verus? fidelis?* and true about or to what? But though he fudged the matter in this record of February 12, when Skilly recanted on March 15, John wrote it down as he heard it said *and as he had therefore remembered it*. And this memory, this lesson in how Lollards talked, did not die here; as John continued in his duties, he discovered what the adjective *trewe* meant, and thus rendered it in Latin when John Godesell, parchment maker, was interrogated on March 18: "Item fatebatur se tenuisse et credidisse quod *quilibet fidelis homo et quelibet fidelis mulier* est sacerdos" (61).

As if to invite some future reader to trace this story, John of Exeter left a trail. As the months of inquisition pass, as he records the errors of one heretic after another, the recantations he composes for them become more and more lurid – more detailed in their denunciations, more colorful in their language, more specific, less formulaic. Increasingly, it seems, he gives the heretics' words back to them to speak at the moment of recantation, and their formulae become his formulae, in a process that seems at times to proceed quite independently of his conscious intent. On August 20, 1429 John Kynget of Nelond recanted before the bishop at the chapel of Bishop's Thorpe. John wrote it, as he did most other recantations, in English for the heretic to pronounce.[25] The first doctrine John Kynget abjured was "that the sacrament of Baptem, whyche the heretikes calle the shakelment of Baptem, doon in water in the fourme custimed in the Churche is of none availe ne to be pondred" (81). The stuffy qualification – "*whyche the heretikes calle* the shakelment of Baptem" – happily serves a double function: the scribe recording distances himself from the polemical word-play in the act of writing, and the accused distances himself, in the act of recanting, from the "heretikes" who still use it.

This double act of distancing was no trivial matter, since the identity of Lollard communities – both the identity they chose for themselves and the identity their prosecutors gave them – based itself largely on a common vocabulary. Wycliffites had worked for decades to forge an English lexicon for matters theological and ecclesiastical, which created a delicate situation for anyone dealing with the heretics. In the absence of a clear and technical

English vocabulary of *orthodox* theology, anyone trying to persuade or refute the heretics had to use a language identified as theirs. A decade or so after John of Exeter died, the Bishop of Chichester, Reginald Pecock, discovered the dangers of sounding like them: his attempts to answer the Lollards on their own terms, with vernacular books aimed at the laity, earned him formal condemnation by the English episcopacy.[26] No such danger threatened John of Exeter in the doing of his job: he was not attempting to persuade or refute, but was only trying to get down their language and apparently keeping himself entertained with its peculiarity. As the investigations proceeded, he learned their jargon and learned *that* it was their jargon. His attention was apparently caught by John Skilly's assertion that "ryngyng of belles in churches availyth to nothyng but oonly to gete mony into prestes purses" (58), for he inserted that qualification repeatedly – whether because the accused all actually used this phrase; because, once used, it became an element in the interrogations; or because the phrase simply took his fancy – in his succeeding reports. He became, so to speak, a proficient in the language.

And as such, some impulse pushed him to capture it in his reportage. Early on, in the testimony of John Skilly, he writes down the classic and uninformative version of the classic Lollard heresy:

Item quod nullus sacerdos habet potestatem conficiendi corpus Christi in sacramento altaris; et quod post verba sacramentalia, a quocumque presbitero quantumcumque rite aut debite sint prolata, remanet purus panis materialis in altari.

(52)

John Skilly may have said this, or acknowledged belief in a proposition posed in these terms; it does not matter; once the magic words *panis materialis* enter the picture, the heresy is certain, since such an opinion denied transubstantiation. This article matches formulations going back to the days of Wyclif himself, and at about the time Bishop Alnwick was conducting his examinations in the Norwich diocese, Bishop Thomas Polton of Worcester was compiling an exhaustive list of questions to be posed in such trials. The first two items on the list are "an post consecracionem sit in altari verum corpus Christi et non substancia panis materialis neque vini" and "si sacerdos habeat potestatem conficiendi corpus Christi."[27] John of Exeter, then, may have written what Skilly said (Lollards *would* adopt the formulae, even the insults, used against them, that is how they came to call themselves "Lollards"), or he may just have written what the bishop said. The latter is the more probable, since the first part of this formulation appears almost to the word a couple of months later in the examination of John Burell, who confesses to a belief "quod nullus sacerdos habet potestatem conficiendi corpus Christi in sacramento altaris"; but this John elaborates the report with an astonishing argument of Burell's:

et quod Deus creavit omnes sacerdotes, et in quolibet sacerdote capud et oculos ad videndum, aures ad audiendum, linguam ad loquendum et omnia membra cuiuslibet hominis: et illud sacramentum quod tales sacerdotes asserunt esse verum corpus Christi nec habet oculos ad videndum, aures ad audiendum, os ad loquendum, manus ad palpandum nec pedes ad ambulandum sed est torta panis facta de farina frumenti. (73)

Treated as I have been treating them in the previous paragraphs, doctrines like this look as I think they looked to John of Exeter: as curiosities, outcroppings of idiosyncrasy amid the formulaic tedium of the records. That is certainly how they appear to the reader of these records. Is there *really* the scholar anywhere who does not learn to skim documents – bishops' registers, chartularies, court rolls, whatever s/he is concerned with – noting the formulae as they slip into place and slowing only when something doesn't work or doesn't fit, when the easy skid of the mind is brought up short with something new or out of place? One advantage in allowing ourselves to see the scribe as a working man who thinks he deserves better is that it draws what I take to be an entirely legitimate analogy between his position and ours: the bishop, after all, did not have to *read* his register: he could order it searched when searching was needed. The landholder who enrolled a charter in chancery did not have to move through documents roll by roll, as Maitland did in disassembling the history of Parliament. The only people who have gone through such documents word by word and formula by formula were the scribes who produced them and the scholars who study them, and in that we can find a sort of kinship.

But the kinship can only take us as far as the scribes themselves went – or as far as they knew themselves to go. Our job is not done when John of Exeter's is, for to the holder of these beliefs, the beliefs were not oddities: the beliefs were their life, and the beliefs could kill them. John of Exeter's job was done once he saw them die or recant; it ill befits any scholar to feel done so quickly, without wanting to know what these beliefs really were for which they accepted, however briefly, this danger. But can the half-attentive scribe allow us to find them?

Many of the Norwich heretics abjured erroneous beliefs about baptism; the articles concerning this sacrament first appear in the Norwich records as what bishops expected to hear on the matter. Polton's register wanted suspect believers to be asked "an puer natus de muliere christiana indigeat baptizari in aqua, vel si baptismum in aqua factum secundum consuetudinem ecclesie sit necessarium ad salutem anime."[28] John Skilly was asked about baptism, and John of Exeter heard the episcopal formula:

Videlicet, quod sacramenta Baptismi facti in aqua necnon Confirmacionis facte per episcopos in forma communi usitata in Ecclesia modice vel nullius sunt virtutis et nichil ponderanda si parentes pueri non baptizati sunt Christiani. (52)

When it came time for recantation and John Skilly heard Richard Caudray, Archdeacon of Norwich ("onus huiusmodi in se suscipiens") forswear his heresies for him, he heard a pedantic transliteration of the Latin:

That the sacramentes of Baptem doon in watir and of Confirmacion doon be a bissop in fourme customed in holi Churche be but of litell availe and not to be pondred if the fadir and the modir of a child hadde Christendom. (56)

Bishop Alnwick must have posed the question in a form like that in Polten's register: Polten's phrase "natus de muliere christiana" contains clearly identical assumptions to the phrase "if the fadir and the modir of a child hadde Christendom." But what Alnwick asked, or at least what John of Exeter recorded, makes an implicit guess about why the sacramental history of the parents should matter: "if the fadir and the modir of a child *hadde Cristendom*." As far as I can tell, this phrase implies that the bishops thought the heretics believed in some process of supernatural inheritance, passing the virtue of the sacrament down through the body of the parents to the child; it is not hard to imagine clerics finding this opinion risible.

But is this what the heretics meant? The repetition of this article from trial to trial brought incremental adjustment to John's record, adjustments he may scarcely have noticed. It also conveys information, which he must have noticed, that allows us to distinguish different strains of theological thought among the suspects. Skilly made his abjuration on March 15; three days later, the parchment maker John Godesell was first examined, and the Latin record of his examination shows a minute difference in the formulation of the baptismal doctrine: baptism, "done in water in the form traditionally used in churches," is dispensable "si parentes infantis sint fideles," a form also used in articles against his wife Sybil (60, 66). A month later, in the articles recorded of John Reeve, glover of Beccles, there is a similarly minute change: baptism is pointless "si parentes infantis nati sint Christiani" (107). But for Reeve there is a vernacular abjuration also: "the sacrament of Baptem done in water. . .is of non avail and not to be pondret if the fadir and modir of the childe be cristened and of Cristene beleve" (111).[29] At about the same time the skinner Richard Grace, also of Beccles, offered a yet more elaborate version of what I think is the same doctrine:

> That the sacrament of Baptem doon in water in fourme custumed of the Churche ys litell to be pondred for as much as whan a child cometh to yeres of discrecion and receyvyth Cristis lawe and hys commaundments he ys sufficiently baptized and so he may be saved withowtyn ony other baptem. (121)

John and Sybil Godesell did not leave behind vernacular abjurations; I would very much like to know what they said when John of Exeter wrote *fideles*. Some indication is given by the supplement to the apparent formulaic version, which appears in Reeve's abjuration, that the parents should be "cristened *and of Cristene beleve*." The specification seems to imply an attitude not simply different from, but quite opposed to, the magical and lineal efficacy of baptism that the bishops seem to have expected the heretics to espouse. The recorded statements suggest simply that the milieu of the Christian family, the beliefs and practices of those parents "of Cristene beleve," is the source of the justified Christian life, that life that Richard Grace speaks of: justification comes from the life and belief of the individual, not the *opus operatum* of baptism, whether that given to the child or to his parents. I am encouraged in this reading by John of Exeter's use of *fideles* – did the Godesells speak of the child of *trewe* Christians? If they did (and in their inquisitions and in no others did John use *fideles* to describe Christian parents), then they invoked not just the Lollard jargon for themselves, but the local, lay standard of social reliability and behavior that everyone was to be able to expect from everyone else.[30]

So John of Exeter recorded several statements that, taken together, allow some understanding of these lay Lollards' beliefs. This does not imply that he himself took any pains to understand them. If he did, his record leaves no evidence of it. Quite the contrary, in fact: it seems to have been an unsystematic and inconsequential curiosity about the language he heard that led him to record fragments of the suspects' own words where he did not have to. It was no part of his job, and for all one can tell, no part of his inclination to understand the words; it was not even really a part of his job to record them. But for that he did seem to have the inclination, and because he did we can try to know their beliefs better than he did. Part of that project involves elaborating and explaining those beliefs. But part also involves distinguishing between them. The opinions about the importance of the family's belief and practice were not the only reason John heard given for the unimportance of the baptismal rite. Hawisia Moone of Loddon, whom Margery Baxter had identified as "secretissima et sapientissima mulier in doctrina W. White" (47), renounced in August, 1430 the opinion

that the sacrament of Baptem doon in watir in forme customed in the Church is but a trufle and not to be pondred, for alle Cristis puple is sufficiently baptized in the blood of Crist, and so Cristis puple nedeth noon other baptem. (140)

The opinion is repeated by John Skylan of Bergh, by John Fynch of Colchester, and by Hawisia's husband Thomas Mone (176, 182). The difference between this formulation and the last suggests the precision with which the heretics' language seems to have shaped John's record: at the same time he records the Mones of Loddon giving this rationale for the rejection of baptism, he also records the opinion of Edmund Archer of Loddon that baptism is unnecessary "if the fadir and modir. . .be of Crist' beleve" (165). These differences do not bespeak any doctrinal disagreement within the local Lollard communities, and certainly not schism. They are not even inconsistent with each other: when the Mones insist that no rite of baptism is necessary for *"Cristis* peple," they apparently speak about those who are in some sense *already* Christians – those, presumably, who like themselves and everyone they would likely have known, were born within the boundaries and beliefs of Christendom and who in that sense inherit their belief. At the same time, the different formulations suggest a difference in tone or emphasis on the elective quality of the rite. Where the former emphasizes disciplines of belief and behavior enforced within the family and the community, the latter emphasizes the *freedom*, in both senses of the word, of divine grace, the gratuitous and already-accomplished quality of salvation.

But if this tonal difference seems fairly unimportant for the Lollard suspects, it is important for us, for the testimonies recorded by John of Exeter present an aspect of lay Lollardy no more regularly audible in the testimony of their friends than in that of their enemies. Anne Hudson begins *The Premature Reformation* with the observation that the history of Lollardy has in the past been written chiefly through the testimony of its enemies, of the bishops and clerics who prosecuted and polemicized against Wyclif and his followers, and that this imbalance must be redressed through scrutiny of their own words, available chiefly through the Lollard treatises that she has been so instrumental in discovering, sorting, dating, and editing. Her book offers a serenely thorough and persuasive defense of Lollard writing and belief, characterizing the movement and its literature as coherent, thoughtful, and courageous, something quite different from the yokel crudity cartooned in McFarlane's classic, witty, and contemptuous portrait of the movement.[31]

The central section of *The Premature Reformation* is a series of three chapters under the general title "The Ideology of Reformation," where Hudson argues that the fractured and apparently random assertions found in vernacular treatises, episcopal registers, and first-person testimonies can be shown to be a coherent and reasoned set of beliefs if they are fit to the template of Wyclif's teaching: the writings of the founder form a conceptual matrix that can elaborate and explain the continuing ideology of the movement. Her approach looks sturdy and productive next to (say) that of Margaret Aston, who uses the Norwich testimony to show how *little* lay Lollards understood of the real intellectual content of Wycliffism, how the attempt by glovers and skinners to grasp Wyclif's theology coarsened it.[32] It is, as I say, a productive approach; it is also a canny one, because it allows her to interpret in two quite different ways the formulaic effect of the records. The Leicester chronicler Henry Knighton said that Lollards all sounded the same. Hudson's implicit explanation of this – she never explains it all in one place, but her intention seems clear – is that there are two different and even opposing reasons for this effect. First, the chief medium by which Lollard beliefs were deliberately catalogued was the inquisition which, as Hudson showed and as I have already noted, tended to proceed as scripted. But second they sounded the same also because they believed the same: the schedule of opinions and beliefs that Wycliffites professed is the schedule of opinions and beliefs that Wyclif had professed and that were perpetuated through writing and through schools.[33]

But all explanations of what is taken for the self-identity of "the" Lollard mind go back to an interested and tendentious assertion of Henry Knighton's. When Knighton spoke of Wyclif's lay followers as mimics of each other, he was speaking in terror:

And even those who were newly converted, those recently begun at imitating this sect, immediately – and wondrously – had exactly the same mode of speech and an identical form of doctrine. And thus both men and women became teachers of evangelical doctrine in the mother tongue. It was as if they were trained in the same school and taught in the lecture hall of a single teacher. It may be held as credible (since it may be believed without doubt) that for those who took up with the initiates of these malicious traps and the supporters of dissension among the worshippers of Christ, the same spirit fit them to the Lollards identically, and inspired them to a conformity of speech, with a burning desire to obey them. From the day they entered, the realm of England has suffered dissension because these violent men have intoxicated it, have incited the son against the father, mother-in-law against daughter-in-law, the servant of the household against its lord, and – what must be mourned – nearly every man against his neighbor.[34]

One might ask (given the relations of the Paston women, for example) whether mother-in-law and daughter-in-law needed help falling into dissension,[35] or whether servant and lord would, without Lollardy, have lived in natural concord. The "burning desire" that Knighton says has "intoxicated" England is a *wonder* that explains to this chronicler, so puzzled by the world, why conflicts he does not understand should ever have happened. The wonder is so powerful that he can convey it only by an absurd comparison: they were like theologians schooled by the same teacher. But what was for Knighton a ludicrous analogy is for Hudson the merest fact: the Lollards speak alike because they studied at the same sorts of schools, under the same sorts of masters.

Knighton describes Lollard style as he does to imply that Lollards do not really speak: that they do not speak of themselves, but of a power that Knighton does not name because he does not need to. *Structurally*, this is not so different from what Hudson describes, more respectful of them as she is: their coherence and sophistication are not their own, but are, proximately or remotely, borrowed from another. Knighton and Hudson, and for that matter Aston, different as they are in their understanding of Lollard communities, all assume that the moment the Lollards really speak their own words and thoughts they become crude and inarticulate.

Hudson *needs* the Lollards to sound like each other; if they are not to be mindless, the mind must be Wyclif's. Whatever lay Lollards can be imagined to have done, they cannot be imagined to have thought for themselves. This, I believe, is the blind spot Hudson needs in order to see new things about Lollard writing. She has almost single-handedly created a field of study by tracing the vernacular writings of the Wycliffite movement – she began with a crucial article on the great Lollard sermon-cycle[36] – and her assumptions here reproduce the ambitions of the sources with which she has worked most productively. For the sermons, tracts, devotional treatises, handbooks, autobiographical accounts – the whole literature of vernacular Lollardy – are *clerical* works, all of them, in the banal sense that they were written by clerics and in the more interesting sense that they, like more orthodox manuals of devotion and belief for the laity, were meant to shape and inform the lay mind with clerical understanding. This is not to imply bad faith on their part, any more than the desire of orthodox clerics to shape and inform the lay mind indicates bad faith on *their* part: it was their job in both cases, and if it amounts to and must be regarded as a hierarchical means of control, it does not follow that this is how they regarded it. But it is to say that there are, at the least, ways in which an unorthodox cleric is more like an orthodox cleric than like his unorthodox flock.

One of the most notorious of the Lollard vernacular treatises was *The Lanterne of Light*, written early in the second decade of the fifteenth century. Apparently popular among the lay Lollards for whom it was written, it issued from a clerical, indeed from an academic, hand to which the conventions of citing canon law came naturally, and the book serves a sort of novitiate manual for the lay believer who would know how ecclesiastics write and talk. For example, after a *distinctio* on biblical figures of the church – virgin, spouse, woman clothed with the sun, *navicula Petri*, and the like – the author says "But how euere we speken in diuerse names. . ., thei techen nought ellis but this oo name, that is to seie the congregacioun, or gedering togidir, or feithful soules" (25), and after quoting Jeremiah's *Maledictus qui opus dei agit fraudilenter* and rendering it "Cursid be he, that doth the werk of God fraudilentli," he glosses the last, Latinate word, "that is to seie, falseli or disceyuabli."[37] These are not vocabulary lessons to help his readers or listeners through the work at hand: the words glossed never appear again in *The Lanterne*. But these passages offer concepts both available to polemical use and current in institutional theology: "congregacioun, or gedering togidir" glosses one of the traditional etymologies of *ecclesia* using a Latinate rendering of *congregacio*.[38] But even while thus instructing them in the ways of clerical discourse, the work reminds them who that discourse ultimately belongs to, and who they must depend on to learn it. Virtually every one of the quotations from biblical, patristic, and canonist writers of *The Lanterne of Light* – and there are hundreds – is given in Latin before it is rendered into English, and while semantically opaque to their intended audience, these Latin passages, sometimes quite long, convey a perfectly clear message: that the author of the treatise can read them while its intended audience cannot.

The work in fact tacitly admits, in certain moments of slippage, that its real ambition is not so much to inform its audience's minds as to replace them. For example, the author cites God's promise, through Jeremiah, to write his law in the hearts of people, but

O ȝe prestis ben muche to blame, þat taken from the peple þe lawe þat God haþ writen him silf in myddis of the herte. . .Certis ȝe lerned neuir þis loore in dedis of þe apostlis.

and he goes on to relate how, in Acts, Philip discovered the treasurer of the queen of India reading Isaiah and wishing to understand it. "Philip took not awey his booke, ne werned him to reede þeronne." The point of this passage is the injustice done to the laity by Arundel's *Constitutions*, which forbade (among other things) the translation of the Bible into English, including the translation even of particular passages. *The Lanterne of Light* flaunts its rejection of the *Constitutions* not only by its blunt and proud insistence on translating such passages exactly and extensively. This passage implies that *The Lanterne*'s author has given back to the communities that read him the text that they ought by rights to have, and that in this he, unlike the English bishops, acts like the Apostle. But in the passage from Jeremiah with which he introduces this assurance, he has been talking about the law written in the *heart*, which suddenly turns out to be identical with the law written in the *book*: to this author, the subjectivity of his readers' faith lives in the writing he gives them; in the Lollard communities for whom he writes, that means that their mind is found only in the community where the book is read, and ultimately in the book itself.

When Hudson describes the sophistication of lay Lollardy, her assumptions are not very different from this author's: the utterances of each embody certain aspects of Wyclif's teaching and the teachings of his academic followers, and enjoy coherence because they refer back to the coherence of Wyclif's system. They can be treated as *thinking* agents because (and, perhaps, *only* because) they are occupied by another's thoughts. I find this model unsatisfying, both because of an *a priori* unwillingness to believe these Lollards incapable of coherently and intelligently appropriating the teachings of their clerical leaders in their own ways and to their own purposes, and because of the evidence offered by the Norwich testimony. When they reject baptism if the parents are *fideles*, their language and the attitudes it embodies bespeak a meaning derived from their own experience of lay life in the small towns and villages of East Anglia, and the reflective theological language of lay experience.[39] They had their own thoughts; their beliefs were no more the pure product of their clergy's instruction that the beliefs of any believers have ever been.

But it is terribly difficult to allow them their thoughts. Even Hudson, so careful and just in her judgments, reacts to an idiosyncratic idea as if it were less idea than inertia: Margery Baxter "ironically" held the opinion that prayer should be made to God alone, "but at the same time was said to pray to William White every day 'ut ipse dignetur intercedere pro ipsa ad Deum celi': *the ingrained habits of medieval piety* prevailed over the recently learned theology." Or as if what was said was not really what was thought: of Baxter's "pragmatic" objection to fasting, "that it was better to finish up left-over meat on Fridays than to get into debt buying fish at the market," Hudson suggests that "this was evidently a secondary reason compared with the theoretical objections to a non-biblical regulation taught by her hero William White."[40] But if instead of looking for "real" Lollardy behind Baxter's statement we simply look at the statements themselves, we might find a theology that is no less consistent than, though different from, William White's.

Before declaring Baxter inconsistent because she denounced the cult of the saints while practicing her own, it might help to wonder what her objection to the cult was. Becket is for her the "official" church saint, and

ille Thomas Cantuariensis quem populus vocat Sanctum Thomam Cantuar' fuit falsus proditor et est dampnatus in inferno eo quod dotavit ecclesias iniuriose possessionibus et suscitavit ac supportavit plures hereses in Ecclesia que seducunt simplicem populum, et ideo si Deus fuerit benedictus idem Thomas fuit et est maledictus, et si Thomas fuerit et sit benedictus Deus fuit et est maledictus, et isti falsi presbiteri qui dicunt quod idem Thomas paciencter sustinuit mortem suam coram altari menciuntur quia tanquam falsus vecors prodictor, fugiendo, occisus fuit in osti ecclesie. (45)

The thought of Archbishop Thomas prompted her to think of Bishop Alnwick and of idolatry. She went on to say that evil bishops like Alnwick would suffer a worse fate than Becket "for thay falsly and cursedly dessyve the puple with thair false mawmetryes and lawes and extorquendas pecunias a simplici populo ad sustentandam ipsorum superbiam, luxuriam et ociositatem" (45). *Mawmetrye*, idolatry, is a significant element in her thought. Worship of the sacrament, for her the merest bread, is "ydolatria" (45); so are indulgences (46); and so, again, is the worship of all images in church (49), which she has already called "ymagines vel cruces *mortuas*" (44). And the fleecing of the faithful is also significant (priests proclaim the necessity of baptism "ad extorquendas pecunias a populo a[d] manutenendos ipsos sacerdotes et cocubinas eorundem" [46]), and, as she says above, is the end and purpose of idolatry and of all sacramental practices. The sacraments, after all, were stipendiary procedures; and this, I believe, lies at the heart of her thinking, motivating it and giving it its coherence.

It helps to explain a particularly suggestive but mysterious sequence in Clyfland's deposition against her:

The said Margery also told this witness that she had often made false confession to the Dean of the Fields so that he would think her of good life; and because of this, he often gave Margery money. And then the witness said to her that she [Margery] had never confessed all her sins to a priest. And the same Margery said that she had never harmed any priest, and therefore would not confess to a priest. . .And the same Margery even said that every man and every woman of her opinion were good priests, and that Holy Church is in the houses of those of her sect. (48–49)

By her false confessions she got money out of the clergy (and not just clergy, but the Cambridge-educated dean of St. Mary in the Fields). There are two things to be said about this process. It quite specifically reverses what she describes as the usual direction of money's flow between clerics and laics; and it quite specifically does in small what Wyclif and his followers had said since the 1370s should be done to the English church as a whole: it liberates some portion of the church's ungodly wealth for the good of the laity. The conceptual center of Wycliffite doctrine, largely repressed, was money; Margery Baxter made it manifest, conceptually supple, and productive of theological categories. Her refusal to confess to a priest because she had never done evil to a priest, for example, supplies the contractual, almost financial notion of confession and forgiveness found in the paternoster – "dimitte nobis *debita* nostra. . ." – but the *economic* character of her theology goes deeper than this, into the images and connections that bind her beliefs to each other.

Baxter's assertion that "Holy Church is in the houses of all those in her sect" differs from both the old Wycliffite definition (that the church is the "number of the predestined," as Wyclif repeatedly said) and that offered by her Norfolk colleagues (that the church "is the soul of every good Christian," as John Burell learned from a fellow servant of Thomas Mone). Eschewing these definitions, eschatological and moral respectively, she situated the church at the center of social and economic existence. Her own house was where her husband "secretly" read to her "the law of Christ" (47–48), where she said one could "see and adore" "the cross of Christ" (her own outstretched arms, 44), where Agnes Bethom, Clyfland's servant, found her cooking "unam peciam de bakon" in proud defiance of the lenten fast (51). She spoke to Clyfland about Lollard beliefs as they were sewing before the fire, and spoke at the same time to Clyfland's *familia*, the servants Joan Grymell and Agnes Bethom (44); when she invited Clyfland to her husband's reading of the *lex Christi*, she invited her to bring the servant Joan as well (47), as presumably she had her own *familia* join in the family's devotion. When she boasted of her husband's trespasses on the property of religious, she mentioned it as something done while returning "ad domum suam propriam" (50).

Baxter's faith was, not automatically but elaborately and consciously, a *domestic* faith, with the house, family, and the maintenance of both at the center of her religious values, a yardstick to take the measure of doctrine. Her argument against the presence of Christ in the eucharist –

if that sacrament were God, the true body of Christ, there would be infinite gods, because a thousand priests and more every day make a thousand gods, and afterwards eat those gods, and once they are eaten discharge them through their hinder parts into the stinking latrine, where you can find plenty of such gods, if you care to sift through it [*perscrutari*]   (45)

appealed to a shared experience in the maintenance of latrines. And so when she spoke of fleecing the "dean of The Fields," her imagination made an immediate connection to the *house* whose income and maintenance the money taken from him went to support. The contrast most persistently implied by her language is between the clergy who gather in people's money for their own pleasures ("to sustain their pride, lechery, and leisure," [45]; "to maintain priests and their concubines," [46]) and the laity who must expend money on necessities, who must "go into debt" if they observe the Friday fast. Her rejecting the fast as uneconomical is, if idiosyncratic, not impertinent, for it obeys an unintended corollary of Wyclif's arguments for disendowment: if the clergy must be despoiled to ease the financial burdens of the laity, then the laity's financial needs and practices are a moral and spiritual norm in themselves.

And St. Thomas of Canterbury violated those needs, "injuriously endowed churches with possessions" (45), and died a coward's, not a martyr's, death "in ostio ecclesie," not, as clerks falsely assert, "coram altari." Baxter had, from a Lollard point of view, plenty to say in Becket's dispraise without this piece of revisionist history. Its real importance, I suspect, lies in the architectural precision she gives to the setting, and the contrast it makes with William White. Becket belongs in *church*, and Baxter's imagination sees in churches the encrustations of luxury: the images that "lewed peyntors glorye. . .with colours" (44), the crosses whose elegance masks the character of an instrument that no more deserves worship than "the gallows on which your brother might be hanged" (44). "God was never in such a church," she says; "he never left, never will leave, heaven" (44). Hudson is mistaken in saying that Baxter rejected the cult of saints; no such rejection appears in the charges or the depositions against her. She rejected the cult of images, including pilgrimage "to any saint" ("ire peregre. . .ad aliquem sanctum" [47], where "sanctum" must mean the *shrine* of the saint), but that is simply part of her rejection of the worship of the rich dead things housed in church buildings. One does not pray to St. Thomas not because one does not pray to saints, but because he was no saint, while William White – whose place was not in churches, but in houses like Baxter's own, where she "gave him refuge, guarding and hiding and concealing him for five days" (41) – was "magnus sanctus in celo" (47).

Baxter did not con her belief from books, but she did not therefore disprize them: she made her beliefs *from* them, and – as John of Exeter seems to have realized – formed her sense of Lollard identity around them. This woman who had "secretly carried the books of the same William White from Yarmouth to Martham and hid them there" (presumably *in her house*) boasted to Clyfland that "she had vanquished [*vincebat*] in court the lord Bishop of Norwich and Henry Inglese and the abbots who were with them" (51). John of Exeter seems to have understood, whether Clyfland did or not, the claim Baxter was making, for his Latin transcript makes her speak the boasts of university debate, of talking theology for victory. He seems so well to have understood the Margery Baxter portrayed in the depositions, the Margery Baxter who seems to have put herself forward as a preacher and theologian, that it is hard to untangle what is his and what is hers, how far he has recorded, how far interpreted, how far (for that matter) invented. The oddly exhaustive alternatives he reports in her condemnation of Becket ("si Deus fuerit benedictus idem Thomas fuit et est maledictus, et si Thomas fuerit et sit benedictus Deus fuit et est maledictus" [45]), pedantic in the precision of tense and mood, recalls the logical conditionals of academic discourse; the report of how she answered the challenge of an unnamed Carmelite of Yarmouth with her understanding of the gospel ("ipsa Margeria. . .exposuit dicto fratri evangelia in lingua Anglicana" [48]]) uses the verb (*exponere*) that conventionally described both academic and homiletic exegesis.

When John of Exeter wrote such lines, was he just reaching for the closest semantic equivalents in his own experience for the sorts of claims Baxter made? Or did Baxter make such claims to clerical and academic prowess? And if the latter, did Clyfland report her words with reasonable accuracy? Or did John makes his guess at what lay behind a mangled report? The point of these questions, actually, is that it is so hard to say, that John's engagement with Clyfland's deposition, and with the woman, presumably present, about whom it was given, creates in the folds of his notary's Latin a character so deeply and satisfyingly readable that one feels hard pressed to judge whether the coherence comes from the subject or the scribe, from reportage or invention. Either he caught, at whatever level of consciousness, and then rendered the quick turns and broad resonances of her thought, *or he created her as a character*, and as a character not merely parodic. Either case bespeaks fascination. In this yielding to attention and interest, he differed from Lollard clerics like the author of *The Lantern of Light*, with his touching faith that his book overwhelms, transforms, *replaces* the minds of his readers; and he differed from the inquisitorial episcopacy, who assumed that recantation and abjuration replaced heretical thoughts with pious ones. He could afford to differ from both because, unlike clerics both Lollard and orthodox, he could, at least in theory and at least institutionally, in his role as scribe and while doing a scribe's work, afford to hear and write the words of the Lollards without judgment and without commitment; he could afford to leave heretics like Baxter their eloquence – and also their mystery. "Illud sacramentum nunquam erit Deus meus, sed magnus antiquus Deus qui nunqum exivit nec exibit de celo erit Deus meus" (51): "That sacrament will never be my God; the great old God who never left heaven and never will leave it, that will be my God." Whatever these words of Baxter's meant, we can be sure that they did not flow from the formulae of notarial skill or of ecclesiastical expectation.

I have not tried to claim that John of Exeter was sympathetic to the heretics. My argument is stranger: that he did not particularly pay attention to them as heretics, and that the boredom of scribal work drove him to record their words; that this sort of detached curiosity could produce a record historiographically more usable than either a hostile or a friendly account, because so little under ideological pressure, or indeed any pressure less vagrant than the need to occupy the mind; *that a chink in the armature of institutional power is the banality of so much of its work.*

Nor have I tried to claim that John's curiosity did the Lollards any particular good. Of course it did them no particular harm – no more, that is, than a less exact, more formulaic record would have done. Those who were executed, or put in danger through their recantations, were no less or more dead or in danger because he let their voices sound: the fullness of his record was for them purely inconsequential. The preservation of their "voice" (if that is what has happened; if that is what it should be called) is an advantage for *us*, not for *them*. But what sort of advantage is it for us? Who are *we* that we should feel this information any advantage? What place (as I asked at the beginning) do we have in this story?

Both the heretics and the bishops thought that there was only one question that mattered in the world, only an urgent (though potentially revocable) decision to *take sides*, with truth or error. It is easy to feel drawn to take sides oneself, to want to intervene on behalf of these lay Lollards, those without privilege of social rank or institutional power, those who found themselves before the bishop's seat for wanting to think about their God. But the two sides exist only from each other: without orthodoxy there is, of course, no heresy, and *vice versa*. There are perhaps those for whom the matters on which Margery Baxter and the rest were examined –

the Real Presence, titles, pilgrimages, images – are live and compelling issues; for the rest of us, there probably can be at most a raw feeling of solidarity with one or another side. While I would not choose to be without that feeling, I cannot pretend that I share Margery Baxter's beliefs any more than I share Bishop Alnwick's, or that she would feel anything but patronized by a sympathy that puts aside the beliefs that were for her the point of dissent; and I cannot in any case imagine that my sympathy does her any good. If as historians we cultivate sympathies, we should in all conscience admit that it is ourselves for whom we cultivate them; and we should perhaps reflect that the figure we most resemble in the scene I've tried to paint is the one who holds the pen and whose investment in the proceedings (beyond of course his professional investment) is in keeping himself awake and aware, getting through days of work that, though well remunerated and hardly on the larger scale of things laborious, still have their *longueurs* and their provocations of restlessness and resentment, and in finding something there worth fixing the mind on. Even when we nourish motives more pointed than this, we ought not to pretend that our work is on our subjects' behalf, or that it is in any direct or unambiguous way political; it is perhaps at most a cultivation of the soul. We may claim other motives than John's, but I am not sure that as historians we can claim any other lineage; like him, we engage with these Lollards, if we engage with them at all, from the safety of privilege and inconsequence.

Notes

1 A longer version of this chapter was discussed at the Center for Hermeneutical Studies, Graduate Theological Union, Berkeley, May 15, 1994. I am grateful to all who criticized and provoked: Robert Brentano, Deborah Lyman, and Anne Middleton (my formal respondents); Stephen Greenblatt, Dorothy Hale, Jeffrey Knapp, Steven Knapp, Geoffrey Koziol, and Chris Ocker; and – most crucially, Jill N. Levin.

2 Norman Tanner, ed., *Norwich Heresy Trials 1428–31*, Camden Fourth Series 20 (London: Royal Historical Society, 1977), p. 77. Subsequent references in the text.

3 Anne Hudson, "The Examination of Lollards," in her *Lollards and Their Books* (London: Hambledon Press, 1985), pp. 125–40.

4 Brian Stock, *The Implications of Literacy: Written Language and Models of*

Interpretation in the Eleventh and Twelfth Centuries (Princeton: Princeton University Press, 1983), pp. 24–30; Michael Richter, *"Urbanitas/Rusticitas:* Linguistic Aspects of a Medieval Dichotomy," *Studies in Church History* 16 (1979): 149–79.

5 See Tanner's description of the hands in and condition of the manuscript, *Norwich Heresy Trials*, pp. 4–6.

6 A translation of the bishop's letter appears in R. N. Swanson, *Catholic England: Faith, Religion, and Observance before the Reformation* (Manchester: Manchester University Press, 1993), p. 267.

7 On all these matters, see Margaret Harvey, "Martin V and the English, 1422–1431," in Christopher Harper-Bill, ed., *Religious Belief and Ecclesiastical Careers in Late Medieval England* (Woodbridge, Suffolk: The Boydell Press, 1991), pp. 59–86.

8 *The Acts and Monuments of John Foxe*, eds. S. R. Cattley and J. Pratt, 8 vols. (London, 1853–70), 6:589. Subsequent references in the text.

9 Norman Tanner, *The Church in Late Medieval Norwich 1370–1532* (Toronto: University of Toronto Press, 1984), p. 50.

10 See, for example, V. H. Galbraith, *Studies in the Public Records* (London: Thomas Nelson, 1948).

11 Michael Camille, *Image on the Edge: The Margins of Medieval Art* (London: Reaktion Books, 1992), p. 24.

12 *Hoccleve's Works: The Regement of Princes* ed. F. J. Furnivall, *Early English Text Society* 72 (London, 1897), line 974.

13 W. K. Wimsatt, Jr. and Monroe C. Beardsley, "The Intentional Fallacy," in Wimsatt, *The Verbal Icon: Studies in the Meaning of Poetry* (Lexington: University of Kentucky Press, 1954), p. 4.

14 David Aers, *Community, Gender, and Individual Identity: English Literature 1360–1430* (London: Routledge, 1990), p. 30.

15 Paul Strohm, "Queens as Intercessors," in his *Hochon's Arrow: The Social Imagination of Fourteenth-Century Texts* (Princeton: Princeton University Press, 1993), p. 106.

16 Susan Crane, "The Writing Lesson of 1381," in Barbara Hanawalt, ed., *Chaucer's England: Literature in Historical Context* (Minneapolis: University of Minnesota Press, 1992), p. 208.

17 See my *Writing and Rebellion: England in 1381* (Berkeley and Los Angeles: University of California Press, 1994), ch. 1, n. 28, and ch. 4, *passim*.

18 Hudson is characteristically circumspect on this matter: see *The Premature Reformation: Wycliffite Texts and Lollard History* (Oxford: Clarendon, 1988), pp. 34–35.

19 *Ibid.*, p. 34 (emphasis mine).

20 Tanner, *Norwich Heresy Trials*, pp. 4–5. I rely on his description of the manuscript, which I have not seen.

21 E. F. Jacob, "Verborum florida venustas," (1933), rpt. in his *Essays in the Conciliar Epoch* (Notre Dame: University of Notre Dame Press, 1963), pp. 203–06.

22 C. R. Cheney, *Notaries Public in England in the Thirteenth and Fourteenth Centuries* (Oxford: Clarendon, 1972), p. 50.

23 Tanner, *The Church in Late Medieval Norwich*, p. 197.

24 Anne Hudson, "A Lollard Sect Vocabulary?" in *Lollards and Their Books*, pp. 165–66.

25 Or rather, in this and many cases, for the heretic to *hear* pronounce. For, like most of his colleagues in error, Kynget claimed that he could not read the indenture ("his eyes were weak," he said; others claimed to be illiterate) and therefore had Master William Ascogh read it for him (p. 33).

26 See E. F. Jacob's essential essay, "Reynold Pecock, Bishop of Chichester," in his *Essays in Later Medieval History* (Manchester: Manchester University Press, 1968), pp. 1–34.

27 Hudson, "The Examination of Lollards" in *Lollards and Their Books*, p. 133.

28 *Ibid.*, p. 133.

29 This formulation also shows that *nati* in the Latin version is a genitive singular modifying *infantis*, not a plural nominative predicated of *parentes*: the point, that is, has nothing to do with any hereditary reception of Christianity or of grace.

30 On *trewthe* as a moral and political standard in English villages and towns, see my *Writing and Rebellion*, ch. 4.

31 K. B. McFarlane, *John Wycliffe and the Beginnings of English Nonconformity* (London: English Universities Press, 1952).

32 Aston, "William White's Lollard Followers" in her *Lollards and Reformers: Images and Literacy in Late Medieval Religion* (London: Hambledon Press, 1984), pp. 71–100.

33 On their schools, see Hudson's dazzling demonstration in *The Premature Reformation*, ch. 4.

34 *Chronicon Henrici Knighton*, ed. Joseph Rawson Lumby, Rolls Series 92 (London, 1895), pp. 186–87.

35 I owe this point to Robert Brentano's wise comment on an assertion made in an earlier version of this essay.

36 Anne Hudson, "A Lollard Sermon-Cycle and its Implications," *Medium Aevum* 40 (1971): 142–56.

37 *The Lanterne of Light*, ed. Lilian Swinburn, Early English Text Society 151 (London: Oxford University Press, 1917).

38 Yves Congar, OP, *L'ecclésiologie du haut moyen-âge: de Saint Grégoire le Grand à la désunion entre Byzance et Rome* (Paris: Editions du Cerf, 1968).

39 This implicit but articulable lay theology has been well described by John Bossy, *Christianity in the West, 1400–1700* (Oxford: Oxford University Press, 1985). His apparent distrust of the medieval laity makes his analysis the more convincing.

40 *The Premature Reformation*, pp. 313, 147.

Index

This index lists names of authors and historical figures, events, and places that appear primarily in the main text; it also provides a guide to subjects and concepts covered in the book. For further bibliographical information, readers should consult the endnotes of individual chapters.

Printed in the United States
47619LVS00003B/228